Retrospecta 42
Yale School of Architecture 2018-2019

Studio

Fall 2018
450a Undergraduate Senior Design Studio....6
1011a M.Arch I First Year Design Studio....8
1021a M.Arch I Second Year Design Studio....17
1061a M.Arch II First Year Design Studio....24
1101a Advanced Design Studio....26
Julie Snow, Surry Schlabs
1102a Advanced Design Studio....30
Simon Hartmann, Michael Samuelian, Andrei Harwell
1103a Advanced Design Studio....34
Adam Yarinsky, Lexi Tsien-Shiang
1104a Advanced Design Studio....38
Peter Eisenman, Anthony Gagliardi
1105a Advanced Design Studio....42
Rossana Hu, Lyndon Neri
1106a Advanced Design Studio....45
Omar Gandhi, Marta Caldeira
1107a Advanced Design Studio....49
Lisa Gray, Alan Organschi
Spring 2019
494b Undergraduate Senior Design Studio....52
1012b M.Arch I First Year Design Studio....54
1022b M.Arch I Second Year Design Studio....63
1111b Advanced Design Studio....70
Pier Vittorio Aureli, Emily Abruzzo
1112b Advanced Design Studio....74
Thomas Phifer, Kyle Dugdale
1113b Advanced Design Studio....77
Brigitte Shim, Andrei Harwell
1114b Advanced Design Studio....81
Yolande Daniels, Gary He
1115b Advanced Design Studio....85
Sandra Barclay, Jean Pierre Crousse, Andrew Benner
1116b Advanced Design Studio....89
Paul Florian, George Knight
1117b Advanced Design Studio....92
Todd Reisz
1118b Advanced Design Studio....95
Anna Dyson, Chris Sharples, Naomi Keena

Design and Visualization

Summer 2018
1000c Architectural Foundations....100
Fall 2018
1018a Formal Analysis....101
1062a Computational Analysis Fabrication....103
1211a Drawing and Architectural Form....104
1224a The Chair....104
1233a Composition....105
1240a Custom Crafted Components....106
1241a Rendered: Art, Architecture, and Contemporary Image Culture....107

Spring 2019
1216b Ornament Theory and Design....108
1222b Diagrammatic Analysis: Recon Modernism....108
1227b Drawing Projects....109
1228b Disheveled Geometries: Ruins and Ruination....110
1242b Architecture and Illusion....111
1243b Graphic Inquiry....112
Summer 2019
1019c Petite Planets: An Ecology of Digital Materiality....113
1019c Scripting and Algorithmic Design: Grid Space....114
1019c Virtual Reality: The Memory Palace....115
1291c Rome: Continuity and Change....115
Technology and Practice
Fall 2018
2021a Environmental Design....118
2031a Architecture Practice and Management....119
2211a Technology and Design of Tall Buildings....119
2234a Material Case Studies....121
Spring 2019
2016b Building Project I: Research, Analysis, Design....121
2022b Systems Integration and Development in Design....124
2219b Craft, Materials, and Digital Artistry....124
2226b Design Computation....125
2230b Exploring New Value in Design Practice....127
Summer 2019
2017c Building Project II: Construction....127
History and Theory
Fall 2018
3011a Modern Architecture and Society....130
3071a Practice: Issues in Architecture and Urbanism....131
3223a Parallel Moderns: Crosscurrents in European and American Architecture 1880–1940....132
3228a The Autobiographical House....133
3265a Architecture and Urbanism of Modern Japan: Destruction, Continuation, and Creation....134
3284a Architectural Writing....135
3286a Architecture after the Rain: Theory and Design in the Post-Atomic Age....135
3289a Bauhaus @ 100....136
3290a Body Politics: Designing Equitable Public Space....137
Spring 2019
3012b Architectural Theory....139
3216a Case Studies in Architectural Criticism....140
3272b Exhibitionism: Politics of Display....140
3283b After the Modern Movement....141
3287b Havana's Architecture: Recent Past and Possible Future....143
3288b MANY....144
3291b GREATS: China's Big Projects 1949-1980....144
Summer 2019
3000c Madrid Summer Program: Deploying the Archive....146

Urbanism and Landscape
Fall 2018
4021a Introduction to Planning and Development....................148
4221b Introduction to Commercial Real Estate......................149
4222a History of Landscape Architecture: Antiquity to 1700 in Western Europe....................................149
Spring 2019
4223b History of British Landscape Architecture: 1600 to 1900....151
4233b Ghost Towns...151
4240b Landscape of Fulfillment: Architecture and Urbanism of Contemporary Logistics..152
Summer 2019
4291c Gothenburg Summer Program: The Urban Atlas..................153
Other Academics
Yale Urban Design Workshop..156
Independent Study...156
M.E.D. Program..157
Ph.D. Program...159

Studio

Studio

Fall 2018

Studio
Fall 2018
450a Undergraduate Senior Design Studio
Turner Brooks

In this course, students learn the architectural implications of contemporary cultural issues and the complex relationship among space, materials, and program. Students designed a 600 square foot studio to accommodate the needs of two distinct users—the scholar and the weaver. The site is set in the woodlands of the Josef and Anni Albers Foundation in Bethany, CT.

Participants
Edward Antonio, Jordan Boudreau, Sungyeon (Kristine) Chung, Mary Catherine Fletcher, Elizabeth Goodman, Amanda Hu, Sheau Yun Lim, Haewon Ma, Andrea Masterson, Deniz Saip, Andrew Sandweiss, Noah Silvestry, Sida Tang, Max Wilson, Noah Strausser

Studio
Fall 2018
450a Undergraduate Senior Design Studio
Turner Brooks
Kristine Chung

The intimate and the dramatic

Within the 600 sq ft limit, two programs are identified: the intimate, regular room for sleeping, and the dramatic, open studio for weaving/studying. The plan pulls them apart, placing all other programs—living, dining, and socializing—in the corridor that connects the bedroom and studio together.

The corridor in between is bent to create an intimate courtyard, covered with pavings inspired by Anni Albers' weaving works. The foldable glass walls facing the courtyard have a wooden screen that mediates the sunlight, while serving as a built graph paper, also inspired by Anni's pattern notebooks. Using the variation in wall thickness, some living infrastructure and furniture are incorporated in the wall.

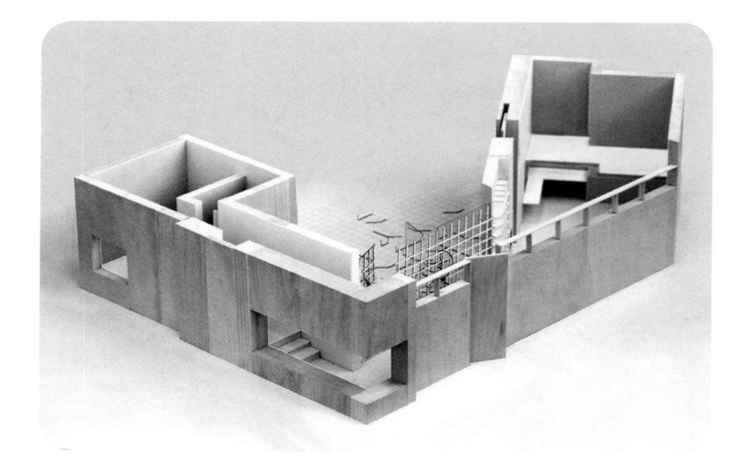

Uniting the scholar and the weaver

Focusing on aspects of design that would unite the scholar and the weaver, I generated this building through the collection of atmospheric moments rather than specifying programmatic spaces. Opportunities for work, play, and sleep are limitless, waiting to be defined by each unique resident. The relationship between light and shadow highlighted by various levels of overlapping space speaks to the purpose of a studio. As a place for contemplation and creation, the studio nurtures sparks of curiosity and imagination.

Studio

Fall 2018

1011a M.Arch I First Year Design Studio

Brennan Buck, Nikole Bouchard, Miroslava Brooks, Nicholas McDermott, Michael Szivos

This studio, the first of the four core design studios, is focused on explorations of form and space, the role and conventions of architectural representation, and concept development in the design process. A sequence of three projects is centered on three distinct representational mediums: image, section, and plan. Program and site are de-emphasized in favor of open formal and spatial exploration sparked initially by appropriation from popular visual culture and constrained by the tendencies of and limitations of image, section or plan. Each medium is employed as both a mode of design and a means of representation. Students are expected to bring a wide range of backgrounds and experience to the studio, and a corresponding variety of approaches and ideas are enabled and encouraged.

Participants

Ife Adepegba, Isa Akerfeldt-Howard, Natalie Broton, Ives Brown, Martin Carrillo Bueno, Christopher Cambio, Colin Chudyk, Jaichen Deng, Janet Dong, Xuefeng Du, Paul Freudenburg, Kate Fritz, Malcolm Rondell Galang, Angelica Gallegos, Kevin Gao, Jiaming Gu, Ian Gu, Ashton Harrell, Liang Hu, Niema Jafari, Alicia Jones, Sze Wai Justin Kong, Louis Koushouris, Tyler Krebs, Hiuki Lam, Pabi Lee, Isabel Li, Mingxi Li, Dreama Lin, Qiyuan Liu, April Liu, Araceli Lopez, Angela Lufkin, Rachel Mulder, Leanne Nagata, Naomi Ng, Louisa Nolte, Alex Olivier, Michelle Qu, Nicole Ratajczak, Heather Schneider, Scott Simpson, Christine Song, Shikha Thakali, Ben Thompson, Sarah Weiss, Max Wirsing, Shelby Wright, Stella Xu, Sean Yang, Peng Yi, Yuhan Zhang, Leyi Zhang, Kaiwen Zhao, Sasha Zwiebel

Jurors

Kutan Ayata, Erin Besler, Benjamin Cadena, Sean Canty, Tei Carpenter, Andrew Holder, Abby Coover Hume, Mariana Ibanez, Parsa Kahlili, Jesse LeCavalier, Stephanie Lin, Jonathan Louie, Dorte Mandrup, Aleksandr Mergold, Jae Shin, Andrew Witt, Michael Young, Mo Zell

Studio
Fall 2018
1011a M.Arch I First Year Design Studio
Brennan Buck
Malcolm Rondell Galang

A variety of distinct performance stages

This project is an unconventional theater that instigates a dynamic interaction between the audience and the performers by integrating the circulation with performance. As opposed to simply having one static auditorium, a variety of distinct performance stages are strategically placed throughout the site that engage the audience to traverse from stage to stage, viewing the play one scene at a time in different settings. Each room/stage is seamlessly connected by curving the corners where two buildings touch and unzipping them, to create a threshold that enables a continuous circulation from stage to stage, and interior to exterior. The theater curates moments where performers entertain outside as audiences watch inside, audiences watch from the outside as performers entertain inside, both audiences and performers are outside, and both audiences and performers are inside. By generating spaces that interweave interior and exterior, the theater provides a multitude of ways for the performers to connect with their audience.

Studio
Fall 2018
1011a M.Arch I First Year Design Studio
Brennan Buck
Angela Lufkin

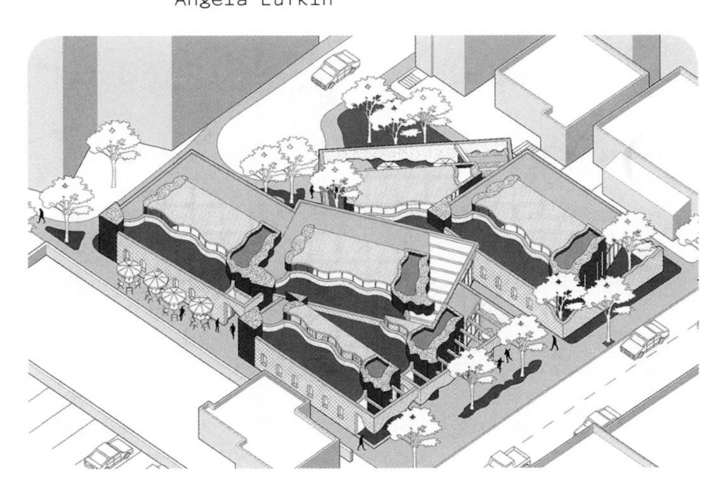

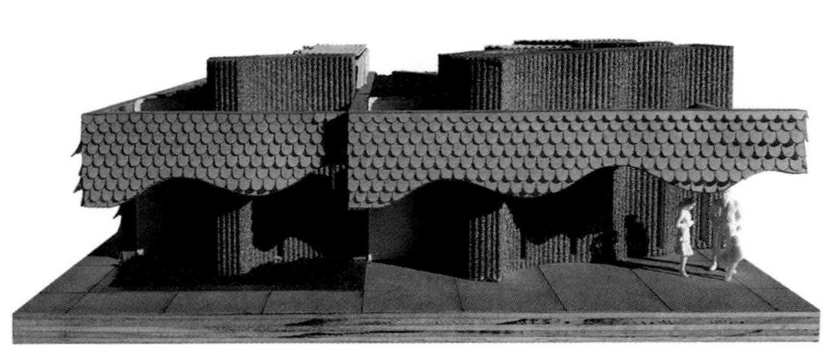

A Hybrid Community Center

This project is a hybrid community center for elderly adults and children, bringing together two groups at the opposite ends of life's spectrum through the medium of storytelling. Formally inspired by the Morgan Blair painting, *Free Stuff/Misc/Etc/Ghosts*, the floor plan is composed of the repetition, rotation, and cropping of a single plan figure to generate a richly varied configuration of interior and exterior space. This operation is tracked through the building in the distinctive reoccurrence of curving, concrete masses, shingled wall planes (marking exteriority), and clipped, graphic partitions (marking interiority). The resulting spaces evoke the whimsical familiarity of a "same, same but different" world which mediates the individual and collective needs of the old and young.

Studio
Fall 2018
1011a M.Arch I First Year Design Studio
Brennan Buck
Louisa Nolte

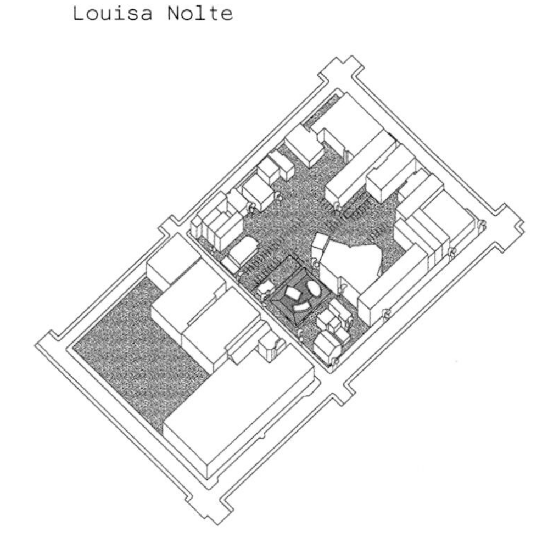

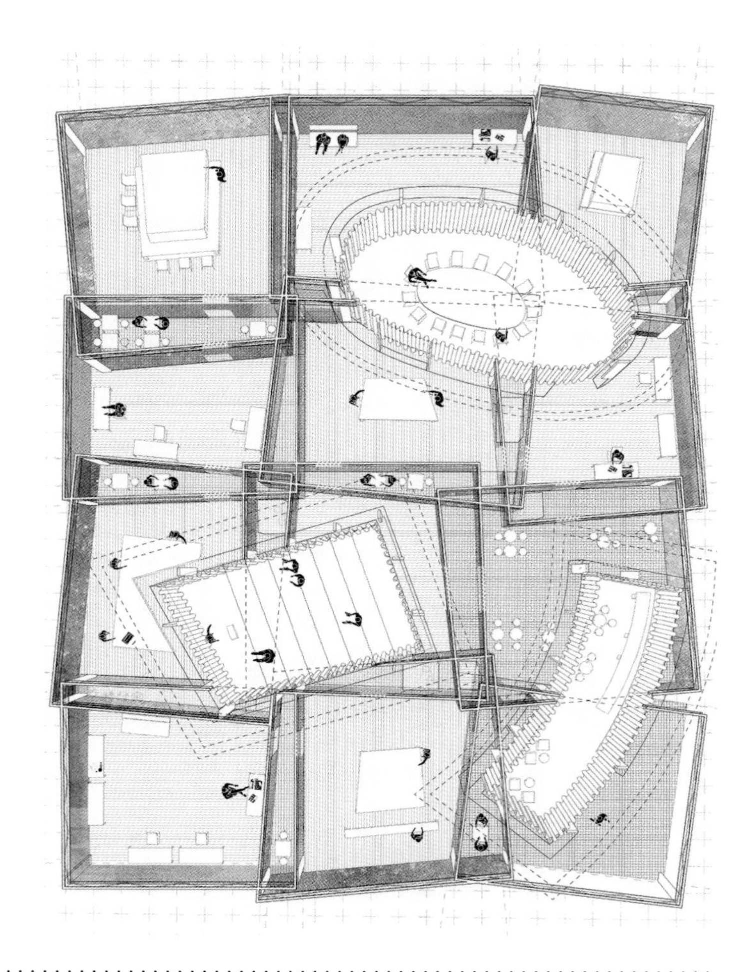

Theoretical and experimental physicists

This is a proposal for theoretical and experimental physicists to collaborate and negotiate. Each group is given a designated rectangle, forming a checkerboard pattern. The overlap of the rectangles are inhabitable. The rooms that are created through the overlap within the scrim walls are used as private rooms in the lab. Large irregular geometries puncture the grid, which are open to the public.

Studio
Fall 2018
1011a M.Arch I First Year Design Studio
Brennan Buck
Heather Schneider

Implied rooms and "hallways" within the heavy masonry arches

Drawing from both the compositional and functional aspects of a circuit board, this project weaves together the traditional architecture of Trappist-style brewing with the laboratory environment of experimental brewing. Just as circuit boards rely on the conductive nature of copper to transfer a current across the board, the experimental brewing relies on stainless steel piping to carry the ingredients through each step of the brewing process, beginning with boiling water in the back and ending with outdoor kiosks that house and distribute the finished product. This scaffolding of pipes carves out implied rooms and "hallways" within the heavy masonry arches of the Trappist brewing program. The fast directionality of the experimental brewing is assuaged by the field of columns and large beer hall, which promote both gathering and wandering.

Nikole Bouchard
Naomi Ng

A convergence of mutative modules that generate overlapping thresholds

The project *Planned, Unplanned* is about pattern and shape. Pattern, as coined by Stan Allen, is a field condition, an interest in the relationship and systemization of parts. It does not regard the resulting form, but the rules that govern it. Shape, on the other hand, serves as an icon. It symbolizes and is complete in itself. Through a constant cycle of image-making and image-(mis)reading, pattern is expressed in plan, while shape is expressed in profile. Like field conditions, the eventual plan is one of many; the pattern is a convergence of mutative modules that generate overlapping thresholds. In profile, however, shape exists as appropriation of the defined building components of Crown Street, College Street and High Street. From High Victorian Gothic roofs to Art Deco ornamented windows, borrowed shapes are assorted and distorted—redefining their purpose in an unfamiliar context, scale and location.

While kept intentionally distinct, the marriage between pattern and shape results in moments of unclarity and ambiguousness. Systemization of patterns ultimately become blurred in navigation, and iconography of shapes become obscured in its distortion.

Studio
Fall 2018
1011a M.Arch I First Year Design Studio
Nikole Bouchard
Liang Hu

A journey with constant variation of compression and expansion

One non-linear corridor weaves through the building connecting programs. It is a journey with constant variation of compression and expansion, light and dark. It provides both intimate moments of specificity and wide open spaces for flexible functionalities. The hit-and-miss break walls conceal and reveal the adjacent programs upon movement, creating visual interactions as well as private moments. The cast concrete of the model exemplifies the material condition of the space, also signifying the aging memory of the built environment that has been cast onto the site.

Studio
Fall 2018
1011a M.Arch I First Year Design Studio
Nikole Bouchard
Scott Simpson

Assembling strange forms appropriated from abstract expressionist paintings

This project—a proposed Karaoke Bar on Crown St in New Haven—theorizes methods of perceiving, inhabiting, and assembling strange forms appropriated from Abstract expressionist paintings. Three 'pods' containing private karaoke suites hover over an open, terraced space with zones for a lounge, a bar, dining spaces, and a larger performance hall—thus facilitating a unique performative privacy across the public spaces. The material strategy abstracts the image of local Stony Creek granite—the pods are wrapped in a printed substrate that imitates the stone while the flooring, a poured terrazzo with varied aggregates, reinterprets the natural source material through a more technological production process and codes various program areas.

Miroslava Brooks
Tyler Krebs

The concept of play as a means to further development

Kindergarten is the beginning of formal education for most children. Thus, it is one of the initial stages in the development of social and communication skills. The proposed building encourages children to traverse a series of varied elevations, scales, adjacencies, and gathering formats. The building is to be explored and interacted with. At this stage in life, students are introduced to various forms of creativity, fundamental knowledge, and exercise: the kindergarten seeks to facilitate environments which are conducive to these learning objectives. Teachers are tasked with being highly adaptable based on the needs of each individual student who, respectively, learns in a variety of manners. Since the needs of the students are varied and continually changing, the architecture sets the stage but does not directly prescribe the play. Children are in constant view of accessible outdoor space as well as the adjacent rooms of the building. This allows children to feel connected to their surroundings yet focused on the task at hand thanks to subtle guiding barriers. Ultimately, the interactive nature of the various bars of the building allow children to use the concept of play as a means to further their development as students.

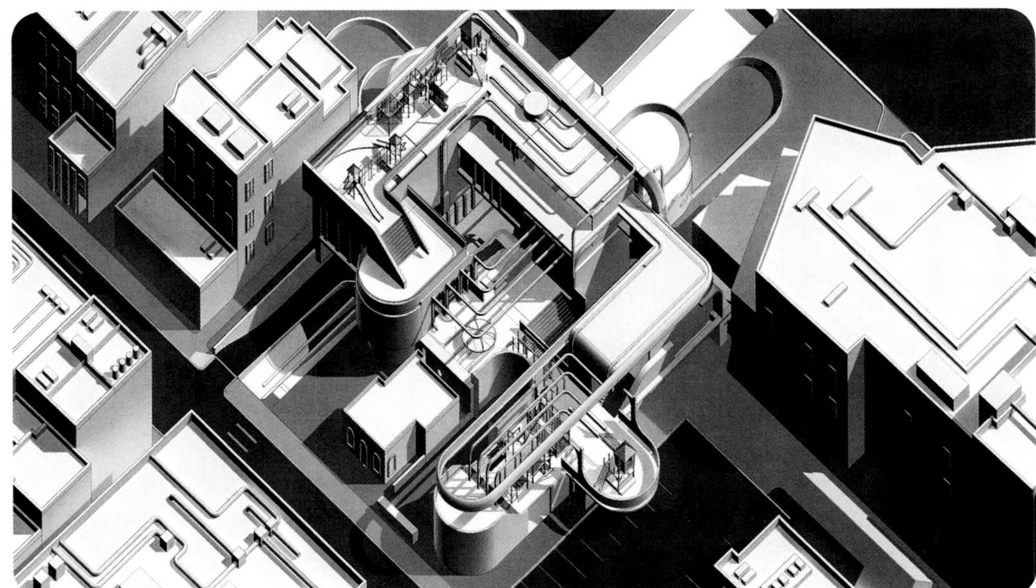

Studio
Fall 2018
1011a M.Arch I First Year Design Studio
Miroslava Brooks
Rachel Mulder

A series of squares shifted and overlapped

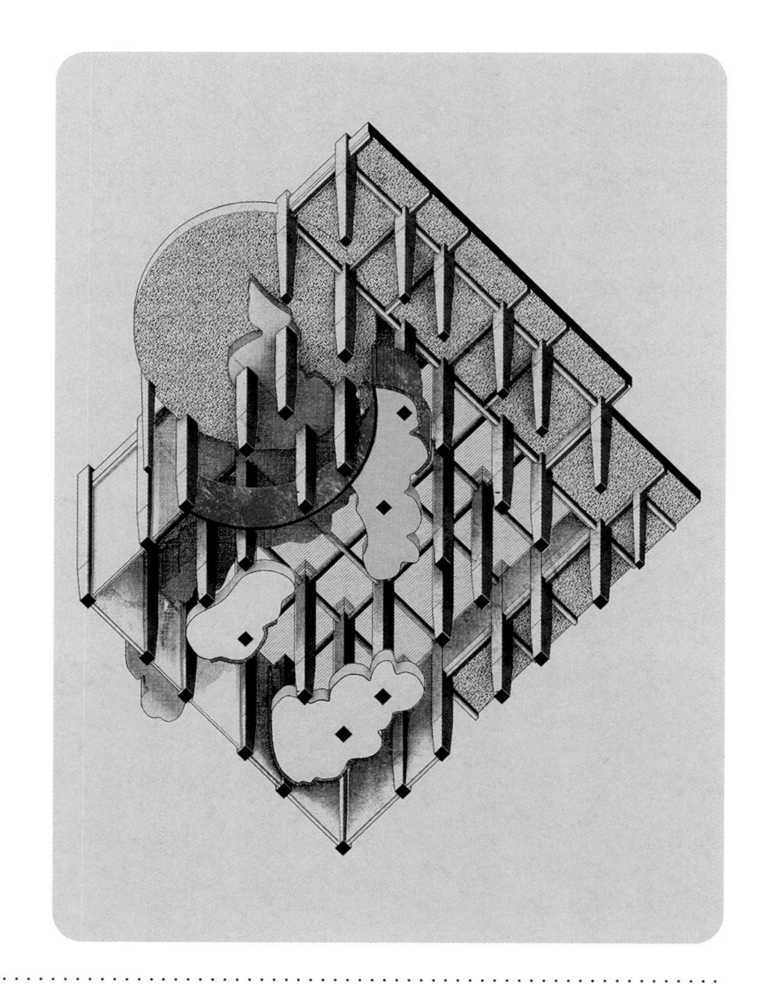

This project proposes a multi-level storefront and small scale garment manufacturing space located on Crown Street in New Haven, CT. Meant for a local garment manufacturer or craftsman, the floorplan is organized in a series of squares shifted and overlapped with a grid of columns. Beginning with a translation of an illustration by Pauliina Holma, and imposing a square grid inspired by SOM's University of Illinois Research Institute, each square floor provides a changing environment for different programmatic needs through elevational shifts and changes in column thicknesses. The dominant grid is broken through shifting of the squares, irregular wavy walls, and overhead cloud-like shapes. These walls are used for retail display, space organization, privacy, and furniture. There is one main entry through a circular atrium on Crown Street. Private manufacturing and office spaces are located on the higher levels, while retail and showroom are located on the lower levels. There is a second entrance in the back accessible through the alley and arcade.

Studio
Fall 2018
1011a M.Arch I First Year Design Studio
Nicholas McDermott
Leanne Nagata

A free and open aquarium of people and animals

This project provides a canopy at its edges and a series of voids that act as a free and open aquarium of people and animals. Inside, crenulated acrylic walls layer views and spaces of fish, lab users, and visitors. The building is suspended mid-block in downtown New Haven.

Studio
Fall 2018
1011a M.Arch I First Year Design Studio
Nicholas McDermott
Sarah Weiss

A field of leaf-like geometries

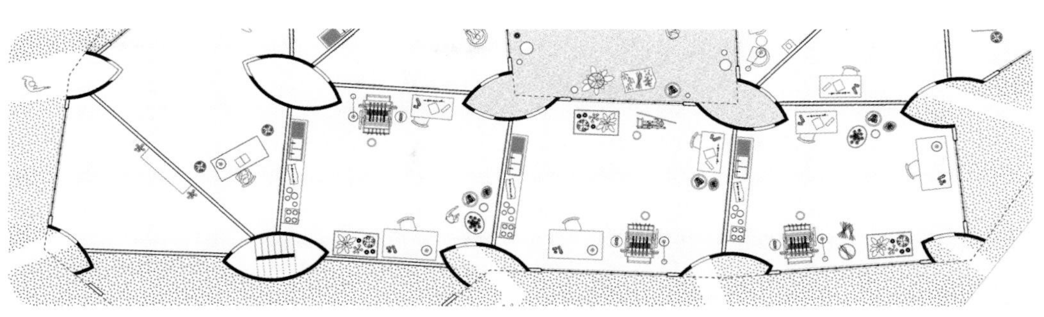

For this project I designed a textile studio center and gallery. In plan, the design is organized about a field of leaf-like geometries, which act as nodes or intersections between studios, galleries, offices, and courtyards. Dividing walls that span between the leaves encase these program specific spaces. These volumes are arranged concentrically, making it possible for each artist to access their own studio from a private door. Once inside, each artist is also able to directly access a central courtyard. Without disrupting this concentric system, the design is grained on a diagonal axis, along which the public gallery's visitors are able to pass through without disrupting the work of the artists. The studio center's second floor is dedicated to administrative offices, which circumscribe a small outdoor space of their own. Along each inhabitant's path, there is the opportunity to interact with other groups at the nodes.

Studio
Fall 2018
1011a M.Arch I First Year Design Studio
Michael Szivos
Louis Koushouris

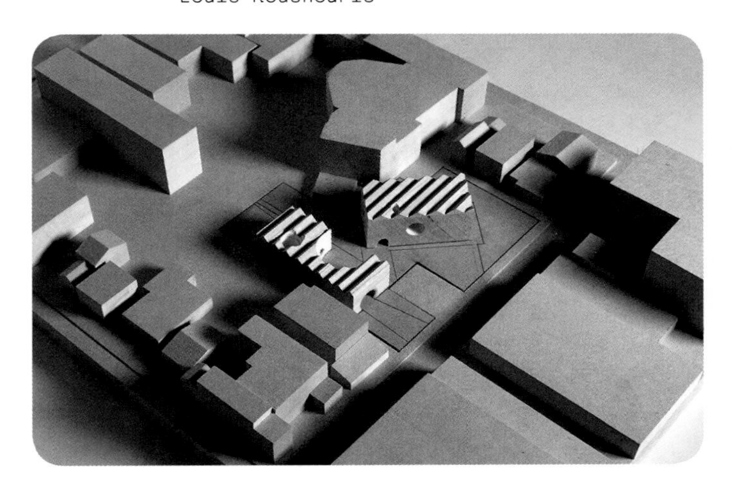

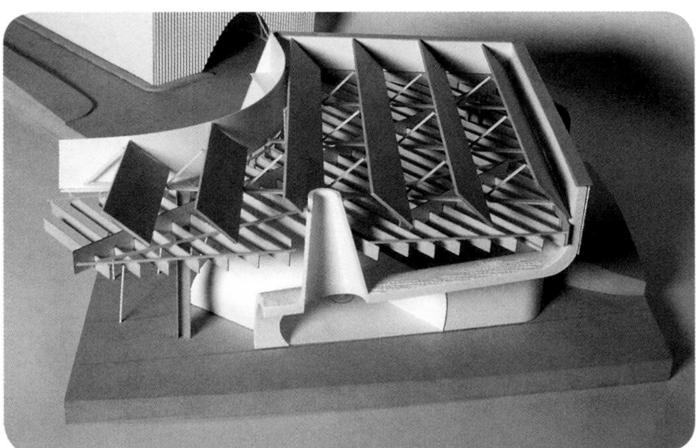

Varying densities and orientations of cones

In this project, titled "Void Fraction", an exploration of porosity informed a process using conic geometry to define a formal language. Cones have unique capacities in optics and projection to create forced perspectives and aligned scenographic views. Varying densities and orientations of cones create eccentric intersections; it is not about the shapes alone, but the relationships between them. Conic sections have formal potential, generating ellipses as well as parabolic and hyperbolic surfaces, allowing immense spatial implications. Rationally organized orthogonal building masses are perforated with conic volumes emphasizing geometric polarity through considered connections of straight/curved, light/heavy, bright/dark, solid/void, connection/bifurcation, and interior/exterior. The duality of two architectural systems reinforce their complementary relationships.

A surface smoothly unifies sharp edges

In this project, titled "Smoothed Fragments", I experimented with multiple ways of establishing surfaces between objects to create unique conditions between the objects. This experimentation was informed by interests in how objects or artifacts can retain their individual identity when being combined under one circumstance. This method is then applied to unique conditions of the site. Four different blocks with their own proportion, program and position are designed responding to the site's four distinct street conditions. Two different kinds of connection were then created between the four blocks. On the exterior, a surface smoothly unifies sharp edges of the four blocks, while it pacifies the difference in scale and proportion. Interior-wise, artifacts representing characters of each block were mixed and combined in a fragmented fashion. Landscape with its own language penetrated between inside and outside, forming a common ground for all the elements.

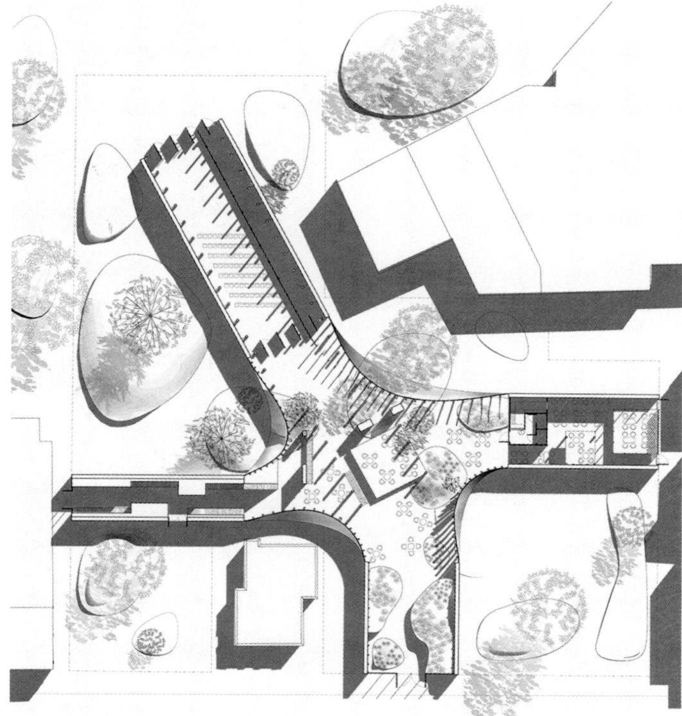

Studio

Fall 2018

1021a M.Arch I Second Year Design Studio

Emily Abruzzo, Annie Barrett, Laura Briggs,
Peter de Bretteville, Iñaqui Carnicero, Martin Finio

Restorative Justice is an alternative to an adversarial criminal justice system. It brings together those who have harmed, their victims, and affected community members into voluntary processes that repair harms. Restorative Justice produces consensus-based plans through face-to-face dialogue that meet the needs victims themselves identify while also supporting the positive development of those who have harmed. This can take many forms, most notably community conferencing models and circle processes.

As interest in Restorative Justice grows nationally, this studio looks at how the design of spaces directly affect human interactions, social processes, and the sharing of experiences. Students designed buildings to support these practices in the context of strengthening communities where restorative practices are needed. In structure and design, each project encourages a feeling of ease and facilitates an organic process of making connections, talking openly, and building community.

Participants

Cristina Anastase, Michelle Badr, Katharine Blackman, Emily Cass, Camille Charbrol, Serena Ching, Page Comeaux, Gioia Connell, Ruchi Dattani, Deo Deiparine, Clara Domange, Miriam Dreiblatt, Helen Farley, Adam Feldman, Nathan Garcia, Michael Gasper, Michael Glassman, Tianyu Guan, Phoebe Harris, Will James, Kelley Johnson, Alex Pineda Jongeward, Andrew Kim, Katie Lau, Eunice Lee, Rachel Lefvre, Zack Lenza, Jackson Lindsay, Matthew Liu, Thomas Mahon, Andrew Miller, Layla Ni, Max Ouellette-Howitz, Jonathan Palomo, Christine Pan, Alix Pauchet, Jewel Pei, Deirdre Plaus, Manasi Punde, Kelsey Rico, Jenna Ritz, Limy Rocha, David Schaengold, Rhea Schmid, Armaan Shah, Baolin Shen, Maya Sorabjee, Arghavan Taheri, Megan Tan, Seth Thompson, Brenna Thompson, Lissette Valenzuela, Rukshan Vathupola, Laelia Vaulot, Darryl Weimer, Xiaohui Wen, Paul Wu, Kay Yang

Jury

Louis Becker, Andrew Berman, Alex Busansky, Brian Butterfield, Ashlee George, Viviana Gordon, Sia Henry, Elijah Huge, Ziad Jamaleddine, Jon Lott , Nadine Maleh, Jennifer Newsom, Megan Panzano, Eeva-Liisa Pelkonen, Benjamin Prosky, Anne Rieselbach, Jennifer Trone

Studio
Fall 2018
1021a M.Arch I Second Year Design Studio
Emily Abruzzo
Page Comeaux

Deep coffers that filter soft light

Sited in Middletown, CT, the building creates new space for the practice of restorative justice, an alternative to the present criminal justice system. By playing up the need for equitable food practices and community space in the city, the building negotiates between two distinct, yet interrelated programs: the community garden and the community justice center. These programs are linked by a central communal kitchen which serves as the point of arrival to and departure from the building. Concrete masonry walls rise from the landscape to support what appears to be a monolithic roof. The roof, composed of thin Corten steel plates, conceals deep coffers that filter soft, diffused light to the spaces below to facilitate the various rituals that occur within.

Studio
Fall 2018
1021a M.Arch I Second Year Design Studio
Emily Abruzzo
Rachel Lefevre

A field of doors which allow private spaces

Restorative justice is a new procedure in progressive criminal justice in which those who are harmed are brought into conversation with the ones who have harmed them. Through a meeting known as the 'circle process', both parties as well as their support systems are engaged in an intense and cathartic mediated discussion about what transpired. This process demands space which accommodates the needs of many through few means. Here, the entire floor plan is created by a field of doors which allow private spaces to open directly into the outside, bring the outdoors in, and allow facilitators to 'reprogram' the building for each group of people—mediating how parties enter and exit, and what spaces would suit them and their needs. The restorative justice center is connected to a series of community spaces which encourage people to become familiar with the building outside of the justice system.

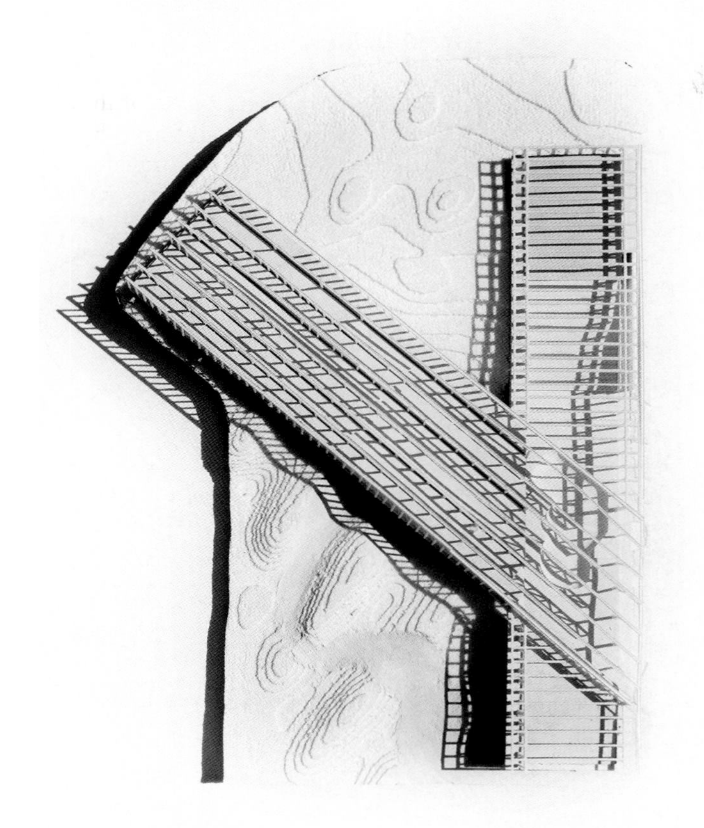

Studio
Fall 2018
1021a M.Arch I Second Year Design Studio
Peter de Bretteville
Emily Cass

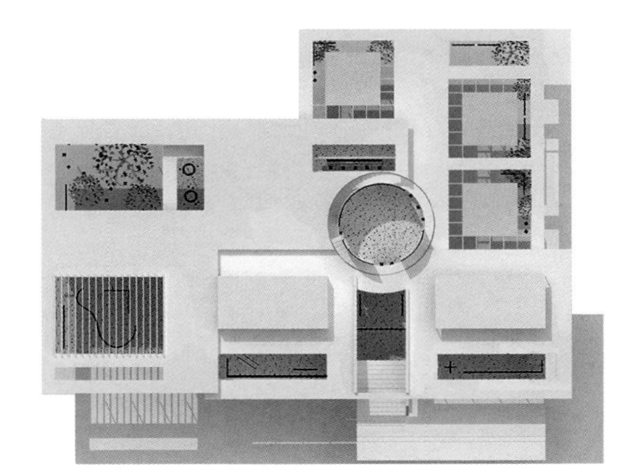

Sunlight and levity across program spaces

This design for a Restorative Justice Center balances the obligation to provide privacy for clients with the simultaneous need to destigmatize restorative justice strategies in our society, which is currently dominated by penal justice. The design embraces the restorative justice circle process as a mechanism to facilitate daily interactions among staff, clients, and the local community.

Rotating around a central circular chamber, the design provides multiple ingress and egress routes, each with differing levels of privacy dictated by program, ceiling heights, sunlight, and vistas. Discrete entrances and sensitive program spaces sit harmoniously alongside a welcoming cafe, bookstore, auditorium, and basketball court which spill out onto more public spaces. Emanating from the central cylinder, the design evenly distributes sunlight and levity across program spaces, marking the center's stark contrast to the typical gravity of penal justice systems.

Studio
Fall 2018
1021a M.Arch I Second Year Design Studio
Peter de Bretteville
Alix Pauchet

Private spaces turn away to overlook a pair of sunken courtyards

The restorative justice process replaces the onus of the justice system from punishment to rehabilitation by bringing victims and perpetrators together in a mediated setting to find appropriate solutions for both. As such, the direct participants of restorative ustice are accompanied by their support system throughout the process. This particularity led to the elaboration of a pair of buildings: one to host direct participants—perpetrators, victims and moderators—the other for indirect participants. This building expresses its programmatic duality in a sidedness whereby its frontage provides a series of communal spaces oriented towards the river, and private spaces turn away to overlook a pair of sunken courtyards. A gradient of densities spans the site, expressed inside through a series of increasingly intimate spaces. The public facades, clad in granite, acknowledge the nearby quarry, while meeting rooms and offices are built from the ground up with rammed earth construction.

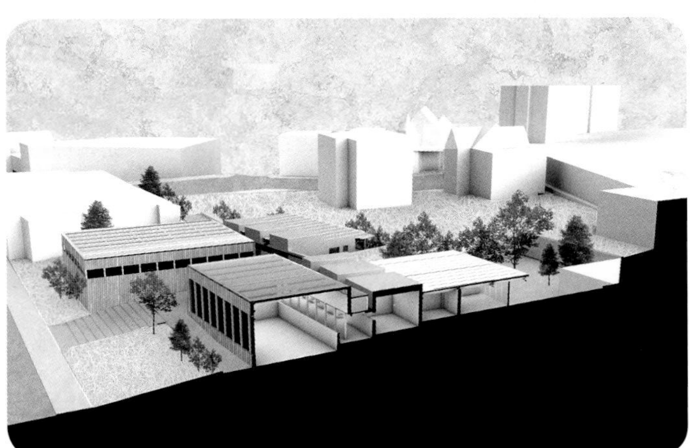

Studio
Fall 2018
1021a M.Arch I Second Year Design Studio
Martin Finio
Matthew Liu

An effort to reduce the institutional qualities of Restorative Justice

"Heide" introduces conceptual and formal maneuvers of play into a restorative justice community center. The site is situated on the main road of Bridgeport, Connecticut, a place lacking in programmed public space, entertainment, and eateries. By playing with the ground plane, the landscape and building share a common element which is used differently in terms of program. The roof structure belongs to the public and fulfills the role of a park and a thoroughfare between Main Street and the train station. Several interpretations of restorative spaces are integrated into the building. The internal plaza serves the auditorium while-whilst also functioning as a gathering space or large circle room. For more serious occasions, underground support rooms are dispersed around the plaza. The outdoor circle room encourages and challenges the City of Bridgeport to utilize the space in any way they see fit in an effort to reduce the institutional qualities of restorative justice.

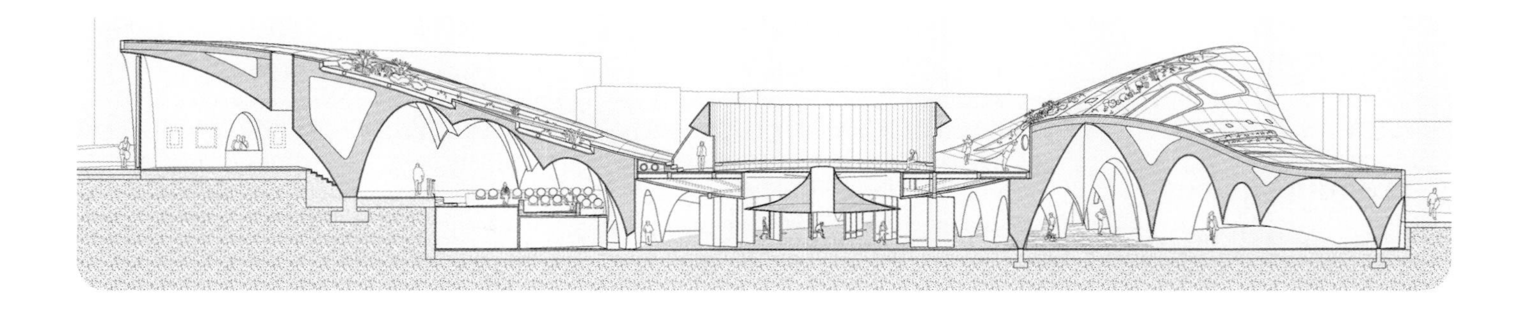

Studio
Fall 2018
1021a M.Arch I Second Year Design Studio
Martin Finio
Manasi Punde

The site as a case study for creating a district for healing

This project studies how the healing practiced within the circle room of a Restorative Justice Center can be amplified and reflected in Bridgeport, Connecticut's urban context. The project introduces a network of productive community-building public spaces, and in turn explores the relationship between restorative justice and community-building spaces. This can be seen at three scales: the scale of the building to the site, the scale of the building to its parts, and the scale of the parts to each other.

Identifying a need for connectedness and community-building spaces within the neighborhood, the project utilizes the site as a case study for creating a district for healing at the neighborhood level. The site acts as a catalyst to create this healing district. Here a new public realm is carved out of the site in addition to proposing the replacement of existing, empty parking lots in the area by productive community-building spaces.

Studio
Fall 2018
1021a M.Arch I Second Year Design Studio
Laura Briggs
Max Ouellette-Howitz

Three towers rise from a continuous base

Located at the edge of a steep site adjacent to one of New London's primary roads, this building stretches to infill a gap in the fabric of the city. Three towers rise from a continuous base in a rhythm that engages the offices of law across the street. Clad in Connecticut granite, these three volumes give weight and permanence to a model for criminal justice reform that asserts itself, not as an alternative, but as a valid and lasting proposition for the future.

The park behind the building is elevated above the street and works its way between the towers. It provides a grassy patch of earth wild with clover and dandelions. Stone walls rise high on either side with breeze coming off the river in the distance and a vista to the city beyond.

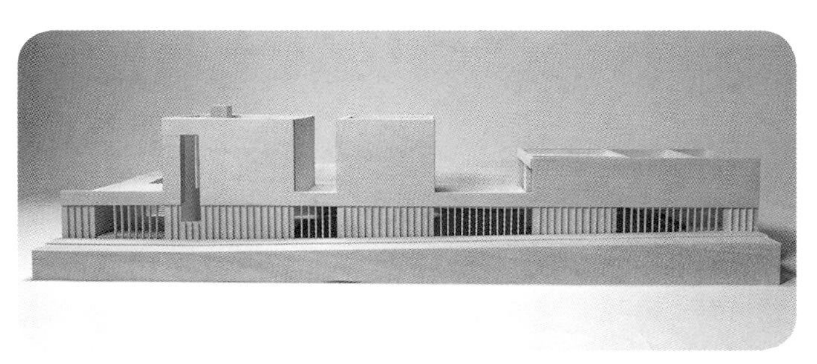

Studio
Fall 2018
1021a M.Arch I Second Year Design Studio
Laura Briggs
Rhea Schmid

A conceptual "node" derived from two paths of research

What I have come to appreciate most about restorative justice is how it promotes and celebrates our ability as self-aware and reflective people to change. Change, however, does not come easily to most of us, especially as it relates to our character. So, how do we capture and highlight that moment when we decide to make a conscious change? What mediates those two states of being, or motivates this transition? How do we celebrate that moment through space? I began to answer these questions through a conceptual "node" derived from two paths of research: one sensitive to the site's adjacent green spaces; the other driven by the circle, an important shape, formally and ideologically, to the program.

Studio
Fall 2018
1021a M.Arch I Second Year Design Studio
Iñaqui Carnicero
Baolin Shen

The building consists of two halves

The Restorative Justice Center in Middletown, Connecticut, provides spaces both for private restorative justice services and public activities within the city. The building consists of two halves: the urban roof, which houses offices and rooms for the restorative circle process; and the urban playscape, which is a landscape of pocket spaces with varying size and height in relation to the streets. The in-between condition of these two halves generates a variety of spaces with different levels of privacy, openness, enclosure, and exposure that are suitable for the different needs of the people. The private spaces of the restorative circle and the public spaces of local activities are intertwined but respected for their required nature.

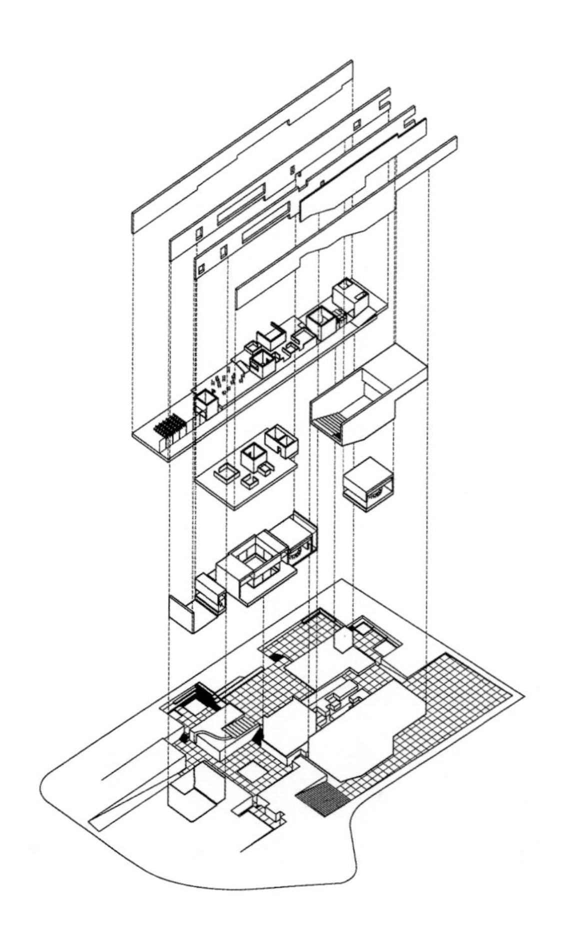

Studio
Fall 2018
1021a M.Arch I Second Year Design Studio
Iñaqui Carnicero
Limy Rocha

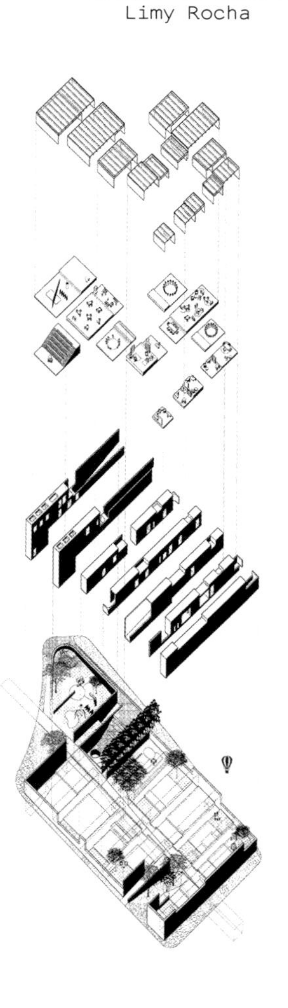

Fuses ground and landscape along an urban stitch

The Restorative Justice Center proposed for Middletown, Connecticut is composed of the interplay between several layers of elements that may inform interaction, passage, function, and quality. By manipulating the ground, concrete walls, wooden in-between rooms, and layered envelope, the center aims to create a world which acknowledges its urbanity at its entry points but also shields from notions of an oppressive judicial system. Creating a world within, the community center fuses ground and landscape along an urban stitch defined by a series of concrete walls. This introduces rooms for communal activity and restorative justice processes as a way to celebrate the culture and identity of its people.

In addition to using an exterior central path that connects it to public amenities and infrastructure, the center also finds ways to inhabit the cross axis and connect to its surroundings. A series of carved concrete walls emerge from the ground. The landscape is reflected, fusing monolithic forms with the natural environment. The wall structures constantly deviate from the central path to provide spaces for the individual within a public context. The rooms outlined by the walls provide an array of spaces for the collective. For functions such as performance, exhibition, work, and reflection, the wooden spaces are open to maintaining views, framing discourse between programmatic adjacencies, and blurring the sense of boundary. The layering of envelope creates a room scale that is discrete and aware of its programmatic function.

Studio
Fall 2018
1021a M.Arch I Second Year Design Studio
Annie Barrett
Deo Deiparine

Public gathering space and intimate private space

In creating an institution for restorative justice practices, a tension emerges between the highly public nature of such an institution and the privacy needed for the "circle process", a reconciliatory process between potentially hostile individuals or parties. The space built for such an institution must accommodate both public gathering space and intimate private space. Rather than designing for a specificity of program, the institution offers a gradient of conditions and sizes that facilitates the diverse needs of a public. The institution's various programming can be sorted into three categories: open, porous, and private. Open spaces allow unrestricted movement and access, serving as a shared commons for all users and visitors of the institution. Programming within the open spaces—galleries, gathering spaces, and recreation areas—are the least prescribed and therefore require the least amount of building intervention.

Studio
Fall 2018
1021a M.Arch I Second Year Design Studio
Annie Barrett
Megan Tan

Structural fins in alternating bays generate space

This project creates a 3D field condition that dissolves the traditional separation between route and destination, room and corridor, in response to the process of restorative justice. The resulting field structure is housed within a simple cube to minimize its footprint and give land back to land. An open plan ground floor is designed to merge with the surrounding landscape visually in the winter and physically in the summer. Structural fins in alternating bays generate space within the depth of the enclosure, negotiating between inside and outside.

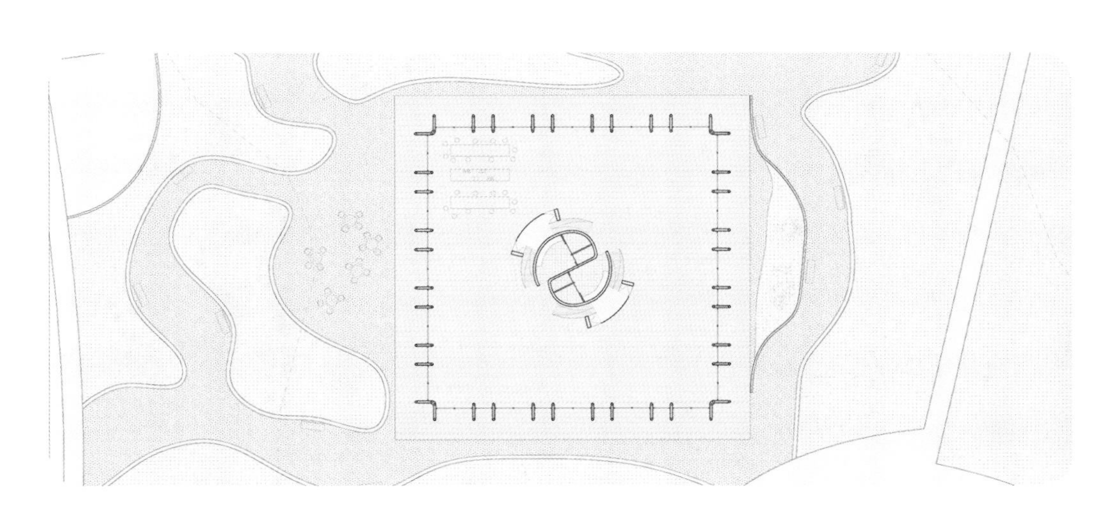

Studio

Fall 2018

1061a M.Arch II First Year Design Studio

Sunil Bald, Joel Sanders

Gallaudet University is the only bilingual liberal arts university in the world that provides education to deaf and hard of hearing students in American Sign Language (ASL) and English. In the fall of 2018, the university updated its 2022 Campus Plan to guide the revitalization of the heart of the campus through the coordinated development of three new mixed-use building projects over the next three to ten-year timeframe.

The Merrel Learning Center (MCL) is one of the buildings under consideration for revitalization in the 2018 Campus Plan Update process. It provides space for book stacks and study rooms, contains one of the largest video/film studios in Washington DC as well as the Gallaudet Deaf History Archives, and a variety of large lecture halls and office space. As a building typology, the university library is undergoing a major transformation in response to major changes in higher education and society at large. Students worked with Gallaudet's DeafSpace Class to envision the new Merrel Learning Center (MLC).

Participants

Hamzah Ahmed, Sara Alajmi, James Bradley, Taiming Chen, Miguel Darcy de Oliveira Miranda, Gretchen Gao, Hojae Lee, Smit Patel, Leonardo Serrano Fuchs, Adam Thibodeaux, Jerome Tryon, I-Ting Tsai, Justin Tsang and Anna Yu

Jury

Hansel Bauman, Stella Betts, Anna Dyson, David Serlin, Brigitte Shim, Ruth Starr and Marc Tsurumaki

Studio
Fall 2018
1061a M.Arch II First Year Design Studio
Sunil Bald, Joel Sanders
Jerome Tryon, Sara Alajmi

An L-shape that wraps around two edges

This project revisits the deaf space manual as it pushes forward the principles of design. It questions architecture and the finality of designed elements, such as walls and floors, to generate new spatial configurations for the noncompliant body, the deaf.

The new intervention is an L-shape that wraps around two edges of the Merrill Library Center in the middle of Gallaudet University in Washington, DC. The proposal hosts new designs that accommodate the deaf needs, such as vibrating floors to alert the users without startling them by tapping on their shoulders. Walls are designed to prevent glare and provide a comfortable environment for sign language users. The composition of these elements allow for visual transactions between spaces, and to better guide users throughout its program. Stacks, reading areas, and meeting rooms are reformed in the new building in order to redefine architecture for the deaf.

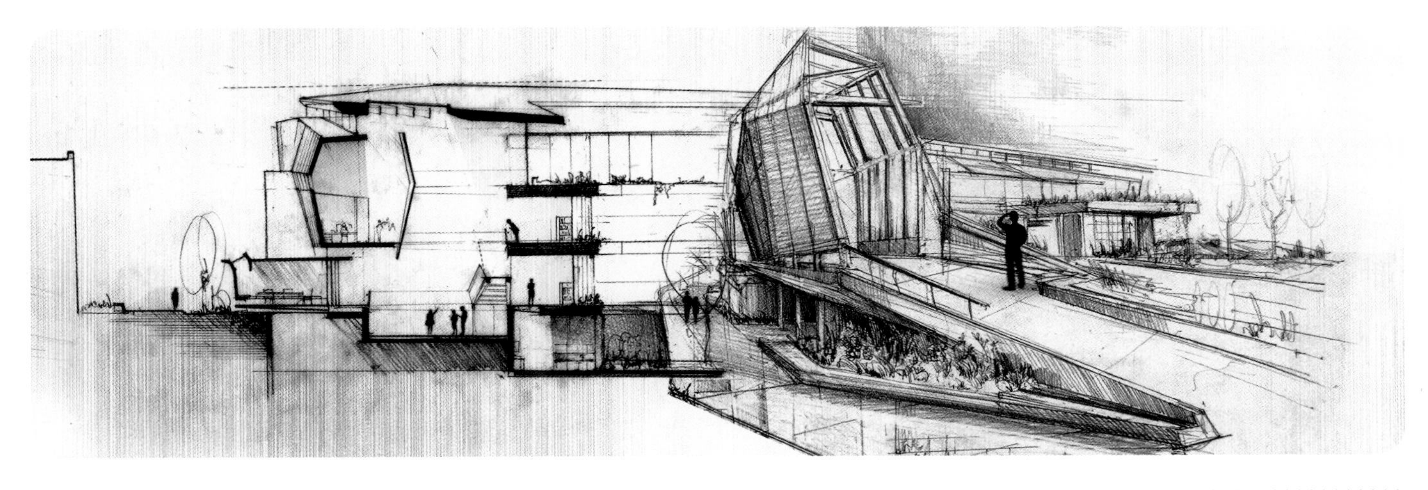

Studio
Fall 2018
1061a M.Arch II First Year Design Studio
Sunil Bald, Joel Sanders
Gretchen Gao, Adam Thibodeaux

Activist Space

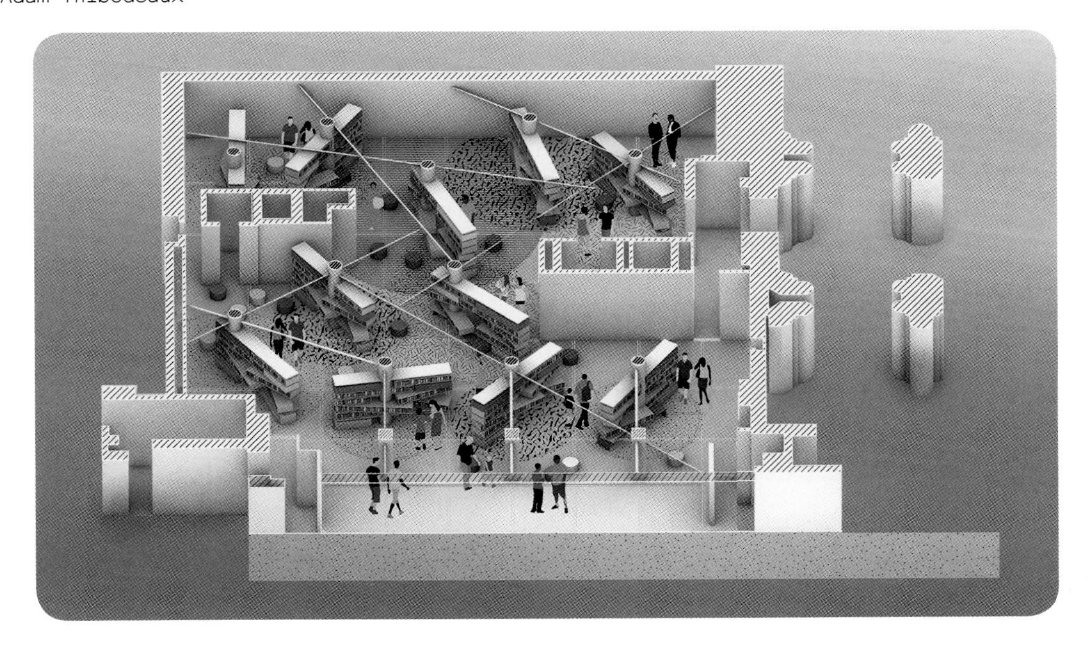

The proposed renovation of the existing library at Gallaudet University is inspired by the history and persistence of activism on campus. A variety of users and scales of interaction are accommodated by reimagining the library program, where all functions exist within an adaptable field of "activist space". The terraced platforms of the existing library are preserved and manipulated sectionally before being infilled with the activist space to open up the site and encourage connection through the campus. Activism is realized as an architectural method, where the new is imagined as a product of the past, and the ultimate goal is to create an open and adaptable hub for interaction.

Studio

Fall 2018

1101a Advanced Design Studio

Julie Snow, Surry Schlabs

The Leatherback Trust is located in Playa Grande, Guanacaste Providence, Costa Rica, a dry tropical forest where water is a precious resource, the lack of which being the principal deterrent to occupation. The Trust has been actively protecting turtle populations on the Playa Grande beach since 1993. Its operations are not restricted to leatherback research and preservation but also necessarily engage social, economic, and political activities. The Trust has a history of Playa Grande citizenship and is a conservator of natural resources.

The studio investigated how architecture creates cultural opportunities while reducing the impact of consumption of energy and water. Students designed a new marine biology station with biology research labs, classrooms, overnight and living facilities for resident biologists, EarthWatch volunteers, and school groups. In addition to living spaces and labs, the new Trust campus provides a separate public building for the community, guides, and tourists to use.

Participants

Kate Altmann, Isabel Balda Moncayo, Sharmin Bhagwagar, Pik-Tone Fung, Varoon Kelekar, Kassandra Leiva, Kola Ofoman, Melissa Russell, Dhruvin Shah, Abigail Smith

Jury

Sunil Bald, Kyle Dugdale, Jeff Goldstein, Joyce Hsiang, Carlos Jiménez, Joel Sanders, Mark Simon, Maryann Thompson, Lexi Tsien-Shiang, Adam Yarinsky

A sense of local community

Costa Rica underwent a dramatic shift in its economy from an agrarian based economy to one based on tertiary services. This was a result of the global decline in beef prices and the resulting rapid deforestation. As a result, there was an increasing reliance on foreign direct investment, the dependence on which presents the country with great challenges. Domestic revenue is relatively low and with shifting global trading patterns, this leaves the economy in a vulnerable position. NGOs working in the country offer temporary employment opportunities before moving on to their next challenges in another region or abroad. The question for the project, therefore, was how to make a building for the Leatherback Trust sustainable and critically stimulate employment opportunities for the local population. The siting and design of the new building sought to contribute to a sense of local community and to encourage responsible development along the road and away from the protected beach.

CJ: From a sustainable point of view, an energy conserving point of view, I think it is a really cool project. But a couple of things about ventilation: A. You discover that ventilation is a matter of wind going over an object creating a negative pressure and that pressure sucking things out of the building. So if you try to ventilate a lot, you don't want to have the negative space inside the structure and you want as much opening on the leave-side; then air will get sucked in and leave at a relatively higher rate. That's a 'Venturi' cone! But you have to locate where you want the ventilation. B. From a technical point of view and based on my personal experience, I mistrust having those openings, in terms of durability. These trusses that use Oak-kind of wood are expensive. I'm certain this truss you are using will rot when it gets wet then dries repeatedly. In order to use your desired material, you almost have to do something like a rainscreen or rubber sheet underneath the roof. On the other hand, I really like your grading from the street to the buildings and thinking about making social places clean. I think you need to think about your building in the same way.

KD: Like here, that's the most successful space. The little porch.

CJ: Yes, like any social building needs a gradation of sociability in the building.

An agroforestry research center with residential units for researchers

Since the 1950s, approximately 60% of Costa Rica's forests have been cleared to make room for cattle ranching and other agricultural practices. The country's commendable efforts in the 1990s to shift the economy from agriculture to eco-tourism have led to a vast decline in deforestation. Nevertheless eco-tourism is viewed as a rather unstable primary source of income. Murren Reserve as a site fell victim to agricultural practices and resulting deforestation. This project combines an agroforestry research center with residential units for researchers. The built volumes, enclosing private spaces such as sterile labs, residences, and libraries, are held in place by permanent wood scaffolding and elevated from the ground. The scaffolding allows for both flexible arrangements of agroforestry test plots on the ground and as containers for public spaces. The community kitchen serves as a central node, where the production, harvesting, and storage of fresh produce encourage community participation in the life cycle of Costa Rican land and its products.

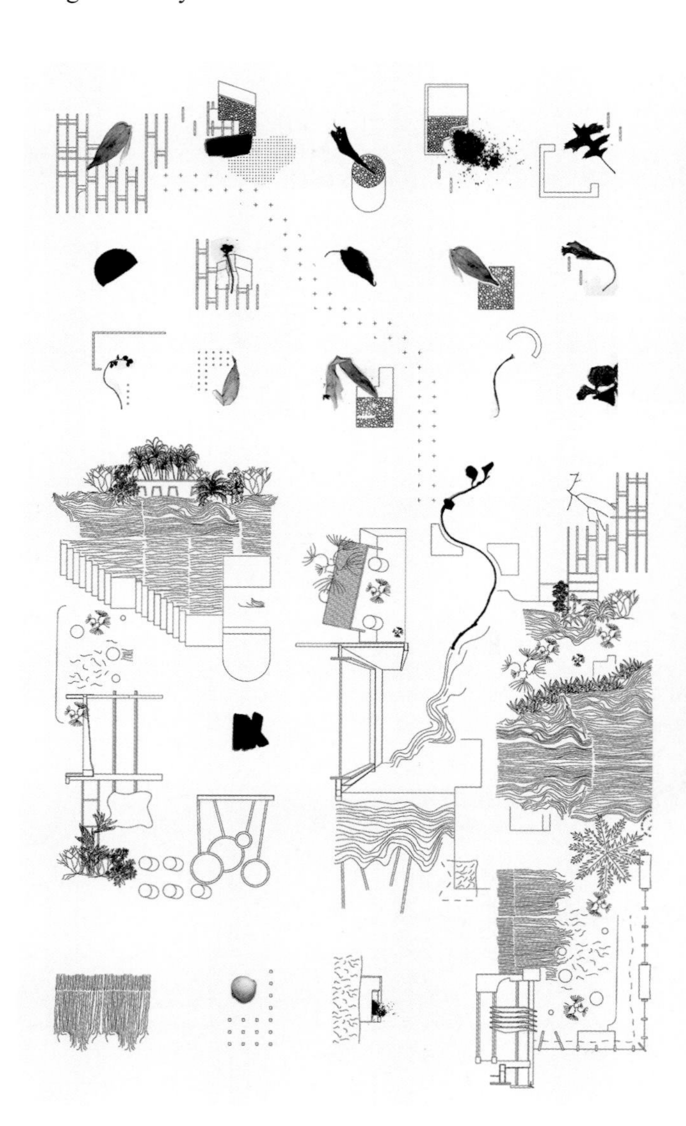

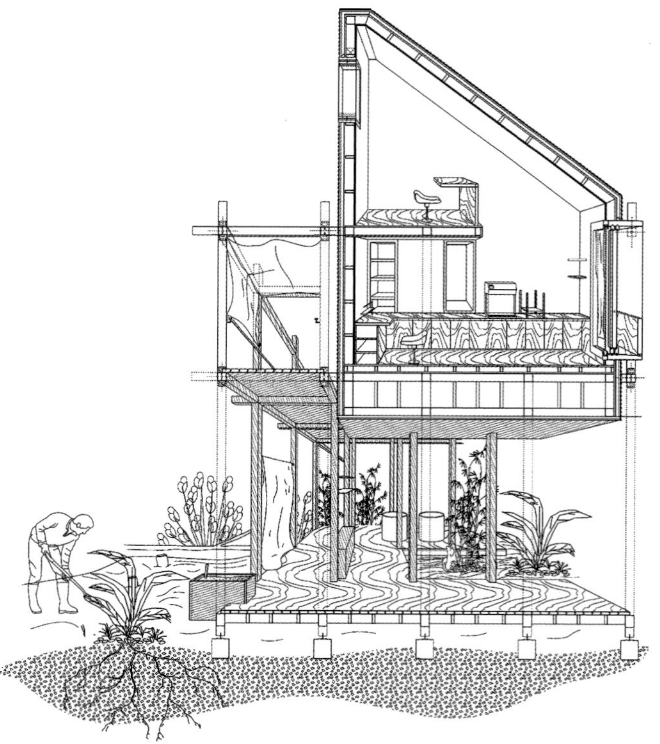

CJ: I think one thing you should reconsider is that you privileged everything with the same scale.

JG: There is more to imply here [in the section]. There is something with the level outdoor spaces and how they are also semi-protected. You seem to have, for this project, set up something like no other and I think you should take advantage of this relatively temporary climate you have created. From year round, spaces might be enclosed but then at some levels you can create something like a mini-garage. It will become more emblematic of the thought you have, making something come out of this place. I'm surprised in the model as well as the plan and the section that the space doesn't feel quite as big.

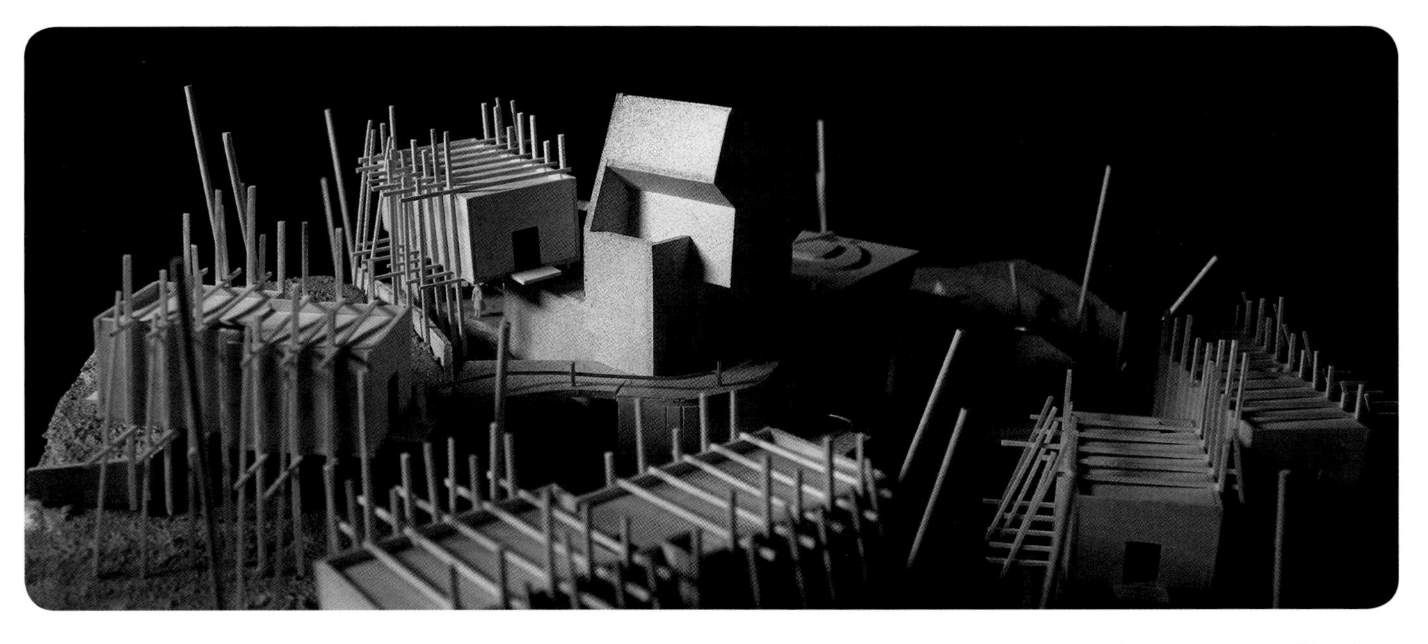

JH: I love the wackiness of it. I think it's amazing and so much fun. I like that it is sort of a hybrid treehouse or vardo and it seems to be a great place to get lost in and run around. It seems exuberant and different from everything else that we have seen today. From here, we can see a lot of dialogues where, somehow, there are both a kind of concrete and heaviness that is institutionally driven verses the lightweight wood structure. This project sort of defies, you know, the neat and polite ways of thinking about architecture, and because it reminds me more of stilts of treehouses or vardos, it has much of that sense of structure that is built for the exterior. You feel like you're partially camping in this part or you're up in the treehouse. It is big but in some way quite condensed that there is a density of experiences that one can get really lost in. I like the excessiveness of it.

CJ: I wish there was more discipline. I like the ephemeral aspect of the buildings but the epicenter of the institution remains, still, sacred. I wish it would have been more into the rock. What I mean is that you need to enjoy the type of environmentalistic hint, and let it come to you excessively.

Two distinct formal and material languages

This project, titled "Leatherback Trust Research Station", builds on The Leatherback Trust's history of promoting turtle conservation by addressing the social context of poaching. The new marine biology station consists of a mix of research labs, scientist residences, and an educational public corridor. The project is built in two distinct formal and material languages. Through this inherent dichotomy, spatial segregation allows for various levels of privacy within the program. The open research labs facilitate maximum passive ventilation and provide visitors with a glance into the inner workings of the station. Residential units are raised to create places of solitude amidst the forest foliage.

Studio
Fall 2018
1102a Advanced Design Studio
Simon Hartmann, Michael Samuelian, Andrei Harwell

Over the last 500+ years, inhabitants and users have left their imprint on Governors Island, not only extracting natural resources and constructing piers, buildings, and fortifications, but by literally modifying the ground and form of the island itself. As use of the island has changed over time, it has been implicated in an ever-evolving set of extended relationships with its context.

The advanced design studio "…And More" begins with this simple provocation, focusing on Governors Island itself as a physical object. Individual architectural explorations consider the island as a place and as an urban condition with a distinct public use within the urban fabric of New York. Rather than deploying standard formulas of urban development or focusing on the picturesque qualities of the island, students instead explored the infrastructures that can connect the island with its surroundings, and described how discreet architectural projects can change the way the island functions within its city and region.

Participants
Melinda Agron, Olisa Agulue, Lani Barry, Brian Cash, Kerry Garikes, Mengi Li, Larkin McCann, Miguel Sanchez-Enkerlin, Mariana Riobom

Jury
Emily Abruzzo, Beat Aeberhard, Amy Green Deines, Edith Hsu-Chen, Eeva-Liisa Pelkonen, Bill Price, Anna Puigjaner, Georg Vrachliotis, Jelena Vucic

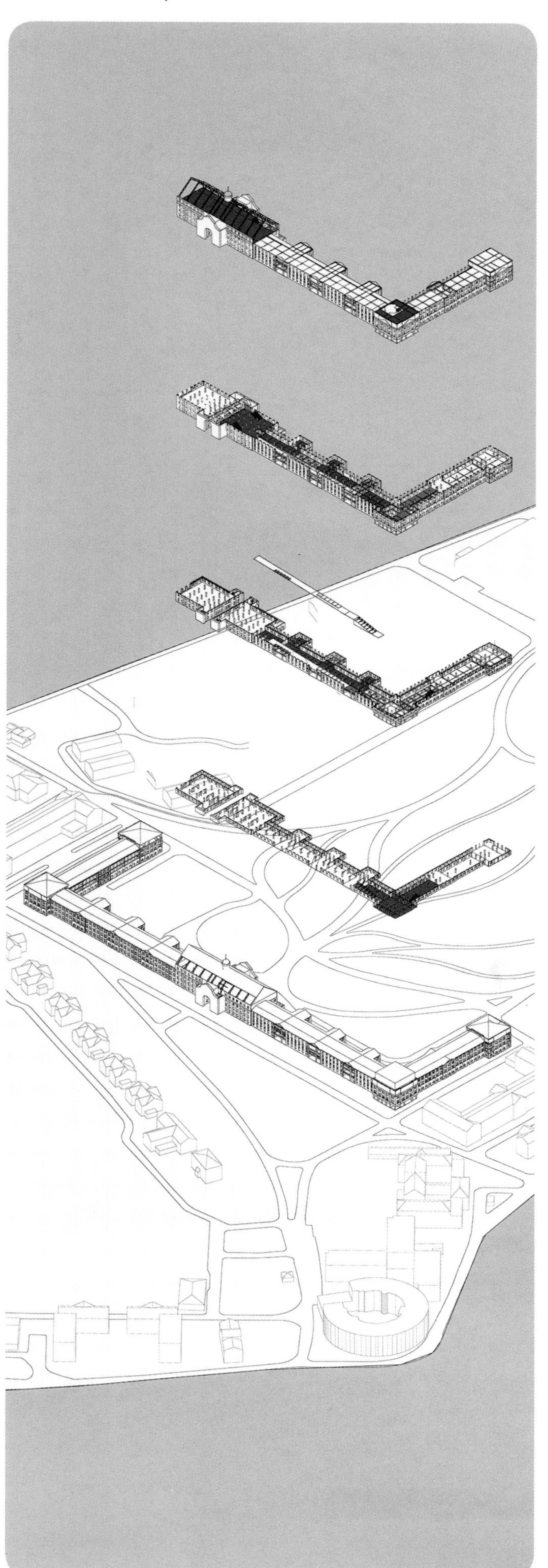

Fourteen separate barracks under one roof

This project, titled "Liggett Hall Transformation", is a proposal to house a cultural institution in the 300,000 square-foot abandoned Liggett Hall by embracing Governors Island as an arts destination for New York City residents. Designed as fourteen separate barracks under one roof, Liggett Hall poses the challenge of how to intervene, yet unify the building as a whole. A proposed ramp connects all floors for visitor access and creates elongated views through the building. The ramp is inserted between the building's relentless post and beam structure, shifting the structural system. The ramp and slight reduction of beams allow visitors to stand at the far west corner of Liggett Hall and see through the grand room above the archway. This ramp, which brings visitors up from the corner to the grand room, is used for installations and exhibits on the journey to the top of the building. Finally, the punctured north facade of Liggett Hall invites the visitors of Governors Island to come inside.

EHC: One of the worst things about Liggett Hall is its length. I really appreciate that you just embraced it's linearity. So having this super long insertion that just re-emphasizes its length is really, really interesting. You took a feature that could be a real drawback, what a lot of people really complain about, it's length, and did something with it. The linearity of the ramp evokes, for everybody, Guggenheim, which is tricky. Guggenheim is a spectacular, iconic building. Building a ramp for a museum, or a gallery, or cultural space is going to pose programming challenges. You've grappled with this. Though it is a gentle slope you may want to punch it up.

ELP: I think a precedent could be the Payne Whitney Gymnasium, an amazing building. It's a neo-Gothic building; it's one of the biggest buildings on campus. It's neo-Gothic but it has this gym inside—I think it's the biggest gym in the world. It's fantastic. You go to the 8th floor and there's the pool. It's like a Koolhaas section of the New York Athletic Association.You have this sort of representation of the facade and behind it weird things happen. You have this representation of building, it has its logic with a lot of length, and you produce this surprising interior which is totally wacko. *laughter*

1102a Advanced Design Studio
Simon Hartmann, Michael Samuelian, Andrei Harwell
Mengi Li (Feldman Nominee)

EHC: Cremation is an ancient practice of many cultures, and for many cultures it's a very singular event, for one person. The family and community come together. In Buddhist culture you accompany the body to the furnace. I've accompanied my grandfather's body. And it was such an intensely private experience with my family. So now you're introducing something that's about a community of multiple cremation ceremonies happening at once. I'm not hearing enough right now about why this should happen on Governor's Island. So it feels a little bit like the idea which you have tried to implement from there.

AD: But then you show us the spreadsheet, a big spreadsheet about how this can generate a lot of revenue. And that's a very valid exercise but it wasn't necessary now. It contradicts your mission which is to introduce an egalitarian sense of community for many people of different backgrounds to come together. There is this key moment in their lives, together. And you had an image of a dollar sign pointing to people, so there's a lot of kind of jarring disjointed or incongruous messages coming together.

MS: Well let me push back on that because I think there's a way to do both. I think you can be sincere and have a real back up justification for it. You have a story about this collective experience that will give people a memory, an imprint about Governor's Island they don't have today. And you know the connection to the water, the connection to time. It's all there, Edith is right. You should start with that. Here's my vision and this is how I do it, and the money's okay too, but it really starts with the 'why', which you didn't really start with, because you do believe it and you do have a story to capture.

Seeking a truly public program is core to the mission of Governors Island. This project proposes a new ritual of death that is of economic, cultural, and social benefit. Positioned on the southern tip of the public park, known as The Hills, the design takes a strategic and conceptual stance incited by Hart Island, the largest potter's field in the United States where unclaimed bodies have been buried in mass graves for decades. In contrast, a sensitively crafted gathering space will provide dignified collective memorial service and cremations each day for anyone who passes in New York City. Cremation are strung together branching off the central hall which is available for alternative programming by visitors, such as conferences, events and celebrations. The architecture orients one to look in and out simultaneously, framing panoramic views of the Statue of Liberty, New Jersey, Lower Manhattan and Brooklyn.

A sensitively crafted gathering space

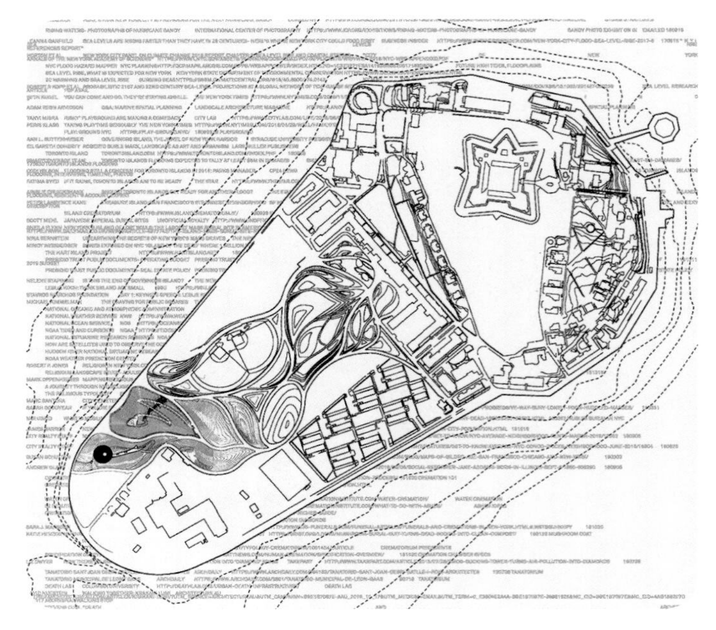

Walkways that act as spaces of intersection

This project proposes a series of residential buildings on Governors Island, leaning on the premise that for the island to truly become a part of the city it must have permanent, year-round residents. The residential blocks—whose architecture implicitly defines a mixed age occupancy—are elevated above public program and walkways that act as spaces of intersection between residents and non-residents. This proposal looks to the future in many senses: it offers a mix of uses and residential types, adapts to changing water levels, and understands that the longevity of Governors Island depends on an architectural proposal that can be re-appropriated over time.

33

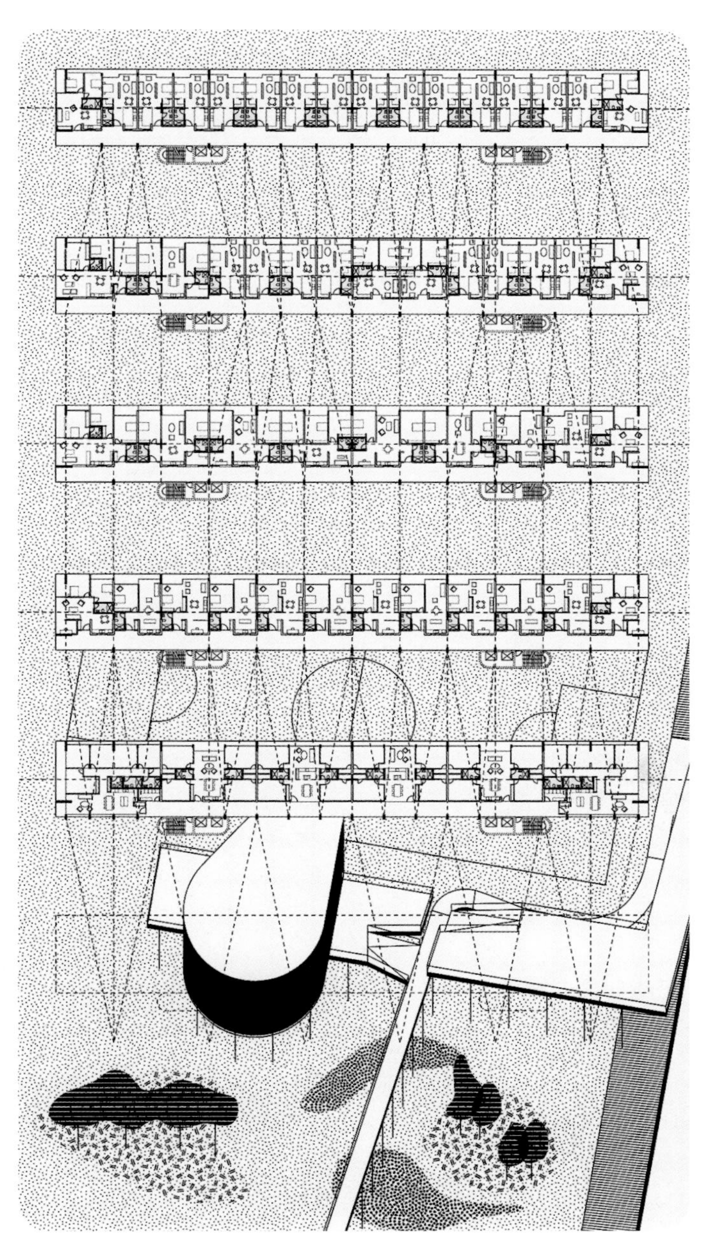

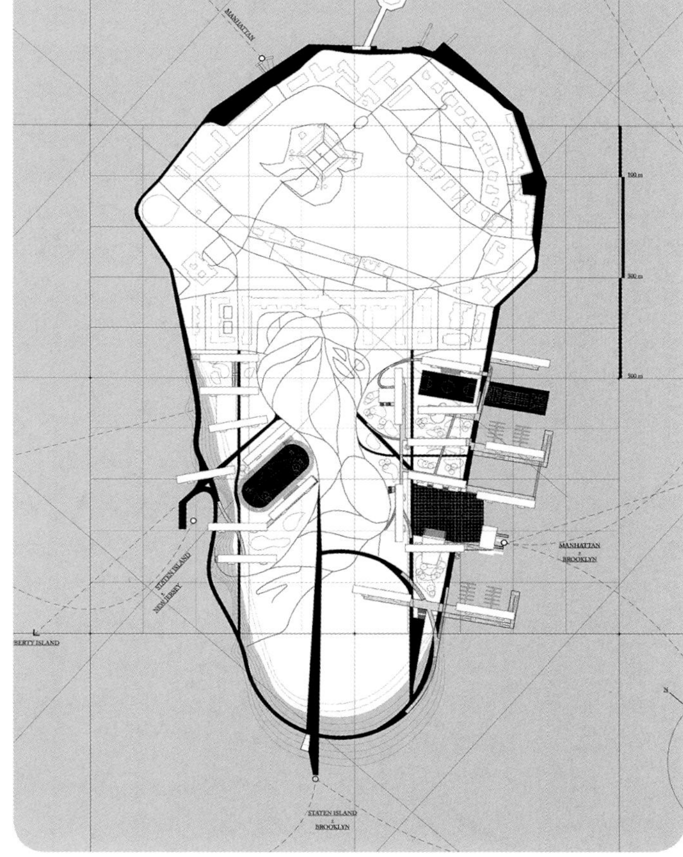

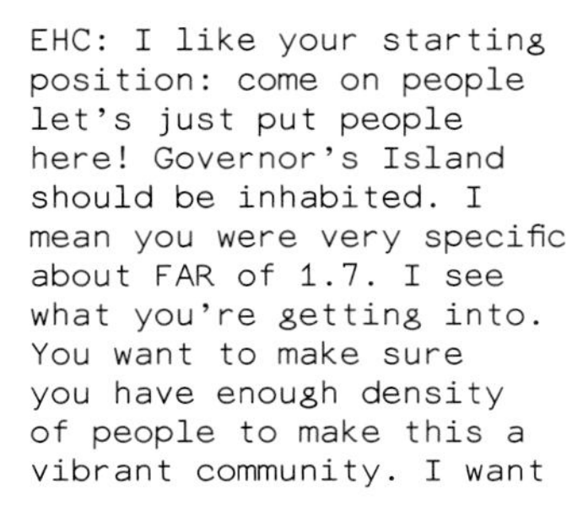

EHC: I like your starting position: come on people let's just put people here! Governor's Island should be inhabited. I mean you were very specific about FAR of 1.7. I see what you're getting into. You want to make sure you have enough density of people to make this a vibrant community. I want to hear more about your thinking about streets. Because the most successful communities have great streets. And I see boardwalks, the ring boardwalk and some internal streets. What is it like to walk along these boardwalks? What do you engage with?

While I love the premise of bringing density here, bringing residential units here, make sure you also build the other stuff. Not just the dwelling units. So this can really be a healthy community because it's providing active storefronts, parks and playgrounds. Talk about the other things that support the health of the community. Otherwise you end up having a Tower on Park development that reads like public housing. So that's the danger here. You have to be focused on the ground plane. The most important part of building development is the first quarter of it and what's happening there.

Studio
Fall 2018
1103a Advanced Design Studio
Adam Yarinsky, Lexi Tsien-Shiang

The interrelationship between individual and social identity is the essence of John and Dominique de Menil's conception of the Rothko Chapel as both place and program. The Chapel building, completed in 1971, is a space for meditation created by Mark Rothko. The Chapel is a platform for social justice symbolized by the adjacent plaza, the reflecting pool, and Barnett Newman's sculpture "Broken Obelisk" which is dedicated to Martin Luther King. Reflecting the shared vision of Mark Rothko and the Menils, the Chapel's identity as a cultural institution is defined through both introspection and exchange.

Through the design of new facilities to support the Rothko Chapel's mission, architecture embodies and extends its identity directly through use and experience. The studio worked across physical and conceptual scales—from the frame of the city, to the institution, to the body as it relates to space and understanding. Both as a process and a product, identity is a filter through which we interpret, commune, and change, as individuals and as a collective.

Participants
Diego Arango, Gwyneth Bacon-Shone, Nicole Doan, Alejandro Duran, Zelig Fok, Erin Kim, Dylan Lee, Jeffrey Liu, Anna Rothschild, Jacob Schaffert

Jury
Barry Bergdoll, Omar Gandhi, Mario Gooden, Chris McVoy, William Middleton, Thomas de Monchaux, Christopher Rothko, Rosalyne Shieh, Sydney Simon, Julie Snow, Yasmin Vobis

Buildings and landscape create layered anticipation

The new buildings and landscape on the site create a series of framed views that lead the visitor toward the chapel and the paintings within. While the existing chapel and plaza are central to supporting the mission of social justice, the new rooms and gardens compliment this mission by providing different environments for people to meet, organize, reflect, or rest. The plan maintains the north-south axis—defined by the chapel, plaza, pool, and obelisk—integral to the introspective character of the Rothko Chapel. By drawing in visitors from the street with views that create incomplete glimpses of this axis, the new buildings and landscape create layered anticipation that supports the original spaces without overpowering them. The chapel and plaza are only fully legible when the visitor inhabits them. On opposite corners of the site, an orientation center and a community events space bracket the site and welcome pedestrians. At the northwest corner, a series of outdoor rooms lead toward the center of the site. The community space on the southeast corner has a ramped interior corridor that frames a limited view of Barnett Newman's Broken Obelisk. The corridor opens to an exterior elevated terrace with views to the reflecting pool, plaza, and chapel.

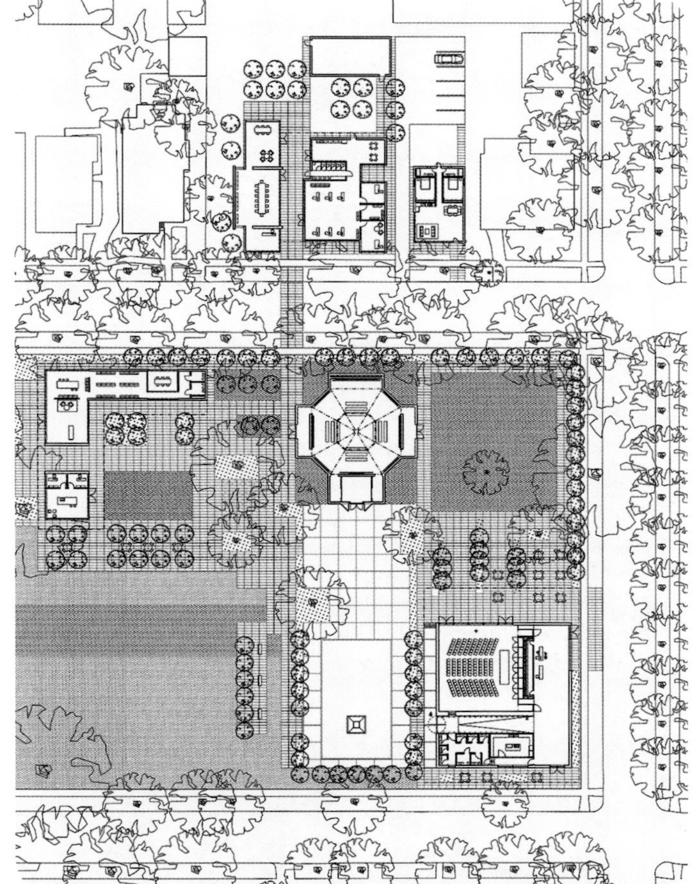

JS: There are some smart things going on in terms of site planning…It seems like the dialogue between the outdoor room, the lawn, to the gathering space, which is sort of semi enclosed—I would say too enclosed—to the space on the West which is an L. There are three different versions of outdoor rooms.

BB: I like the making of a kind of "roomness", the kind of yes-a-room and not-a-room…is it a room, is it not a room, is it part of the outside…
I applaud the opaqueness.

JS: I think that the idea of the subtlety of the glimpse, or fragmented view, I think is really interesting because there's plenty of spaces to use as a totality, you've given several opportunities for that, but to begin to frame glimpses is great. For instance the image where you just see a fragment of a door and a tree against that sort of wall seems like a very poetic way to approach something pretty intense.

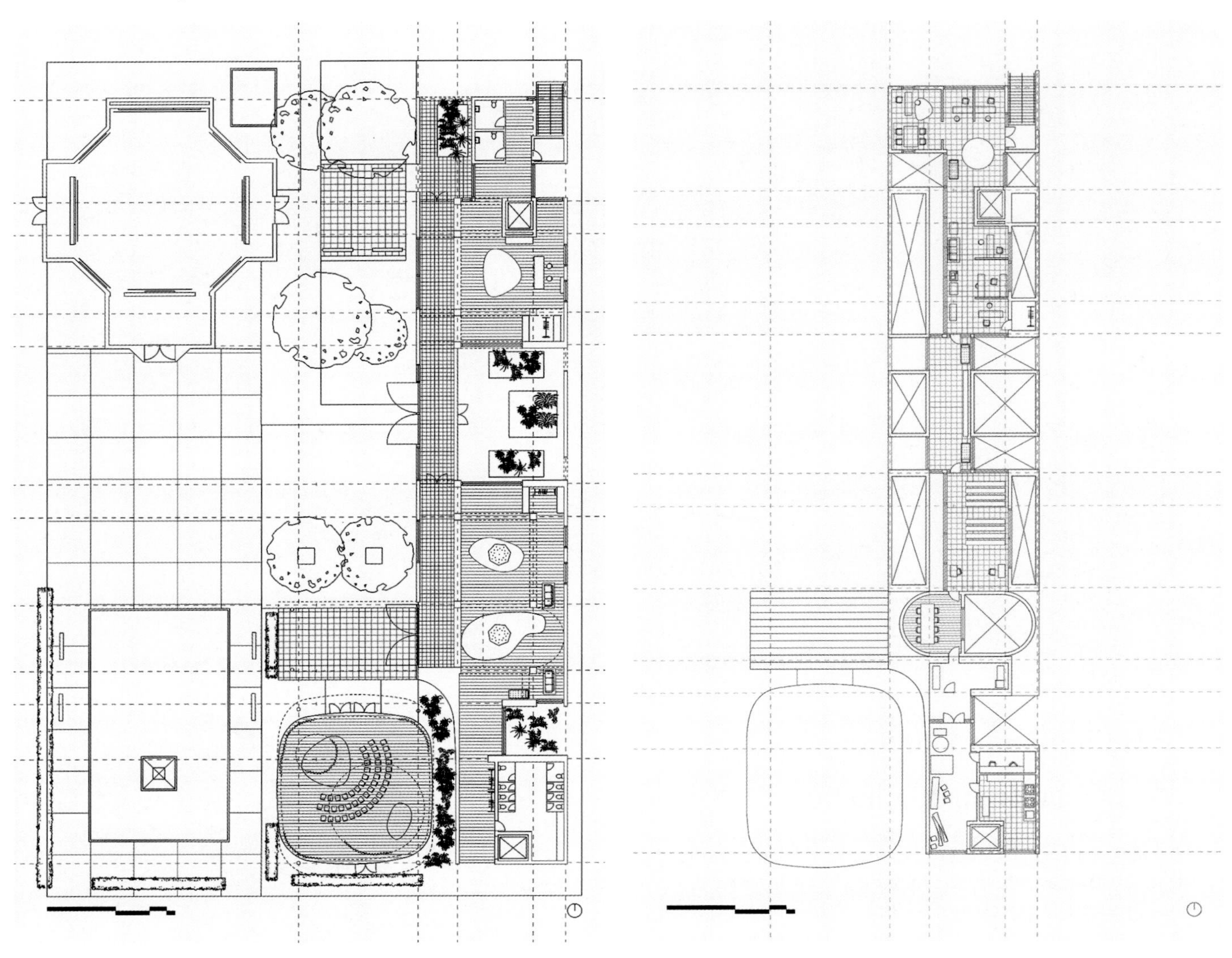

A sequence of enclosed and open-air spaces

Suburban Houston, Texas is an unexpected setting for a world-class artistic campus. Walking amid the rows of bungalows, one would never expect to find an object-building as strange, powerful, and yet unassuming as the Rothko Chapel. Yet there it is, welcoming all who find it with open arms. This proposal structures the relationship between the chapel and its context—namely, the suburban neighborhood of Montrose and the rest of the Menil campus. A sequence of enclosed and open-air spaces come together to bound the site's perimeter; the boundary they create activates the site, formalizes the transition between the interior of the chapel and the street, and places the chapel into a clearer relationship with its context. New program space is housed within a building on the site's eastern edge—this building acts as an activated edge for the Menil campus and prepares visitors for the experience of entering the chapel itself.

CM: I think the idea of creating this boundary. A building that's not a building, a kind of wall, is an interesting idea. It reinforces the field around the Chapel. But then to literally make it wall-like in reality? Sometimes it's interesting to do the opposite of what's expected. In other words, you're making a wall. Sometimes it's interesting to make a relationship with something just by doing the opposite.

A cross axis of buildings focused on gathering and social justice

The Rothko Chapel is an unaffiliated non-profit spiritual organization focused on personal meditation, communal gathering, and global social justice. The balance between contemplation and action bring visitors together from around the world to their small campus to experience the fourteen monumental paintings by Rothko that define the octagonal hall of the chapel building. Here visitors can behold the monolithic broken obelisk sculpture that acts as a counterpoint to the paintings in the outdoor reflecting pool. The goal of my project was to heighten this dialectic by framing it with the campus expansion, while forming a cross axis of buildings focused on gathering and social justice. The project creates a defined campus language while respecting the integrity and power of the existing chapel.

CM: This is a strange project. It actually seems to be quite interesting to me to itemize the program so the chapel building seems to be just one of a number of buildings. It almost becomes a bit anonymous. It makes the power of the project come down to how you detail it. So whether or not, let's say, it's brick and it's running bond—that level of detail. To the level of detail of glazing. Is it a steel sliding window system? How does this track to the detail of the ceiling? I think it's that kind of level of subtlety that will make this project sing. To me, at an overall scale, I can buy this. It seems quite smart. But now I want to dig into how is this constructed.

Studio
Fall 2018
1104a Advanced Design Studio
Peter Eisenman, Anthony Gagliardi

New Haven, Connecticut is famous for having one of the few remaining planned nine square grids. While the central square contains the historical town green, there is little else on the periphery of the nine-squares that records the figure with any positive difference. Because of the demolition of the Coliseum and the imminent removal of the South Orange Public Housing Project, there is an entire neighborhood-scale area in the city with no spatial or programmatic resolution.

To address this issue, students produced a project for a site in New Haven bounded by George Street on the north side, Church Street on the west, the railroad tracks on the east, and Union Station on the south. Students questioned the urban ground, its lack of grain or grid, and the unstructured gap between legible forms.

Participants
Kunhee Chang, Nancy Chen, Orli Hakanoglu, Nicholas Miller, Evan Sale, Luke Studebaker, Christopher Tritt, Minquan Wang, Issy Yi, Winston Yuen

Jury
Miroslava Brooks, Brian Butterfield, Henry Cobb, Preston Scott Cohen, Cynthia Davidson, Rossana Hu, Elisa Iturbe, Lyndon Neri, Caroline O'Donnell, Nicolai Ouroussoff, Ingeborg Rocker, Anthony Vidler, Sarah Whiting, Guido Zuliani.

Latent within the city is a modular grid system

The historic "mat building" tends to fail urbanistically due to the homogeneity of its own system; it can be read as oppositional to its urban context. Examples of such mat buildings include Le Corbusier's Venice Hospital (1965) and Candilis-Josic-Woods' Free University in Berlin (1963). As a response, we proposed a mat building whose modular grid system and massing derived not from an internal logic divorced from that of its surroundings, but from one found within the heterogeneous built environment of New Haven.

Latent within the city is a modular grid system for a mat building: the nine square. This form exists in downtown as well as in the Hill neighborhood. The scalar relationship between these two instances of nine square grids is exploited within each level of the proposed urban-scale building.

The organization of enclosed and open space on each level is derived through a process of grid-based abstraction from the distinct built environments of each of the nine square neighborhoods. While these derivations share an organizational logic, they differ in their form, use, and scale. At its edges, the mat building frays and integrates into the vacancies of its immediate urban context, blurring the boundary between city and building.

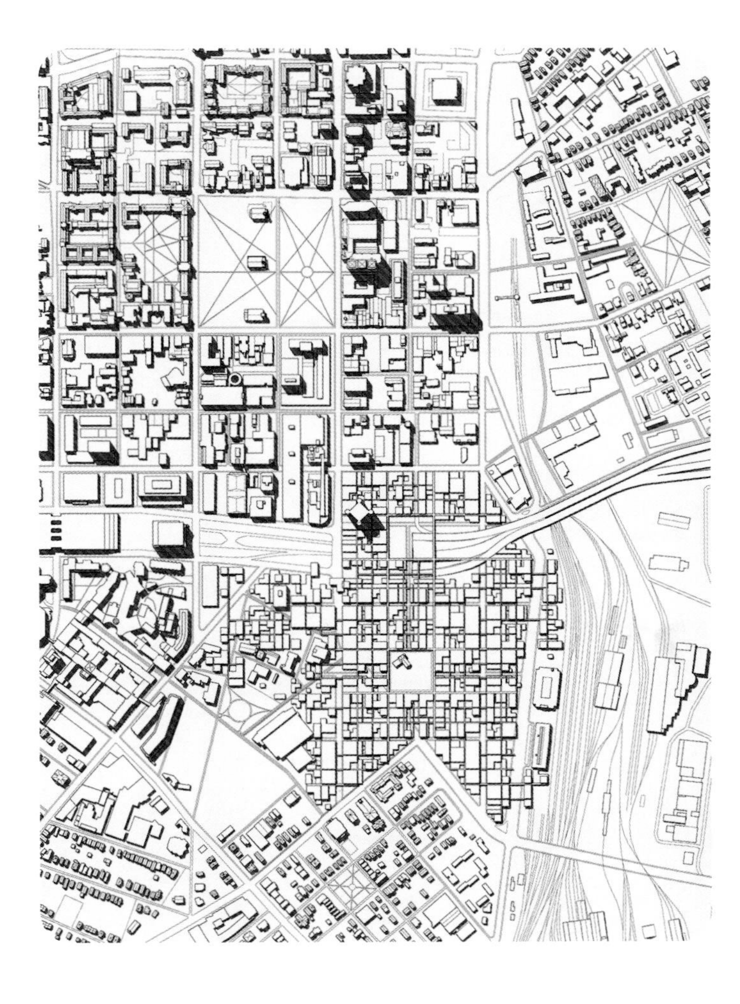

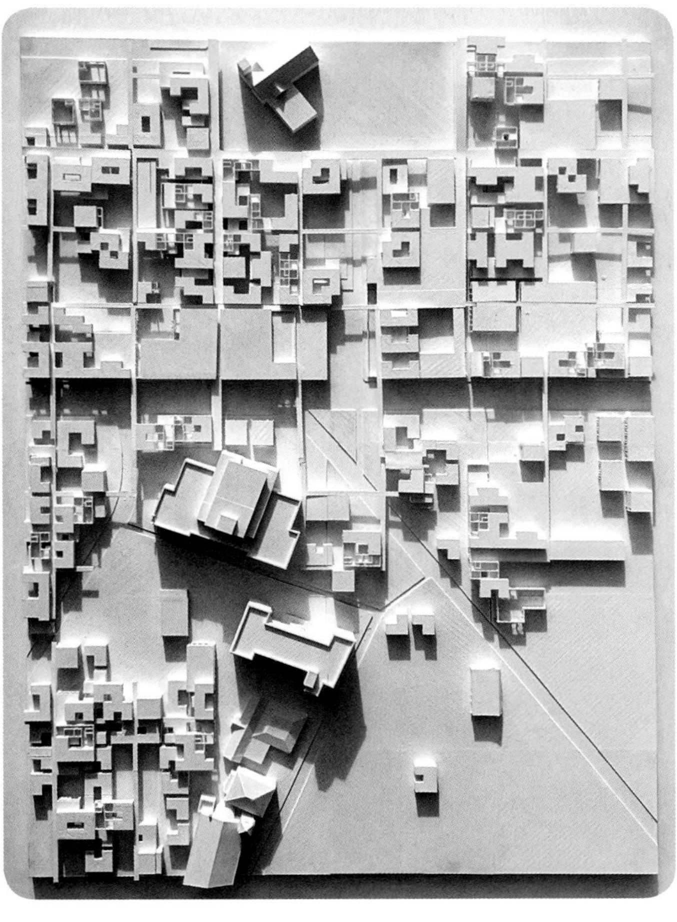

SW: Do you think you were too faithful to the mat typology? Does a mat typology always have to be orthogonal? Surely this assignment is to take a typology, and through that collision with site, invent something new. I think here, you've invented something new. I would even go further and say, okay, if this is the project and we're taking this system and that system, those are not the only two systems on the site. There are curvilinear systems there too that need to be tested into the system to create more variety.

TV: I would say that there's a possibility of doing an explicit mat and an implicit mat. I think that is an implicit mat, the single-level cross, but you're also doing an explicit mat with your streets in the air.

PSC: I think the thing that attracts me here is not that it is two grids coming together, it's the dual scale that is starting to occur. One tiny scale of objects that belong to the smaller grid; the bigger ones are even able to retain their integrity, occasionally clipped in certain ways to establish special conditions. It looks like urban texture even though it was generated by this very abstract method. And also, I believe it could use multiple programs; it's more realistic to imagine an integration of what you're calling 'public services'. But you can't possibly cover this entire territory with commercial or public space. It'd have to serve the entirety of New Haven, or more. So this could be very fine grain, in certain areas spotted with shops or whatever they may be, and most of that could be housing or offices.

The incursion of a metonymic quadrant of the four into the nine

The New Haven urban form is dominated by a nine square urban plan. This project emphasizes a latent four square plan adjacent to the original nine square. As a formal equivalent that also impinges on the nine square, the four square introduces dualism and dissonance in order to weaken the cohesive image of the nine square. Formally, the project maintains the dissonance between the four square and nine square by simultaneously taking two approaches to their relationship. First, the qualitative differences between the two organisms are left unresolved in the incursion of a metonymic quadrant of the four into the nine. Second, this quadrant is carved away by a supple contextual grid that represents the smoothing of the transition between the two squares. The resulting figural void introduces a linear public space between Union Station and Downtown. This form counters the central hierarchy of the New Haven Green.

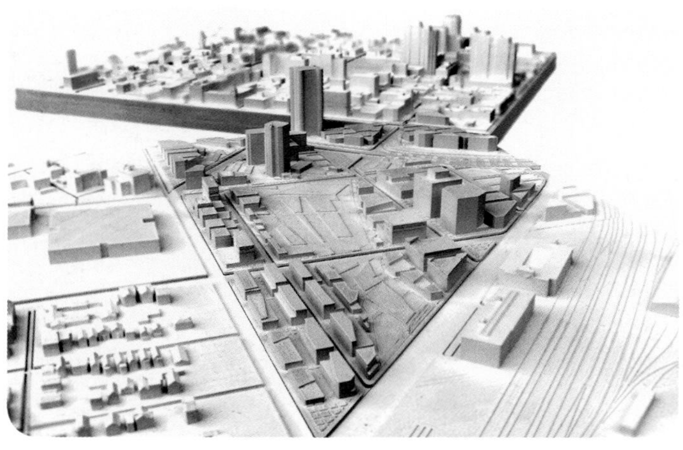

CO: I see it diagrammatically in your project, but in plan I don't think the four-square is legible.

BB: I don't think the four-square needs to be legible, you just need the figure reading against the orthogonal. So I think you're raising a really important point; I think it behooves you. It behooves you to articulate when you can drop what your process is or what you made significant for the reading. So the question is legibility. I don't think this is a project that demands legibility of process, which is interesting in your realm. You say that New Haven is your precedent, but it's truly here. And I think that process is part of what you're not showing us.

RH: It's related to my question. When you moved from the nine-square to the four, which logic did you employ? Did you take four of the nine and enlarge it to become four? Or did you take the one square and divide by four?

Displacing the monocentric and polycentric ideal cities

The organizing logic of the New Haven nine square cannot be extended outward. We instead identify a four square latent in the Hill neighborhood. We articulate the space between, and by implication the rest of the space in the city, as an interstitial north/south square grid.

The four square creates an opposition to the original nine square and the monocentric ideal city that it describes. By building the remaining area as a homogenous field, we formally reinforce both figures while challenging the rationality of either. The north/south grid is itself weakened by a competing system of circulation and buildings that depends on neither of the figures nor on any regular grid.

By displacing the monocentric and polycentric ideal cities from an assumed open ground, we transform holistic forms into a composite city. The new ground both accentuates edges and enables connection.

CD: It's significant to use a building grid as your urban instigator and if you extrapolated from that and made an argument about how urbanism relates to architecture and vice versa. There's a kind of zooming in and out that is very naturalized in your project. I like the simplicity of the argument and the approach. I just think that it would affect the nine-square and four-square as urban-scale interventions. You're building figures that are sitting rather than figures in buildings within an urban fabric. It's a very interesting inversion but you're not owning up to it. For me, that's the key invention of the project. You're making an argument; the diagram with the little hand sketch that said you had the two figures against a gridded background isn't clear. Because usually you'd have figures in a fabric be the buildings in a neutral urban grid. You're saying the two urban grids, the nine-square and the four-square, are forming two figures in a neutral fabric. And that neutral fabric is built form; it's architecture, it's not urbanism. And you don't seem to be running with that idea, which I'd say, is a softball.

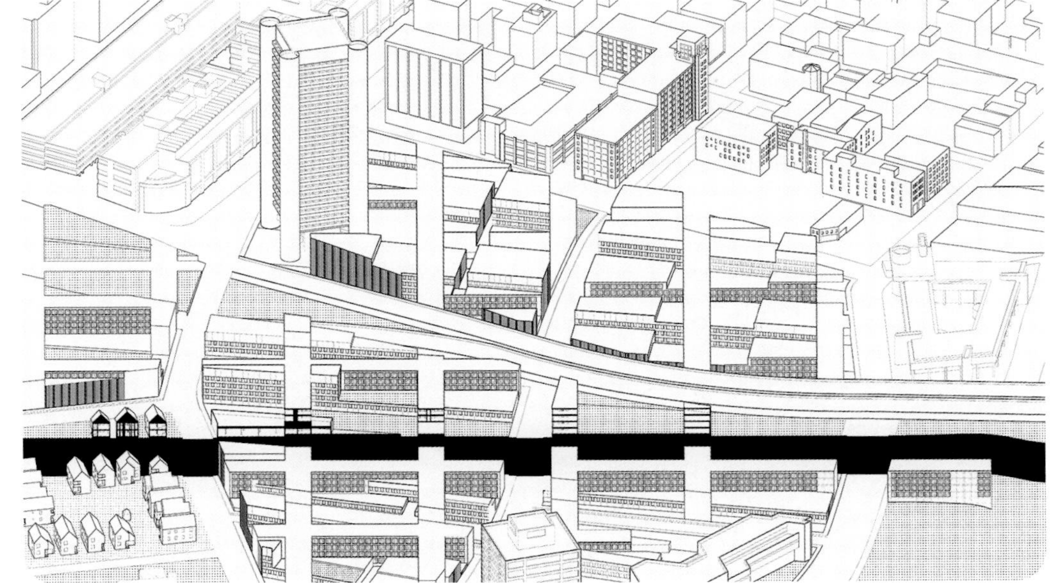

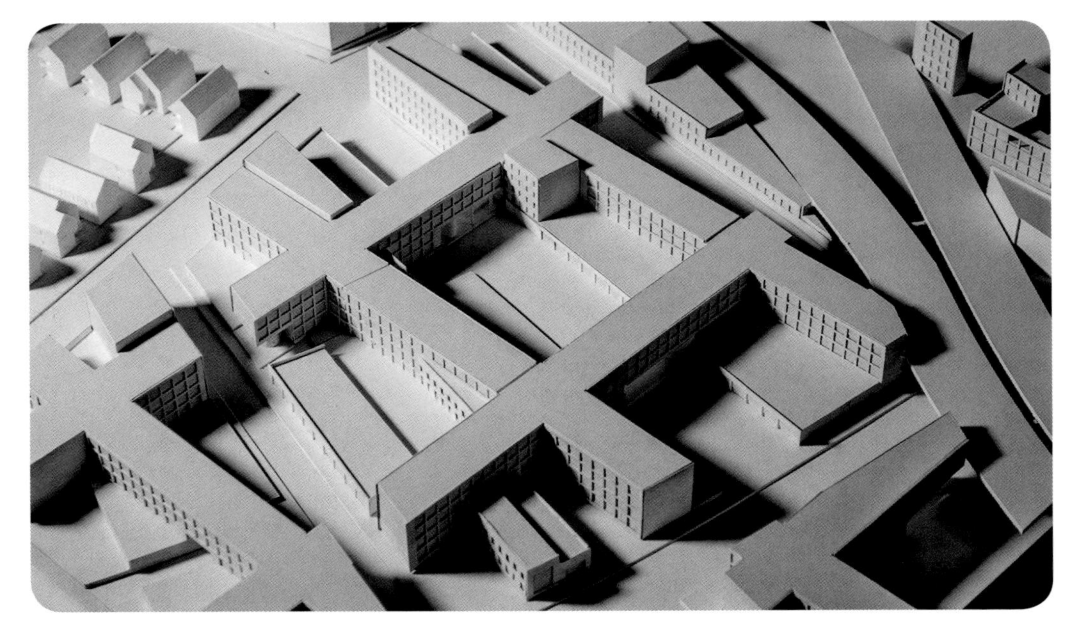

Studio

Fall 2018

1105a Advanced Design Studio

Rossana Hu, Lyndon Neri

Nostalgia tends to be taken dismissively or negatively in both architecture and general culture. Charles Maier aptly states: “Nostalgia is to longing as kitsch is to art.” This studio is based on the premise that nostalgia, rather than being reductive, offers a productive means to engage with issues of heritage, collective memory, displacement, and urban renewal.

The studio explores how reflective nostalgia may offer a new model for adaptive reuse in the context of China. China’s growth is unprecedented; it holds the record for the fastest growing economy in history, and the race towards urbanization is resulting in a vast landscape of anonymous cities. Urban transformations happen quickly and entire neighborhoods and streetscapes are altered seemingly overnight. There are certainly iconic monuments that have been preserved, but the commercialization of these relics renders them incapable of representing the depth of the city’s culture. Our test case for the studio looked specifically at Shanghai and the remnants of its tumultuous industrial heritage.

Participants

Tayyaba Anwar, Sissi Guo, Dimitris Hartonas, Jennifer Lai, Minakshi Mohanta, Iven Peh, Vivian Tsai, Lucia Venditti, Matthew Wagstaffe, Ray Wu, Katrina Yin

Jury

James Dallman, Laurie Hawkinson, Zhang Ke, Grace La, Julie Snow, Nader Tehrani, Calvin Tsao, Billie Tsien, Tod Williams

Studio
Fall 2018
1105a Advanced Design Studio
Rossana Hu, Lyndon Neri
Jennifer Lai

New variations of moving and staying in space

This project integrates the streetscapes and everyday activities found in Shanghainese life into a hotel. By introducing the streetscape throughout the hotel, the traveler is able to interact with the local community and initiate different exchanges. The insertion of the streetscape also creates new thresholds for local participation. Working with the constraints of the existing structural grid on site, portions of the existing slabs are removed and new programmed spaces are added. This design brings about new variations of moving and staying in space.

43

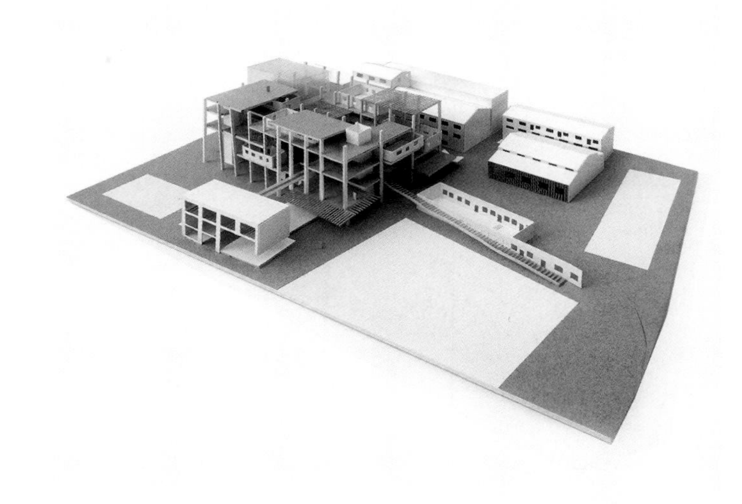

CT: There is a potential here, where you can test how far you can set the tone and then allow things to happen because you are orchestrating all these open spaces according to your imagination. Let's say 'we imagine it and then let someone finish it'. Like an artist doing an exquisite cadaver, he paints it and it has a life of its own, and another artist can finish it.

BT: I think this project is kind of an 'architecture without architects' that has a very strong, either, intellectual or physical framework, but the architecture you are saying is left to the people who live to furnish or to inhabit the interstitial space.

TW: If the street is truly public, how do you make sure in some conceptually legal way to define what is open to everyone and what is not. Here, although you have done good work in bringing that back together, I think it is very difficult to know what is actually private and what is public.

Studio
Fall 2018
1105a Advanced Design Studio
Rossana Hu, Lyndon Neri
Ray Wu

A walled garden with demolished Maoist-industrial nostalgia

"Teahouse as the Other" is an adaptive-reuse of an industrial site situated within a residential neighborhood in Jing'an, Shanghai. The program of the hotel is augmented by an other, in this case, the Chinese teahouse typology. A walled garden with demolished Maoist-industrial nostalgia taking the place of fake mountains and water features complements the stripped main structure which houses an open air teahouse on the first two floors and accommodations on the remaining three. Towards the street a visual boundary is maintained by the entry gate and the indistinct main building, masking the presence of a garden.

GK: So, I want to ask you a question. Do you feel comfortable with people … because you have provided the most beautiful handmade piece of paper. Do you feel like you would want to have other's make their marks or would you want to control their marks? Because that's a very … it's an attitude about how you want to work as an architect. Are you making a paper where everyone can apply their ideas, or would you want to be in control?

RW: I think I would want to be in control in the beginning. That's when I'm allowed to have control. Then at one point, I'm going to have to let it go, that's just how I see it.

NT: At what point are you going to let it go? *laughter* No this is a serious question.

RW: When you build it.

NT: So your assumption is that you will fight to the death until it's built?

TW: That's great.

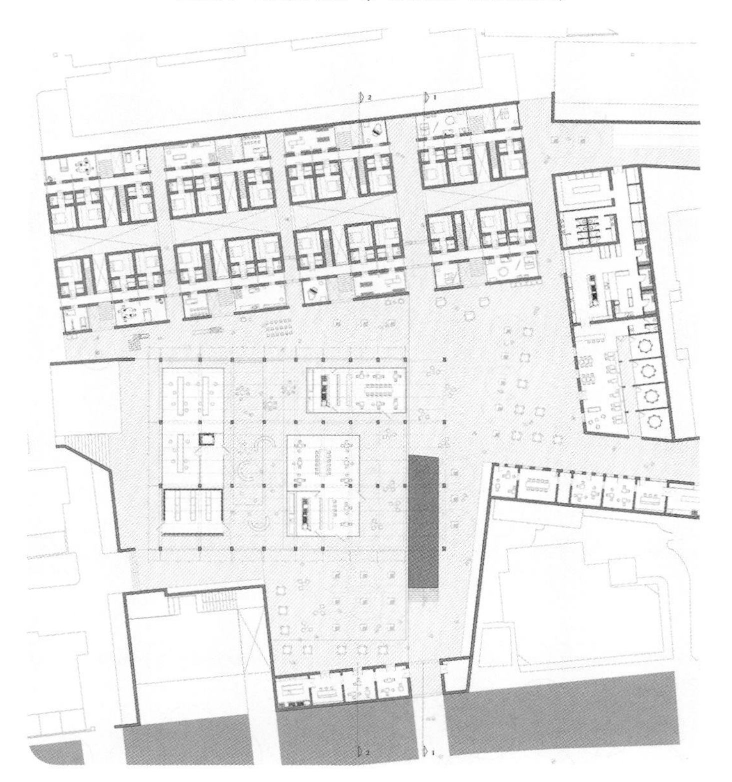

Rethinking the room as the most basic unit of architectural space

The hotel typology introduces an opportunity for the rethinking of the room as the most basic unit of architectural space. It is a typology that is built around the idea of minimizing individual space in favor of the collection of both spaces and functions that would otherwise be compressed into private units. This idea is not only at the core of the hotel's functional structure, but it also represents a critical model for those who think more radically about new forms of inhabitation and cohabitation.

The strategy for adaptive reuse is to introduce the new architecture as a landscape on top of which the old sits. This landscape articulates, in the simplest way, the complex geometries that bound our site, while maintaining and multiplying the perspectives of the main building from outside and from within. The main building, intact in its façade from the first floor up, is wrapped with a transparent structure that adds a new layer to encourage dialogue between the old and new.

TW: Just so I can understand, I've been in Colombia in a building that was all Airbnb. This is not just a building that is all Airbnb. Is that correct? What is the difference between something which has been built as a whole system, is purchased, and you neither live in it or rent it?

LV: To me, it would be key to have most of the units rented permanently because then that community can begin to grow and visitors can come and plug themselves into that community. Rather than having it serve, absolutely temporal, Airbnb people. In an ideal world, maybe this would be a cooperative base model.

TW: I think that's an interesting idea. That if a person rents a space more permanently, they then would make it more theirs. And thus you'd begin to see a differentiation between one which is more hotel and one which is not. Look, it's a beautiful scheme, very very well done; beautiful perspectives. But I'm not clear how we can interrogate the idea to see if it's a good idea.

Studio
Fall 2018
1106a Advanced Design Studio
Omar Gandhi, Marta Caldeira

The crux of Sendack's Where the Wild Things Are is that imagination transforms the environment: a solitary child is liberated by his imagination. The story centers on ideas of growth, survival, and change inspired simultaneously by real and fictive worlds. What is the impact of imagining a new landscape, and where do ephemeral experiences crafted within the mind overlap with those occurring in the natural/physical world?

This studio challenged students to design a campus of creatures on the property of Rabbit Snare Gorge as a series of interventions that used methods of biomimicry to produce specific functional qualities. Students explored progressive strategies for diverting, mitigating, and integrating climate, in all its forms. The studio explored the evolution of architectural responses to building in a region of extreme climatic conditions: Inverness, Nova Scotia. Through a blend of traditional and contemporary approaches, the studio evolved a methodology toward a climatically-responsive, regionally inspired architecture.

Participants
Lara AlKhouli, Katherine Barymow, Nino Boornazian, Haylie Chan, Sunny Cui, Kate Fisher, Ryan Hughes, Jincy Kunnatharayil, Ben Olsen, Colin Sutherland

Jury
Andrew Benner, Stephanie Davidson, Perla Delson, Rossana Hu, Jimenez Lai, Lyndon Neri, Brigitte Shim, Adam Yarinsky

The act of play at the building level

The metric of time could be disrupted by the vastness of the landscape, as the various rhythms of the waves, the trees, and the expansive horizon instill in us a different understanding of space. If we look back to our childhood, we always wanted to grow up quickly in order to perform as adults are only allowed to do. While trying to understand the complexities of the world around us using the little things that we know, we turn to imagination to fill in the rest.

In response to the aging population in Nova Scotia, I wanted to explore how architecture could bridge the generational gap between children and adults by rethinking the conventional use of architecture. The project, a nursery home and a summer camp, takes on a long and linear dimension, seemingly slowing down the metric of time. It embraces the children's misreading of architecture with the act of play at the building level: a bunk bed tower, an outdoor TV room, and stairs as moveable seats. At the same time, the project encourages unlearning for the elderly through their spontaneous meetings with the visiting children. Globally, the project acts as a mediator between the calmness of the center and the chaos of the forest, serving as the protector of this community.

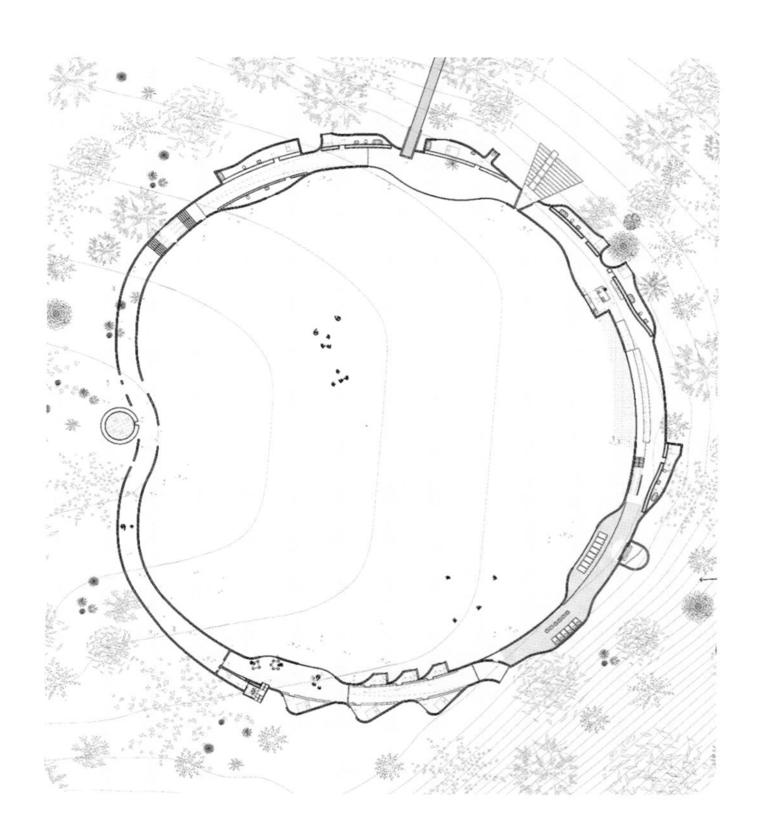

JL: First, it's a really beautiful project. It's fantastic. The plan is so elegant. I mean I could talk about the slightly deformed circle. In Japanese culture, the notion of wabi-sabi is when something is imperfect; we are able to connect with the imperfection and empathize with the sadness. So I think there's that sensibility here. The other thing, to continue with the Japanese references … obviously the White 'U' of Toyo Ito, in fact the first built project of Ito, is a story precisely about the differentiation of inside and outside. I guess the main contrast is that, for him, his sister, who became a widow, wanted the outside to be the back of house, and the inside to be the front of house. So this reversal of front and back of house created an intimate domestic courtyard. The front of house places emphasis on the courtyard as a secret social space for the people in that house, only. The thing about Ito is by introducing something like the 'U' he effectively eliminated the notion of corners, as you have.

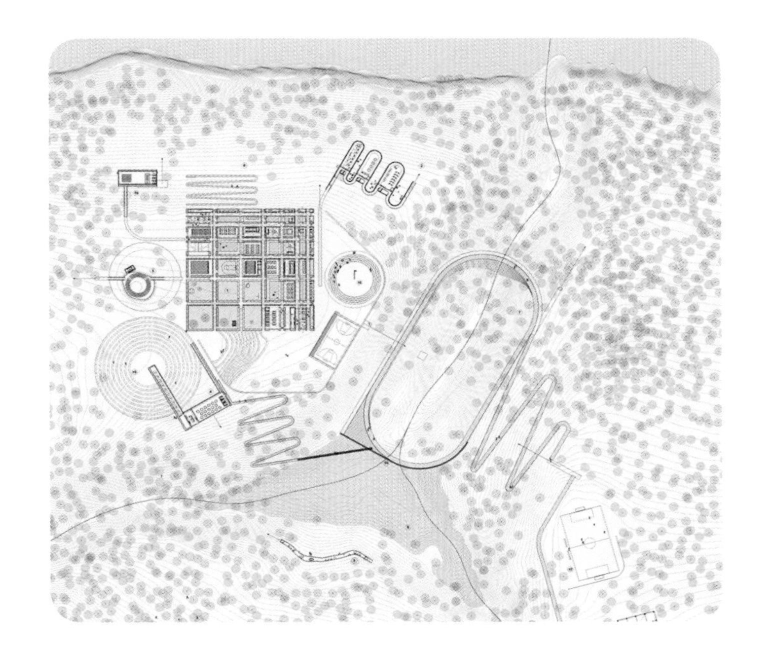

A logarithmic pattern of indoor and outdoor space

Seeking creative strength through an immersion into nature has long been a practice of many artists. This project, "The Forum", generates a moment of collective gathering in a landscape of monumentality. Proposed as a creative arts camp for children, the project is sited on a fifty-acre oceanfront site in Inverness, Nova Scotia. Through a series of topographic investigations, the architecture establishes a new ground plane through the medium of the horizontal. Atop the crest of the site sits the climax of the project, the living pavilion. Sitting in a delicate relationship with the existing topography, a logarithmic pattern of indoor and outdoor space is projected from a new horizontal datum which sits four feet above grade at its minimum and thirty-two feet above at is maximum. The play between the natural ground and the projected pattern generates a dynamic system of space that changes in both plan and section simultaneously. The resulting volume is then inhabited by the users of the site, establishing a structure for the exchange of ideas, the formation of new relationships, and a reframing of the natural landscape.

LN: You're probably not going to hear a lot of bad stuff. There is a lot of positive here, Ryan, I mean I absolutely love it. But if I'm looking at your site plan it seems like as individuals they are very strong together. I start to wonder. I mean they are so strong … but I start to wonder. I think you are very good with your forms, so you know that this is the practical aspect, but you didn't put it in here. It's a little bit awkward. All these paths that come here, in relationship with your object, are actually very strange. It could be tenuous. I could see if you started to build the model, you would say, 'no I'm not going to put it in there, it's just not pretty enough.' But I know it's right here. *laughter* Also, it's just a little bit awkward. You know the shape wants to be something else and yet it ends up as an object–it wants to be part of the circulation. The praise will come because it's amazing. The facilities you've created here. At mid-review, you didn't even have that second layer, and that's just really strong. It reminds me of Valerio Olgiati's own house, in Portugal. Because it's bringing a whole different perspective to this landscape. And you've achieved that, in an amazing way. It's just that there are all these tensions that I am more curious about.

JL: I'm going to try to slingshot into something else; I don't know where it'll land. I'm thinking of the composition of the campus, as the grid carries it at the seams. It reminds me of earlier, when we talked about Berlin and Hejduk, or maybe even a Campo Marzio moment, when the figures are supposed to be messy. I think the rotation of the objects that create these acute and obtuse angles between buildings is an interesting way of organizing expansions and contractions. I would say, yes, there are some awkward moments, but I quite enjoy the awkward moments between the shapes. The reflected ceiling plan was a really amazing reveal. You sort of treated our ceiling as a facade itself which reads very strongly.

The walls slip and splay, organizing space

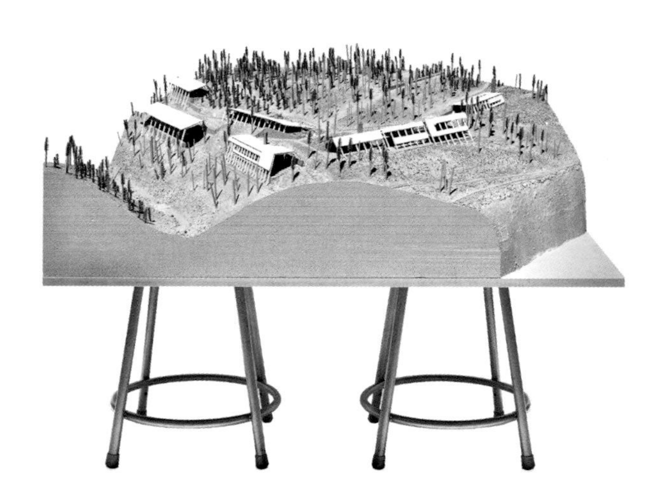

The lodges at Broad Cove Banks shape the ground using the retaining wall as a primary architectural device. Here, the ground is not a background element against which figures are understood but the primary material for place and space-making. The thickened ground of Broad Cove Banks hosts space, circulation, and landscaping. Long lines of architecture and landscape are inscribed along the contours, blending into the grade. The buildings lodge into the ground, their thin width and long length giving them volume without apparent mass. The walls slip and splay, organizing space, circulation, and landscape. They define edges and levels, produce gaps for sunlight and entry, and distinguish between enclosed and open space. Lodging the campus in the thickened ground suggests that we don't just tread on this earth, but that we belong to it.

JL: As a campus of creatures, do they have nicknames?

BO: Uh. *smiles* they don't have nicknames yet. But they have centipede-like forms which might invoke nicknames. There are six here, but I've shown four at the outposts here.

AY: They're mascara brushes. *laughter*

SD: I love that though, it's great.

AB: It seems to imply that there's a spectrum between the active man and nature. There's some really sensitive work here, especially when you're making those animated moves like the wall. The only thing that I am sort of wishing is for more of the other steps that span between wild and that grounded, rooted move. It seems like there could be a wider range. Even in the one's where you are stepping [towards nature] a little bit; it seems very tentative. You're not really reaching out to the wild and blending a little bit more. There are moments where it starts to do it, but I'm curious about what drove you to stay close to its initial area?

BO: Each of these buildings are associated with a kind of territory. So I just wanted to find the forwardmost edge with the hope that it would actually start to blend beyond. There's a moment where the edge ceases to be inhabitable, I would hope that would become the implied edge.

Studio
Fall 2018
1107a Advanced Design Studio
Lisa Gray, Alan Organschi

The LifeCycle Studio explored advanced approaches to the design of sustainable buildings in the urban housing sector. Guided by circular economic principles, students conducted research and developed designs for new modes and configurations of urban dwelling. By considering both upstream, ecological benefits and downstream improvements in public health, students engaged some of the most deeply entrenched problems of contemporary global society. Ultimately, the studio examined ways in which circular economic principles can promote a new design culture, one that leverages abundant and underutilized environmental resources and addresses pressing global environmental crises.

The LifeCycle Studio was conducted collaboratively with an advanced Master level studio at the Department of Architecture at Aalto University in Otaniemi, Finland. Both studios worked on the same architectural project—a program of new, high density housing for Jätkäsaari, an urban development zone in a former industrial district on Helsinki's western waterfront.

Participants
Dana AlMathkoor, David Bransfield, Davis Butner, Martin Man, Javier Perez, Misha Semenov, Priyanka Sheth, Melissa Weigel, Millie Yoshida, Ethan Zisson

Jury
Andy Bernheimer, Peggy Deamer, Anna Dyson, Rosalie Genevro, Simon Hartmann, Pekka Heikkinen, Matti Kuittinen, Antti Lehto, Mae-Ling Lokko, Tanya Luthi, Alexander Purves, Philip Tidwell, Kim Yao

Studio
Fall 2018
1107a Advanced Design Studio
Lisa Gray, Alan Organschi
Davis Butner, Millie Yoshida (Feldman Nominees)

A catalog of self-sustainable systems

Proposing a new mode of sustainable urban habitation in Helsinki, Finland, “RAMPED” applies a circular economic approach to the 2018 Helsinki Housing Reform Competition brief, calling for a mixed use apartment complex and 400 parking spaces to be phased out as Helsinki strives to become car-free over the next decade. This proposal consists of a catalog of self-sustainable systems that comprise flexible and accessible apartments and amenities, adaptable to a variety of sites and domestic lifestyles in the new urban development of Jätkäsaari. The proposal considers the scale of the parking unit as the basis for a unifying modular system. The system can adapt from parking into housing and amenity space, in addition to flexible wet wall and wet block components, geothermal and radiant heat reuse, gray water systems, and timber frame construction techniques.

50

MK: This is a stupid question, but did you enjoy doing this studio? *laughter*

AO: We actually told them to do everything, step by step. *laughter* It was a horrible time.

HH: But a few words about parking, because everything else was so clear. How did you end up with this?

DB: Well we were assigned to different topics in our studies while in Finland. Mine was on ramps and parking geometries. I was fascinated with all of the options that were available and the lack of solutions on how they could be adapted to living environments, but it didn’t seem far away or hard to marry the two.

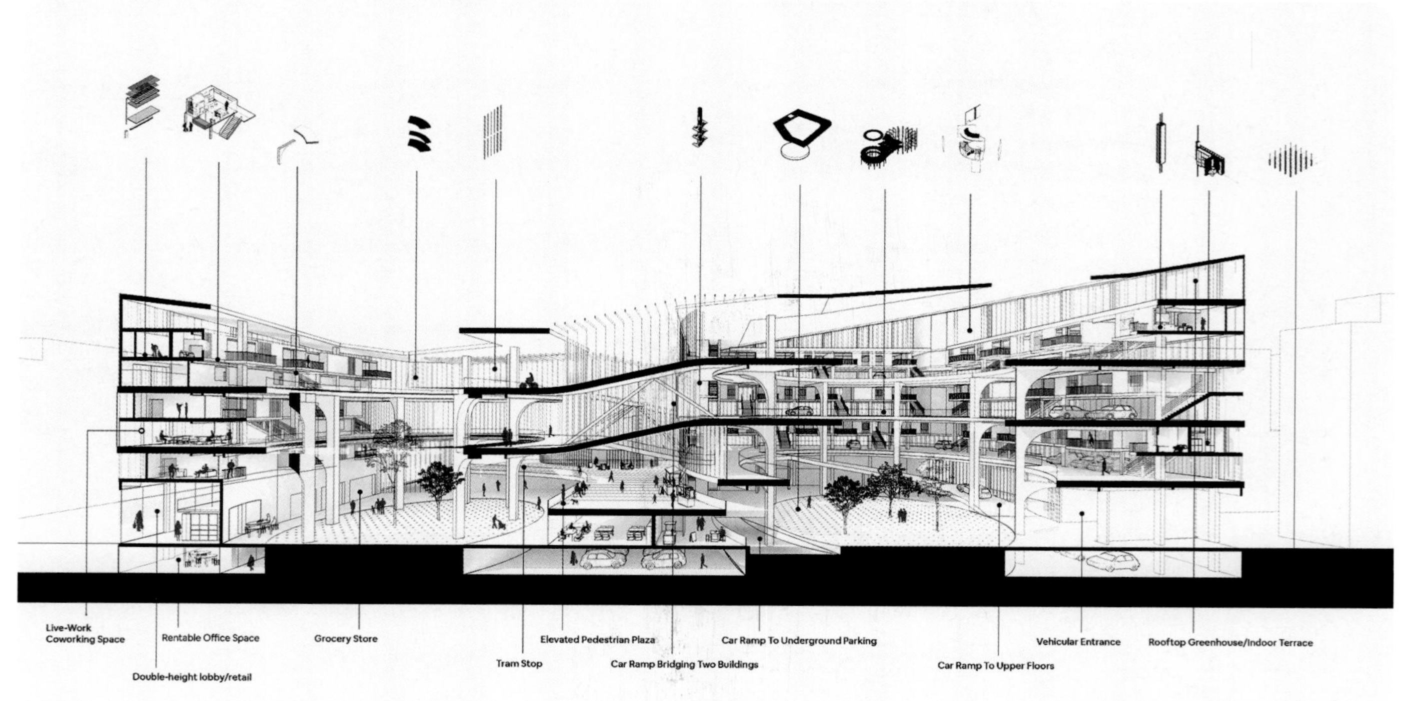

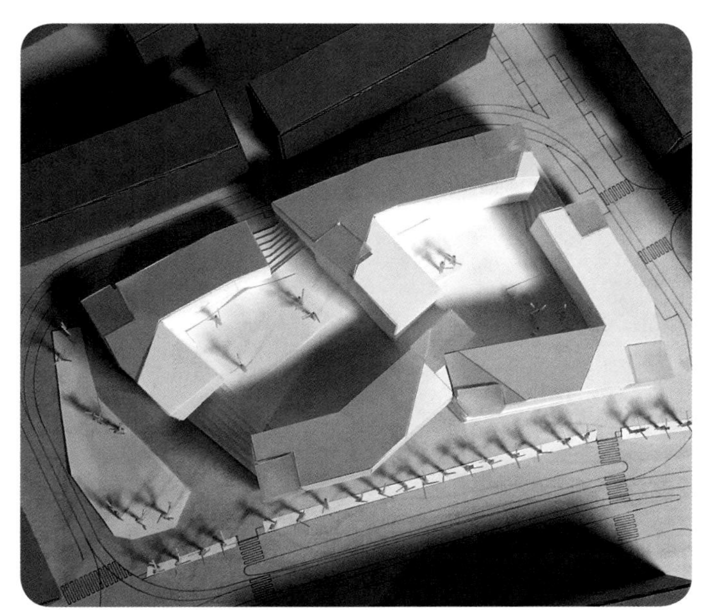

Organized sharing economy

The man-made peninsula of Jatkasaari is the newest developing neighborhood of Helsinki, Finland. Formerly a shipping hub, the area is being developed to address a growing housing crisis in the city as more and more people are moving from the country to the capital city. As a major importer of goods and energy, Finland is conscious of its material expenditure and the life-cycle of its buildings. I looked towards examples of co-housing which allow for residents to enjoy a greater number and quality of amenities through an organized sharing economy.

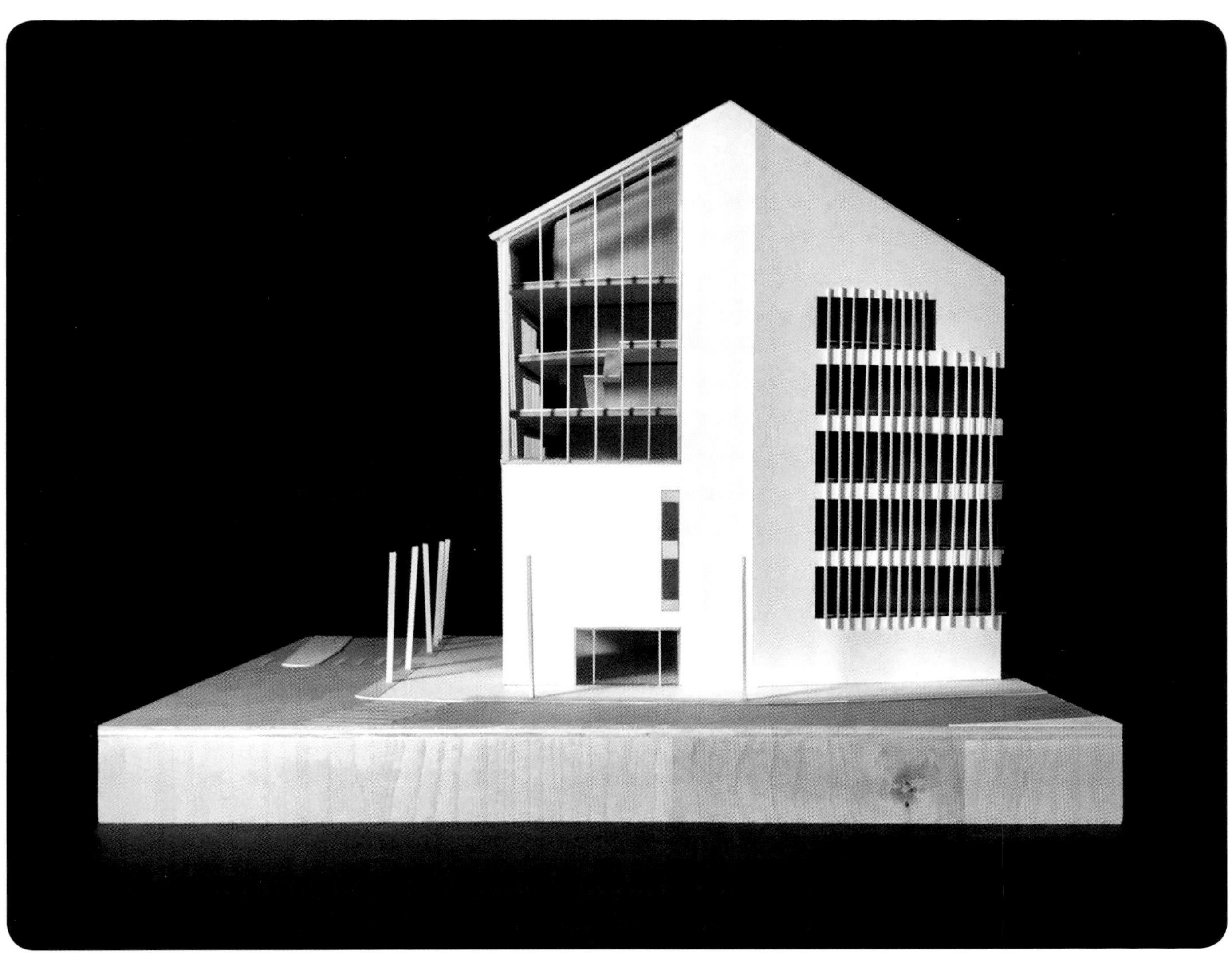

AP: It's very nice work Javier. The form is very beautiful and sculptural and of course looks very typical, or local.

AD: I think it's a very intriguing and intelligent way of trying to reuse these empty spaces. It's tricky, it's almost like one of your critiques of those spaces is that they just weren't big enough to have a gathering or social space. You've definitely provided that. Another interesting thing is that you're giving thermal height spaces to these surfaces. I definitely feel that there's a threshold condition after which people feel comfortable. Something that is very fascinating is that instead of just extending horizontally you've decided to do it vertically. I think it's very very intriguing and could possibly be a very successful way for people to find their niches in a social space, but to also have privacy.

Studio
Fall 2018
1107a Advanced Design Studio
Lisa Gray, Alan Organschi
Melissa Weigel, Ethan Zisson

Pinwheel structured CLT towers

AP: This is a very nice, different proposal. The tectonic style and structural system used is very differently.

AL: I only have one question, did you think about introducing more natural light in the interior?

MW: We thought that having two points of exposure was right. We also eliminated this corridor space to make up for the lack of exposure. But we were aware of this issue.

EZ: Because we were asserting these balconies into every corner with two planes of light coming in, it felt like it was getting a lot of glass and a lot of light. We were able to get this facade that has momentary pop-outs instead of expansive glazed conditions.

Embracing the Finnish forest as both metaphor and material, this project proposes a light-filled and flexible mixed-use development. The thick base rises from grade to accommodate the city's required parking and creates a walkable terrain to host community programs on top. The apartments rise above in pinwheel structured CLT towers. Each apartment has two exposures to allow for greater quantity and variety of light in Helsinki's dark winters. The space is designed to change with the needs of the community. The large spans of parking contain removable panels to transform into usable space in a post-car city and the apartments allow for great variation in unit type and size. The facade panels take inspiration from vernacular shingles and add texture and scale to the form.

Studio

Spring 2019

Studio
Spring 2019
494b Undergraduate Senior Design Studio
Steven Harris, Gavin Hogben

Students in this course assembled an array of distinct architectural elements into a landscape ensemble. Students assessed the character of the elements and the relations developed among them, while maintaining an open attitude to their functional definitions or utilities. The semester's main topic and project was a City of the Dead constructed on Miami's Biscayne Bay.

Participants
Edward Antonio, Jordan Boudreau, Kristine Chung, Mary Catherine Fletcher, Elizabeth Goodman, Amanda Hu, Sheau Yun Lim, Haewon Ma, Andrea Masterson, Deniz Saip, Andy Sandweiss, Noah Silvestry, Noah Strausser, Sida Tang, Max Wilson

Studio
Spring 2019
494b Undergraduate Senior Design Studio
Steven Harris, Gavin Hogben
Kristine Chung

Cemetery on water

Conceived as a City of the Dead, this cemetery on water is a series of linear structures that protect the City of the Living. Situated at the border between Biscayne Bay and the ocean, the structures function as a breakwater by accumulating and reinforcing the existing sand flats.

The building blocks of this infrastructural project have a physical connection to the individual: the cremated ashes are cast into individual monuments, which use the material remains of the dead to create and enclose a physical space for commemoration. Each of these monuments contributes to the linear extension of the breakwater, corresponding exactly to the progression of time.

Studio
Spring 2019
494b Undergraduate Senior Design Studio
Steven Harris, Gavin Hogben
Sida Tang

A field of columbaria

This project, “Living Memorials”, is an aquatic system of columbaria in the barrier islands of Biscayne Bay. These concrete stelae forms make up a field of columbaria lining the intertidal environment of the bay. Informed by biodiversity in the area, the columbaria contain niches and perforations for differing lifeforms, from anchors for seagrass and acropora, to shoals for sea turtles, to roosts for seabirds. The effects of the winds, tides, light, and sediment are the variables in the algorithmic backbone of the project, and the changing geometry and arrangements dynamically respond to create diverse ecosystems amidst the columbaria.

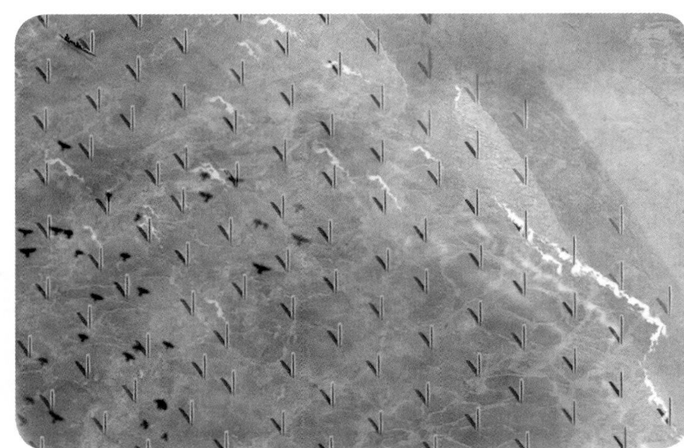

Studio
Spring 2019
1012b M.Arch I First Year Design Studio
Trattie Davies, Sunil Bald, Peter de Bretteville, Joeb Moore, Miriam Peterson

At certain moments in time and specific moments of education, it is critical to consider directly and holistically the systems in which we reside to find edges, determine relevance and question seemingly inherent outcomes. In this studio we address the elusive topic of dwelling, confronting factors of material, site, program, time, and change as entrées to design thinking. Dwelling as a concept is multi-varied and interpretable. At a minimum, it involves occupation but can grow to encompass shelter, security, domesticity, family, community, society, and environment, all requiring consideration of the transient nature of life.

In this studio, students considered and defined dwelling from the varying perspectives of program, site and materiality in relation to the creation of space. As an invention, architectural thinking has the capacity to project possible worlds, integrating real, speculative, and imagined fictions. In this extended experiment, projects open up the range of diversity of the built environment, offering extraordinary speculations, proposals, and outcomes for how we may live.

Participants
Ife Adepegba, Isa Akerfeldt-Howard, Natalie Broton, Ives Brown, Martin Carrillo Bueno, Christopher Cambio, Colin Chudyk, Rosa Congdon, Jiachen Deng, Janet Dong, Xuefeng Du, Paul Freudenburg, Kate Fritz, Malcolm Rondell Galang, Anjelica Gallegos, Kevin Gao, Jiaming Gu, Ian Gu, Ashton Harrell, Liang Hu, Niema Jafari, Alicia Jones, Jae Jung, Sze Wai Justin Kong, Louis Koushouris, Tyler Krebs, Hiuki Lam, Pabi Lee, Isabel Li, Mingxi Li, Dreama Lin, April Liu, Qiyuan Liu, Araceli Lopez, Angela Lufkin, Rachel Mulder, Leanne Nagata, Naomi Ng, Louisa Nolte, Alex Olivier, Michelle Qu, Nicole Ratajczak, Heather Schneider, Scott Simpson, Christine Song, Shikha Thakali, Ben Thompson, Sarah Weiss, Max Wirsing, Shelby Wright, Stella Xu, Sean Yang, Peng Ye, Yuhan Zhang, Leyi Zhang, Kaiwen Zhao, Sasha Zwiebel

Jury
Emily Abruzzo, Ramona Albert, José Aragüez, Annie Barrett, Stella Betts, Julian Bonder, Brennan Buck, Karen Fairbanks, Leslie Gill, Jaffer Kolb, Amy Lelyveld, David Leven, Toshihiro Oki, Megan Panzano, Laura Raicovich, Lyn Rice, Nathan Rich, Karla Rothstein, Rosalyne Shieh, Michael Szivos, Marc Tsurumaki, Dragana Zoric

Intersections form residual eccentric conditions

This project is situated on the Allen Street median in New York City's East Village. It is a street, a liminal place of circulation. Walking, biking, driving cars/buses, trains, represent scales of orbits in a broader constellation of movement. The only constant is change. Five hundred years ago the site was a lush natural landscape, two hundred years ago tenement housing, one hundred and fifty years ago the EL train and widened street, and at present, subways and bikes. Historical precedents inspired the idea to posit new means of movement through space.

The building is a housing typology massed in response to adjacent facades. It is organized rationally in an orthogonal grid, then intersected by paths that deviate, like warp and weft of textiles. Paths both physically and visually connect discrete places. They define edge conditions, allowing sectional shifts. Intersections form residual eccentric conditions, becoming public and semi-private space. Dwelling is manifested as a result of movement in the public realm.

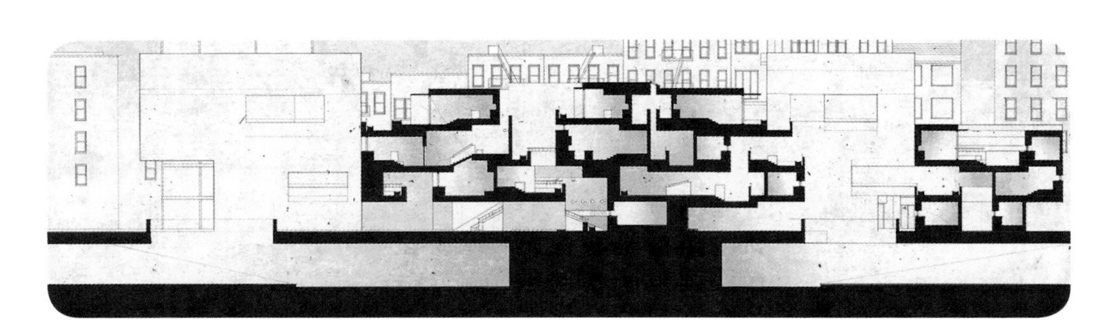

Studio
Spring 2019
1012b M.Arch I First Year Design Studio
Trattie Davies
Rachel Mulder

A moving sensorial palace

This project, titled "Love in Blobs/Lovin' Blobs", considers the meaning of dwelling through experience, resiliency, and what it means to feel loved. It begins with an investigation of flamingos who migrate to mate in the harsh environment of the Andean Salt Flats of Chile. During the day, the UV rays burn hot and at night the temperature drops so low the flamingos are frozen in place. While here, they collectively dance across flats until they pair off to mate. Situating itself in the East River, Lovin' Blobs is a moving sensorial palace that finds its permanent home in Hallett's Cove. Through material experimentation, it challenges our understanding of dwelling by offering a space to experience sensation, touch, smell, sight, and to consider relationships with ourselves, others, and the city.

Studio
Spring 2019
1012b M.Arch I First Year Design Studio
Trattie Davies
Ben Thompson

A protracted subterranean arcade

Using Freudian Psychoanalysis, the existing Beaux-Arts bathroom at Allen and Delancey is interrogated and illuminated. The derelict structure becomes the vestibule for an extrusion which functions as a protracted subterranean arcade open to the public. Above this internalized thoroughfare, apartments clad in steel populate the roof, acknowledging the materiality and rhythm of the since demolished elevated train. Iron grate apertures, both vertical and horizontal, pour light into the lower arcade from the street; the deep shadows simulate the light of the street life under the absent elevated line. Both apartment dweller and public coalesce into the hallowed bathroom portal. The design collapses the gap between past and present, what is repressed and what is illuminated, in an attempt to acquiesce the breadth and trauma of history.

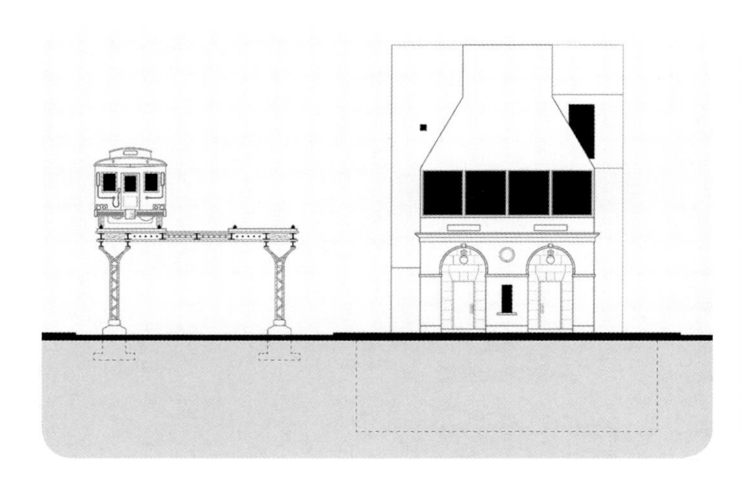

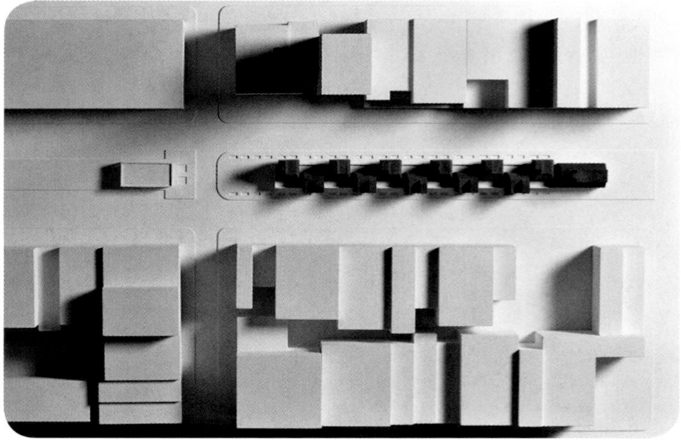

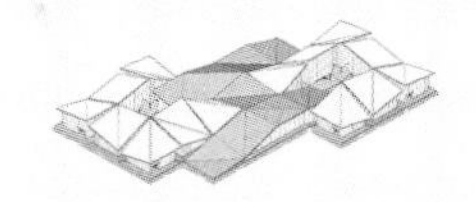

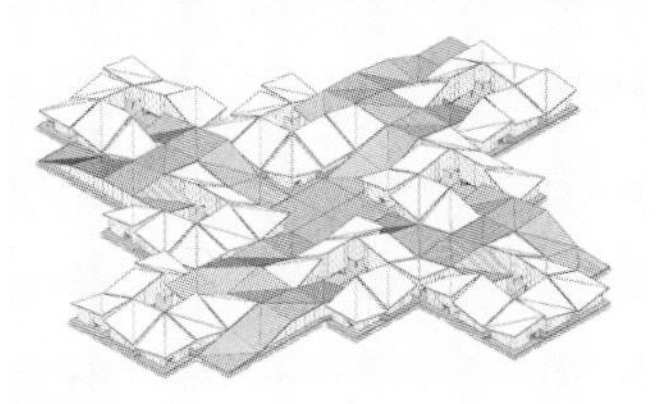

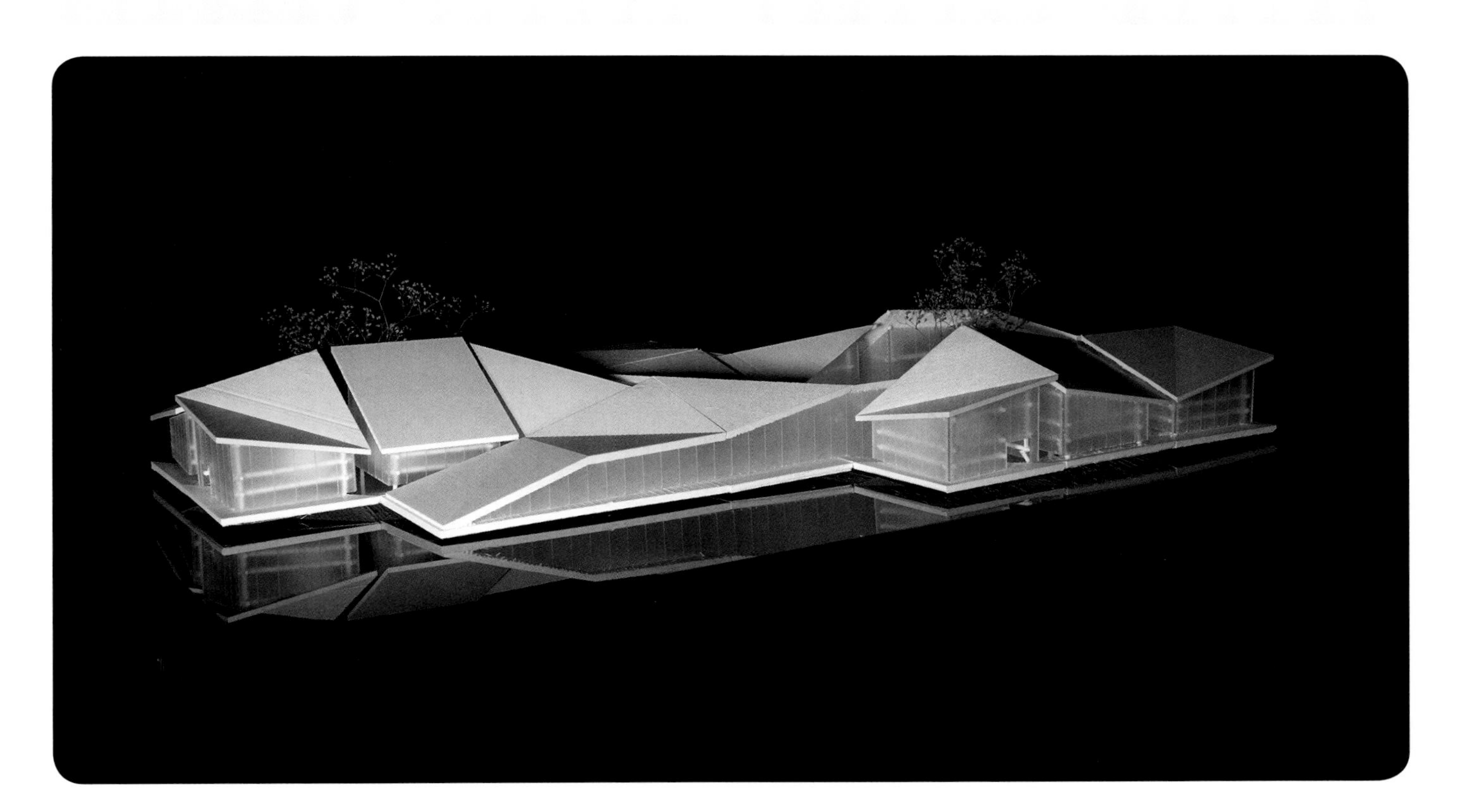

Floating architecture

This project is a direct response to the impacts of rapid urbanization, housing shortage, and significant increase in sea level, rainfall, and flooding caused by climate change in coastal areas. Because of the accelerating rate of rising sea level, coastal areas require urgent adaptation and innovative building strategy. By developing floating architecture, the project eliminates the need for grading, foundation construction, or any site specific preparations. The project is able to be rapidly deployed, expanded, and adapted to any coastal area.

Though the project can expand indefinitely, the initial design provides dwellings for thirty-two individuals. The dwellings consist of several micro-communities made up of eight individual units. The community is designed to interlock and continue to grow independently from the existing land. Each unit in each micro-community interlocks together to form a shared green space in its core. Two micro-communities can then be interlocked together to create a larger green space and a shared enclosed amenity space. Finally, four or more micro-communities can be interlocked together to create a continuous green walkway and shared amenities throughout the entire floating community.

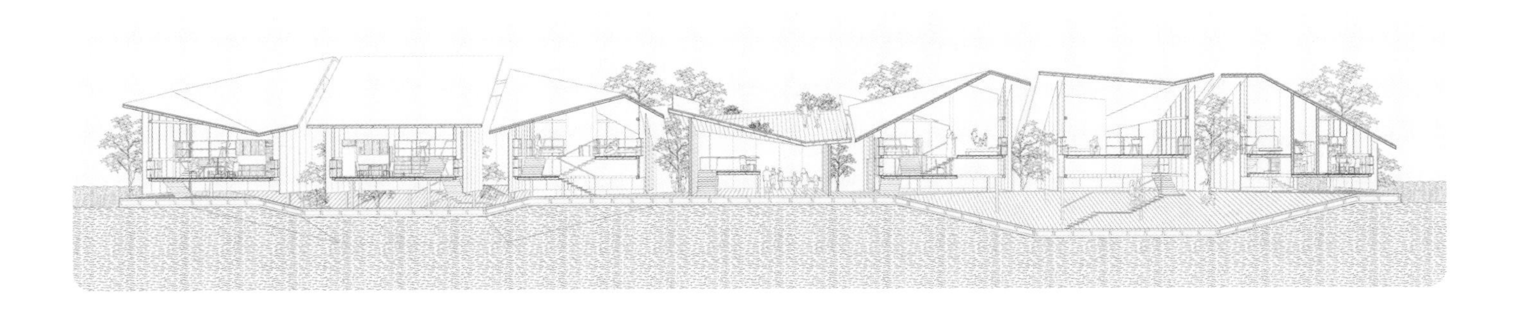

Studio
Spring 2019
1012b M.Arch I First Year Design Studio
Sunil Bald
Araceli Lopez

Feasible dwellings that ultimately find an end

This project parallels in program to a "tiny village". The towers maintain a central core where the necessary components of dwelling occur: cultivating, cooking, eating, and storing. The central core, materialized in scaffolding to allow for gardening and natural growth, holds the largest footprint within the tower. The small perimeter allows for a place of resting. The towers are maintained by a datum with a means of purifying available to those who inhabit the tower, and those outside of the urban village. The tiny villages themselves are not meant to be permanent structures; rather, they are feasible dwellings that ultimately find an end. Similarly, the form of the towers allows for the ultimate death of drowning underwater.

Studio
Spring 2019
1012b M.Arch I First Year Design Studio
Peter de Bretteville
Naomi Ng

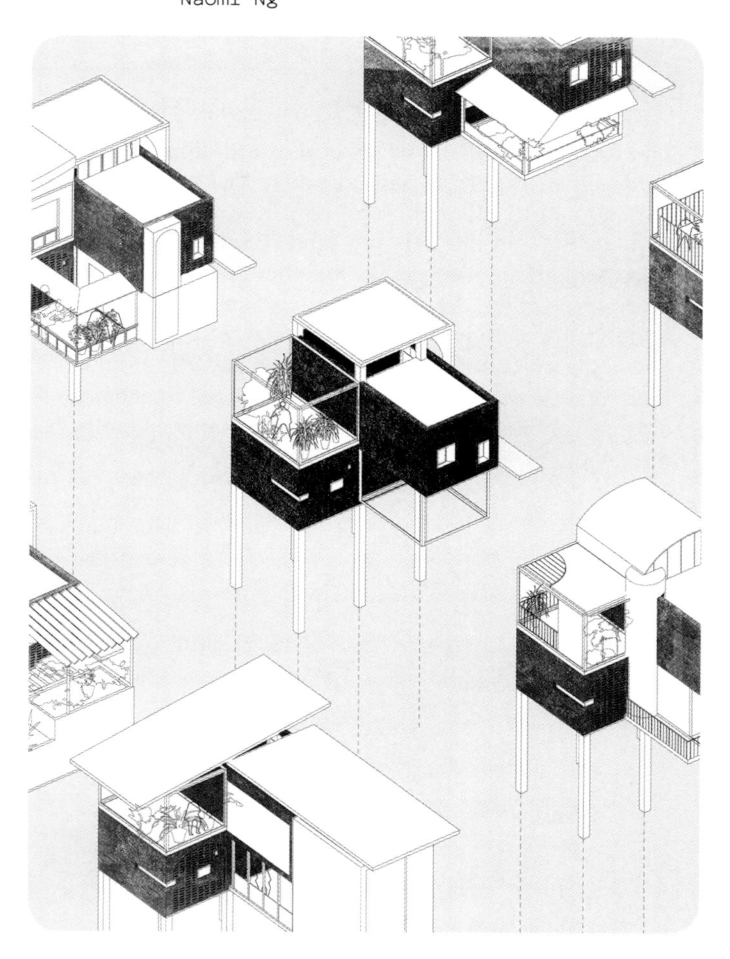

The life of a building

Our lifecycle and architecture are somewhat like palimpsests. Stripped wallpaper revealing those of a previous tenant, castings of formwork, and spackling where frames were once mounted. Death is not demarcated by physical dilapidation, nor does it follow a linear chronology. Like a palimpsest, overlays simultaneously conceal and reveal signs of one's own past; the life of a building could be brought into an afterlife as signs.

This project involves a series of twelve dwelling units (places of the living) that hover above the Marble Cemetery New York (places of the dead). To encourage the cyclical process of construction, demolition, and reconstruction as a palimpsest, the design provides each individual an initial lofted unit that satisfies essential dwelling needs, along with three times its potential expandable space. This promotes participatory authorship, customization and demolition—so architecture, material, and its inhabitants can evolve and decay together in time.

Playfully monstrous

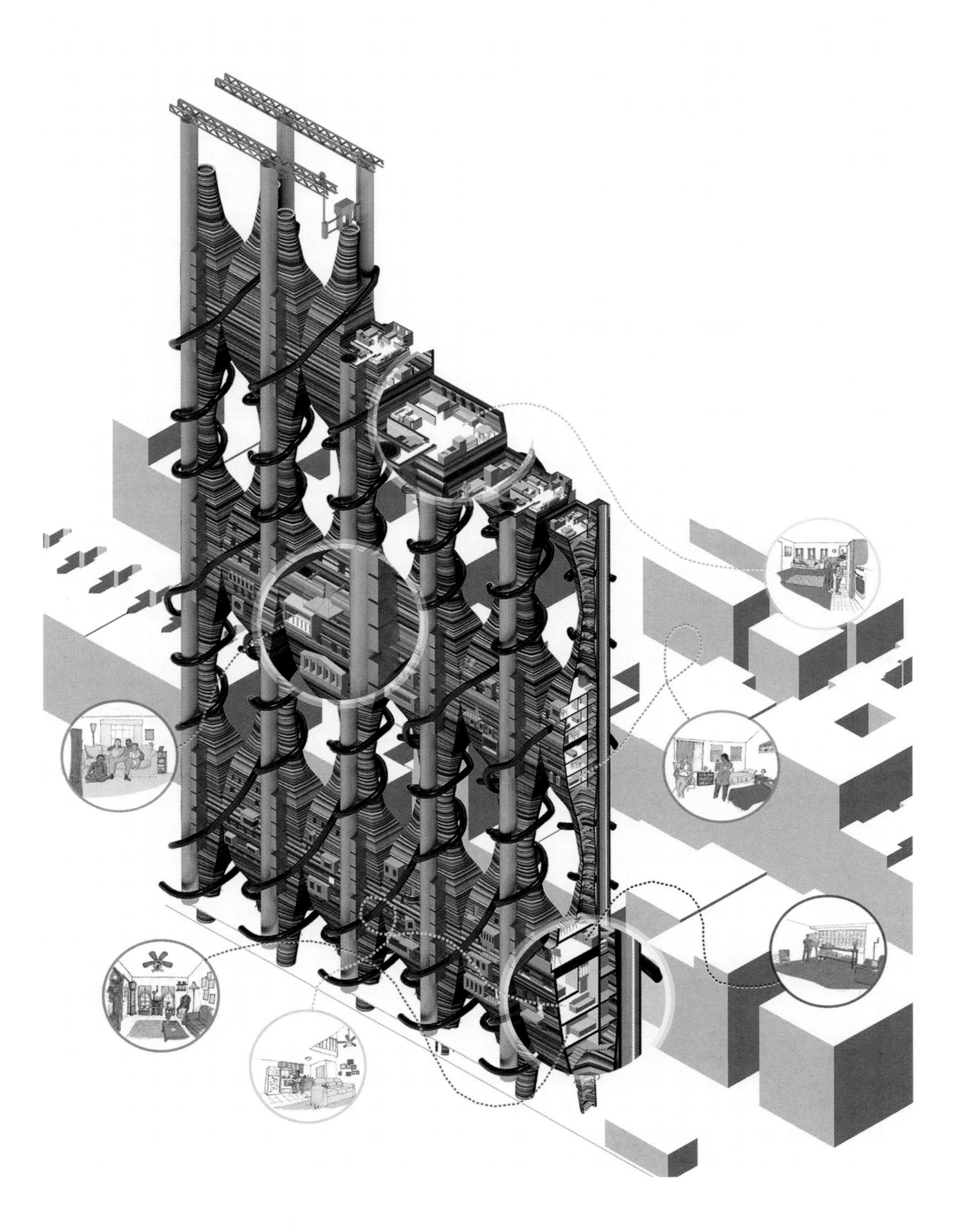

The Lower East Side is a neighborhood in a constant state of transition; traditionally an immigrant neighborhood, it has now become a site of gentrification. This proposal uses architecture as a way of reading the passage of time and memory. The building is a playfully monstrous form which exists at the urban scale of New York, but gives authority to the inhabitants to modify their own floor plan and façade. The building is 3D printed over the course of one hundred years where each month a different colored layer is printed from recycled plastics, mimicking geologic formations as a marker of time. Exterior elevators and fire escape slides allow for open floor plan interiors. Residents can build out over the street and use the building as a base on which to grow their apartment units. The expansion, contraction, and manipulation of the units serves as a memory of the lives of the individual inhabitants.

Studio
Spring 2019
1012b M.Arch I First Year Design Studio
Joeb Moore
Mingxi Li

A ruin on its first day of construction

This project originated from two books.

Book I is a Truman Capote autobiographical novel planted with grass inside the pages. The growth of plant life stiches the book together until the human narrative becomes illegible.

Book II is a collage of family life cycle in Halen Estate and clips of people doing parkour within the project. What this book reveals is the very long process of life phases in contrast to the eruption of momentary events.

This project is sited in New York Marble Cemetery. Visitors step into the space knowing that it's dedicated to the deceased, yet only plant life is visible in sight. The program is a thirty unit dwelling complex that roughly mimics a monastic way of living, with two floors of individual cells sandwiching a double-height public space for dining and events. The building stands with the awareness of becoming a ruin on its first day of construction.

Studio
Spring 2019
1012b M.Arch I First Year Design Studio
Joeb Moore
Qiyuan Liu

An escape from urban life

Based on the study of social death, this project reengages people who have lost the ability or will to communicate with the social environment. Between the public passage penetrating through the community and the apartments for the autistic group, there is a third space wrapped up by a porous continuous surface serving as protection for the residences and a buffer between private and public life. The privacy of the apartments is further secured by the entrance and windows. From the units, only the third space and the sky are seen, making this community an escape from urban life, though it is in the middle of it.

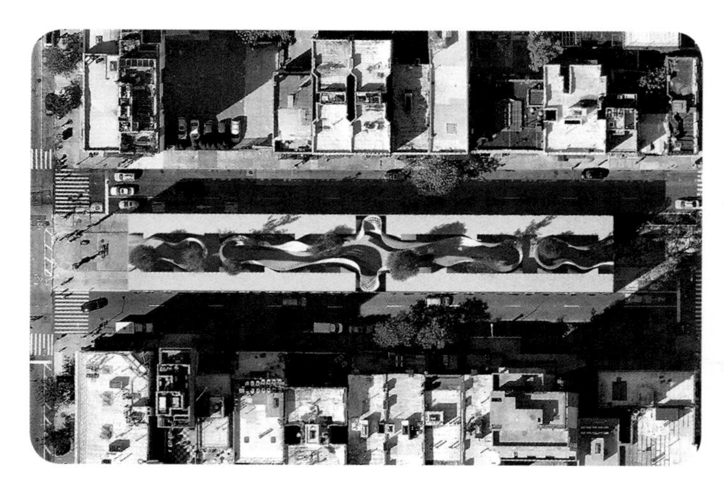

Like a DNA strand

This project is an epitome of the history of Chinese immigrants in the Lower East side of Manhattan in the twentieth century. It is a reflection of the relationship between the past, the future, and the present.

This collective house starts with ten family units. The residents share cooking and dining space with their neighbors, growing food together on the roof deck, and taking care of each other. Residents also share space with visitors by starting small business on the ground floor. The ten units grow vertically when the next generations come and semi-communal space develops. When the cycle plateaus, newborns come and the old go simultaneously, keeping the units at a certain height. Family units can intersect with others as dwellers marry and families grow. The entire structure stays flexible but stable because of the bonds between families, like a DNA strand. The project can grow horizontally along the street and transform into a "micro-city" over many generations.

61

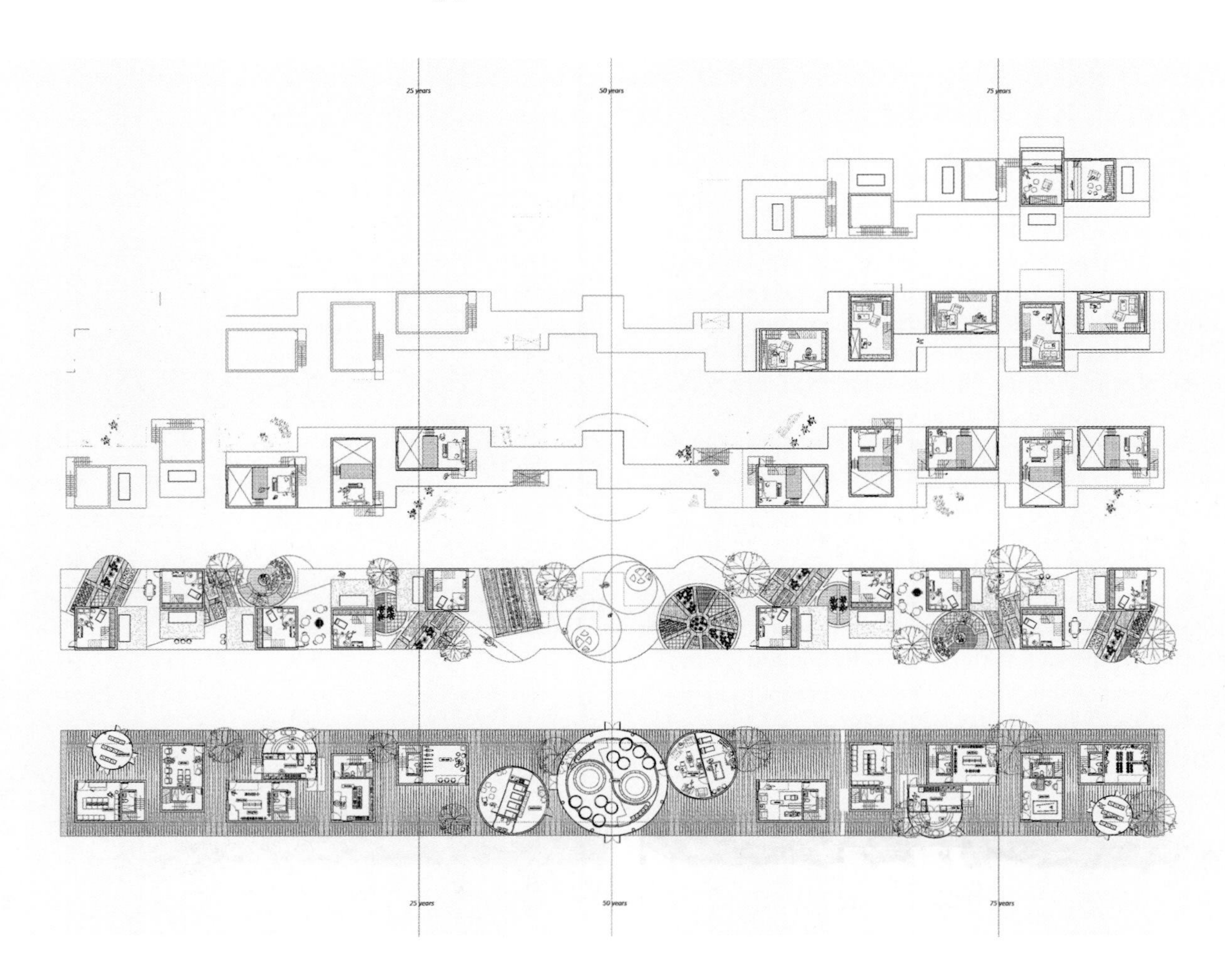

Studio
Spring 2019
1012b M.Arch I First Year Design Studio
Miriam Peterson
Natalie Broton

Traces of grid and spaces for light

By observing a map of Manhattan, we can see that there are two distinct organizational systems. The first is the city grid. The second is where the grid breaks and circulation becomes dynamic and fluid. This occurs in parks. In each system, however, there is cross-pollination, where grids bleed into park pathways, and winding park perimeters determine city grid boundaries. Rem Koolhaas in Delirious New York tells us that these conditions exist in section as well, beginning with the invention of the elevator. This project utilizes the relationships between park and city to create a series of dwellings on the Median at Allen and Delany in Manhattan.

Today, the median is a public space, and to retain its identity as an open area, the dwelling interventions are lifted over the median. The ground floor, the park, is complete with foliage, bike paths, a playground, community gardens, and pathways. The second floor contains seven dwellings. Each room is separated by space that is pinched to allow for light as a transition between each room. The growth of the tree canopy, originating in its placement in the park, is what determines the perimeter of these dwellings. The third floor is the densest both in foliage and in dwellings. It emulates the identity of the city, leaving traces of grid and spaces for light to reach each floor. By humbling the architect's authority over nature and space, these dwellings pursue a romantic relationship with nature, even in the density of the city.

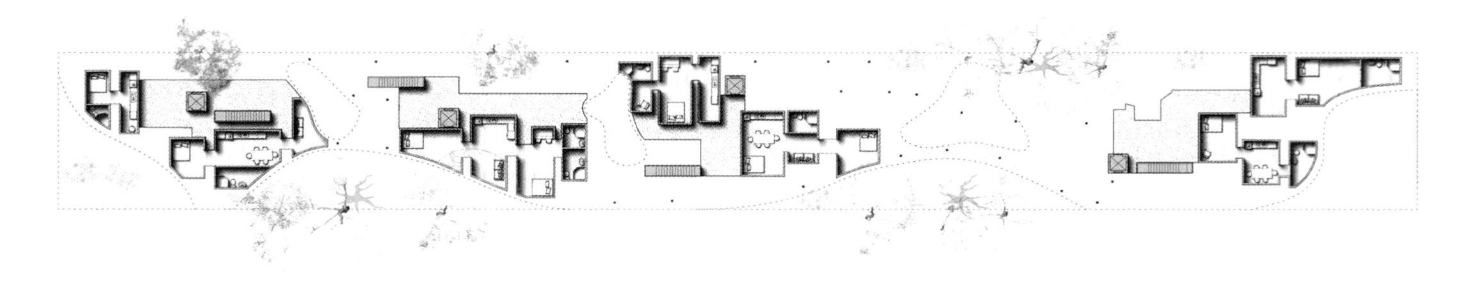

Studio
Spring 2019
1012b M.Arch I First Year Design Studio
Miriam Peterson
Hiuki Lam

A reinterpretation of tenement housing

The project is based on a series of precedent studies of dwelling for family and individuals, as well as analysis of tenement housing as a dwelling prototype in the Lower East Side of Manhattan. The redundant circulation patterns in the tenement housing provide an opportunity to rethink the interchangeability of the same plan layout for different inhabitants just by altering doors and passages. The project is treated as a reinterpretation of tenement housing by extracting elements including fire escapes, backyard/lightwell, and the front-back-side relationship. The unit chunk is made up of fixed servant space and flexible served space. With metal meshes wrapping the building, different levels of transparency and depth can be read on the façade. This project looks closely at the most subtle and ordinary architectural elements and anticipates big changes in the entire building, which evolve with time.

Studio

Spring 2019

1022b M.Arch I Second Year Design Studio

Aniket Shahane, Anthony Acciavatti, Alicia Imperiale, Jesse LeCavalier, Bimal Mendis, Dragana Zoric

The Marx Brothers playground, a 1.5 acre parcel located on 2nd avenue between 96th and 97th streets, is aptly named. Not only were the famed siblings born a short distance from this site in Manhattan, more recently it has become the stage for an urban slapstick of sorts. The City of New York plans to sell the playground to a private developer based on the claim that the parcel is technically a playground, not a park. While the threat of losing public space can be seen as antithetical to one idea of "City", the competing sets of values that are fueling this particular Marx Brothers show are also, in many ways, symptomatic of a healthy city—one that produces both conflict and celebration by embracing difference.

While this studio studied the Marx Brothers playground site, it was also just as interested in sites that may be implicated by the variety of interconnected urban issues embedded in this project. It may be more accurate to claim that this studio was interested in the sites that are or could be impacted by the urban situation that has created the Marx Brothers project as much as the playground, itself. Students selected their own sites and articulated the relationship of site to situation.

Participants

Cristina Anastase, Michelle Badr, Katharine Blackman, Emily Cass, Camille Chabrol, Serena Ching, Gioia Connell, Ruchi Dattani, Deo Deiparine, Clara Domange, Miriam Dreiblatt, Adam Feldman, Nathan Garcia, Michael Gasper, Michael Glassman, Tianyu Guan, Phoebe Harris, Will James, Kelley Johnson, Andrew Kim, Katie Lau, Eunice Lee, Zack Lenza, Jackson Lindsay, Matthew Liu, Thomas Mahon, Andrew Miller, Layla Ni, Jonathan Palomo, Christine Pan, Jewel Pei, Deirdre Plaus, Kelsey Rico, Jenna Ritz, David Schaengold, Rhea Schmid, Armaan Shah, Baolin Shen, Maya Sorabjee, Arghavan Taheri, Megan Tan, Seth Thompson, Laelia Vaulot, Darryl Weimer, Xiaohui Wen

Jury

Miroslava Brooks, Eric Bunge, Cynthia Davidson, Trattie Davies, Joe Day, Elizabeth Goldstein, Theodore Hoerr, Elisa Iturbe, Alexandra Lange, Peter Macapia, Mariana Mogilevich, Alan Plattus, Quilian Riano, Shawn Rickenbacker, Elihu Rubin, Susanne Schindler, Surry Schlabs, Rosalyne Shieh, Brigitte Shim, Georgeen Theodore

Studio
Spring 2019
1022b M.Arch I Second Year Design Studio
Aniket Shahane
Serena Ching, Deirdre Plaus

Reinvigorated 24/7

This project explores urbanism through a series of design explorations and interventions for the nighttime population in New York. Given the scale of this population, the density of 24/7 businesses and workers in the Marx Brothers neighborhood, and the long-accepted closing of parks during nighttime hours, the Marx Brothers Playground presents a unique opportunity to investigate and challenge this condition.

Night shift workers are able to move freely between reinvigorated 24/7 amenities and open spaces due to the scale of surface treatments and lighting, architectural forms and edge conditions, and the rezoning of blocks in the Upper East Side neighborhood. These simple design strategies draw long-overdue attention to this 15% of the population through urban solutions towards a healthier, safer night culture in the Marx Brothers neighborhood.

Studio
Spring 2019
1022b M.Arch I Second Year Design Studio
Aniket Shahane
David Schaengold, Darryl Weimer

Ellie

Once upon a time, in New York City, the trains used to run high up in the sky. / But there was a problem… / It was too noisy. / So they tried putting the trains underground. / But there was still a problem… / Building the tunnels was a big interruption. / So finally, after many years, they put the trains way underground. / As deep as a tall building is tall. / And it worked! / Everything was very quiet, and there were no interruptions. / But there was still a problem. / It took way too long to build tunnels. / Nobody knew what to do... / One day a friendly monster named Ellie came to New York. / Wherever she went, people came to see her. / It was a Party! / Ellie wanted to do something nice for everyone in New York. / She had a brilliant idea… / What if wherever Ellie went they built tunnels right underneath her? / New Yorkers like to be interrupted if the interruption is a Party! / She started working right away. / With Ellie's help, they built a new tunnel all up and down Second Avenue in no time flat. / The mayor was so grateful he gave her the key to the city.

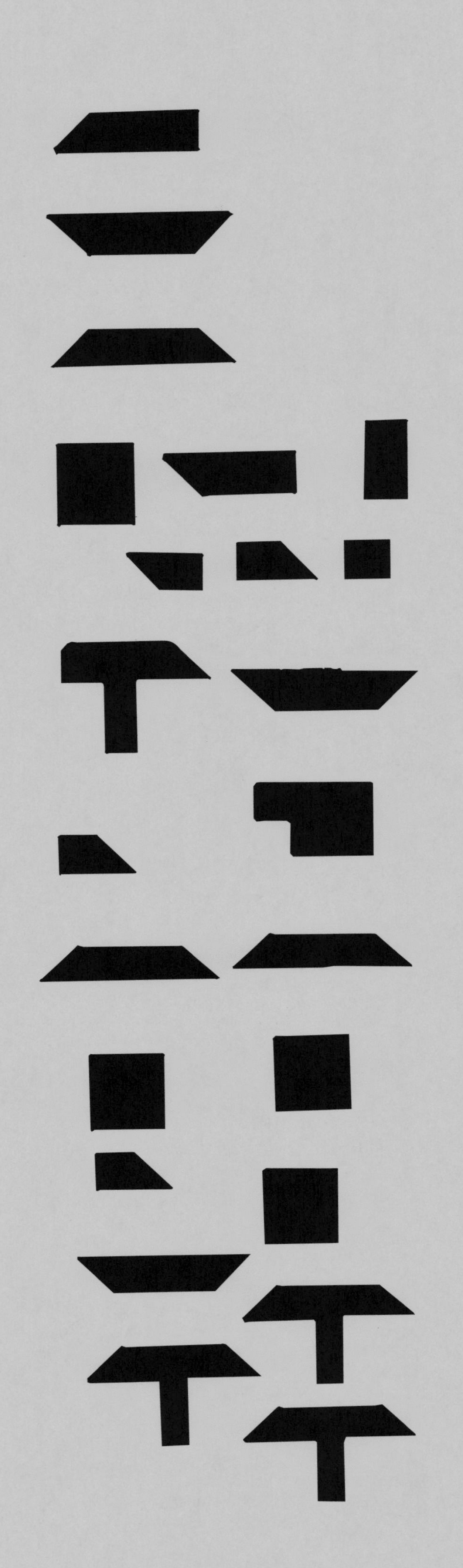

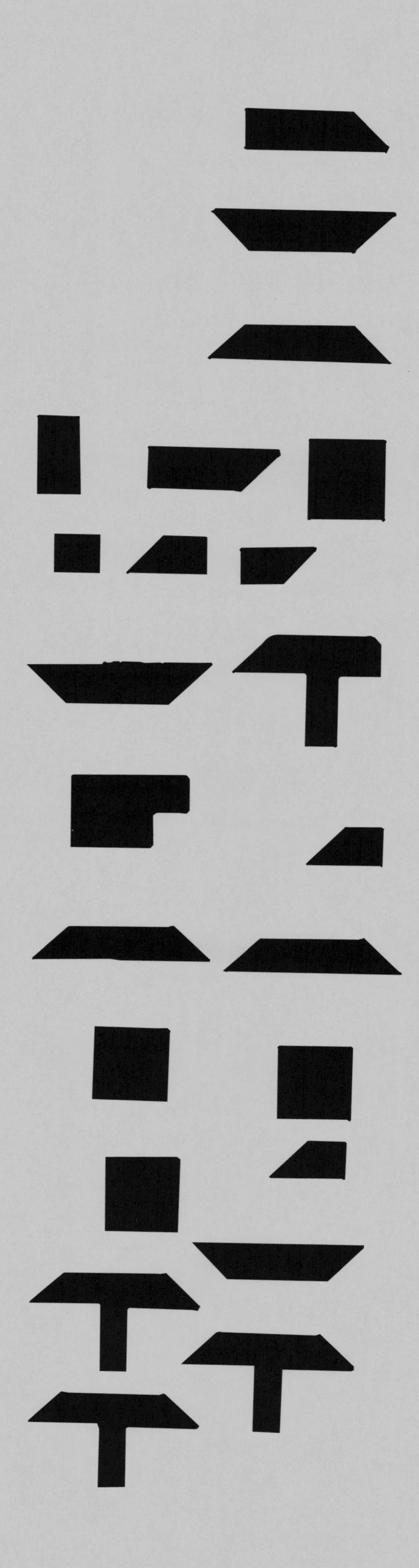

Studio
Spring 2019
1022b M.Arch I Second Year Design Studio
Anthony Acciavatti
Rachel Lefevre, Max Ouellette-Howitz

Islands programmed for play

Historically, the East Harlem waterfront was topographically rich: a series of tidal marsh islands fed by surrounding creeks and streams. Indeed, before the 20th century, East Harlem was a collection of islands and bridges. Today, East Harlem is a flattened tabula rasa, a product of decades of infill which created new grounds. This project proposes a method for erasing this tabula rasa while reconnecting the city to the waterfront and its history of islands and bridges. The creation of a canal which feeds an intermodal hub connecting a new ferry network to the newly completed Q subway line serves as the lifeblood of the site. A series of islands programmed for play line the edges of the canal. A network of pedestrian bridges cross between the islands, while the islands themselves act structurally for private and public development which also spans between them. This technique provides the city with a strategy for encouraging development through publicly owned soft-site interventions.

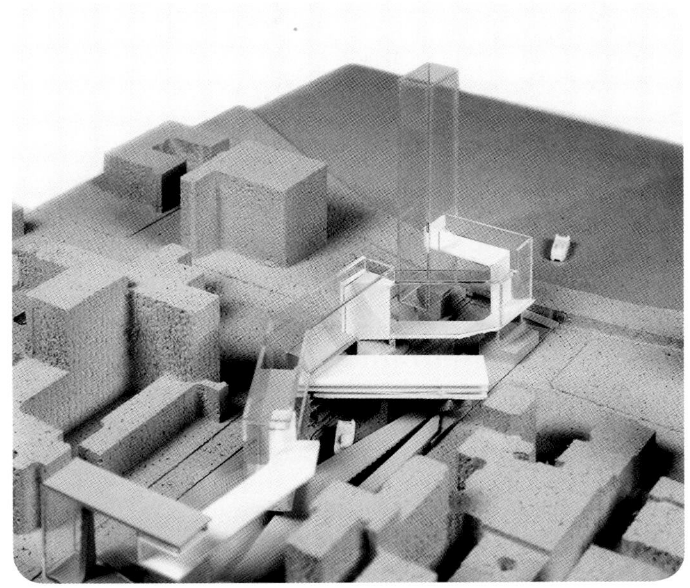

Studio
Spring 2019
1022b M.Arch I Second Year Design Studio
Anthony Acciavatti
Limy Rocha, Brenna Thompson, Rukshan Vathupola

Find a loophole

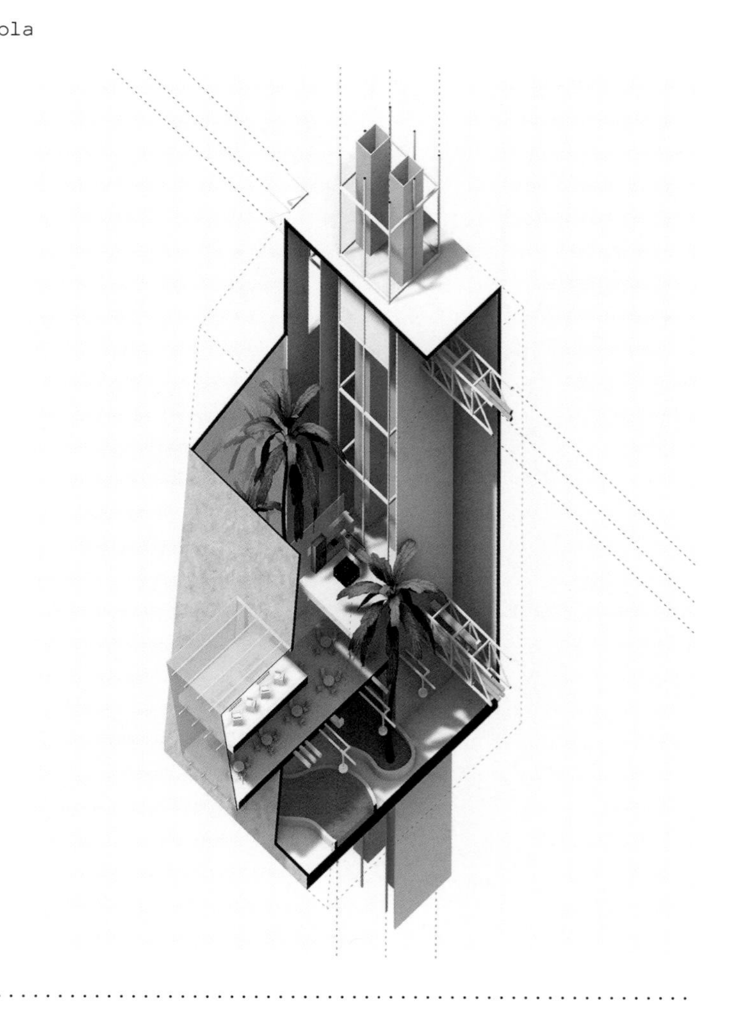

We have developed a game of improvisation between the architect, developer, open space advocates, the department of education, the parks department, mayor, governor, and the surrounding communities to create excess public realms through the deployment of loopholes.

The game exists as a continuous cycle:

1. Isolate a need/program shared by the communities of the Upper East Side and East Harlem
2. Find a loophole
3. Establish a spatial connection between Steps 1 and 2
4. Use Step 3 to anticipate a socio-economic shift
5. Repeat Step 1

Through loopholes, the communal life of the city can re-emerge from within the throes of modern planning by divesting the power of individual developers into a larger collection of the individuals of a community. The environment of New York is then brought to a human scale by redefining itself as a series of successive plays between flexible and public spaces. The inhabitants are transformed into generators of space, allowing the city to exist as a series of iterations through time, constantly evolving and adapting from within. The best kept secret in planning has been uncovered, and we look forward to the consequences.

Studio
Spring 2019
1022b M.Arch I Second Year Design Studio
Bimal Mendis
Phoebe Harris, Kelley Johnson

Small interventions

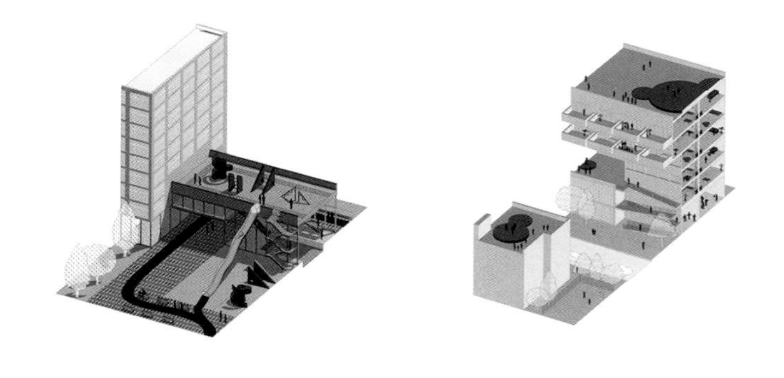

East Harlem has a robust existing system of educational programs, community based non-profits, and recreational space, yet this area still has major issues surrounding education and public health. This project ties together the existing system of public and private initiatives through small interventions. These interventions generate community based feedback loops that increase in scale while still exaggerating each site's individual characteristics. These spaces are enhanced with unique interventions, determined through analysis of issues at the neighborhood scale while utilizing existing community assets. Focused on the nine Jointly Operated Playgrounds, or, J.O.P.s, in East Harlem, we have studied each one's existing community partners and adjacent community programming. We have identified the existing characteristics of the space that can be amplified by the J.O.P. This network of site specific parks work together as a network to help serve the needs of the East Harlem neighborhood.

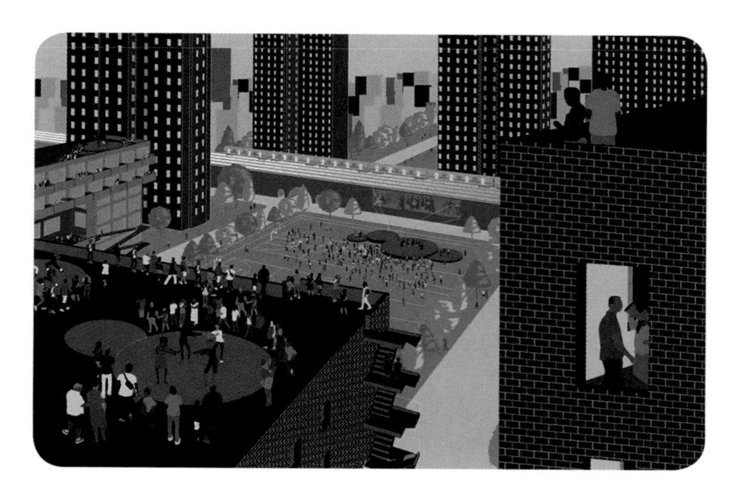

Studio
Spring 2019
1022b M.Arch I Second Year Design Studio
Bimal Mendis
Kelsey Rico, Maya Sorabjee

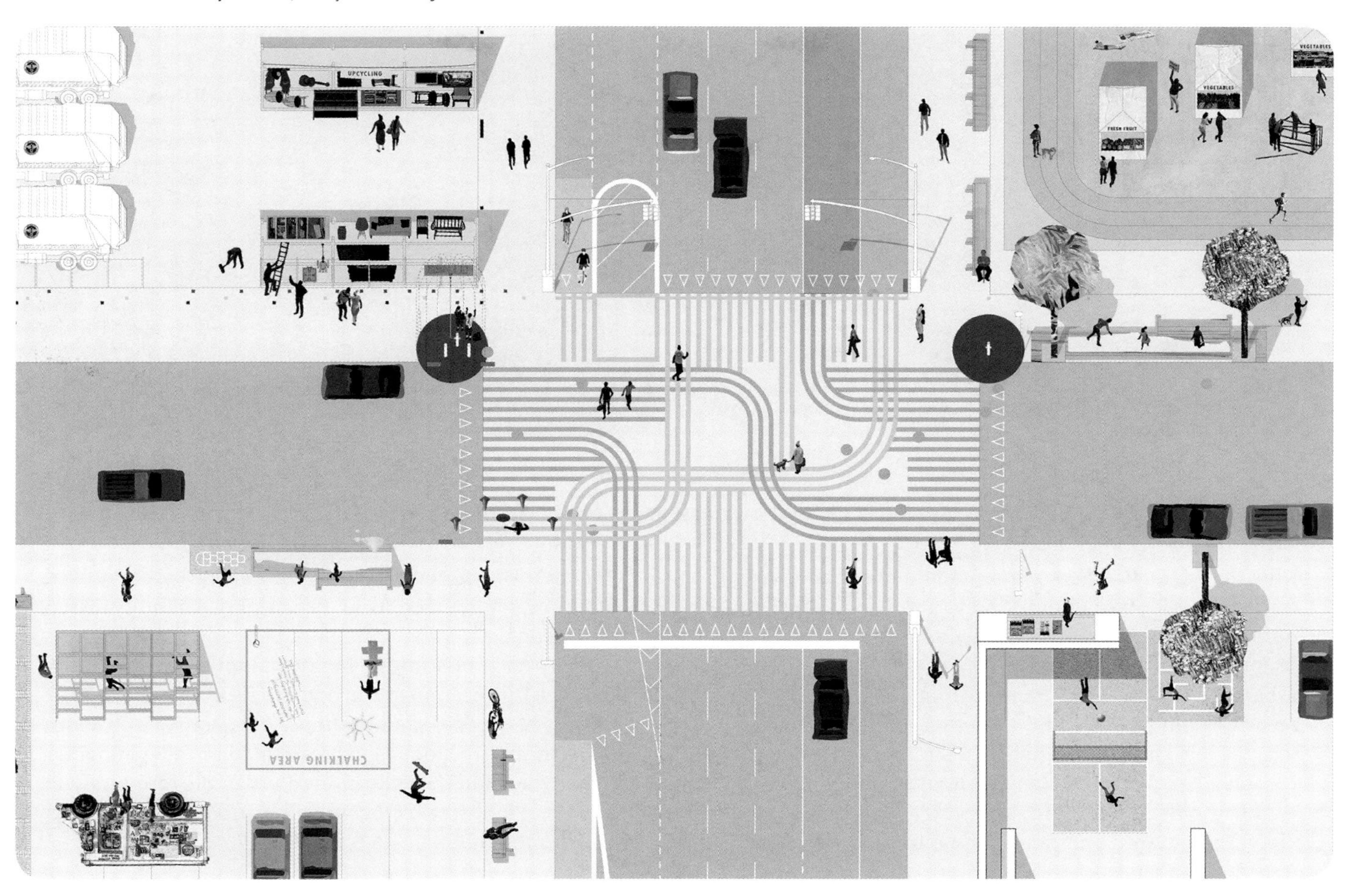

A city authored by many

This project titled, “The Public Lab for Allied Education”, or “PLAE”, is a community organization devoted to the protection of the street as a space of play, welfare, and education. PLAE collaborates with municipal agencies across the five boroughs in order to use the street as a medium of urban intervention, ensuring its future as an inclusive public amenity. Working with various institutions in East Harlem and tapping into existing sources of city funding, the recent initiatives of PLAE test radical ideas about the city and its streets, engaging in a program of resurfacing that brings with it educational and employment opportunities. In doing so, we are committed to reconsidering the extent and possibilities of the public, working with communities to collectively redefine the term. We envision a city authored by many, comprised of a robust network of streets that are ultimately owned by no one, but belong to everyone.

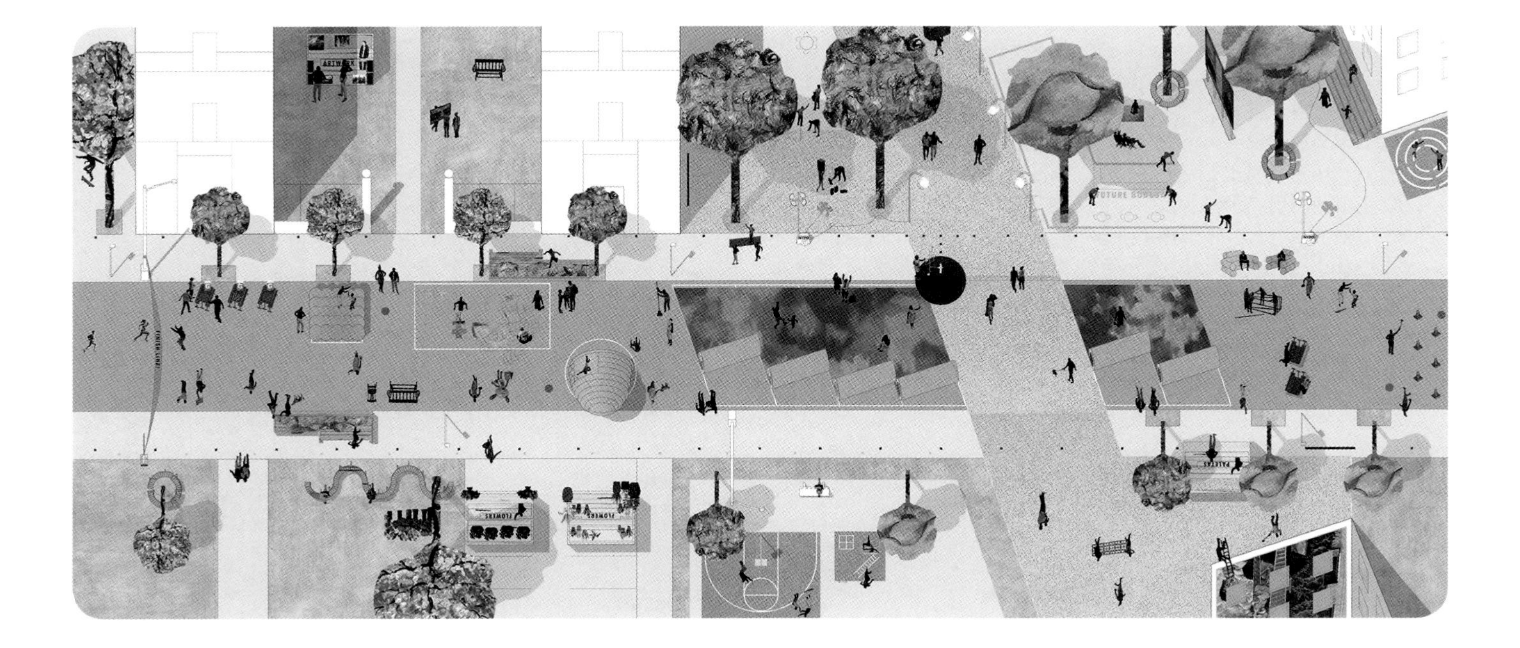

Studio
Spring 2019
1022b M.Arch I Second Year Design Studio
Dragana Zoric
Eunice Lee, Jewel Pei

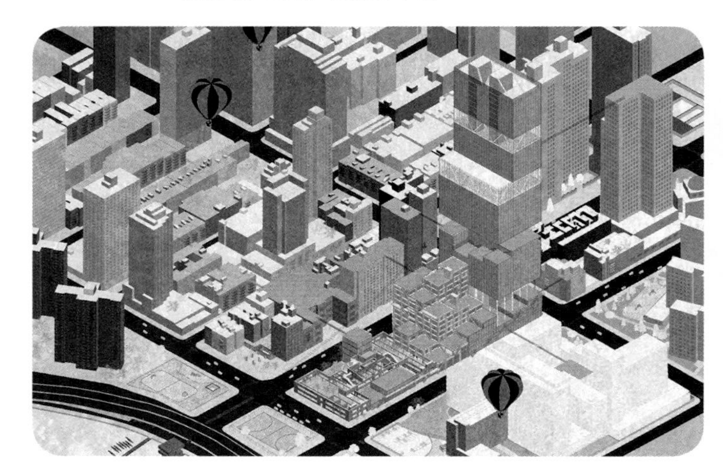

A multilayered urban playground with unexpected obstacles

Like the Marx Brothers playground, many open spaces for public-play are under a constant threat of redevelopment. Instead of resisting these developments, we propose urban strategies to reclaim underused space as urban playground in an ever growing city. With different techniques of drawing and collaging, our project reimagines the city through the lens of a child.

Our first urban strategy reinvents the playground typology with the Transfer of Development Right (TDR) program. High-density developments on Jointly Operated Playground sites require a nearby underused site to be repurposed as an urban playground forested with nature.

The second strategy creates a network of play by connecting the unused urban elements such as back alleys, fire escapes, and rooftops. This network provides children the freedom to explore the city independently. The city becomes a multilayered urban playground with unexpected obstacles and possibilities for interactions with the community.

Studio
Spring 2019
1022b M.Arch I Second Year Design Studio
Dragana Zoric
Rhea Schmid, Armaan Shah

Maintaining an honest porosity

Cities, like New York, are designed for an image that tends to serve its administrators as opposed to its citizens. Reappropriating the Marx Brothers Jointly Operated Playground, or J.O.P., as an opportunity to question this status quo, "CO-OP Campus" explores education as a strategy for a socially-driven urbanism.

Located in the educationally disenfranchised neighborhood of East Harlem, the campus situates itself within District 79, a network of alternative education programs. The campus embraces these programs, including the pre-existing technical school, and sees opportunity to better integrate the various training, support, and recreational initiatives into the city fabric.

This set of synergistic activities engages a ground plane that shifts and reacts to an extruded shed canopy, built to delineate the campus whilst maintaining an honest porosity. COOP Campus traces the humble J.O.P. partnership from a past reliance on development towards a future where development amplifies the voices that deserve an urbanistic presence.

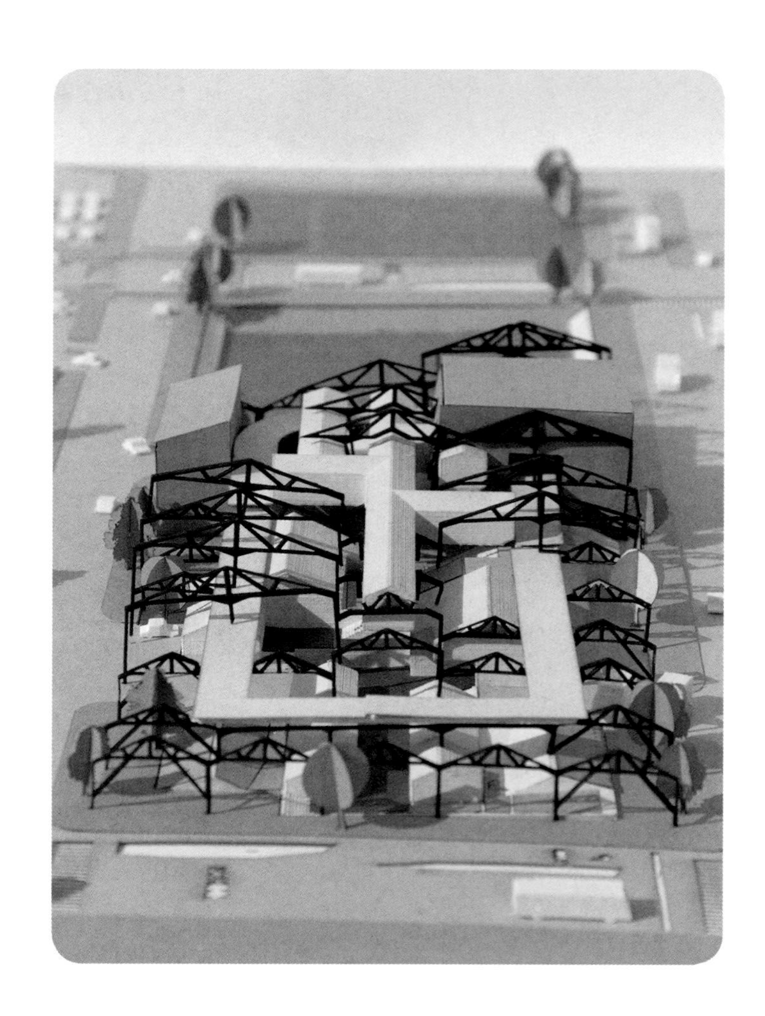

Studio
Spring 2019
1022b M.Arch I Second Year Design Studio
Alicia Imperiale
Emily Cass, Michael Gasper, Seth Thompson

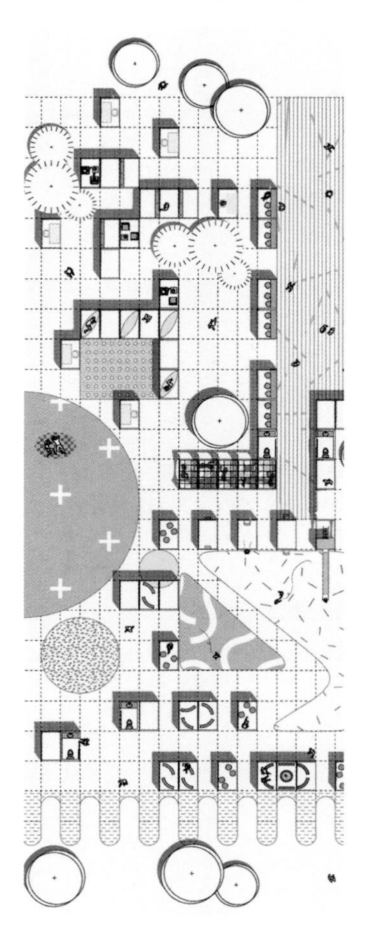

Traveling modules of public resources

The future of Jointly Operated Playgrounds in NYC is in jeopardy as developers seek to profit from their real estate. Using heatmaps of GIS data, we indexed infrastructure, demographics, and public resources to identify the neighborhoods that would most benefit from investment in local playgrounds. Our research also uncovered a recurring NYC motif: unused scaffolding from Local Law 11 facade inspections.

Our proposal turns scaffolding into a structural system to host traveling modules of public resources: libraries, community gardens, bathrooms, health clinics, gathering spaces, food stalls, marketplaces, and reflection areas. We envision a constant reorganization and movement of modules around the city, as buildings undergo different phases of construction and community needs change over time.

Studio
Spring 2019
1022b M.Arch I Second Year Design Studio
Alicia Imperiale
Michael Glassman, Andrew Kim

A more powerful agent for public good

The Educational Construction Fund, or EDF, is the primary steward of the site, responsible for the proposal and implementation of a private development that enables the building of new school facilities.

As a public benefit corporation the ECF sits between public and private, raising questions about the opportunities and challenges of delivering public goods, like schools and parks, with private investment. While the benefits of building schools are clear, the interests of private development do not always align with those of schools and neighbors.

Following extensive research into the history of the ECF's existing projects, we propose a transformation of the organization for present and future. The improved ECF is transparent, seeks out community involvement, and tests innovative mixed-use practices. With a new set of principles guiding development, could the ECF be a more powerful agent for public good?

Studio
Spring 2019
1111b Advanced Design Studio
Pier Vittorio Aureli, Emily Abruzzo

For centuries, architecture, urban design, and planning have been mobilized in order to remove any form of commoning, and enforce a fixed regime of land ownership as the ultimate form of both city and rural land. For this studio, each project offered a possible reinvention of the settlement form from the present regime of land use to a situation in which land will be used in common and ownership will be limited to the minimum indispensable.

This studio focused on the Roman Agro, the region that surrounds the city of Rome. Despite its clearly discernible topographic form, which has defined the landscape of Rome for millennia, the Agro is a vast suburban area where growth over the last century has been propelled mostly by appropriation and building speculation. Each student or group of students worked on a specific toponimo and proposed a strategy of gradual transformation based on the sharing of spaces and resources.

Participants
Diego Arango, Haylie Chan, Sunny Cui, Nicole Doan, Varoon Kelekar, Jeffrey Liu, Martin Man, Leonardo Serrano Fuchs, Gus Steyer, Lucia Venditti, Issy Yi

Jury
Anthony Acciavatti, Tatiana Bilbao, Angelo Bucci, Esther da Costa Meyer, Yolande Daniels, Gary He, Alicia Imperiale

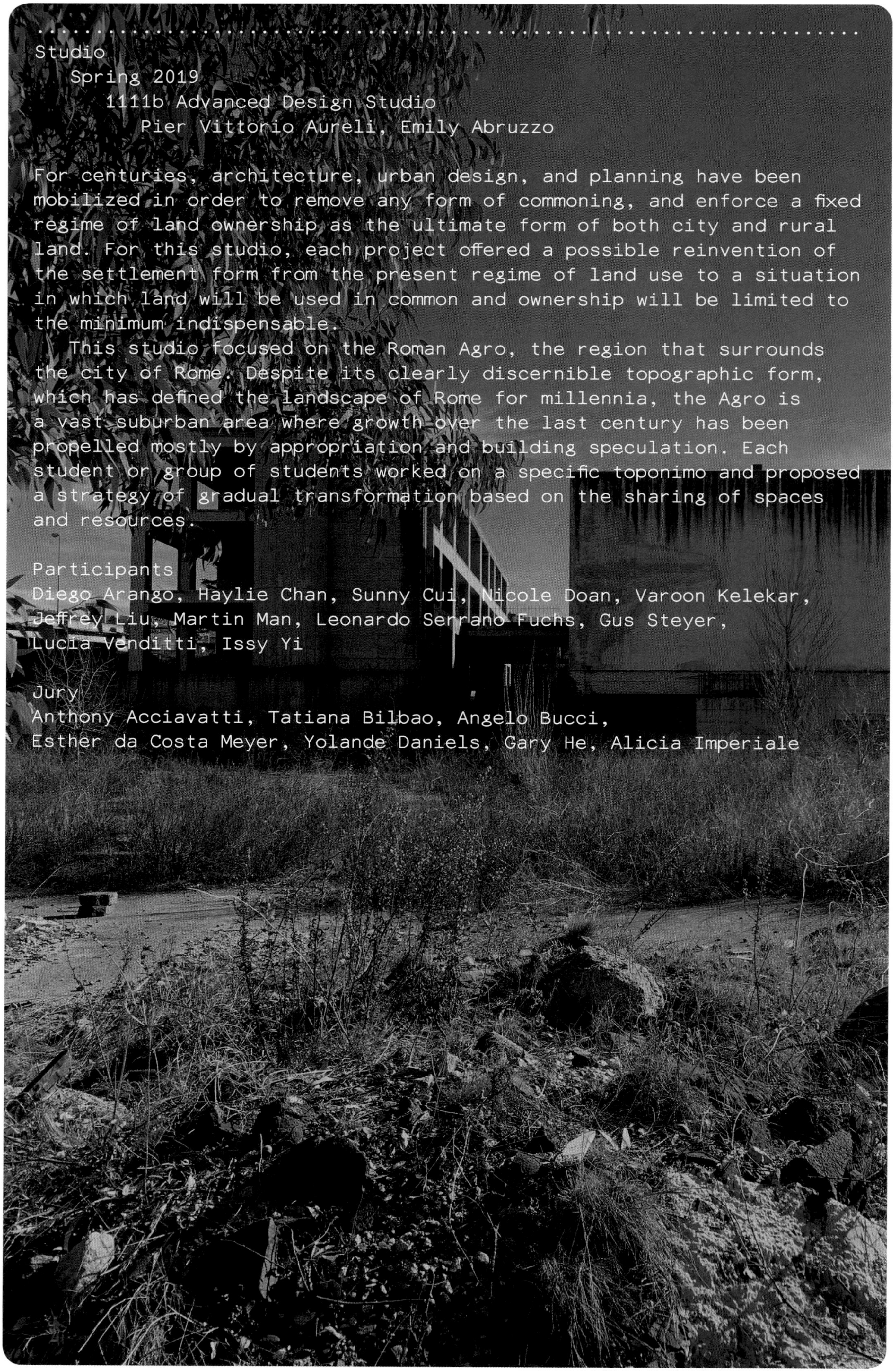

Tear down walls to create new, open spaces

This project reclaims the existing grid—typically used as a disciplinary and expansionary technology—to create spaces that foster negotiation and practices of commoning. These very practices are in opposition to the regimen of private property that the grid has historically been used to uphold. In the earliest phases of the project, neighbors tear down walls to create new, open spaces for gardening, leisure, and rituals. As more people eliminate the distinction between their plots, they appropriate the street that once served as car access for individual homeowners. These neighbors will be able to collectively acquire and farm arable land adjacent to the settlement. Any revenue from this enterprise would be used to build modular structures that can become either workspaces or homes that support new residents as well as alternative forms of kinship. Each new block is close to small-scale civic interventions along Giardini's edge. In turn, the blocks form an altered grid supported by larger public spaces, of which the focal point is a large open field along the Via Polense.

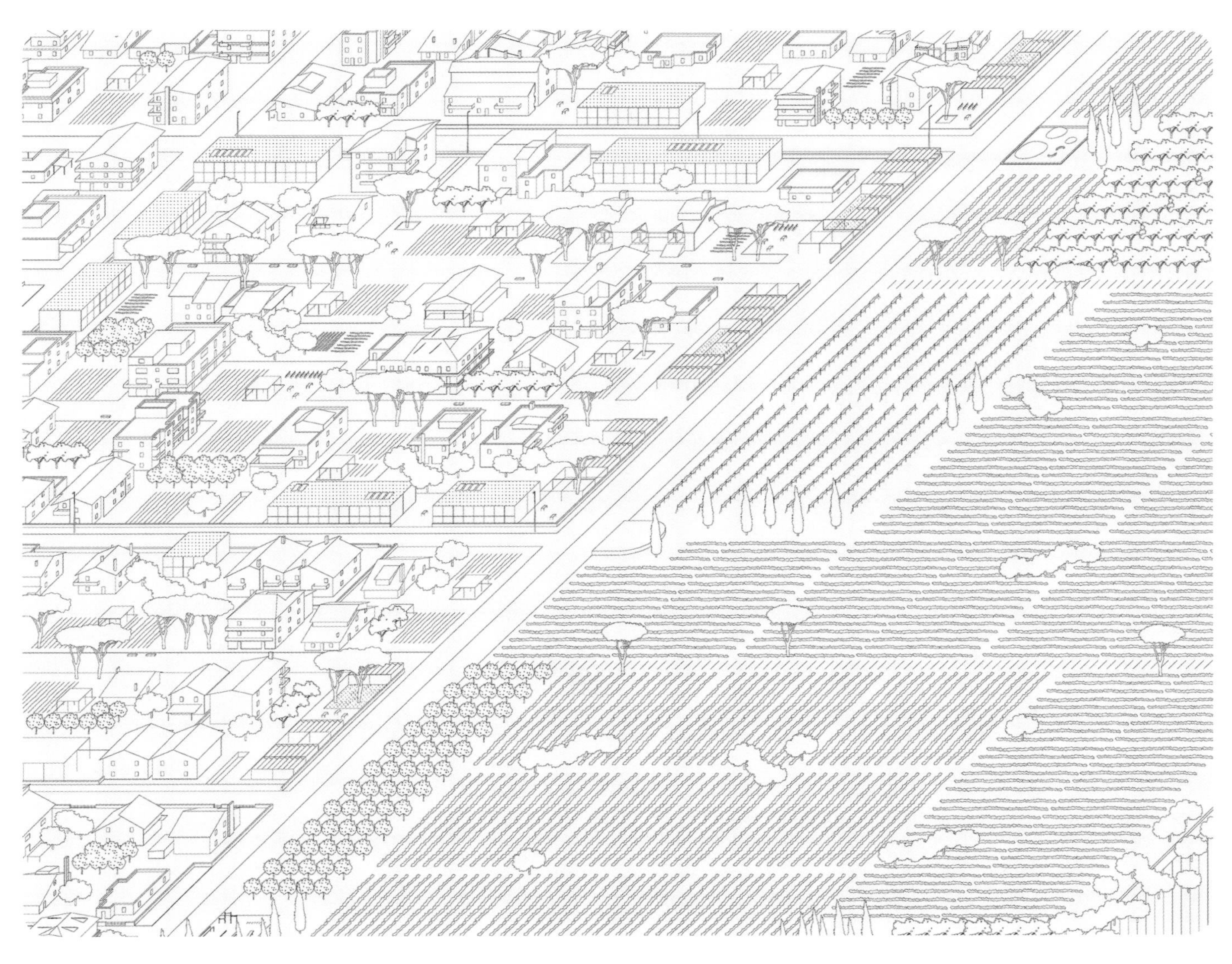

TB: The opportunity of this place is that it is not completely open but also not rural. Then why not transform them into the idea of the city, which is part of the public nor to the idea of the rural area because you have, for example, these paved roads. By asking these questions we can then start to really imagine the idea of a common and instead of transforming all these little things into little cities and then replicating them.

PVA: I agree that there may be an emphasis on gardening and agriculture, but really, this is a culture that is part of this area of Europe. It empowers people to work more in the service industry and in the public sector where there exists an ontological crisis of people not being able to see what they have been able to produce. This project is very didactic of an extreme form of commitment to commoning, or shall I say commoning is an extreme form of commitment, otherwise it would not work. I don't want to repeat myself but the monastic model is really important in understanding that self-sufficiency is not just a matter of survival but the way to come together and to ritualize themselves and to take an alternative form of life. I think in this project you arrived to a point where you have to introduce a certain division of labour which is a reminder to ourselves that commoning is not the barbecue in your backyard garden kind of thing, like you see everywhere in those illegal coffee shop in New York. Commoning requires a lot of ambition and commitment.

Studio
Spring 2019
1111b Advanced Design Studio
Pier Vittorio Aureli, Emily Abruzzo
Haylie Chan, Jeffrey Liu

A legible infrastructure for new communal rituals

Albuccione is an informal settlement where development has occurred along slender, linear agrarian fields. The physical constraints of this linear settlement has forced residents to perform domestic labor in informal sheds outside their primary residence. With an aging population that is forced to partially dwell in shoddily-built structures, Albuccione is facing a crisis of care. Nonetheless, the deconstructed condition of domesticity presents an opportunity to reinvent reproductive labor as a shared public ritual rather than one belonging to the private domestic sphere. This project reconstitutes the household as a linear strip of collective rooms for the commoning of care: single-story assisted living units with communal spaces where residents engage in shared rituals of reproductive labor. Though this process of commoning operates as a ground-up protocol, it eventually reorganizes the structure of the settlement as a whole according to the logic of communal care and provides the settlement with a legible infrastructure for new communal rituals of domesticity.

ECM: I think this is a beautiful project, and I love the way you used two different typologies: the low villas and then the palazzina. While we are seeing the end project here, I also really like all the difficulties that you ran into during the documentation on site. I would really like to complement that as you have to work with the people there.

PVA: For this project, especially, and also in the others of course, we are very critical but there's never the assumption to be judgemental and to go there and build a beautiful housing project. I think the photography is a way to understand the seeds of possibilities. At the same time, there's also the concern of not to romanticize. For example, this was one of the very few places where we enjoyed the informality because when we met other settlers, there was a clear boundary between public and private space. Somehow in this case, it is one of the most informal settlements. In this multifamily plot, there's some kind of exposure of domestic life. There's a fine line between making architecture and finding a way to understand that there is also sometimes very positive things in what is actually there. I think, in this project, this dilemma which was never solved, in a way, is actually very, very powerful.

Ritualized relationship with the landscape

Located at a tri-point of three municipalities—Rome, Guidonia, and Tivoli—the settlement of Martellona has been overseen by the state. The settlement is characterized by sparse population, with buildings spread throughout its expansive arable territory, traversed by the Aniene river. These factors enable Martellona to sustain population growth and become, in the last stage, autonomous in terms of food production.

Gardens are one of the most strategic urban elements that serve as catalysts for social and cultural activities, as well as new forms of labor. The phasing towards commoning starts by promoting horticulture and crop rotation based on subsistence. A collective identity is established as neighbours cooperate and negotiate during collective cultivation and harvesting. Tending, producing, cooking, eating, and sharing form a choreography which celebrates the self-sufficiency of the settlement and its ritualized relationship with the landscape.

A series of punctual interventions along the territory provide platforms for life in common. The Casali and the Cippi are placed according to a structuring grid that is overlaid and oriented to engage with existing contingencies and potentials. The Casali host storages, shared kitchens and dining areas, libraries, childcare facilities, clinics, and other public amenities. They are central communal spaces for each of the commoning units. The Casale is designed in modules, which enable its ad hoc expansion as the community grows. Smaller elements, the Cippi, are spread along the fields, hosting agricultural and public uses or gravitate towards the river, marking a new relationship of the inhabitants with the Aniene.

TB: I love your idea and as a village, it is programmatically very nice—you have it all—but I do think that there is an innocence of thinking that all these Casali will just appear there and attract a lot of people. There's a lack of thinking that this could become a hub for agriculture in a lively way so that they will attract labour from other places and that the neighbour will be able to attach to those Casali, no?

AB: Well, to that, I think your first step would need to be the subtraction of boundary. It has to overcome the limit of properties. When I saw the scheme, I was actually not sure whether this is the boundary. What I think would be a step forward, is what the studio has already suggested: you make an institution as commons. The community makes the institution through the construction of the Casali and will be able to provide for themselves. Then the question is how many?

Studio

Spring 2019

1112b Advanced Design Studio

Thomas Phifer, Kyle Dugdale

In January of 1972 the artist Donald Judd moved to the isolation of Marfa, Texas, to escape the growing commercialism of the New York City art scene. It was in Marfa, surrounded by the open desert landscape, that he sought to build a world for himself, for his family, and for his work. Today, however, Marfa is firmly on the international art map. No longer a place where “only 10 visitors might drift in annually”, by 2016 the number of visitors had risen to 40,000, such that Marfa is now “popularly perceived as an outpost of Manhattan in Far West Texas” (Josh Franco).

Marfa now participates in that same culture it tried to escape, perpetuating the partnership between art and capital. To respond to this issue, students designed not for artists, but for visitors, aiming both to preserve the qualities that first attracted Judd to Marfa, and to deepen the impact of Judd’s legacy.

Participants

Sharmin Bhagwagar, Davis Butner, Pik-Tone Fung, Kerry Garikes, Sissi Guo, Changming Huang, Larkin McCann, Nicholas Miller, Javier Perez, Aslan Taheri, Millie Yoshida

Jury

James Carpenter, Jean Pierre Crousse, Lisa Gray, Frank Harmon, Brian MacKay-Lyons, Beka Sturges

Walls that thicken progressively to contain space

This project, "Between Land, Dust, and Skies", proposes a more immersive experience of Marfa than is currently afforded. The two components—a point of arrival and individual sleeping accommodations—are in two different locations: the point of arrival in town, and the residences in the desert. The residences and their connecting pathways are partially or completely underground which allows for an investigation of the relationship between the body and the ground. The building for arrivals stitches the city blocks together using walls that thicken progressively to contain space as one navigates through the building. By eschewing any preconceived notions that come with the imagery of Marfa, the project addresses those elements of Marfa which create a sense of place like no other: its vastness, its walls and streets, the dust that never leaves your fingertips, and Marfa's skies that continue to fascinate visitors and locals.

JPC: Could you do six instead of five buildings? *laughter* I think you should go against the rules because the project is about the imposition of the landscape and the insertion of sunken space. I like the welcome center because it is a building that is very respectful as it accommodates other buildings and, at the same time, it creates a new world of choices. The gesture is not shy, nor banal. It's not ruled by the context.

MKL: The context is always doing a lot of work. Glenn Mercutt always says the situation gives eighty percent and he does twenty percent of the work. This is a very wise approach and you are pretty young to be so wise about that. You know, fantastic I think.

Studio
Spring 2019
1112b Advanced Design Studio
Thomas Phifer, Kyle Dugdale
Pik-Tone Fung

Bringing the desert into town

Each year, more and more people make the journey through the seemingly endless desert to visit Marfa. In light of this, the project honors the vast landscape as art itself by bringing the desert into town and elevating it thirty inches. This podium serves as a public space, and a sunken garden in the middle features colorful native plants. Stepping down into the arrivals building, visitors find an open-air coffee bar on one side and a reception area on the other. Sitting above the podium, the five long, narrow houses are identical in plan but vary in section, where tilted planes carefully control daylight. Sited in the middle of the town, this project does not prescribe a path for people to follow, but instead encourages them to discover the town on their own, wandering outwards until they find themselves in the open desert landscape once again.

FH: I have a tiny suggestion that you might not expect. As your original premise was that you want people who came here to experience the town, how hard would it be to have steps, actually, here? So then I can leave my building and go to the town. You can give the place a connection. Right now, I feel like I'm sitting there like a perfume model; they are a little unrelated to the site. Regarding the stairs, people will instinctively know, once they go up the steps, if they are in a private land.

BS: Yes, I have this question too. If you see the plan, which we are all really taken with, you have to send a very strong message about inviting people because since you lifted it up, what are your moves that give it back to the public? I actually think the trees aren't helping you because of this idea of bringing the desert into town and finding ways to bring this sidewalk to come down to the town. Because you have created such a private space, it wouldn't be weird if people moved in and out of these buildings from the town.

Studio
Spring 2019
1112b Advanced Design Studio
Thomas Phifer, Kyle Dugdale
Millie Yoshida

Dialogue with the desert environment

Between the in-town arrival building and the five residences on the outskirts of Marfa, this project explores light as threshold, linear sequence, and tectonic design through the materiality of rammed earth. Through the process of reductive design and dialogue with the desert environment, the buildings are boiled down to bare essence, revealing the open-ended linear circulation as opportunity for public space amidst the isolation in the vast landscape.

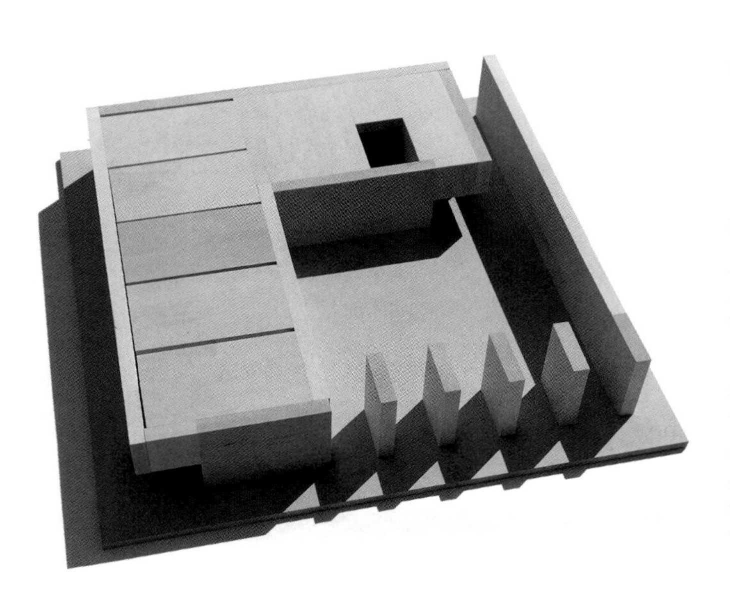

JPC: The idea of relating people together and being in their own spaces are very good ideas. However, there is a problem when this becomes a rule and not a possibility. In fact, the rule should not be about opening but about serenity. Something that works in the landscape as an object might not work as well as a space. If those houses follow the topography, you could always have this relationship but not oblige them to look at one another. That would be much richer even if it means the project would be less abstract in the landscape.

BMKL: I think there would be a way to mess up the current condition and keep your idea by making the ground drop and the roof stay.

JPC: You would follow the topography and keep the same height at the top.

BMKL: Yes, that's the trick.

Studio
Spring 2019
1113b Advanced Design Studio
Brigitte Shim, Andrei Harwell

Housing as an urban architecture acts as a robust frame for public life. The dwelling is a frame for our everyday lives. Is it time for housing to do more? Can housing linked with other programmes reshape our cities in vital and unexpected ways?

This studio investigates and explores hybrid prototypes that intertwine housing, sustainability, and landscape, and links them with cultural programs resulting in innovative models for city building. The studio worked with the Honolulu Art Museum and designed propositions for a vacant site in downtown Honolulu owned by the museum. Each student developed a new prototype for the Honolulu Art Museum's urban city block interrogating the ways that housing, museums, and social condensers can be combined providing a catalyst for rethinking the future of downtown Honolulu.

Participants
Melinda Agron, Tayyaba Anwar, Nino Boornazian, Zelig Fok, Orli Hakanoglu, Mengi Li, Ben Olsen, Jen Shin, Colin Sutherland, Adam Thibodeaux, Ray Wu

Jury
Ceren Bingol, Craig Buckley, Kenneth Frampton, Inès Lamunière, Chris McVoy, Alan Organschi, Todd Reisz, Dean Sakamoto, Billie Tsien

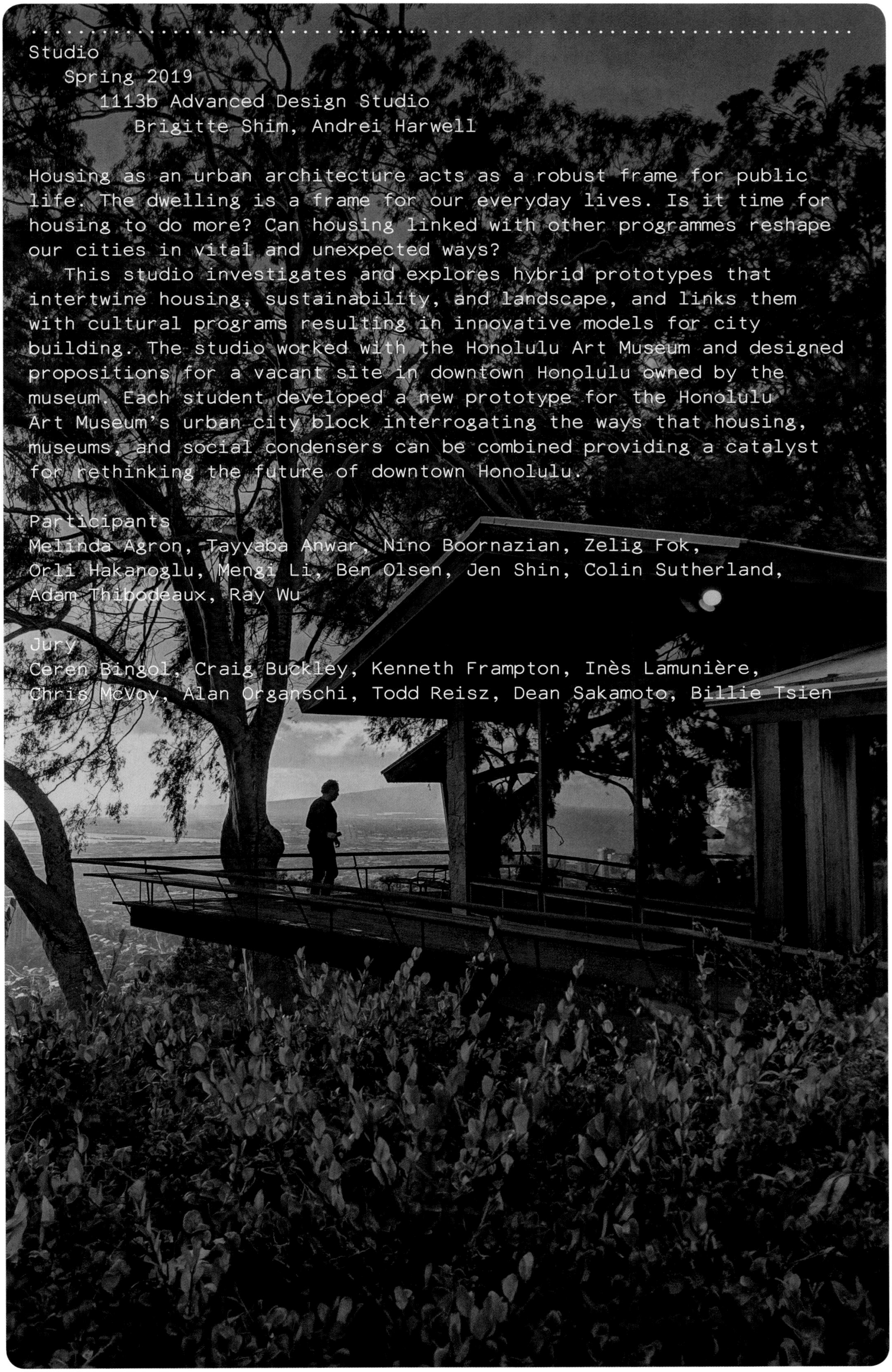

Architecture cannot exist in isolation

Hawaii holds and projects an identity of a utopic 'paradise island' to the world, yet struggles with defining its architectural individuality. This project, titled "Thinking Inside the Box", acknowledges that architecture can only provide a framework to the city, allowing the design to respond to the customs and needs of its inhabitants and grow with time. It enables the emergence of intimate spaces on the ground and in the sky, where the locals have the opportunity to form relationships with travelers.

Architecture cannot exist in isolation, devoid of influences that it relies on for its operation. It is contingent to the global and local impacts, and believes that the 'box', a volume that is provided to the inhabitant, behaves like a living organism, and provides fluidity within itself, allowing for impulsive spaces of variability and transition.

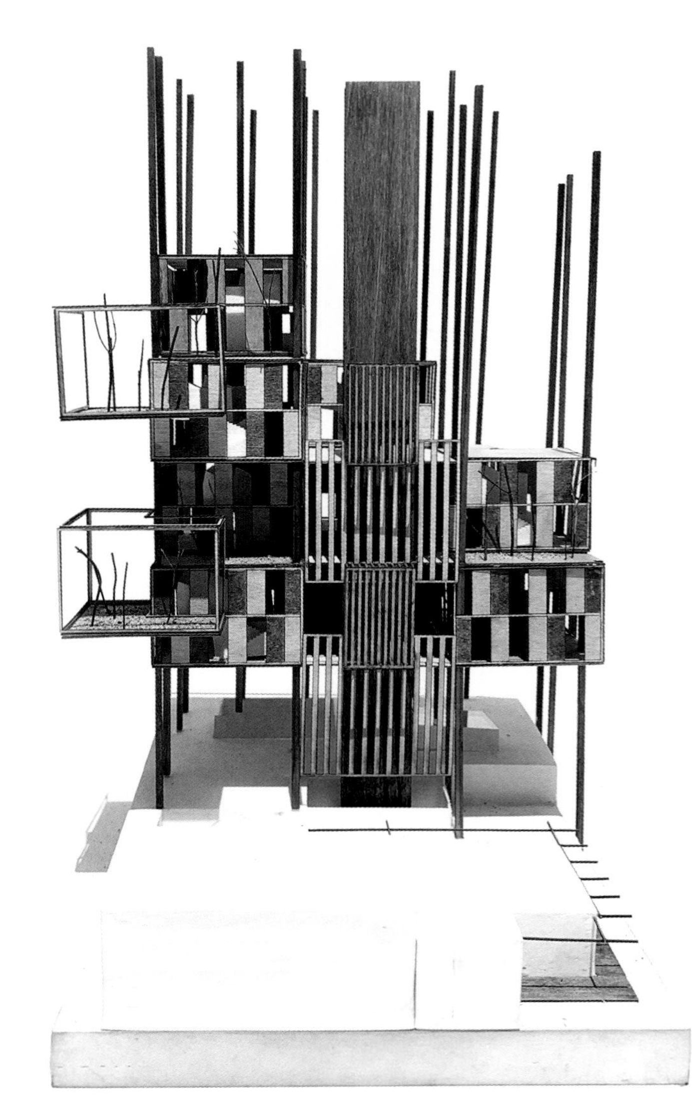

CM: Beautiful presentation. Amazing drawings and models. Maybe you can learn something from your initial roots though? It started as a rational project from the ideas of globalization, but it can actually turn to a project driven from localization, where you can say that you're doing an exclusive project. I would never move out if I got a spot in here. So it's not a transient community, I think, with local artisans and local community members. You can still have a rational architecture but rooted in a good cause. So maybe it doesn't have to be globalization.

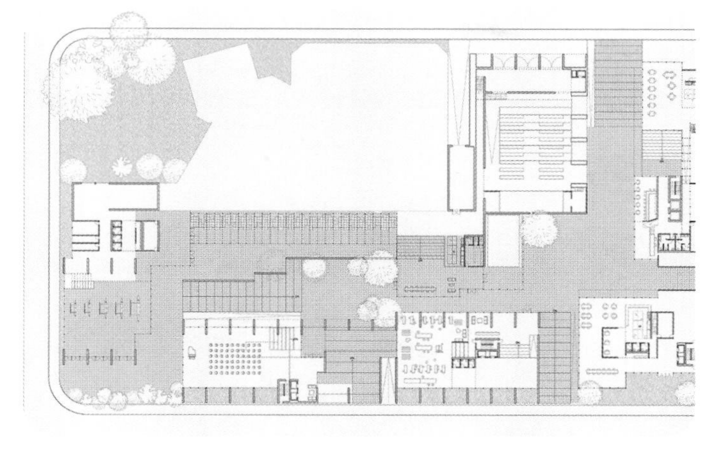

KF: I think it's a beautiful scheme. I think the way you get into the scheme, the whole continuity and public access, has many virtues from that point of view. But when you come to the boutique hotel, I don't quite understand why it breaks up into these two bits. Could it be not broken up? For example, when you look at the affordable housing, you have this kind of communal bay that is looking out, right? I think it's more logical, given the overall scheme, for the communal areas to look *in*. You could have added more units and given more continuity to the overall form. I think there's enormous potential here.

DS: The museum is a challenge because it has a shitty entry. It's too close; you only have about twenty feet for that entry. People hate it—it's too steep. They're talking about entering off to the side. They're talking about creating an iconic entry here. So why I think this is brilliant is that [the entry] puts pressure on Victoria Street, a narrow street, which could become part of that place. And you create this passage through the housing—maybe you combine your residential and hospitality at the end—and this becomes a generous, open place that relates to the park. Urbanistically, I think that's it.

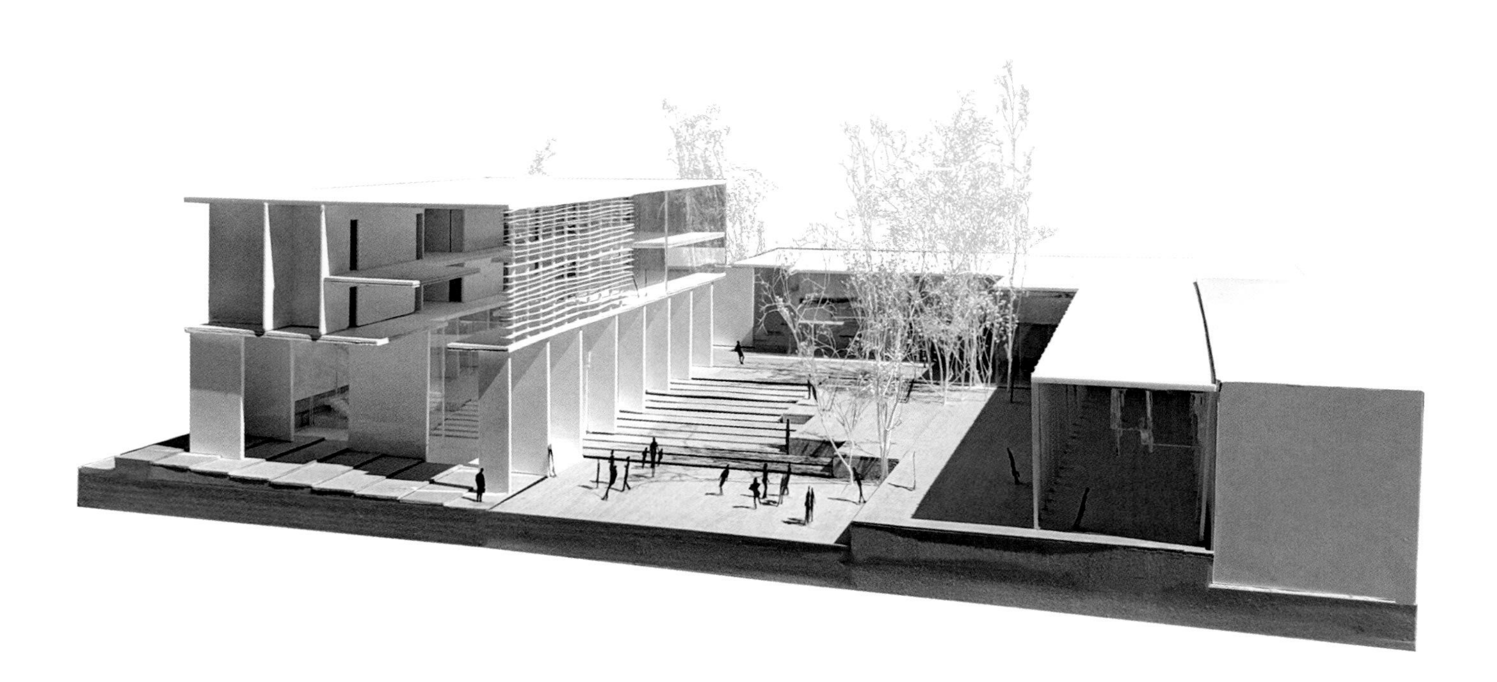

Moments of serendipitous collision and exchange

"Living by Design" is a mixed-use building in downtown Honolulu featuring a boutique hotel, affordable housing, and a design center. Located adjacent to the Honolulu Museum of Art (HMA) and the HMA School, it strengthens the identity of this existing arts node. While hotel and housing both fundamentally deal with the act of dwelling, a rift likely exists between their residents in terms of their respective socioeconomic status and relationship to Hawaii. Thus the various components of the design center are used to bridge together these two worlds, as well as to link the building to its urban arts context. Instead of being encapsulated within a standalone building, the various components of the design center appear throughout the site, animating the entire complex and serving as a platform to bring together residents of the hotel and affordable housing alike. Art and design manifest as galleries to the west, a spine of visible storage to the north, artist studios in the affordable housing units to the south, and as informal pocket galleries throughout the corridors of the hotel to the east. Connecting all of these elements is a generous public realm whose series of interconnected courtyards serve not only as gathering spaces, but also as outdoor circulation, offering moments of serendipitous collision and exchange among residents, visitors, and the broader community.

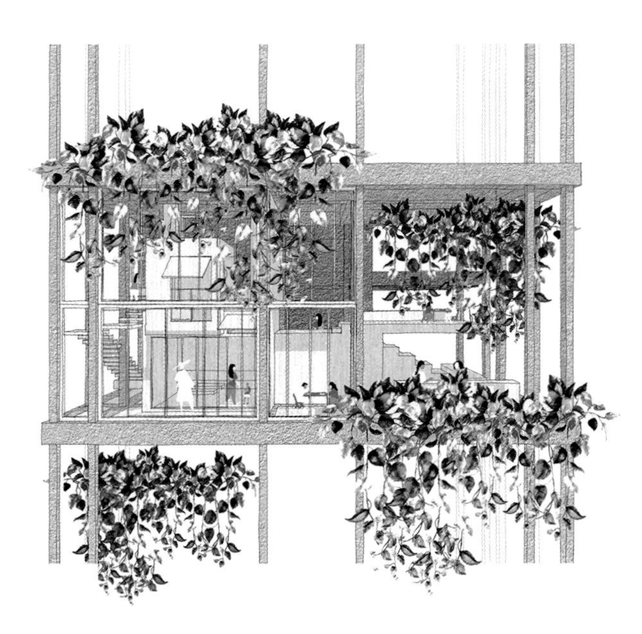

Community members are agents of their own spaces

"Ho'oponopono/To Make Right" examines past and present colonization of Hawaii through a framework of privileging Native Hawaiian intelligence and lifeways. This project imagines the growth of a community that moves toward the reversal of the Mainland imported-paradise-ideal still pervasive throughout Honolulu today by making space for the practice of art, life, and the creation and documentation of knowledge. It subverts the given brief—boutique hotel, design institute for Native Hawaiian cultural objects, and affordable housing—into a Center for Living and Healing Arts, affordable housing, and short-stay housing for scholars whose work touches on Hawaiian and indigenous knowledge. Through semi-public courtyards, flexible unit modules, and shared patterns of living, Ho'oponopono treats all spaces as a pool of resources. Here, community members are agents of their own spaces and collectively cultivate their work in making right the problems that continue to plague native communities such as homelessness, economic marginalization, and degradation of culture and land. By respecting and making space for Hawaiian knowledge and lifeways, Ho'oponopono stands as a small but important step in the material form of Hawaiian sovereignty.

AO: I think gateway buildings, which are very grounded in a nice way, create threshold. I don't think the other languages which are more elevated or more itemized, can. I was going to ask you if you're hiring? *laughter* I think the presentation is incredible. Exceptional premises, really beautiful. The drawing techniques are really beautiful and yet, it's very rigorous. These diagrams, for me, with the cubes, are problematic. It's the only thing I don't like. Because I think you've actually found an architecture with a lot of different ways of describing closure, openness, and porosity. I think I was bugged by that at the midterm and it's still in that model. You have absolutely stripped it of that, and I think it's actually really sophisticated.

CM: One, you've started organizing the site through space formed by buildings. Two, you reinvented the program; I hope you continue to do that. As architects, that's important rather than taking program as it is. And the way you've done it through this connection with history and rethinking it from the way it's been, let's say, distorted, is great. The third thing is you used the module to create a kind of finer grain. The only critique I have is once you break up the scale so much, the public nature and scale of the courtyard space gets lost. Notice the elevations along the courtyards get lost.

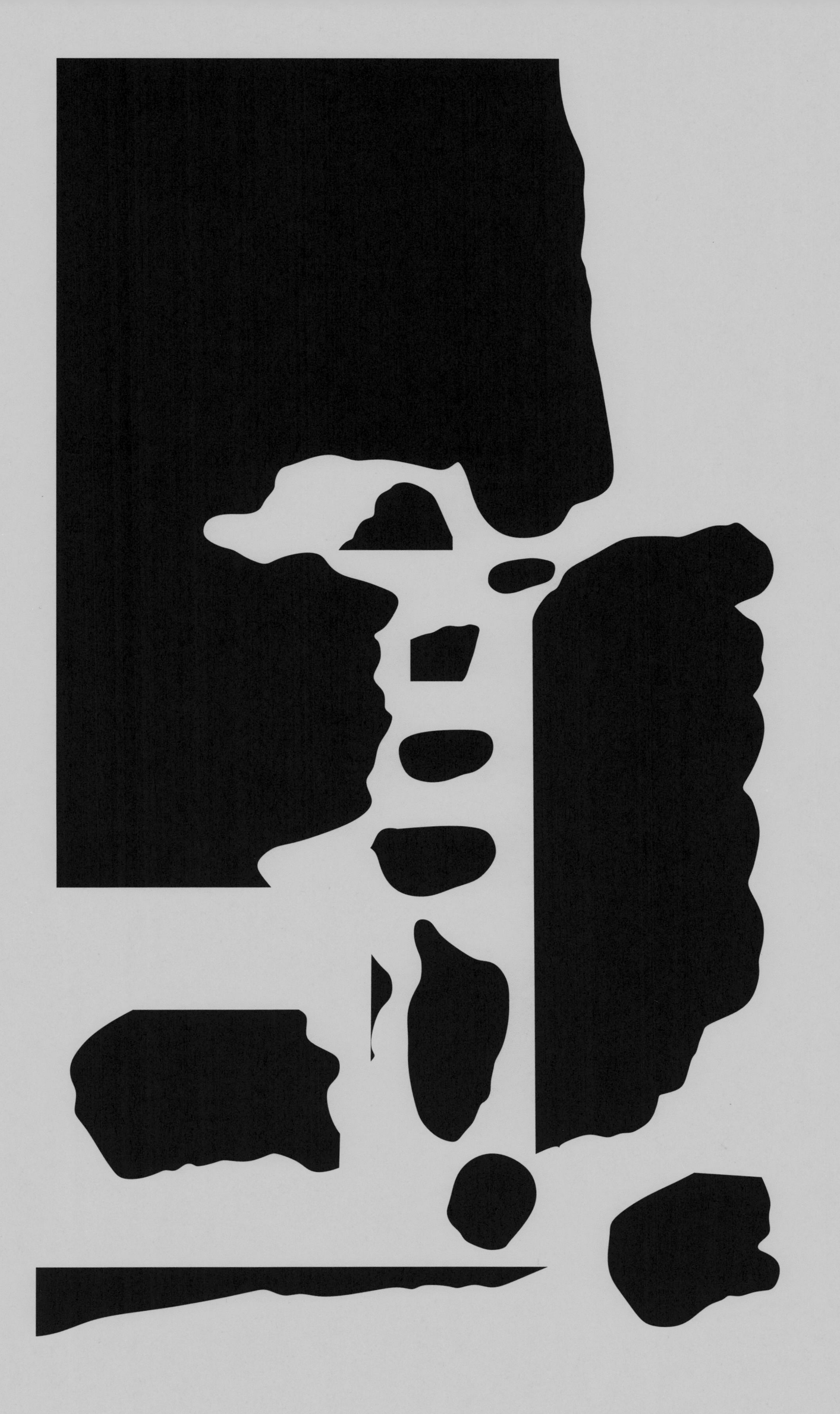

César Pelli 1926-2019

“Most architects know that there are some buildings that speak. Very few buildings sing and very many are mute. And this really is perhaps one of the most important things to be concerned about when one designs any building.”

Dean of YSoA 1977-1984
Founder of Retrospecta 1977

Retrospecta 42

V Letter from the Dean
VII Letter from the Editors
VIII Lectures
XIII North Gallery Exhibitions
XV Symposia
XVIII Jim Vlock First Year Building Project 2018 Open House
XIX Publications
XX Paprika!
XXII Student Organizations
XXII Awards
XXIII Happenings
XXIV Donors
XXVII Students
XXVIII Faculty
XXIX Index

Letter from the Dean

The Dean’s office has a wall of bookshelves. They are full of beautiful books by or about great architects, many of them faculty members, visiting faculty, and graduates of the School; also volumes on Yale’s architectural history and its campus as well as all the volumes of Perspecta. Perhaps the most alive of the books and journals that fill the wall, Retrospecta presents the work of today’s students and our most recent graduates. It has a consistent immediacy and addresses the viewer in the present tense, showing students in the midst of engaging the challenges of the moment.

This issue of Retrospecta covers the design studio and course work of the 2018-2019 academic year. It includes lectures, symposia, and student-run events. Our students, as is well reflected here, are interested in global problems as they relate to architecture and the built environment. They are passionate about exploring design solutions that can lead to positive change—addressing issues like the need for livable cities and the impact of the built environment on climate change. However, this does not lessen their interest in form-making, technology, materiality, and beauty. In fact, I would say it enhances it.

At the Yale School of Architecture we remain committed to helping all our students enrich and expand their passions, broaden and enhance their knowledge, and become architects who will change the world. Our goal is that they have both an individual voice and a commitment to the common good; and a strong philosophical position in their creative work while respecting the creative motivations of others. Architecture can be defined both narrowly and broadly. It is indeed the designing of buildings, but it also the shaping of the world. We teach both here.

Deborah Berke

CHIPPERFIELD

Letter from the Editors

This is a book
of lists, works, artifacts, scraps, cities, islands, worlds, lifecycles, ecosystems, conversations, cocktails, critiques, clouds, bubbles, waves, natures, playgrounds, buildings, borders, broadsheets, birdies, long nights, stories, memories, and people.

Natalie
Ives
Colin
Justin

Lectures

Dean Berke: “As many of you know, we host a reception following our lectures, and in a minute, I will invite you all upstairs to the gallery on the second floor of this building for tonight’s reception. As many of you also know, at our receptions we serve a cocktail, connected in some way to the speaker and their work. This research is done by Assistant Dean Andrew Benner, so I thank him in advance for his choices this semester. Tonight’s cocktail is a drink called the ‘Inverted Manhattan’. It is essentially a Manhattan with the ratio of rye to vermouth reversed. Andrew’s description was that ‘it evokes an inverted image of Manhattan as might be seen reflected in the water from Governors Island. See you on the second floor.”

August 30, 2018
Michael Samuelian
Civic Engagement in New York City

> “How can development be redefined in terms of the public sector, thinking about how architects, specifically designers, can engage the public in a way that many of us traditionally haven’t?”

Michael Samuelian is the Fall 2018 Edward P. Bass Distinguished Visiting Architecture Fellow at the Yale School of Architecture and the President at the Trust for Governors Island.

Evening Cocktail: “Inverted” Manhattan (sweet vermouth, rye whiskey, bitters)

September 6, 2018
Anab Jain
Other Worlds Are Possible

> “The very fact that the current world view requires infinite growth in a finite world demonstrates that it will collapse. We have no choice but to see outside the current paradigm, because the current paradigm will fail. The only question is: what will we birth in its place?”

Anab is co-founder and director of Superflux, a London and India based speculative design practice. Jain is the recipient of the Award of Excellence ICSID, UNESCO Digital Arts Award, and Grand Prix Geneva Human Rights Festival, and has received awards from Apple and the UK Government’s Innovation Department. He work has been exhibited at MoMA New York, V & A Museum, Science Gallery Dublin, National Museum of China, Vitra Design Museum, and Tate Modern.

Evening Cocktail: “Weiss Gespritzt” (Gruener Veltliner Wine, Voslauer mineral water)

September 20, 2018
Georgeen Theodore and Tobias Armborst
Oh, the Places You’ll Go!

> "We wanted to develop a practice in which serious urban research and scholarship would be directly tied to applied creative practice."

Interboro Partners, a Brooklyn-based architecture, urban design, and planning firm led by Tobias Armborst, Georgeen Theodore, and Daniel D'Oca.

Evening Cocktail: “The Interboro” (genever, amaro, dry vermouth, apple cider, bitters)

September 27, 2018
Christopher Hawthorne
Unfinished City: The Contentious Rise of the Third Los Angeles

> “The city is still restless, even squirming and certainly unfinished. But more and more it would like to sit for a time and have a chance, for once, to take stock. It’s not quite a retrospective, but it’s a start.”

Christopher Hawthorne (Yale College '93) is the first Chief Design Officer of the City of Los Angeles and served as the architecture critic for the Los Angeles Times for fourteen years.

Evening Cocktail: "The Last Word" (gin, green chartreuse, maraschino liqueur, lime juice)

October 11, 2018
Rossana Hu and Lyndon Neri
Reflective Nostalgia

"The place that we come from sets the stage for many of our architectural and design explorations. We want to share that condition with you tonight—a contextual framework of our operative modes as architects. We bring forth a few issues that started out as problems. We needed to confront working on projects that became obsessions that kept coming back again and again, surfacing and resurfacing, sometimes consciously, and at other times, utterly unintentional."

Lyndon Neri and Rossana Hu are the founders of the Shanghai-based architecture firm Neri & Hu and are the Fall 2018 Norman R. Foster Visiting Professors at the Yale School of Architecture.

Evening Cocktail: "Chrysanthemum #3" (Drumshanbo Gunpowder Gin, dry vermouth, Benedictine, lemon juice, absinthe)

November 1, 2018
Julie Snow
Invisible Site

"The social and cultural territory of projects seems to offer a rich ground for architectural and urban design investigation. The social dynamic of public space, or the work space for that matter, blends ideas of social interaction, inclusivity and equity, as well as security and safety. The cultural context can provide investigative avenues for history, values and cultural patterns."

Julie Snow is a founder of Snow Kreilich Architects and the Fall 2018 William B. and Charlotte Shepherd Davenport Visiting Professor at the Yale School of Architecture.

Evening Cocktail: "Ballerina in Work Boots" (Russian vodka, dry vermouth, extra dry cider)

November 8, 2018
Omar Gandhi
Defining a Process

"Having worked for several wonderful firms, I knew how they had worked—but how was I going to work? What was my process going to be? I decided I was going to do as little as possible; I was going to take the information that was given to me—about climate, about context, about materiality-and was just going to play with that."

Omar Gandhi is an architect based in Nova Scotia and the Fall 2018 Louis I. Kahn Visiting Assistant Professor at the Yale School of Architecture.

Evening Cocktail: "Les Suetes" (Canadian Whiskey, maple syrup, ginger beer, lime)

November 12, 2018
Simon Hartmann
HFF. Alternate Endings

"When we founded the office, we were at the kitchen, and we said we want to build; we want to build internationally and we want to have collaborations. That was the mission statement at the kitchen table. Because that was a time in 2003 in Switzerland you had a lot of people who went into academia; they did just enough to get into academia. My English colleagues, there were a lot of them, would say they could work on their theoretical position while not building. We wanted to build before we could say anything interesting."

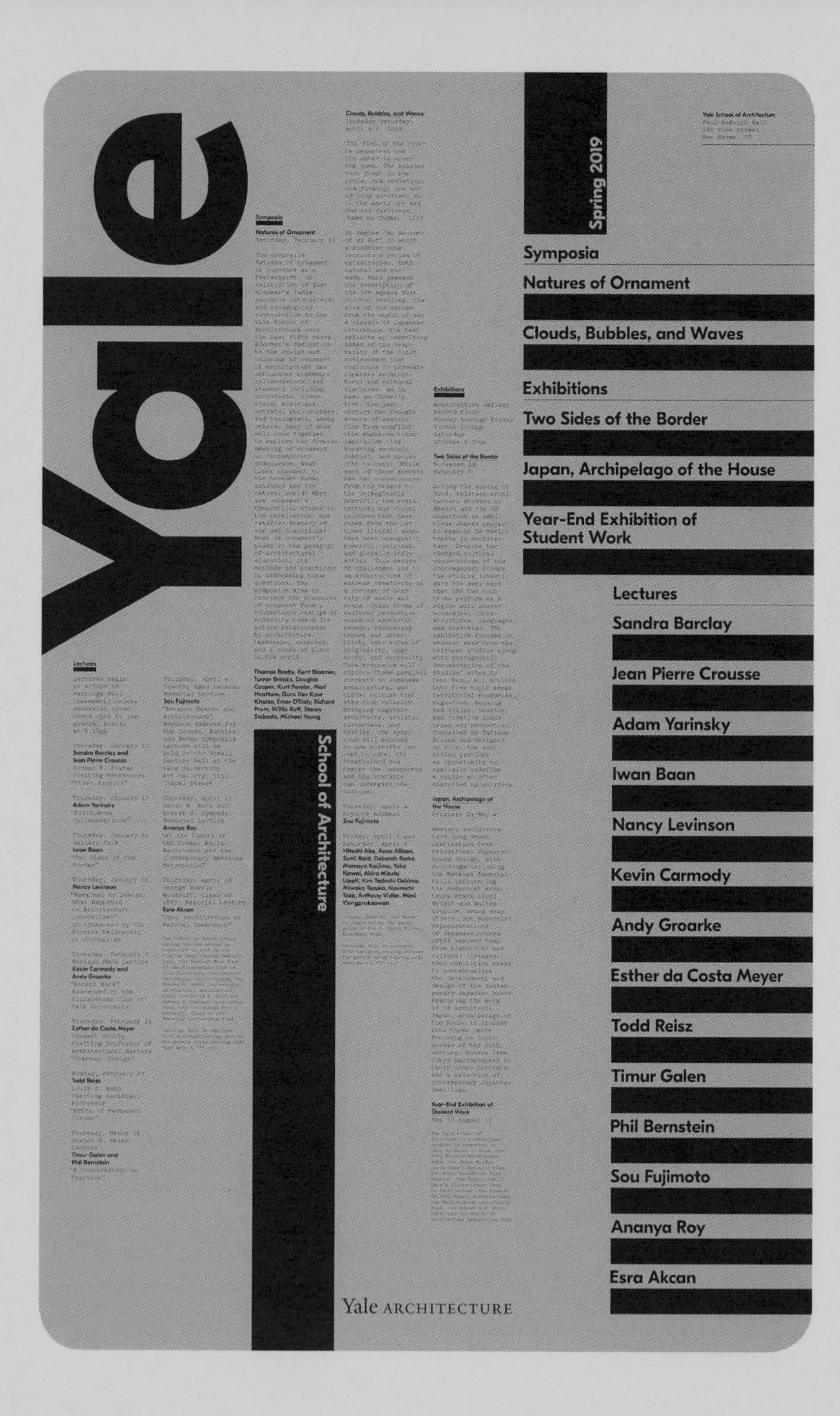

Simon Hartmann is a co-founder of Basel-based HHF Architects and the Fall 2018 William Henry Bishop Visiting Professor.

Evening Cocktail: “The Kanton” (Suze, Barenjager, tonic, lemon)

November 15, 2018
Anna Dyson
Transforming the DNA of the Built Environment

“What would it mean in this day and age, to have a truly symbiotic relationship between architectural practice and research, in a way that borrows from other models? Almost everything in the anthropocene is seen as an urban act. If we were to look at what we are measuring, projecting and, drawing—what is the measuring stick?”

Anna Dyson is the Hines Professor of Sustainable Architectural Design at the Yale School of Architecture and the Yale School of Forestry and Environmental Studies. She is also the founder of the Center for Ecosystems in Architecture at Yale (CEA).

Evening Cocktail: “ELM” (birch liqueur, gin, cream soda)

November 29, 2018
Francesco Casetti
Spectral Visions, Enclosed Public

“My interest in media and space is ultimately the idea that space matters, because it is a medium. We mediate through space and in space. After all, the idea is that you, architects, and us, media people, in some sense are doing the same job, or at least facing the same problems.”

Casetti is the Thomas E. Donnelley Professor of Humanities and Professor of Film Studies at Yale. His work specializes in the semiotics of film and television and the role of cinema in the context of modernity.

Evening Cocktail: “The Bicycle Thief” (Campari, gin, grapefruit juice, lemon juice, simple syrup, seltzer)

January 10, 2019
Sandra Barclay, Jean Pierre Crousse
Other Tropics

"In every project we do, our first effort is to find good questions that will guide us and our design process. Not pretending to find the answers, but with the aim to think about the means we have at our disposal, and the meaning or sense our building should convey."

Sandra Barclay and Jean Pierre Crousse are the founders of Barclay & Crousse, a Lima-based architecture firm, and are the Spring 2019 Norman R. Foster Visiting Professors at the Yale School of Architecture.

Evening Cocktail: “Chilcano” (pisco, lime juice, ginger beer, bitters)

January 17, 2019
Adam Yarinsky
Posthumous Collaborations

“Architecture is grounded in a part of a complex web of physical and social relationships. We frame our practice as research or inquiry into these conditions and develop strategies about program and process as well as the craft of building out of engaging the conditions which we are working within.”

Adam Yarinsky is a partner at Architecture Research Office and was the Fall 2018 Eero Saarinen Visiting Professor at the Yale School of Architecture.

Evening Cocktail: “Corpse Reviver #2” (gin, Lillet, lemon juice, Cointreau)

January 24, 2019
Iwan Baan
Two Sides of the Border

"When the Berlin wall fell there were sixteen border fences around the world and today there's almost sixty-five, either built or under construction. The wall, while an ancient security strategy, has a purpose to repel, but in fact, walls generate a magnetic field, especially visible in these areas like Tijuana."

Iwan Baan is a leading international architectural photographer and among the most ubiquitous presences in the architecture profession today. This lecture accompanies the exhibition, "Two Sides of the Border," conceived by Tatiana Bilbao and curated by Nile Greenberg. Baan photographed a series of landscapes and structures throughout the US and Mexico to examine the regional ties between people, cultures, and economies.

Evening Cocktail: "Two Sides of the Border" (mescal, Balcone's Baby Blue Bourbon, lime juice, tamarind soda, Topo Chico Mineral Water)

January 31, 2019
Nancy Levinson
Marginal by Design: What Happened to Architectural Journalism?

"Architecture is a discipline with such a rich history of periodical literature. Journals and magazines in print and online, are critical markers of our global design culture. They at once disseminate and reflect that culture, while also influencing it. And yet it's not often we step back and analyze the workings of our journals and magazines."

Nancy Levinson (Yale College '78) is editor and executive director of Places Journal. Since arriving at the journal in 2009, she has led its transition from print to digital, advanced the editorial mission of public scholarship, and overseen the launch of Places Books. Previously she was founding director of the Phoenix Urban Research Lab at The Design School at Arizona State University, and before that, a founding editor of Harvard Design Magazine at the Harvard Graduate School of Design.

Evening Cocktail: "A Cocktail of Two Cities" (gin, lemon juice, champagne)

February 7, 2019
Andy Groarke
Mortal Bodies

"We're interested in the capacity of architecture to raise questions in the viewer, where experience of its physical presence can be shared, discussed, and assemble people in a way that unrealized projects, or other representations of architecture cannot. We're interested in how the physical properties of architecture may reveal other meanings or relate to other ideas beyond themselves through the realm of experience."

Andy Groarke is a founding director of London based architecture practice Carmody Groarke, established in 2006 with Kevin Carmody. Groarke had previously worked with David Chipperfield Architects and Haworth Tompkins Architects in London.

Evening Cocktail: "Queen Elizabeth" (dry vermouth, Benedictine, lime)

February 21, 2019
Esther da Costa Meyer
Chareau: Design

Student: I found that the use of two different materials, one that was really refined and that was more industrial, beautiful in [Chareau's] work. I was wondering if there was any social argument behind that?
ECM: The politics were complicated. When he was struggling, he had to let go of his skilled craftsmen whom he worked with for decades. There was a politicization, although his wife was much more openly political than

he was. He was a man who was moody, shy, brilliantly gifted, but sat on fences. He was never as overtly political as some of his clients.

Esther da Costa Meyer teaches modern architecture and contemporary architecture at Princeton University. She is the Spring 2019 Vincent Scully Visiting Professor of Architectural History at the Yale School of Architecture.

Evening Cocktail: "The Mary Pickford" (rum, pineapple juice, maraschino liqueur, grenadine)

February 25, 2019
Todd Reisz
Myths of Permanent Cities

"For once, architecture seems urgent and necessary, as if lives depended on its expedited transport over hostile landscapes and on your safe arrival on the other side. You, and the other sharply dressed consultants, are the highest paid in the elite circuit of global experts on cities. You are worth helicopter transport."

Todd Reisz, architect and writer on the cities of the Arabian Peninsula, is editor of multiple books. He has taught at the Harvard Graduate School of Design and the Yale School of Architecture, returning to the latter this semester as the Louis I. Kahn Visiting Assistant Professor.

Evening Cocktail: "Suffer No Fools" (genever, Kentucky bourbon, lime juice, ginger beer, bitters)

March 28, 2019
Timur Galen and Phil Bernstein
A Conversation on Practice

PB: When you left practice for the development world, what was the view of what architects did and how did that affect your decision to make a change?
TG: The first step on leaving practice was to move to New York and take a junior development role on a building for which Gordon was the curtain wall consultant. I have to say, it's always better to be lucky than good. Coming to New York in the middle of the 80s, there was a class of leaders in the profession who had had two lifetimes of experience in a decade. There was just so much going and I had the unbelievable good fortune to be mentored by a number of those people.

Timur Galen is an Executive Vice President at The Related Companies.

Phil Bernstein (YC '79, M. Arch '83) is Associate Dean at the Yale School of Architecture where he has taught since 1988.

Evening Cocktail: "Court-side" (gin, elderflower liqueur, lime juice, simple syrup, rhubarb bitters, champagne)

April 4, 2019
Sou Fujimoto
Between Nature and Architecture

"A lot of difficulties can happen, but still we should be optimistic and open doors to new futures. If you can enjoy the whole situation, you can make something interesting, exciting–something that people feel a part of. Then, you can make a breakthrough. Be honest–this is the most important thing. Be honest to the project, to the client, regulations, and yourself too."

Sou Fujimoto is an architect with offices based in Tokyo and Paris. This lecture is the opening keynote of the Clouds, Bubbles, and Waves symposium at the Yale School of Architecture.

Evening Cocktail: "Cloudy with Bubbles" (shochu, Calpico soda, seltzer)

April 11, 2019
Ananya Roy
At the Limits of the Urban Racial Banishment and the Contemporary American Metropolis

AR: In conceptualizing the American metropolis as a post-colony, I will practice what postcolonial critique as well as the black radical tradition has repeatedly staged, which is a re-working of the West itself.

Ananya Roy is the Renee Luskin Chair in Inequality and Democracy at the UCLA Luskin School of Public Affairs.

Evening Cocktail: "Mulholland Drive" (Calle 23 reposada tequila, ginger beer, lime juice)

April 18, 2019
Esra Akcan
Open Architecture as a Radical Democracy

Kyle Dugdale: What would you say is the correlation between the quality of the architecture, in the terms you are studying of hospitality, and status of the architects whom we've come to respect from our education?
EA: Today I looked at Moldenhauer and Siza, in the book I looked at others. They had varying responses to immigration laws. Some of them were very ignorant and didn't care, but some of them were ironic, some subversive. So it's really very different, based on different architects.

Esra Akcan is an Associate Professor at Cornell University and Director of the Cornell Institute for European Studies.

Evening Cocktail: "Vinkara Narince" (Turkish white wine)

August 30–October 6, 2018
Stepwells of Ahmedabad

Believed to be one of the five tattva (elements) from which all life is derived, water has been revered in the Indian sub-continent since times immemorial. Among the various types of water structures found throughout India, stepwells are an indigenous and divergent phenomenon found extensively in regions of Gujarat, Rajasthan, and North-Western India.

The Stepwells of Ahmedabad exhibit is a collective initiative of a group of architects from Ahmedabad to highlight the historical, architectural response to the age-old problem of providing drinking water while touching upon the tangential social, ecological, and cultural aspects of stepwells.

Curated by Priyanka Sheth, Tanvi Jain, and Riyaz Tayyibji

October 11–November 15, 2018
A Seat at the Table

It is well known that the profession of architecture is still largely a man's world. But its educational institutions appear to be in better shape: today, male and female architecture students graduate at equal rates. Still, despite this hopeful statistic, there are many subtle ways in which architecture schools remain far from inclusive.

In July 2018, Equality in Design sent two surveys to approximately 86 schools around the world, seeking to assess the educational climate of architecture and its ability to provide an equitable experience to its students, regardless of their gender identification. The results trickled in over the next few months, reaching a total of 779 responses. The results, some forming common threads, and other forming divergent opinions, were showcased in this exhibit.

Curated by Equality in Design

November 29, 2018–January 3,2019
Redevelopment: The Story of Church Street South

Designed as an affordable housing development in 1968 by then-Dean of the Yale School of Architecture, Charles Moore, Church Street South is in the midst of a rapid transformation today under a new redevelopment project. This exhibition explores the methods of city planning, the madness of redevelopment, and the meaning to be found in all of it.

Curated by Jonathan Hopkins, MED 2019

January 10–February 16, 2019
HUTONGism

HUTONGism is an ongoing research project that collectively explores the potential of the hutong, a type of urban vernacular in Beijing, as a living condition in a highly dense environment. Contemporary hutongs contain alleyways, courtyard houses, and service elements such as shops and restaurants. We imagined the hutong as a collective house: alleyways as living rooms, courtyard houses as bedrooms, shops as pantries, and restaurants as dining rooms. Residents share this house with each other and with visitors. Different from high-rise residences, its collective attributes suggest alternative ways of living in high density. We consider the hutong as an inspiration for vibrant urban community.

Curated by Baolin Shen and Jingqiu Zhang

February 21–March 30, 2019
Sounding Sacred

In contemporary architectural practice, absent of any overarching religious dogmas, what constitutes ‘sacred’ space? Given the diverse images of sparsity, intimacy, introspection, and communal ritual that the term ‘sacred’ conjures, can architects effectively design spaces of universal reverence? Is the notion of sacred architecture intuitive? Is it learned? Must it be considered from an aural, as well as visual perspective? By analyzing the acoustical characteristics of religious vernacular typologies, we hope to better understand the ways in which aural practices shaped their design and can inform architects envisioning future spaces of reverence.

Curated by M. Isabel Balda, Davis Butner, and Evan Sale

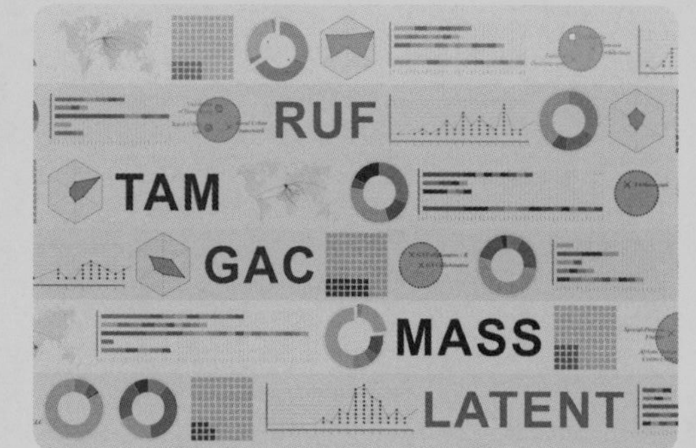

April 4–May 4, 2019
Let’s Talk Business

Let’s Talk Business presents the work of six social-impact, humanitarian architectural practices, or architect-led agencies, through their evolving business models. The exhibition introduces topics related to sustainable funding, project management, office structure, and networking to provide an alternative lens by which we may learn, consider, and critique work with a strong social agenda.

Curated by Vittorio Lovato

Symposia

February 23, 2019
Natures of Ornament

The symposium Natures of Ornament is convened as a Festschrift, in celebration of Kent Bloomer's indispensable intellectual and pedagogical contribution to the Yale School of Architecture over the last fifty years. Bloomer's dedication to the design and thinking of ornament in architecture has influenced academics, collaborators, and students that include architects, historians, musicians, artists, philosophers, and biologists, among others, many of whom will come together to explore the diverse meaning of ornament in contemporary discourses. What links ornament to the broader human sciences and the natural world? What are ornament's theoretical stakes in the intellectual and material history of our own discipline? What is ornament's place in the pedagogy of architectural education, its methods and practices? In addressing these questions, the symposium reorients the discourse of ornament from a contentious vestige of modernity toward its active relationship to architecture, landscape, urbanism, and sense of place in the world.

Speakers

Sunil Bald, Yale University
Thomas Beeby, Yale University
Deborah Berke, Yale University
Kent Bloomer, Yale University
Turner Brooks, Yale University
Douglas Cooper, Carnegie Mellon Univ.
Kurt Forster, Yale University
Mari Hvattum, The Oslo School of Architecture and Design
Guru Khalsa Dev Kaur, Architect
Emer O'Daly, Architect
Richard Prum, Yale University
Willie Ruff, Yale University
Stacey Sloboda, University of Mass., Boston
Michael Young, The Cooper Union

Interview with Kent Bloomer

R42: You have a clear dedication to the Yale School of Architecture, having taught here for over forty years, for which we are immensely grateful. What do you see that is particularly special about this place and these people?

KB: Yale University's campus, magnificent architecture, and direct contact with the New Haven Green are extraordinary and inspiring. An ideal place for a School of Architecture which was conceived within the humanities and fine arts. YSOA inherited a project which exceeds the mandate of a purely professional school, per se, as it embraced history, philosophy, forestry, etc. Especially today, a balance between a liberal broad reaching curriculum and "professional" studies is a fragile project, yet one that has been enforced by the School's leadership, faculty, visitors, and students for the half century I have been on board.

R42: You have a background in physics and architecture from MIT, and went on to study sculpture here at Yale. Did your interest in—maybe we could say obsession with—ornament come first, or did it develop through teaching and practice?

KB: Perhaps my "obsession" with ornament has been fueled by a reaction, a defense against the negation and misunderstanding of the subject and practice of ornament, rampant in the architecture academy at large. As a child I had a rich and natural understanding of ornament and its dependence on the objects being ornamented. After WW2, into my student years, an "official" negation began to pervade the practice of architecture. Yet in my lifetime I have not encountered a single credible argument to support the removal of "ornament" from the requirements of professional education in both architecture and art. How can we critique and grow an otherwise timeless discipline by eliminating its presence and ignoring its function? My passion is my emotional expression to right

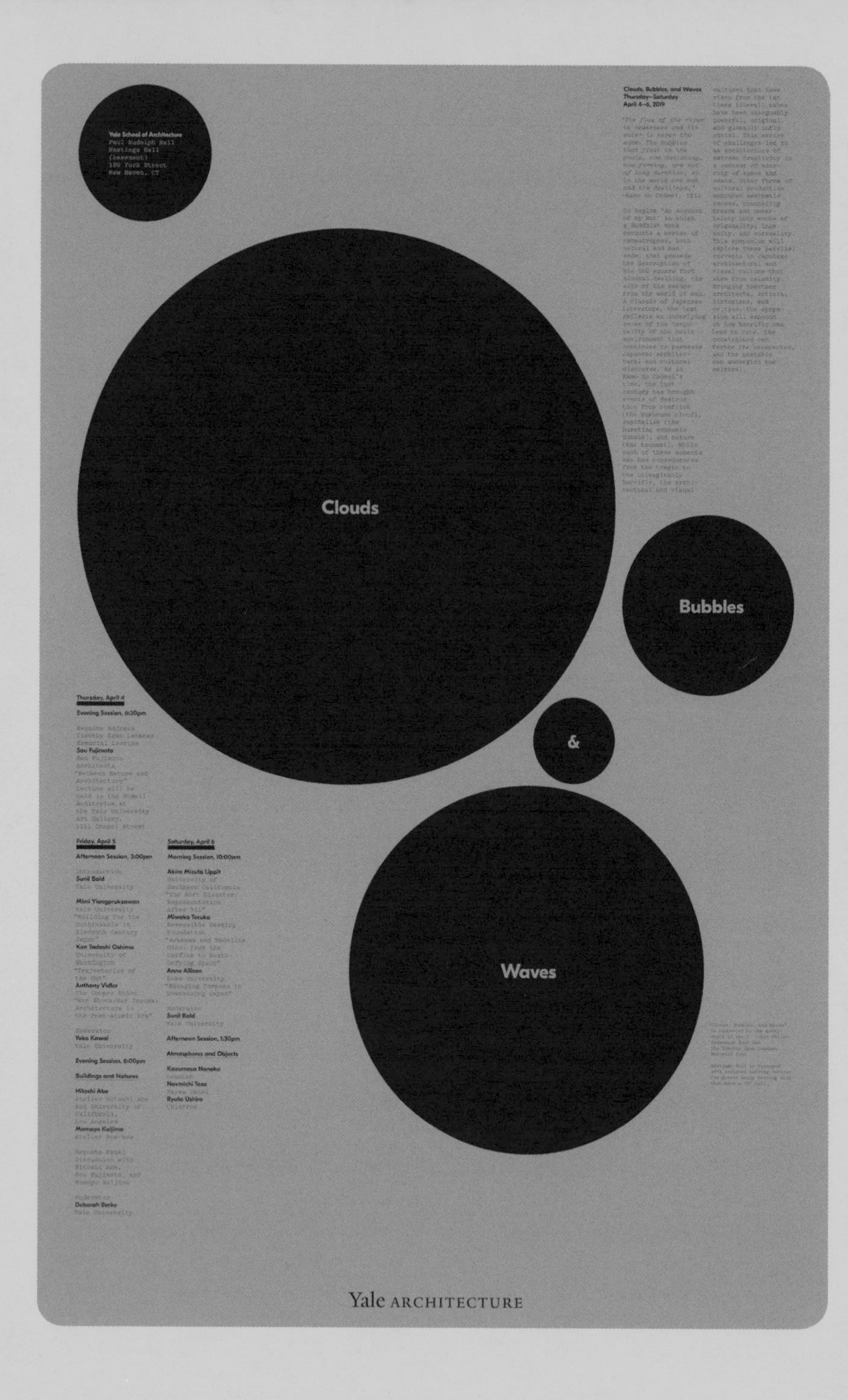

a wrong. Universities and hopefully professional schools are constituted to protect and explore, not to index or forestall knowledge.

R42: How has the conversation about ornament changed during your time at Yale, and where do you think the future lies?

KB: While the word “ornament” has been more frequently uttered in the last fifteen years of conversation in halls of architecture its profound identity is mushy and its means of functioning compared to those of decoration, pattern, art, visual language etc. remain very confused. Dictionaries verge on being liabilities because the extraordinary beginning, the etymology of ornament remains submerged, deteriorated, and spoiled. Many have taken to talking about something they have not rigorously studied. However I am intuitively optimistic that the worst is receding. Ornament may once again become essential to the working vocabulary of design.

R42: As someone who has experienced a lifetime of studies, what advice do you have for this year’s graduating class?

KB: Perhaps, contrary to my praise of the broad spectrum of the humanities and science (to govern our study of architecture), I also recommend the critical importance of studying an “amount” of specialized or limited knowledge. Such depth means digging a deep walled off hole into some fragment or cousin of the designers major responsibilities such as an esoteric mechanical detail, a rare type of geometry, a remote province of culture, a mysterious figure of ornament, or a moment in time. Such an effort to hyper focus on a very special agenda should eventually be judged or incorporated into the body of general broad spectrum knowledge. Even if the general knowledge (the big picture) may be regarded as superficial compared to extremely specialized items of knowledge their conflation can produce a magic of inspiration. It is the combining or collision of differences (the electron, proton, and molecule) that realizes energy.

R42: What’s next for Kent Bloomer?

KB: Besides staying connected to my practice (in the concept and scribble processes) I have commitments to myself to write more about teaching and designing, and to others, to lecture here and there. Meanwhile I have a growing interest in exploring ornament in music. American jazz is a goldmine. I began that conversation years ago with Willie Ruff. I am particularly looking at the syntax between bebop and boogie woogie (bebop riffs and phrases ornamenting the seminal blues). I can bang some that out on my Hammond B-3.

Parallels with music in relation to ornament were outstanding in Bach. My sense is that sidestep will reinforce my fascination with architectural ornament. Any ideas?

April 4-6, 2019
Clouds, Bubbles, and Waves

“The flow of the river is ceaseless and its water is never the same. The bubbles that float in the pools, now vanishing, now forming, are not of long duration: so in the world are man and his dwellings.” -Kamo no Chomei, 1212

So begins ‘An Account of my Hut’ in which a Buddhist monk recounts a series of catastrophes, both natural and man-made, that precede the description of his 100 square foot minimal dwelling, the site of his escape from the world of humanity. A classic of Japanese literature, the text reflects and underlying sense of the temporality of the built environment that continues to permeate Japanese architectural and cultural discourse. As in Chōmei ’s time, the last century has brought events of destruction from conflict (the mushroom cloud), capitalism (the bursting economic bubble), and nature (the tsunami). While each of these moments has had consequences from the tragic to the unimaginably horrific, the architectural and visual cultures that have risen from the (at times literal) ashes have been unarguably powerful, original, and globally influential. This series of challenges led to an architecture of extreme creativity in a context of scarcity of space and means. Other forms of cultural production embraced aesthetic excess, channeling trauma and uncertainty into works of originality, ingenuity, and surreality. This symposium explores these parallel currents in Japanese architectural and visual culture that stem from calamity. Bringing together architects, artists, historians, and critics, the symposium expounds on how horrific can lead to cute, the constrained can foster the unexpected, and the unstable can undergird the cultural.

Speakers

Hitoshi Abe, Atelier Hitoshi Abe and University of California, Los Angeles
Anne Allison, Duke University
Sunil Bald, Yale University (Moderator)
Deborah Berke, Yale University (Moderator)
Sou Foujimoto, Sou Fujimoto Architects
Momoyo Kaijima, Atelier Bow-Wow
Yoko Kawai, Yale University—Moderator
Akira Mizuta Lippit, University of Southern California
Kazumasa Nonaka, teamLab
Ken Tadashi Oshima, University of Washington
Miwako Tezuka, Reversible Destiny Foundation
Novmichi Tosa, Maywa Denki
Ryuta Ushiro, Chim↑Pom
Anthony Vidler, The Cooper Union
Mimi Yiengpruksawan, Yale University
Midori Yoshimoto, NJ City University

Mimi Yiengpruksawan
Building for the Unthinkable in Eleventh-Century Japan

"Ghosts are an important residue. What the anthropologist Anna Ting calls, "the vestiges and signs of past ways of life still charged in the present; ghosts which are recently riding on the winds of the anthropocene". If humanity is going to have a future, in an age of surveillance and capitalism and machine intelligence, we need to pay attention to ghosts."

Anthony Vidler
War Shock/War Trauma: Architecture in the Post-Atomic Era

I return to Japan, and to the remarks from its most recent Pritzker Prize recipient, on a collage that he produced in 1968, entitled "Re-Ruined Hiroshima", in an article titled "The Future City lies in Ruins", he wrote: "as a boy of fourteen, I saw the cities of Japan burn to the ground before my very eyes. Running through the dilapidated streets like an animal, I escaped the incendiary bombs, but not the complete and utter destruction of everything I knew. All the physical objects in my world and everything around me disappeared. It seems as if the entire fabric of life, even the bonds of family and other human relations, turned to piles of rubbish. There wasn't a cloud in that sky over the Japanese archipelago the day Japan surrendered. The summer sun cast sharp black shadows on the ground. It was silent. Time stopped. It was the end of history. All that so clearly constituted the future disappeared. One had to call it a void. As I stood long in that void, only the blue sky came up. My mind and body dropped away and I had no mental capacity to be self-aware. To recall a few of those moments, I believe it was a feeling of despondency under the blue skies. At that time, the spectacle that spread before me was the plane of the burnt ruins."

Keynote Panel Discussion with Hitoshi Abe, Sou Fujimoto, and Momoyo Kaijima, and and Deborah Berke (moderator).

DB: The question I want to ask the three of you, is that given the crisis, it seems that you did not make "capital-A" architecture or magazine-ready architecture. You made a different kind of architecture. Do you think that response to crisis, changes architecture? The second part of the question is, has your response to that crisis, [the earthquake], now that it's eight years ago, changed the architecture you make today?

MK: In 2000 I lived in Tokyo and I also was teaching at the University of Art. Not really in the center of Tokyo but in a rural area. So I was able to visit the area and do research. Then the earthquake came. The earthquake caught my interest. Something interesting that happened was we tried to share how to recover (from earthquakes) among our colleagues and friends. We did several seminars, every month or two months with my friends who are architects. We tried to be collaborative.

HA: We tried to listen to everybody carefully to feel what naturally had to be done. Then suddenly, almost naturally, something emerged from the situation. The architectural design is not something from our side, it's more from the situation. But we should be very careful and focused to make a nice interaction with the whole situation.

NT: I compare Maywa Denki and Muji. For example, Maywa Denki make fish-bone extension cord. Muji make extension cord. Maywa Denki makes instrument. Muji does not make instrument—so can not compare. So I make Muji instrument.

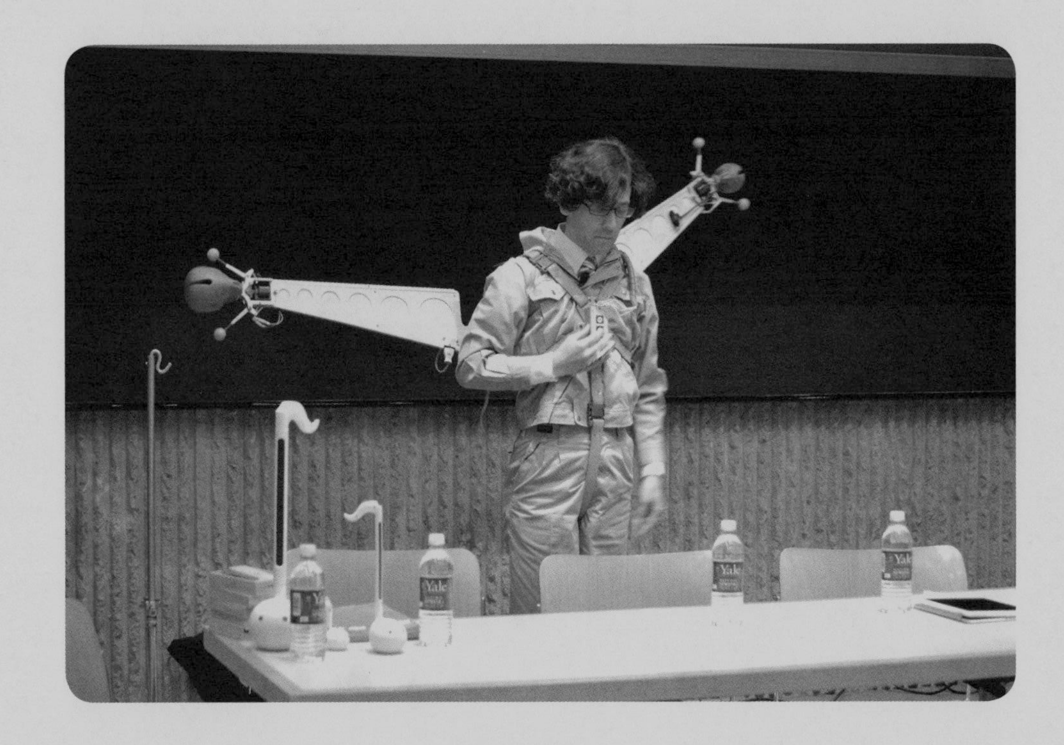

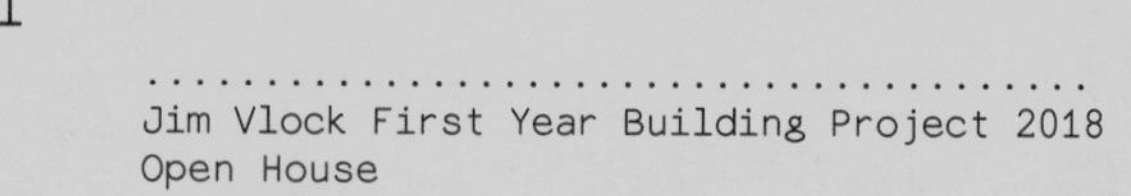

XVIII

Jim Vlock First Year Building Project 2018
Open House

On October 15, 2018, an open house was held to celebrate the completion of the 2018 Jim Vlock First Year Building Project with community members of YSoA, Columbus House, and the New Haven Hill neighborhood.

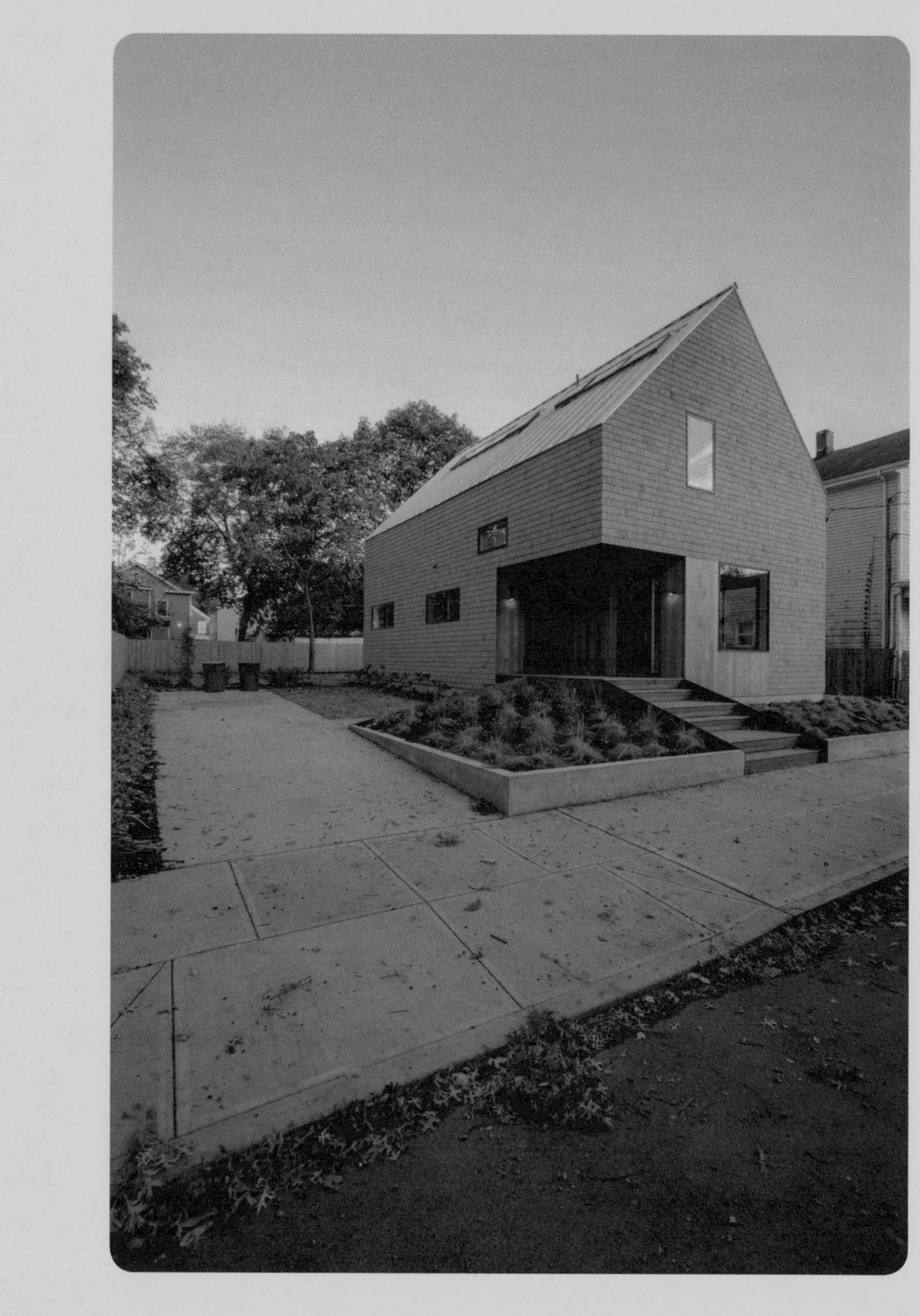

Publications

The following books were published by the School of Architecture in 2018-2019

Harlem:
MART 125
Jonathan Rose, Sara Caples, and Everardo Jefferson
Yale School of Architecture/ The Edward P. Bass Distinguished Visiting Architecture Fellowship

Harlem Studio, Mart 125, features the Edward P. Bass Visiting Distinguished Architecture Fellowship with developer Jonathan Rose and with Kahn Visiting Assistant Professors, Sara Caples and Everardo Jefferson who set the students on the task to design a new building across from the Apollo Theatre on 125th Street in Harlem. The book was edited by Nina Rappaport and Jenny Kim ('16). The books below were published by the School of Architecture and distributed by Actar and designed by MGMT.Design.

Mexican Social Housing: Promises Revisited focuses on the Louis I. Kahn Visiting Assistant Professorship studio of Tatiana Bilbao. It was published by INFONAVIT (Institute of the National Fund for Worker's Housing) and designed by Sociedad Anónima and distributed by Actar.

The Diamonds of American Cities presents the work of Edward P. Bass Visiting Distinguished Architecture Fellow Janet Marie Smith, vice president of the Los Angeles Dodgers, and Alan Plattus and Andrei Harwell, Yale faculty members. The challenge to the students, was to analyze ballparks and their urban ramifications in a two-phased project, one each for a minor and a major league team. The book was edited by Nina Rappaport and Ron Ostezan ('18), designed by MGMT.Design, and distributed by Actar.

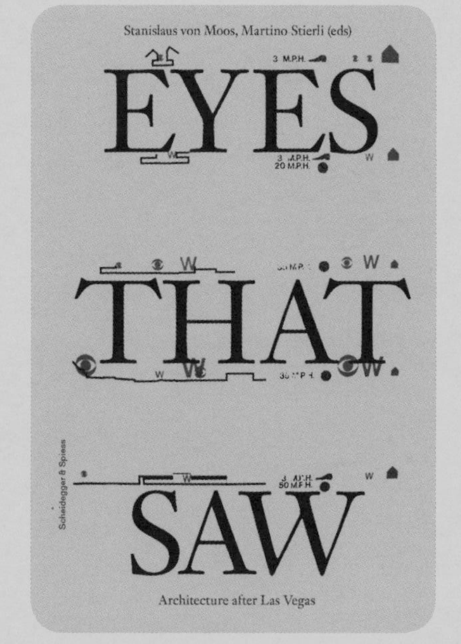

The book Eyes that Saw features a collection of scholarly essays based on the conference held at Yale celebrating the fortieth anniversary of the 1968 epochal Las Vegas Studio led by Robert Venturi, Denise Scott Brown, and Steven Izenour. Three Yale studios brought students out into the world as a way to both analyze and then design projects and, in doing so, transformed architectural education. The book was designed by Bruno Margreth; edited by Stanislaus von Moos, Martino Stierli, Nina Rappaport, and Ann Holcomb; and is co-published by the Yale School of Architecture and Scheidegger & Spiess.

....
Paprika!

Paprika! is the often-weekly broadsheet of the Yale School of Architecture. Founded in the summer of 2014, Paprika! is named after the vibrant orange carpets in the pits and auditorium of Rudolph Hall, the epicenter of student life at the Yale School of Architecture.

We are of, by, and for students of art and architecture. Our submissions are open (paprika.ysoa@gmail.com); our meetings are open; we receive zero fiscal support from the school, and YSOA exercises no editorial control.

Fall Coordinating Editors
· Katie Lau
· Andrew Economos Miller
· X. Christine Pan

Spring Coordinating Editors
· Page Comeaux
· Nicole Doan
· Alejandro Duran

Web Editor
· Seth Thompson

4-00 Internal Memo
August 30, 2018
Editors: Katie Lau, Andrew Economos Miller, X. Christine Pan
Graphic Designer: Rosa McElheny

4-01 Tourism Revolution
September 13, 2018
Editors: Simone Cutri, Mengi Li, Ben Olsen, Evan Sale
Graphic Designer: Simone Cutri

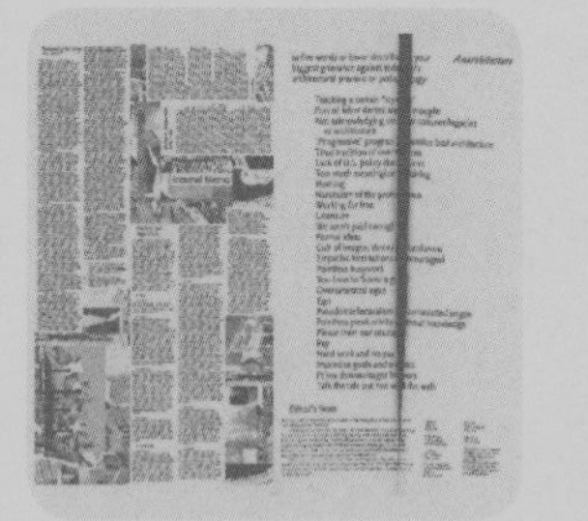

4-02 Anarchitecture
September 20, 2018
Editors: Tayyaba Anwar, Sharmin Bhagwagar
Graphic Designers: Kayla Arsadjaja, Evan Chang

4-03 Energy
October 4, 2018
Editor: Jack Hanly
Graphic Designer: David Knowles

4-04 Duck, Duck, Shed
October 11, 2018
Editors: Michael Glassman, Darryl Weimer
Graphic Designers: Maria Candanoza, Hyung Cho

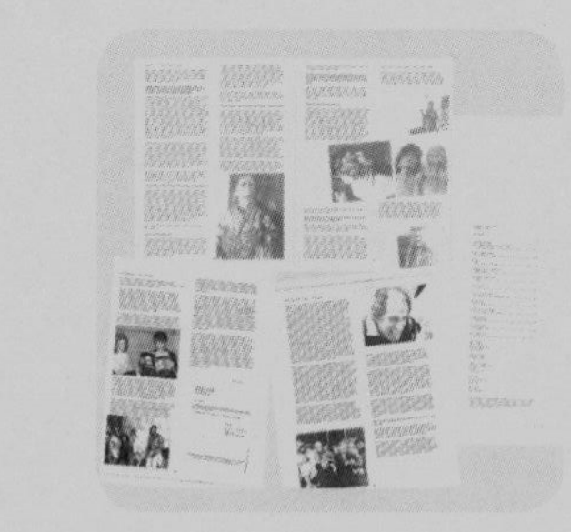

4-05 Halloween II
October 25, 2018
Editors: Nicholas Miller, Matthew Wagstaffe, Ethan Zisson
Graphic Designer: Steven Rodriguez

4-06 “Vernacular”
November 1, 2018
Editors: Nicholas Miller, Matthew Wagstaffe, Ethan Zisson
Graphic Designer: Jinu Hong

4-07 An Image for the Present
November 8, 2018
Editors: Willis Kingery, Seth Thompson
Graphic Designers: Seth Thompson, Willis Kingery

4-08 Illusion, Deception
November 15, 2018
Editors: Nicole Doan, Dina Taha
Graphic Designers: Micah Barrett, Zack Robbins

4-09 Temperature
January 10, 2019
Editors: Page Comeaux, Nicole Doan, Alejandro Duran
Graphic Designers: Da Woon Jeon

4-10 Same Same, But Different
January 24, 2019
Editors: Michael Glassman, X. Christine Pan
Graphic Designer: Evan Chang

4-11 Just What the Doctor Ordered: Health and Architecture
February 7, 2019
Editors: Kate Altmann, Winston Yuen
Graphic Designers: Tuan Quoc Pham, Orysia Zabeida

4-12 Cite Analysis
February 21, 2019
Editor: Andrew Economos Miller
Graphic Designers: Laura Huaranga, Minhwan Kim

4-13 Phantasy
February 28, 2019
Editors: Nicholas Miller, Matthew Wagstaffe, Ethan Zisson
Graphic Designers: Hyung Cho, Steven Rodriguez

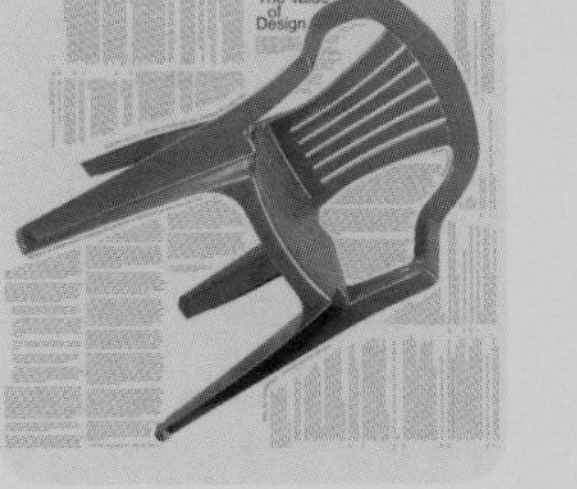
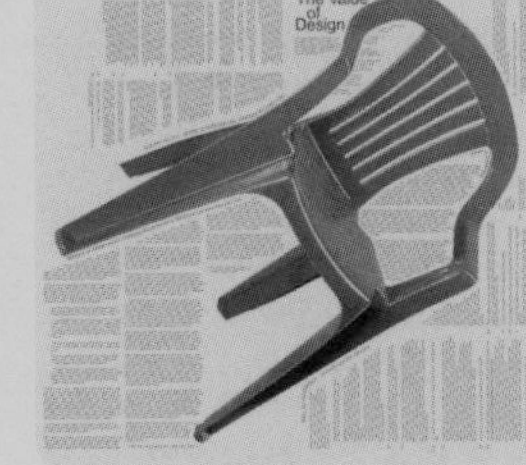

4-14 The Value of Design
March 28, 2019
Editors: Cyndi Chen, Liwei Wang
Graphic Designers: Kyla Arsadjaja, Maria Candanoza

4-15 Ca(non)
April 4, 2019
Editors: Priyanka Sheth, Dina Taha
Graphic Designers: Jinu Hong, Yuanbo Wang

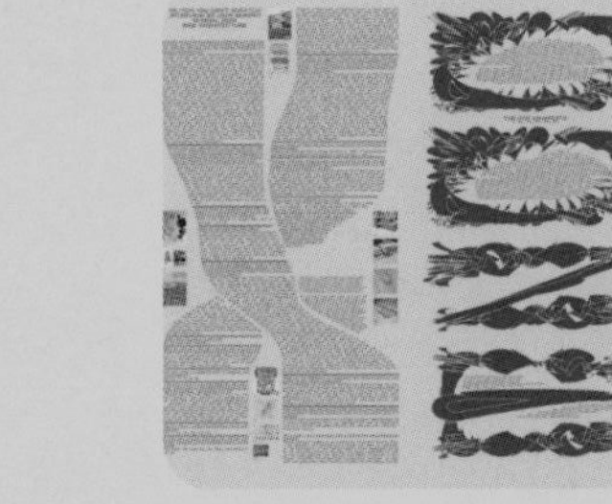

4-16 The Ooz
April 11, 2019
Editors: Tayyaba Anwar, Jack Murphy
Graphic Designers: Herdimas Anggara, Julia Schäfer

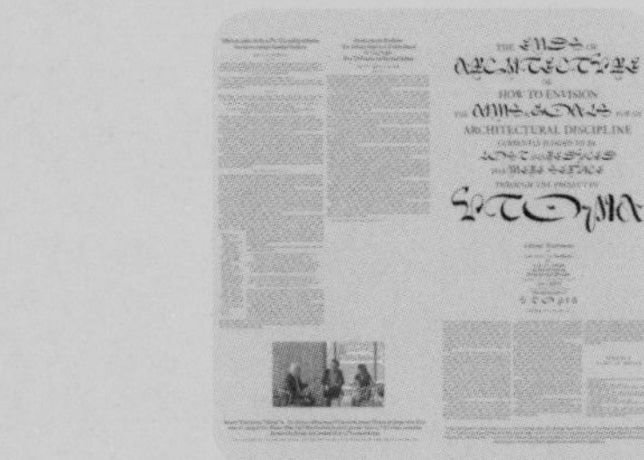

4-17 Ends of Architecture
April 18, 2019
Editors: Camille Chabrol, Deo Deiparine, Martin Man
Graphic Designers: Tania Alvarez Zaldivar, Zack Robbins

Student Organizations

Badminton
Students pair up and enter a tournament each year to compete in the fourth floor pit.

Built Environment and the Environment Group (BE^2)
An organization jointly run between the Yale School of Architecture and the Yale School of Forestry and Environmental Studies that focuses on the intersection of the built environment with the environment.

Christian Fellowship
Meets weekly over coffee and muffins to encourage community and provide a venue for conversations on topics related to Christianity, faith, and architecture.

Equality in Design (EiD)
A coalition of students committed to expanding access to the discipline and profession of architecture, as well as critically engaging with architecture's social and political context and implications

Green Action in Architecture (GAIA)
Devoted to addressing sustainability and environmental health and wellbeing issues within the school, as well as promoting broader discussion of environmental consideration as they pertain to architecture generally.

Indigenous Scholars of Architecture, Planning, and Design
A collective student group focused on increasing the knowledge, consciousness, and appreciation of indigenous architecture and planning.

Outlines
An advocacy and social group for lesbian, gay, bisexual, transgender, queer, and all students.

Paprika!
The often-weekly broadsheet and the epicenter of student life at the Yale School of Architecture.

Perspecta
The oldest student-edited architectural journal in the United States internationally respected for its contributions to contemporary architectural discourse with original presentations of new projects as well as historical and theoretical essays.

Soccer
An intramural soccer team that competes against Yale University's other graduate and professional schools.

YSoA East
Dedicated to fostering critical discourse and knowledge of Eastern architecture. The aim of the group is to consolidate and drive interest for eastern architectural and urbanist trends.

Awards

Faculty Award

Professor King-lui Wu Teaching Award
· Surry Schlabs

Student Fellowships

William Wirt Winchester Traveling Fellowship
· Sharmin Yezdi Bhagwagar
· Ryan Thomas Hughes

Gertraud A. Wood Traveling Fellowship (awarded 2018)
· Menglan Li

George Nelson Scholarship (awarded 2018)
· Miguel Sanchez Enkerlin
· Melissa Kendall Weigel

David M. Schwarz / Architectural Services Good Times Award
· Zelig Siu Lum Fok

Student Medals and Prizes

American Institute of Architects Henry Adams Medal
· Miguel Sanchez Enkerlin
Alpha Rho Chi Medal
· Nicole Magsaysay Doan
William Edward Parsons Memorial Medal
· Lucia Venditti

The H.I. Feldman Prize
· Ryan Thomas Hughes

The H.I. Feldman nominees

Fall 2016 (awarded 2017)
· Minquan Wang

Fall 2017
· Dimitris Hartonas
· Minquan Wang

Fall 2018
· Sara Al Ajmi '20
· Diego Arango
· Sharmin Yezdi Bhagwagar
· Davis Samuel Butner '20
· Ryan Thomas Hughes
· Menglan Li
· Evan Daniel Sale
· Christopher Dylan Tritt
· Jerome Tryon '20
· Lucia Venditti
· Millie Yoshida

Spring 2018
· Dimitris Hartonas

Spring 2019
· Diego Arango
· Sharmin Yezdi Bhagwagar
· Ryan Thomas Hughes
· Erin Hyelin Kim
· Jincy George Kunnatharayil
· Hsin-Ju Lai
· Mariana São Pedro Riobom
· dos Santos
· Jennifer Shin '20
· Jerome Tryon '20
· I-Ting Tsai '20
· Justin Hin Yeung Tsang '20
· Lucia Venditti
· Matthew Leo Wagstaffe
· Winston Gee Kong Yuen

Wendy Elizabeth Blanning Prize, awarded 2018
· Hsin-Ju Lai

Sonia Albert Schimberg Prize
· Hsin-Ju Lai

Janet Cain Sielaff Alumni Award
· Menglan Li

Moulton Andrus Award
· Lani Mei Barry

The Drawing Prize
· Erin Hyelin Kim

Gene Lewis Book Prize
· Diego Arango

David Taylor Memorial Prize B. Jack Hanly
· Matthew Leo Wagstaffe

Student Internships

Takenaka Corporation Summer Internship (awarded 2018)
· Iven Peh Sze Kiat

David M. Schwarz / Architectural Services Summer Internship and Traveling Fellowship (awarded 2018)
· Benjamin D. Olsen

Happenings

Aug 31, 2018 Equality in Design Brown Bag Lunch Series 01 with Kishwar Rizvi · Sep 6, 2018 – In Memory of MJ Long (M.Arch '64) MJ's legacy will continue through the pedagogy at the school, the generations of students she inspired, and the many pioneering buildings she designed. Deborah Berke Dean, Yale School of Architecture · Sep 14, 2018 Dear YSOA, We invite your contributions to Paprika Vol. 04 Issue 05: 'Duck, Duck, Shed.' · Sep 28. 2018 Guest lecture – 1st Oct – Decoding urban in an emerging economy: Indian, by Shaleen Singhal · Sep. 27, 2018 CITY + Architecture event, Lunch with Design, Bitches · Oct 2, 2018 Net Zero Carbon Buildings Lunch Talk by our guest speaker Alex Co · Oct 8, 2018 Friday at 1pm: Ben Shepherd, The Nature of Building Resilience · Oct 9, 2018 Yale School of Art: Women Breaking the Canons of Practice by Andrea Fraser · Oct 12, 2018 Yale Arts Mixer by Outlines: Share your work; read a poem, monologue, play new tunes. · · Oct 17, 2018 Tomorrow 1pm: Sean Godsell, "An Austrailian Architecture" · Oct 22, 2018 This afternoon, the Yale World Fellows program will host Mokena Makeka for a discussion on the role of architecture in the face of increasing inequality. · Oct 22, 2018 The Annual Halloween Party is coming up and it's time to get spooky! · Oct 22, 2018 Isabelle Doucet will present a talk entitled "Resistant Architecture: (Hi)stories that Make a Difference." · Oct 29, 2019 Brown Bag Lunch Series, Ann Murrow Johnson · Oct 30, 2018 Architecture Forum Nov. 6th: Patricia Ekpo and Mia Kang · Nov 5, 2018 THURSDAY 11/8 Professor Marianne LaFrance will present her research titled Subtle and Not So Subtle Sexism. · Nov 5, 2018 EiD Ally Skills Workshop for Men, Friday 1pm. Join us in conversation with Andrew Westover · Nov 7, 2018 Sultan Sooud Al Qassemi "Modern Architecture in Gulf" · November 10, 2018 Outlines is showing A Single Man. It's queer and architecture-y and gorgeous looking. · Nov 8, 2018 Today at 1: Access, Accountability, Architecture: Charles Davis II in conversation with Summer Sutton. · Nov 9, 2018 Stefano Romagnoli is here to talk about his work on energy landscapes in South America. · Nov 9, 2018 Kendall Nicholson on The Changing Face of Architectural Education. · Nov 13, 2018 Please join Dean Berke and Dean Bernstein for a YSoA Town Hall on Wednesday, 14th at 1pm · Nov 15, 2018 Bryan Young – Material Case Studies Lecture · Nov 26, 2018 _Wednesday: Julia Gamolina, founder and author of Madame Architect, a website devoted to the stories of women architects. · Nov 26, 2018 Tonight: Architecture Forum – Kadambari Baxi, "Three Collaborative Projects" · Nov 29, 2018 Lunch Lecture today on Urban Heat Island: Theory, Measurement, and Mitigation by Prof. Xuhui Lee · Dec. 4, 2018 Tomorrow night, the final teams of this year's badminton tournament will be squaring off in the Finals and Semi-Finals! · December 8, 2018 Your presence is requested for a Bauhaus party. Sat 12.15.18, civil twilight: 4:22pm, northeast stair · Jan 16, 2019 Eduardo Luque talk titled "Perspectives." Friday. · Jan 17, 2019 Today: "Employment Strategy & Opportunities in Today's Market" by Phil Bernstein · Jan 22, 2019 Koyaanisqatsi (1982) Screening Tonight – 7:15 – Hastings · Jan 24, 2019 Today at 1pm: Jason McLennan on the future of the Green Building Movement · Feb 4, 2019 Feb. 6th: Career Workshops; Salary Negotiation with Nancy Alexander & Amy Wrzesniewski ; Designing Your Resume & Work Samples with Luke Bulman · Feb 4, 2019 This week we will be seeing the 1971 Australian film, Walkabout in Hastings at 7.15pm · Feb 6, 2019 Today: "Bay Area Urbanism: Architecture, Real Estate, and Progressive Community Planning in Postwar America" by Matthew Gordon Lasner. · Feb 10, 2019 Water Abundance in Architecture with David Hertz · Feb 11, 2019 TONIGHT! Ayala Levin at the Architecture Forum; "Biography and Contradiction: Unpacking Denise Scott Brown's 'African View' of Las Vegas" · Feb 12, 2019 Tonight's feature for the Spring Film Series is Mon Oncle. · Feb 18, 2019 Tonight! Resume and Work Sample Strategy with Rob McClure · Feb 18, 2019 Brown Bag: A Discussion on Surveillance and Black City Life with Simone Browne. · Feb 18, 2019 Friday, February 22 at 1pm: Mari Hvattum "Style" · Feb 19, 2019 Spring Film Series Tonight: "Safe" by Todd Haynes · Feb 21, 2019 Make Architecture Indigenous Again: Guest Lecture by Chris Cornelius today at 11:30am · Feb 25, 2019 "Perspectives on Practice." Tuesday: Leticia Wouk Almino, Antonia Devine, Violette de la Selle · Feb 26, 2019 Tomorrow at 3: Fred Kent & Kathy Madden – "Placemaking: Building a Global Campaign" · Mar 1, 2019 In memory of Kevin Roche DFAH '95 (1922-2019), world-famous modern architect and inspirational member of the Yale and New Haven design community. · Feb 28, 2019 Happy birthday Frank Gehry! · Mar 4, 2019 Adrienne Brown, "How Do You Represent a Problem Like Institutional Racism?" · Mar 6, 2019 YSoA Prom 2019: Retro Future; Saturday, April 13th · Mar 25, 2019 Florian Sauter of Sauter von Moos will present "Surreal Presence" today at 1pm. · Mar 25, 2019 Career Panel- How to Start a Firm 101 with Kimberly Brown, Miriam Peterson, Ryan Salvatore. · Mar 27, 2019 Architect and Engineer Nic Goldsmith will present "Mass to Membrane" today at 1pm · Apr 1, 2019 24 CITY by Jia Zhangke _MOVIE NIGHT TOMORROW! · Apr 9, 2019 Finals got you down? Come watch Game of Thrones to keep things in perspective. 9 PM @ Hastings · Apr 9, 2019 Please join Kahn Visiting Assistant Professor Todd Reisz and Sultan Sooud Al Qassemi for a day-long symposium on architecture of the Gulf cities this Friday · Apr 11, 2019 Secret surprise Happy birthday song for Peter de Bretteville at 2pm · Apr 12, 2019 MISSING STOOL: Mint condition padded grey heavy duty 6400 model with chrome leg extensions, made by National Public Seating Corp in Clifton New Jersey, Looks like all the other stools, Please return to 6th floor scrap metal depot · Apr 12, 2019 Family, Planning: On Balancing Home and Office. Featured guests are Perla Delson, Mait Jones, Oliver Freundlich, Vrinda Khanna, Robert Schultz, Laura Pirie, Aicha Woods, Caleb Linville, Carmel Greer · Apr 20, 2019 YOGA in the PIT Happening Now! · Apr 22, 2019 Tonight at 6:30: Kathleen James-Chakraborty and Gary He · Jun 3, 2019 In Memory of Stanley Tigerman (B.Arch '60, M.Arch '61)

Donors

The Yale School of Architecture is grateful to all those who provided financial support during the period July 1, 2018–June 30, 2019.

Friends:
- Anonymous (5)
- Kevin Dale Adkisson '12 B.A.
- Nancy Alexander '79 B.A., '84 M.B.A.
- Judy Hart Angelo
- Michael Corcoran Barry '09 B.A.
- Sid R. Bass '65 B.A., '83 M.A.H.
- Sasha C. Bass
- Mercedes T. Bass
- Dean Deborah L. Berke, '16 M.A.H.
- William L. Bernhard '54 B.A.
- Michael Bierut
- Kent C. Bloomer '59 B.F.A., '61 M.F.A.
- Carolyn Brody
- John A. Carrafiell '87 B.A.
- James C. Childress
- Fred W. Clarke III
- Carol B. & Douglas E. Cohen
- Richard D. Cohen
- Sylvia Cohn
- Mr. & Mrs. Daniel T. Coleman
- Claire Creatore
- Edgar M. Cullman, Jr. '68 B.A.
- Peggy & Richard M. Danziger, Esq. '63 LL.B.
- Sevra Francesca Kaarl Davis '00 B.A.
- Sheila L. de Bretteville '63 B.F.A., '64 M.F.A.
- Richard D. DeFlumeri
- Ronald M. Druker
- Jodie & John L. Eastman
- Cynthia Davidson & Peter Eisenman
- Mr. & Mrs. Michael Eisner
- George L. Farias '80 B.A.
- Paul Florian
- George T. Fournier
- Jeanne Gang
- John S. Gattuso
- Frank O. Gehry '00 D.F.A.H.
- M. Ian G. Gilchrist '72 B.A.
- Melanie A. Ginter '78 B.A., '81 M.S.
- Paul J. Goldberger '72 B.A.
- Elsbeth & Edward Haladay
- Andrew Philip Heid '02 B.A.
- Stephen J. Heyman
- Judith Hudson '88 M.F.A.
- Maria D. Hummer-Tuttle & Robert Tuttle
- Mrs. Walter A. Hunt
- James L. Iker
- Adam Inselbuch
- Elise Jaffe + Jeffrey Brown
- Barbara Jakobson
- Isaac Kalisvaart
- Susie Kim
- Ken Kuchin
- Penelope Laurans
- Elizabeth Lenahan
- Leonard Levie
- Jane A. Levin, Ph.D. '72 M.Phil., '75 Ph.D.
- Richard C. Levin '72 M.Phil., '74 Ph.D., '13 L.H.D.H.
- Dr. Keith G. Lurie '77 B.A.
- Catherine W. Lynn, Ph.D. '78 M.A., '81 Ph.D.
- Anne Kriken Mann
- Timothy D. Mattison, M.D.'73 B.A.
- Ann & Gilbert Maurer
- Margaret McCurry
- Bruce McLanahan '57 B.A.
- Susan Mead
- Kathryn Milano
- William I. Miller '78 B.A., '05 M.A.H.
- Paul Everett Needham '11 B.A.
- Mrs. David L. Niland †
- Helen W. Nitkin
- Brian O'Looney '90 B.A.
- Jean Lattner Palmer
- Pamela & Edward Pantzer
- Professor Richard B. Peiser '70 B.A.
- Cesar Pelli '76 M.A.H., '08 D.F.A.H.
- Rafael Pelli '78 B.A.
- Katie Ridder & Peter Pennoyer
- Gregory Matthew Perez '11 M.B.A.
- Kathryn L. Perkins
- Leslie Marden Ragsdale, Esq. '90 J.D.
- William L. Rawn III '65 B.A.
- William K. Reilly '62 B.A., '94 M.A.H.
- Richard M. Reiss '81 B.A.
- Eve Hart Rice, M.D. '73 B.A., '15 M.A.H.
- Anya Robertson
- Joseph B. Rose '81 B.A.
- Carolyn Greenspan & Marshall S. Ruben, Esq. '82 B.A.
- Jeffrey J. Salzman '75 B.A.
- Julie Schindler '89 B.A.
- Stephen A. Schwarzman '69 B.A.
- Norman C. Selby '74 B.A.
- Brenda Shapiro
- Dr. Teresa Silberman
- Katherine Farley & Jerry I. Speyer
- Barbaralee Diamonstein-Spielvogel & Carl Spielvogel
- Mr. & Mrs. Craig Stapleton
- Eleanor & John Sullivan
- Jeff C. Tarr
- Billie Tsien '71 B.A.
- Benjamin Villa
- James Von Klemperer
- Betty L. Wagner
- Jill Westgard
- Mathew D. Wolf
- Peter M. Wolf '57 B.A.
- Pei-Tse Wu '89 B.A.
- Arthur W. Zeckendorf

Corporations, Foundations, and Matching Gift Support:
- a chance…fund, inc.
- The American Endowment Foundation
- Ammor Architecture LLP
- The Barclays Bank PLC
- Big Ass Fans
- The BPB & HBB Foundation
- Carolyn S. Brody Family Foundation
- Centerbrook Architects & Planners
- ConocoPhillips
- The David and Lucile Packard Foundation
- David M. Schwarz Architects, Inc.
- Deborah Berke & Partners Architects
- Diogenes Charitable Foundation
- Earl & Brenda Shapiro Foundation
- Eisner Foundation, Inc.
- Elisha-Bolton Foundation
- Erving and Joyce Wolf Foundation
- The Fidelity Charitable Gift Fund
- Genga Family Properties, LLC
- Gensler & Associates
- Grace Court Foundation, Inc.
- Greater Washington Community Foundation
- Jackson Walker LLP
- The Jaffe Family Foundation
- The JCT Foundation
- The Jewish Communal Fund
- Jewish Community Foundation of Metrow
- Joseph B. Rose Foundation
- JP Morgan Asset Management
- Kemp Mooney Architect
- Kohn Pedersen Fox Associates PC
- Kraus Family Foundation
- Luckey LLC
- Marble Architecture
- The National Philanthropic Trust
- The New York Community Trust
- Pelli Clarke Pelli Architects, Inc.
- Richard H. Driehaus Foundation
- Robert A.M. Stern Architects, LLP
- Robert A.M. Stern Family Foundation
- Schwab Fund for Charitable Giving
- The Speyer Family Foundation
- Steven Robinson Architects
- T.S. Kim Arch Fellowship Foundation
- Vanguard Charitable
- Wells Fargo Community Support Campaign
- Yale Club of New Haven

Yale School of Architecture Alumni Donors:

1937
- Richard G. Hartshorne, Jr. †

1949
- Theodore F. Babbitt
- Jack Alan Bialosky, Sr.
- Prof. Charles H. Brewer, Jr.

1952
- James A. Evans
- Prof. Emeritus Wm. S. Huff
- Donald C. Mallow

1953
- Milton Klein
- John V. Sheoris

1954
- Boris S. Pushkarev
- Thomas R. Vreeland, Jr.

1955
- Sidney M. Sisk

1956
- Richard W. Chapman
- Walter D. Ramberg

1957
- Ernest L. Ames
- Edwin William de Cossy
- Richard A. Nininger
- William L. Porter

1958
- James S. Dudley
- Mark H. Hardenbergh
- Allen Moore, Jr.
- Malcolm Strachan II

1959
- Bernard M. Boyle
- Frank C. Chapman
- Louis P. Inserra
- Herbert S. Newman
- Earl A. Quenneville
- Carolyn H. Westerfield

1960
- Larence Newman Argraves
- James B. Baker
- Thomas L. Bosworth
- Richard S. Chafee
- Bryant L. Conant
- John K. Copelin
- Michael Gruenbaum
- Raymond F. Liston †
- Oscar E. Menzer
- Robert A. Mitchell
- Konrad J. Perlman

1961
- Edward R. Baldwin II
- Paul B. Brouard

· Peter Cooke
· Warren Jacob Cox
· Francis W. Gencorelli
· Charles T. Haddad
· W. Eugene Sage
· Bradford P. Shaw
· Yung G. Wang

1962
· Richard A. Hansen
· Tai Soo Kim
· Keith R. Kroeger
· James Morganstern
· Leonard P. Perfido
· Renato Rossi-Loureiro
· Meredith M. Seikel
· Donald R. Watson
· Myles Weintraub

1963
· Austin Church III
· Ward Joseph Miles
· F. Kempton Mooney
· Louis H. Skidmore, Jr.
· William A. Werner, Jr.

1964
· Philip Allen
· Theoharis L. David
· Charles D. Hosford
· Judith A. Lawler
· Dr. Charles L W. Leider †
· Robert J. Mittelstadt
· Joan F. Stogis

1965
· Thomas Hall Beeby
· H. Calvin Cook
· Richard C. Fogelson
· Peter L. Gluck
· Norman E. Jackson, Jr.
· Isidoro Korngold
· Thai Ker Liu
· John I. Pearce, Jr.
· Alexander Purves
· Elliot A. Segal
· Mason Smith
· Robert A.M. Stern
· Frederick C. Terzo
· Leonard M. Todd, Jr.
· Jeremy A. Walsh

1966
· Andrew Andersons
· Emily Nugent Carrier
· Richard C. Carroll, Jr.
· James Scott Cook
· John S. Hagmann
· William F. Moore

1967
· William H. Albinson
· Prof. Edward A. Arens
· R. Caswell Cooke, Jr.
· Gunter Dittmar
· Charles M. Engberg
· Alexander D. Garvin
· Howard E. Goldstein
· Glenn H. Gregg
· Chung Nung Lee
· John W. Mullen III
· Theodore Paul Streibert
· Darius Toraby

1968
· Frederick S. Andreae
· Robert A. Busser
· Gail H. Cooke
· Peter de Bretteville
· Richard M. Donnelly
· John Fulop, Jr.
· Christopher C. Glass
· John Holbrook, Jr.
· Peter C. Mayer
· Prof. Peter Papademetriou
· Franklin B. Satterthwaite Jr., Ph.D.
· Donald R. Spivack
· John J. Vosmek, Jr.
· James C. Whitney, Esq.

1969
· Stephen Harris Adolphus
· James E. Caldwell, Jr.
· Samuel R. Callaway, Jr.
· Robert J. Cassidy
· David B. Decker
· James M. Gage
· Harvey R. Geiger
· Jane L. Gilbert
· William H. Grover
· Peter Hentschel
· Roderick C. Johnson
· Raymond J. Kaskey, Jr.
· David H. Lessig
· John H. Shoaff
· Kermit D. Thompson

1970
· Richard F. Barrett
· Roland F. Bedford
· Paul F. Bloom
· F. Andrus Burr
· Ronald C. Filson
· Brin R. Ford
· George T. Hathorn
· John D. Jacobson
· Kathrin S. Moore
· James V. Righter
· Laurence A. Rosen
· Daniel V. Scully
· Walter C. Upton
· Jeremy Scott Wood
· William L. Yuen, Esq.
· F. Anthony Zunino

1971
· William A. Brenner
· An-Chi H. Burow
· Mazie Cox
· Mark J. Ellis
· John Jayner
· H. Rodriguez-Camilloni

1972
· Marc F. Appleton
· Paul B. Bailey
· Edward P. Bass
· Frederick Bland
· Phillip Mack Caldwell
· Roberta Carlson Carnwath
· Heather Willson Cass
· William A. Davis, Jr., Esq.
· John H. T. Dow, Jr.
· Karel Voss Fisher
· Joseph A. Ford III
· Coleman A. Harwell II
· Mark L. Hildebrand
· William H. Maxfield
· David B. Peck, Jr.
· Jefferson B. Riley
· Mark Simon
· Henry B. Teague
· Brinkley S. Thorne
· Carl H. Wies
· George Vincent Wright
· Roger Hung Tuan Yee

1973
· Judith Bing
· Hobart Fairbank
· J.P. Chadwick Floyd
· Stephen R. Holt
· Everardo A. Jefferson
· Nancy Brooks Monroe
· Karen Rheinlander-Gray
· Steven C. Robinson
· Michael J. Stanton
· William A. Sterling
· Stephen C. Thomson
· R. Jerome Wagner
· John W. Whipple
· Robert J. Yudell

1974
· Gordon M. Black
· Sara E. Caples
· Eric A. Chase
· William E. Odell
· Thomas C. Payne
· Barbara W. Ratner
· Barbara J. Resnicow
· David M. Schwarz
· George E. Turnbull

1975
· Tullio A. Bertoli
· Douglas J. Gardner
· Margaret R. Goglia
· Keith B. Gross
· Susan L.M. Keeny
· Edwin R. Kimsey, Jr.
· Francis C. Klein
· Larry W. Richards
· J. David Waggonner III

1976
· Benjamin M. Baker III
· Shalom Baranes
· Henry H. Benedict III
· Anko Chen
· Stefani Danes
· Barbara R. Feibelman
· James R. Kessler
· Roy T. Lydon, Jr.
· Eric Jay Oliner
· Herschel L.D. Parnes
· Adrienne K. Paskind
· Stuart N. Silk
· Barbara Sundheimer-Extein
· Scott Van Genderen

1977
· Calvert S. Bowie
· Louise M. Braverman
· Bradley B. Cruickshank
· W.J. Patrick Curley
· Stephen R. Hagan
· Jonathan S. Kammel
· James Hirsch Liberman
· Kevin P. Lichten
· Randall T. Mudge
· Davidson Norris
· Paul J. Pugliese
· Andrew K. Robinson
· Stephen M. Tolkin
· Alexander C. Twining

1978
· Philip H. Babb
· Frederic M. Ball, Jr.
· Paul W. Bierman-Lytle
· Shiao-Ling Chang
· Kenneth H. Colburn
· Kathleen Anne Dunne
· Lisa J. Gelfand
· Cynthia N. Hamilton
· William S. Mead
· William Hall Paxson
· Daniel Arthur Rosenfeld
· Julia Ruch

1979
· Steven W. Ansel
· Jack Alan Bialosky, Jr.
· James Leslie Bodnar
· Richard H. Clarke
· Jeffrey P. Feingold
· Bradford W. Fiske
· Patti Lee Glazer
· John Charles Hall
· Gavin A. Macrae-Gibson
· George R. Mitchell
· Thomas N. Patch

1980
· Jacob D. Albert
· Turan Duda
· G. Peyton Hall
· Stephen W. Harby
· Robert S. Kahn
· Mariko Masuoka
· Ann K. McCallum
· Julia H. Miner
· William A. Paquette
· Joseph F. Pierz
· Beverly Field Pierz

1981
· Richard L. Brown
· Michael B. Cadwell
· Mark Denton
· Brian E. Healy
· Mitchell A. Hirsch
· T. Whitcomb Iglehart
· Lawrence N. Lam
· Jane Murphy
· Frances H. Roosevelt
· Spencer Warncke
· Diane L. Wilk

1982
· John A. Boecker
· Domenic Carbone, Jr.
· Bruce H. Donnally
· Eric J. Gering
· Raymond R. Glover
· Kay Bea Jones
· John E. Kaliski
· Charles F. Lowrey, Jr.
· Theodore John Mahl
· Paul W. Reiss
· William H. Sherman
· R. Anthony Terry

1983
· Maynard M. Ball
· Anthony Stephen Barnes
· Phillip G. Bernstein
· Carol J. Burns
· Margaret D. Chapman
· Stuart E. Christenson
· Ignacio Dahl-Rocha
· Jane Backus Gelernter
· William H. Gilliss
· Stefan Hastrup
· John Lam
· Erica H. Ling
· Elisabeth N. Martin
· Elizabeth Ann Murrell
· Nicholas J. Rehnberg
· Jacques M. Richter
· Gary Schilling
· Brent Sherwood
· Robert J. Taylor
· Nell W. Twining
· Michael R. Winstanley

1984
· Bruce R. Becker
· Marti M. Cowan
· Teresa Ann Dwan
· Douglas S. Dworsky
· Ruth Slobin Harris
· Blair D. Kamin
· Elizabeth M. Mahon
· David Chase Martin
· Sharon Matthews
· Timothy G. McKenna
· Kenneth E. McKently
· Scott Merrill
· Jun Mitsui

· Lawrence S. Ng
· David L. Pearce, Ph.D.
· John R. Perkins
· Ted Trussell Porter
· Jennifer C. Sage
· Marion G. Weiss
· Sarah E. Willmer

1985
· Barbara A. Ball
· Rasa Joana Bauza
· William Robert Bingham
· M. Virginia Chapman
· Michael Coleman Duddy
· Olivia H. Emery
· Siamak Hariri
· Lucile S. Irwin
· Charles H. Loomis
· Peter B. MacKeith
· Chariss McAfee
· Joseph A. Pasquinelli
· Roger O. Schickedantz
· R. David Thompson

1986
· Timothy Burnett
· Margaret J. Chambers
· Tim Culvahouse
· Robert E. Day
· David J. DiGiacomo
· Carey Feierabend
· David J. Levitt
· Nicholas L. Petschek
· J. Gilbert Strickler
· John B. Tittmann

1987
· Stuart A. Basseches
· Mary Buttrick Burnham
· William D. Egan
· E. Baker Goodwin
· Elizabeth P. Gray
· Christopher S. Hays
· Andrew B. Knox
· Douglas S. Marshall
· Timothy Day Mohr
· Lilla J. Smith
· Duncan Gregory Stroik
· Andrea M. Swartz
· William L. Vandeventer
· Lester Y. Yuen

1988
· Atowarifagha I. Apiafi
· Hans Baldauf
· Andrew D. Berman
· Cary Suzanne Bernstein
· John David Butterworth
· Aubrey Leon Carter III
· Allison Ewing
· Natalie C. Gray-Miniutti
· Drew H. Kepley
· Ann Lisa Krsul
· Thomas Fleming Marble
· William B. Marquand
· Oscar E. Mertz III
· David H. Must
· Nicholas Alfred Noyes
· Alan W. Organschi
· Elaine M. Rene-Weissman
· William Taggart Ruhl
· Gilbert P. Schafer III
· Matthew Viederman
· Li Tze Wen
· Robert Duncan Young

1989
· Edward R. Burian
· Larry G. Chang
· Darin C. Cook
· John DaSilva
· Steve Dumez
· Kevin S. Killen
· Stephen D. Luoni
· Giovanni Pagnotta
· David J. Rush
· Rossana H. Santos
· Margaret Sherman Todd
· Robert Ingram Tucker

1990
· Charles Bergen
· Kristen L. Hodess
· Jeffrey E. Karer
· Marc D. L'Italien
· David M. Levine
· Peter J. Newman
· Alison W. Horne-Rona
· Mildred I. Sung
· Scott Wood

1991
· David M. Becker
· Peter J. Brotherton
· Kimberley J. Rodler
· Alexander M. Stuart
· Dr. Susan E. Sutton
· Kevin Wilkes
· Heather H. Young

1992
· Kelly Jean Carlson-Reddig
· Betty Y. Chen
· Perla Jeanne Delson
· Timothy Craig Durfee
· Frederick Adams Farrar II
· Bruce Marshall Horton
· Maitland Jones III
· Douglas Neal Kozel
· James Arthur Langley
· Daniel P. Towler-Weese
· Marc A. Turkel
· Marion Converse Winkler

1993
· Gregory Miller Barnell
· Benyamin Ber
· Timothy Charles Geisler
· Richard G. Grisaru
· Louise J. Harpman
· Michael A. Harshman
· Celia C. Imrey
· Jordan J. Levin
· Gitta Robinson
· Allen Douglas Ross
· Evan Michael Supcoff
· Katherine D. Winter

1994
· Brendan Russell Coburn
· Mark C. Dixon
· Pamela J. Fischer
· Paul W. Jackson
· Vrinda Khanna
· William J. Massey
· Tania K. Min
· Eeva-Liisa Pelkonen
· Albert J. Tinson
· Mimi H. Tsai

1995
· Andrew K. Anker
· Carolyn Ann Foug
· Ann Kim
· George Craig Knight
· Johannes Marinus Knoops
· Aaron Matthew Lamport
· Michael Henry Levendusky
· John Christopher Woell

1996
· Andrew C. Backer
· Jasmine Benyamin
· Douglas C. Bothner
· John B. Clancy
· Don M. Dimster-Denk
· Russell S. Katz
· Michael V. Knopoff
· Chung Yin J. Lau
· Arthur J. Lee
· Alexander Francis Levi
· Thomas A. Lumikko
· Nancy Nienberg
· Steven A. Roberts
· David A. Thurman
· Mai-Tse Wu

1997
· Richard Kasemsarn
· Drew Lang
· Peter Downing Mullan
· Bertha A. Olmos
· David Jason Pascu
· Jeffery Ryan Povero
· Linda Caroline Reeder
· Ian Mark Smith
· William James Voulgaris
· Shawn Michael Watts

1998
· Thalassa Alexandra Curtis
· Melissa L. Delvecchio
· Marjorie K. Dickstein
· Clifton R. Fordham
· Hahn Joh
· Emily Sheya Kovner
· Karl A. Krueger
· Elizabeth P. Rutherfurd
· Dean S. Sakamoto
· Paul D. Stoller
· Jennifer L. Taylor
· Gretchen V. Wagner

1999
· Colin Christopher Brice
· Kimberly Ann Brown
· Adrienne James
· Bruce D. Kinlin
· Katherine E. Sutherland

2000
· Benjamin Jon Bischoff
· Bing Bu
· Dominique Diana Davison
· Joseph Shek Yuen Fong
· Oliver Edmund Freundlich
· Christopher Scott Herring
· Donald Wayne Johnson
· Thomas Matthew Morbitzer
· Ronald Michael Stelmarski
· Michael James Tower

2001
· Ghiora Aharoni
· Claude Daniel Eshaghian
· Mark Foster Gage
· Jeff Allan Goldstein
· Christopher M. Pizzi
· Adam Joseph Ruedig
· Elizabeth Weeks Tilney
· Juliana Chittick Tiryaki
· Can M.A. Tiryaki
· Zhonggui Zhao

2002
· Sarah Marie Lavery
· Yansong Ma

2003
· Andrew William Benner
· Marcos Diaz Gonzalez
· Li-Yu Hsu
· William L. Tims

2004
· Pu Chen
· Stephen Yuen-Hoo Chien
· Spencer Walker Luckey
· James C. Nelson III
· Benjamin Rosenblum
· Na Wei
· Damian Delafield Zunino

2005
· Ralph Colt Bagley IV
· Brent Allen Buck
· Jennifer N. Carruthers
· William Michael Dudley
· Jonah C. Gamblin
· Ruth Shinenge Gyuse
· Derek James Hoeferlin
· Brandon F. Pace
· Brett Dalton Spearman
· Nicholas Martin Stoutt

2006
· Benay Alena Betts
· Angel Paolo Campos
· Michael Joseph Grogan
· Sean A. Khorsandi
· David Nam

2007
· Gabrielle Eve Brainard
· Brook G. Denison
· Christopher Hsin-An Lee
· Adrienne E. Swiatocha Turner

2008
· Marc Charles Guberman
· Whitney M. Kraus
· Yichen Lu
· Jacob I. Reidel
· Leo Rowling Stevens IV
· Alberto B. Zamora

2009
· Matthew A. Roman
· Rebecca B. Winik

2010
· Helen B. Bechtel
· Daniel David Colvard
· Jacquelyn Page Wittkamp Hawkins
· K. Brandt Knapp
· Scott Brandon O'Daniel
· Tal Schori

2011
· Kipp Colby Edick
· William Grandison Gridley
· Alexandra Fox Tailer

2012
· Kathryn L. Perez
· Ian Gordon Starling
· Laura Clark Wagner

2013
· Antonia M. Devine
· Amy G. Mielke
· Altair L. Peterson
· Ryan Salvatore
· Paul C. Soper III
· Katharine J. M. Storr

2014
· Ali John Pierre Artemel
· Mary F. Burr
· Danielle Davis
· Cristian A. Oncescu
· Craig M. Rosman
· Constance M. Vale

2015
· Elena R. Baranes
· Lauren E. Raab

2016
· Shayari Hiranya De Silva
· Shuangjing Hu
· Nicolas Thornton Kemper

2017
· Alex O. Kruhly
· Maxwell T. Mensching
· Georgia M. Todd
· Robert J. Yoos

2018
· Caitlin E. Baiada
· Abena A. K. Bonna
· David Alston Langdon
· Margaret F. Marsh
· Pierre Thach

Tribute Gifts in Honor of
· Thomas Hall Beeby
· Deborah Berke
· Kent C. Bloomer
· Paul B. Brouard
· Frank O. Gehry
· Philip Grausman
· Leonard Levie
· Robert A.M. Stern

Tribute Gifts in Memory of
· Constance M. Adams
· John E. Decell
· Robert P. Hammell
· Timothy E. Lenahan
· Carroll L.V. Meeks
· James E. Palmer
· Myron B. Silberman
· David E. Taylor
· Stanley Tigerman
· Robert Charles Venturi, Jr.
· Ronald Wagner

† denotes deceased donors

....

Students

M.Arch I Year 1
· Adepegba, Ifeoluwa
· Akerfeldt-Howard, Isa M
· Broton, Natalie Alexandria
· Brown, Ives Banerjee
· Cambio, Christopher James
· Carrillo Bueno, Martin
· Chudyk, Colin Douglas
· Congdon, Rosa Elinor
· Deng, Jiachen
· Dong, Yichen Janet
· Du, Xuefeng
· Freudenburg, Paul Kieran (joint degree program, M.E.M. School of Forestry & Environmental Studies '22)
· Fritz, Kate Marie
· Galang, Malcolm Rondell Belmonte
· Gallegos, Anjelica Sanchez
· Gao, Yangwei Kevin
· Gu, Jiaming
· Gu, Yi Ian (joint degree program, M.B.A. School of Management '22)
· Harrell, Ashton Rutledge
· Hu, Liang
· Jafari, Niema
· Jones, Alicia Irene
· Jung, Hyun Jae
· Kong, Sze Wai Justin
· Koushouris, Louis Alexander
· Krebs, Tyler C
· Lam, Hiuki
· Lee, Hye Min Pabi
· Li, Mingxi
· Li, Yidong Isabel
· Lin, Simeng Dreama
· Liu, Qiyuan
· Liu, Yuyang April
· Lopez, Araceli
· Lufkin, Angela M
· Mulder, Rachel E
· Nagata, Leanne Kiyomi
· Ng, Naomi Jemima
· Nolte, Louisa Charlotte Emily
· Olivier, Alexandra Nicole
· Qu, Mingyang Michelle
· Ratajczak, Nicole Aleksandra
· Schneider, Heather Mary
· Simpson, Scott Austin
· Song, Christine Yeasul
· Thakali, Shikha Lhamu
· Thompson, Benjamin LaTour
· Weiss, Sarah Anna
· Wirsing, Max N
· Wright, Shelby
· Xu, Chuqiao Stella
· Yang, Sean Mingjue
· Ye, Peng
· Zhang, Leyi
· Zhang, Yuhan
· Zhao, Kaiwen Kevin
· Zwiebel, Sasha Fisher

M. Arch I Year 2
· Anastase, Cristina Laura
· Badr, Michelle Feroz
· Blackman, Katharine La Polt
· Cass, Emily J
· Chabrol, Camille
· Ching, Su Yen Serena
· Comeaux, Page Thomas
· Connell, Gioia Montana (joint degree program, M.E.M. School of Forestry & Environmental Studies '20)
· Dattani, Ruchi
· Deiparine, Deo Antonio
· Domange, Clara Andrée
· Dreiblatt, Miriam Helen Sinkoff
· Farley, Helen Catherine
· Feldman, Adam Howard
· Garcia, Nathan A
· Gasper, Michael Thomas
· Glassman, Michael Drew
· Guan, Tianyu
· Harris, Phoebe Webster
· James, William Packer
· Johnson, Kelley Pauline
· Kim, Andrew David Kisung
· Lau, Katie Nicole
· Lee, Eunice Young
· Lefevre, Rachel N
· Lenza, Zachary A
· Lindsay, Jackson Thomas
· Liu, Matthew
· Mahon, Thomas Patrick Friesen
· Miller, Andrew James
· Ni, Pianra Layla
· Ouellette-Howitz, Max
· Palomo, Jonathan
· Pan, X Christine
· Pauchet, Alix Marie Louise (joint degree program, M.E.M. School of Forestry & Environmental Studies '21)
· Pei, Jewel
· Pineda Jongeward, Alexandra Louise
· Plaus, Deirdre Marie
· Punde, Manasi
· Rico, Kelsey Rebecca
· Ritz, Jenna Leigh
· Rocha, Limy Fabiana
· Schaengold, David A
· Schmid, Rhea Isobel
· Shah, Armaan Bobby
· Shen, Baolin
· Sorabjee, Maya
· Taheri, Arghavan
· Tan, Si Hen Megan
· Thompson, Brenna Leigh
· Thompson, Seth Colburn
· Vathupola, Rukshan Eranga
· Vaulot, Laelia Kim-Lan
· Weimer, Darryl Thomas
· Wen, Xiaohui
· Wu, Paul
· Yang, Kay

M. Arch I Year 3
· Agron, Melinda Marlén
· Agulue, Olisa Ugo
· Arango, Diego
· Bacon-Shone, Gwyneth Amanda
· Barry, Lani Mei
· Boornazian, Antonino B
· Bransfield, David Hunter
· Bruce, Samuel David (joint degree program, M.E.M. School of Forestry & Environmental Studies '20)
· Butner, Davis Samuel
· Cash, Brian Jeffrey
· Chan, Haylie Hoi Ki
· Chen, Shiyan Nancy
· Cui, Yipeng Sunny
· Duran, Alejandro
· Fisher, Kate Nicole
· Fok, Zelig Siu Lum
· Fung, Pik-Tone
· Garikes, Kerry Danaher
· Hakanoglu, Orli
· Hughes, Ryan Thomas
· Kim, Hyelin Erin
· Lai, Hsin-Ju Jennifer
· Lee,Dylan
· Leiva, Kassandra Maria
· Li, Menglan
· Liu, Jeffrey Zhenhua
· Man, Martin
· McCann, Larkin Patrick Daniel
· Miller, Nicholas Alexander
· Monge Kaser, Samantha (joint degree program, M.B.A. School of Management '20)
· Muydinov, Rashidbek
· Ofoman, Kola Anita
· Olsen, Benjamin D
· Peh, Iven Sze Kiat
· Rothschild, Anna Jordan Bodeen
· Russell, Melissa A
· Sale, Evan Daniel
· Sanchez-Enkerlin, Miguel
· Schaffert, Jacob S
· Semenov, Misha
· Smith, Abigail Li
· Steyer, Charles Augustus Pearso (joint degree program, M.E.M. School of Forestry & Environmental Studies '20)
· Studebaker, Luke Claude
· Sutherland, Colin Hollingworth
· Tritt, Christopher Dylan
· Tsai, Wei-Shih Vivian
· Velaise, Alexander (joint degree program, M.B.A. School of Management '20)
· Wagstaffe, Matthew Leo
· Wang, Li Wei (joint degree program, M.B.A. School of Management '20)
· Weigel, Melissa Kendall
· Whitcombe, Daniel (joint degree program, M.B.A. School of Management '20)
· Wu, Ray
· Yi, Issy
· Yin, Xiaoyue Katrina
· Yoshida, Millie
· Yuen, Winston Gee Kong
· Zisson, Ethan Norris

M. Arch II Year 1
· Ahmed, Hamzah
· Alajmi, Sara S A A M
· Bradley, James M
· Chen, Taiming
· Darcy de Oliveira Miranda, Miguel
· Gao, Yuchen
· Huang, Changming
· Lee, Ho Jae
· Patel, Smit Ramesh
· Serrano Fuchs, Leonardo
· Thibodeaux, Adam
· Tryon, Jerome John
· Tsai, I-Ting
· Tsang, Hin Yeung Justin
· Yu, Borou Anna

M. Arch II Year 2
· AlKhouli, Lara Yasser
· AlMathkoor, Dana
· Altmann, Kate Eleanor
· Anwar, Tayyaba
· Balda Moncayo, Isabel
· Barymow, Katherine J
· Bhagwagar, Sharmin Yezdi
· Chang, Kunhee Blair
· Doan, Nicole Magsaysay
· Guo, Shiyua Sissi
· Hartonas, Dimitris
· Kelekar, Varoon Chandan
· Kunnatharayil, Jincy George
· Mohanta, Minakshi
· Perez, Javier
· Sao Pedro Riobom Dos Santos, Mariana
· Shah, Dhruvin
· Sheth, Priyanka Sanjeev
· Shin, Jennifer Yunhee (joint degree program, M.E.M. School of Forestry & Environmental Studies '20)
· Taheri, Aslan
· Venditti, Lucia
· Wang, Minquan

M.E.D. Year 1
· Bushman, Holly

M.E.D. YEAR 2
· Hanly, Jack
· Hopkins, Jonathan
· Simon, Maia
· Taha, Dina

- Zhang, JingqiuPh.D
- Ciardullo, Christina
- Giannakopoulou Karamouzi, Iris
- He, Gary Huafan
- Issaias, Theodossis
- Khan, Ishraq
- Mankiewicz, Phoebe
- Michielli, Zachariah
- Pacula, Nicholas
- Pretorius, Mandi
- Printz, Gabrielle
- Sutton, Summer
- Tobey, Aaron
- Turturo, David
- Jia, Jane Weng

Undergraduate Junior
- Abdi, Hafsa
- Adeoye, Angel
- Brown, Charelle
- Chan, Trevor
- Davis, Hana
- Fandrich, Elena
- Galvan, Sebastian
- Gormley, Carina
- Hedges, Julia
- Hurtado, David
- Hwang, Arthur
- Jacobs, Jane
- Melin-Corcoran, Mari
- Nagano, Karin
- Nicolosi, Graceann
- Pales, Ash
- Potter, Sophie
- Rimm-Kaufman, Sam
- Saldarriaga, Daniel
- Saunders, Margaret
- Tebbetts, Kas
- Thompson, Adam
- Villanueva, Valeria
- Wauer, Reanna
- Yap, Mary (Eli Whitney Program)

Undergraduate Senior
- Antonio, Edward Joe
- Boudreau, Jordan
- Chung, Sungyeon Kristine
- Fletcher, Mary Catherine
- Goodman, Elizabeth
- Hu, Amanda
- Lim, Sheau Yun
- Ma, Haewon
- Masterson, Andrea
- Saip, Deniz
- Sandweiss, Andrew
- Silvestry, Noah
- Tang, Sida
- Wilson, Max
- Strausser, Noah

Fall 2018 Graduation
- Nelson, Cameron
- Wu, Kaifeng

....

Faculty

Dean
- Deborah Berke

Associate Dean and Associate Professor Adjunct
- Sunil Bald

Associate Dean and Senior Lecturer
- Phillip Bernstein

Assistant Dean, Director of Exhibitions, and Critic
- Andrew Benner
-

Assistant Dean and Associate Professor
- Mark Foster Gage

Assistant Dean and Assistant Professor
- Joyce Hsiang

Assistant Dean, Director of Undergraduate Studies, and Assistant Professor Adjunct
- Bimal Mendis

Hines Professor of Sustainable Architectural Design and Professor of Forestry and Environmental Studies
- Anna Dyson

Charles Gwathmey Professor in Practice
- Peter Eisenman

J.M. Hoppin Professor of Architecture
- Robert A.M. Stern

Professor Emerita
- Peggy Deamer

Professor Emerita of Architecture and American Studies
- Dolores Hayden

Visiting Professor Emeritus
- Kurt Forster
- Alexander Purves

Professor and Director of the Master of Environmental Design Program
- Keller Easterling

Professor
- Alan Plattus

William B. and Charlotte Shepherd Davenport Visiting Professor
- Julie Snow (Fall 2018)
- Pier Vittorio Aureli
- (Spring 2019)

Norman R. Foster Visiting Professor
- Lyndon Neri & Rossana Hu (Fall 2018)
- Sandra Barclay & Jean Pierre Crousse (Spring 2019)

Vincent Scully Visiting Professor
- Anthony Vidler (Fall 2018)
- Esther da Costa Meyer (Spring 2019)

Eero Saarinen Visiting Professor
- Adam Yarinsky (Fall 2018)
- Yolande Daniels (Spring 2019)

Edward P. Bass Distinguished Visiting Architecture Fellow
- Michael Samuelian (Fall 2018)

Robert A.M. Stern Visiting Professor
- Paul Florian (Spring 2019)

Daniel Rose Visiting Assistant Professor in Urban Studies
- Jesse LeCavalier (Spring 2018-2019)

William Henry Bishop Visiting Professor
- Simon Hartmann (Fall 2018)
- Thomas Phifer (Spring 2019)

Louis I. Kahn Visiting Assistant Professor
- Omar Gandhi (Fall 2018)
- Todd Reisz (Spring 2019)

Louis I. Kahn Visiting Professor
- Brigitte Shim (Spring 2019)

Visiting Professor
- Chris Sharples (Spring 2019)

Professor Adjunct
- Kent Bloomer
- Turner Brooks
- Alexander Garvin
- Steven Harris
- John D. Jacobson
- Joel Sanders

Associate Professor
- Kyoung Sun Moon
- Eeva-Liisa Pelkonen
- Elihu Rubin

Critic
- Emily Abruzzo
- Anthony Acciavatti
- Annie Barrett
- Nikole Bouchard
- Kyle Bradley
- Laura Briggs
- Miroslava Brooks
- Brennan Buck
- Marta Caldeira
- Iñaqui Carnicero
- Trattie Davies
- Peter de Bretteville
- Kyle Dugdale
- Anthony Gagliardi
- Andrei Harwell
- Gavin Hogben
- Adam Hopfner
- Alicia Imperiale
- Elisa Iturbe
- George Knight
- Amy Lelyveld
- Nicholas McDermott
- Joeb Moore
- Timothy Newton
- Miriam Peterson
- Surry Schlabs
- Aniket Shahane
- Rosalyne Shieh
- Michael Szivos
- Lexi Tsien-Shiang
- Dragana Zoric

Senior Critic
- Martin Finio
- Alan Organschi

Lecturer
- Victor Agran
- Maya Alam
- John Apicella
- Anibal Bellomio
- Ezio Blasetti
- Dorian Booth
- Kipp Bradford
- Luke Bulman
- Alastair Elliott
- Dov Feinmesser
- Bryan Fuermann
- Kevin Gray
- Erleen Hatfield
- Robert Haughney
- Kristin Hawkins
- Larry Jones
- Amir Karimpour
- Yoko Kawai
- Beom Jun Kim
- Jennifer Lan
- Gina Narracci
- Kari Nystrom
- Laura Pirie
- Victoria Ponce de Leon
- Daniele Profeta
- Craig Razza
- Pierce Reynoldson
- Kevin Rotheroe
- Edward Stanley
- Philip Steiner
- Celia Toche
- Adam Trojanowski
- Carter Wiseman
- Cynthia Zarin

Instructor
- Nathan Burnell

Scientific Researcher
- Mohamed Aly Etman
- Naomi Keena

Associated Faculty, Michael H. Jordan Professor at the Yale School of Management
- Amy Wrzesniewski

Director of Communications
- AJ Artemel

Lead Administrator
- Regina Bejnerowicz

Senior Administrative Assistant, Academic Support
- Terence Brown

Operations Manager
- Zelma Brunson

Senior Administrative Assistant–Lectures, Exhibitions, and Special Events
- Richard DeFlumeri

Director of Advanced Technology
- Vincent Guerrero

Senior Systems Administrator
- Robert Liston

Registrar, Title IX Coordinator, and Admissions Administrator
- Tanial Lowe

Financial Aid
- Andre Massiah
- Adelia Palmieri

Students

- Adepegba, Ifeoluwa 102, 122
- Alajmi, Sara S A A M 25, 93, 144, XXII
- AlMathkoor, Dana 94, 120,
- Altmann, Kate Eleanor 27, 82, 127, 131, XXI
- Anwar, Tayyaba 78, 109, 125, XX, XXI
- Arango, Diego 35, 71, XXII
- Bacon-Shone, Gwyneth Amanda 96
- Badr, Michelle Feroz 144, 154
- Balda Moncayo, Isabel XIV
- Barry, Lani Mei XXII
- Bhagwagar, Sharmin Yezdi 28, 75, 106, 132, XX, XXII
- Bradley, James M 103, 126
- Broton, Natalie Alexandria 62, 125
- Brown, Ives Banerjee 114
- Bruce, Samuel David 86,156, XIV, XXII
- Bushman, Holly 144
- Butner, Davis Samuel 50, 152, XXII
- Cash, Brian Jeffrey 94
- Carrillo Bueno, Martin 122
- Cass, Emily J 19, 69, 112, 136
- Chan, Haylie Hoi Ki 46, 72
- Chen, Shiyan Nancy 149
- Chen, Taiming 83, 103, 120
- Ching, Su Yen Serena 64, 134, 154
- Chung, Sungyeon Kristine 6, 53
- Comeaux, Page Thomas 18, 124, 146, XX, XXI
- Congdon, Rosa Elinor 104
- Coombs, Robert 138
- Cui, Yipeng Sunny 73, 119
- Darcy de Oliveira Miranda, Miguel 97
- Deiparine, Deo Antonio 23, 132, 154, XXI
- Deng, Jiachen 122
- Doan, Nicole Magsaysay 109, XX, XXI, XXII
- Duran, Alejandro 36, 127, 142, XX, XXI
- Fok, Zelig Siu Lum 107, 109, 111, XXII
- Fritz, Kate Marie 113
- Fung, Pik-Tone 76
- Galang, Malcolm Rondell Belmonte 9, 57, 100, 102, 114, 123
- Gao, Yangwei Kevin 130
- Gao, Yuchen 25
- Garikes, Kerry Danaher 31
- Gasper, Michael Thomas 69
- Glassman, Michael Drew 69, 113, 135, 148, XX, XXI
- Gu, Jiaming 122
- Guo, Shiyua Sissi 105, 111
- Hakanoglu, Orli 39, 79, 137
- Harrell, Ashton Rutledge 102
- Harris, Phoebe Webster 66, 116, 144
- Hartonas, Dimitris 140, XXII
- Hopkins, Jonathan XIII
- He, Gary Huafan 70, 81, 130
- Hu, Amanda 7, 138
- Hu, Liang 12, 122
- Hughes, Ryan Thomas 47, 87, 119, XXII
- Jafari, Niema 102
- Jett, Robert 144
- Johnson, Kelley Pauline 66, 118, 133, 154
- Jung, Hyun Jae 122
- Katz, Jenny 138
- Kelekar, Varoon Chandan 29, 108
- Kim, Andrew David Kisung 69, 112
- Kim, Hyelin Erin 94, XXII
- Koushouris, Louis Alexander 15, 55, 123, 137
- Krebs, Tyler C 13, 102
- Kunnatharayil, Jincy George 90, 119, 156, XXII
- Lai, Hsin-Ju Jennifer 43, 84, XXII
- Lam, Hiuki 62
- Lau, Katie Nicole XX
- Lee, Eunice Young 68, 126, 154
- Lee, Ho Jae 97, 106, 138
- Lefevre, Rachel N 18, 65, 118, 145, 146, 151
- Lenza, Zachary A 140
- Li, Menglan 32, XX, XXII
- Li, Mingxi 60
- Li, Yidong Isabel 16, 115
- Lim, Sheau Yun 136
- Lin, Simeng Dreama 122
- Lindsay, Jackson Thomas 105, 154
- Liu, Jeffrey Zhenhua 72
- Liu, Matthew 20, 124
- Liu, Qiyuan 60
- Liu, Yuyang April 123
- Lopez, Araceli 58
- Lufkin, Angela M 9, 102
- Mahon, Thomas Patrick Friesen 121, 152, 154
- Man, Martin 119, XXI
- McCann, Larkin Patrick Daniel 119
- Mezey, Claudia 144
- Miller, Andrew Economos XX, XXI
- Miller, Nicholas Alexander 40, 150, 152, XX, XXI
- Minto, Alison 141
- Mohanta, Minakshi 144
- Mulder, Rachel E 14, 56, 102, 137, 153
- Nagata, Leanne Kiyomi 14
- Ng, Naomi Jemima 11, 58, 115, 122
- Nolte, Louisa Charlotte Emily 10, 123
- Ofoman, Kola Anita 151
- Olsen, Benjamin D 48, XX, XXII
- Ouellette-Howitz, Max 21, 65, 121
- Pan, X Christine 113, 139, 148, XX, XXI
- Patel, Smit Ramesh 120
- Pauchet, Alix Marie Louise 19, 116, 124
- Peh, Iven Sze Kiat 110, XXII
- Pei, Jewel 68, 126, 148
- Perez, Javier 51, 106, 127
- Pineda Jongeward, Alexandra Louise 124, 154
- Plaus, Deirdre Marie 64, 124, 141
- Punde, Manasi 20, 143, 154
- Rico, Kelsey Rebecca 67
- Rocha, Limy Fabiana 22, 66, 144
- Russell, Melissa A 94
- Sale, Evan Daniel 41, 133, 142, XIV, XX, XXII
- Sanchez-Enkerlin, Miguel 33, 88, 119, XXII
- Sao Pedro Riobom Dos Santos, Mariana
- Schaengold, David A 94
- Schaffert, Jacob S 37, 91, 119
- Schmid, Rhea Isobel 21, 68, 116, 141, 148
- Schneider, Heather Mary 10
- Semenov, Misha 149
- Serrano Fuchs, Leonardo 73
- Shah, Armaan Bobby 68
- Shen, Baolin 22, 154, XIV
- Sheth, Priyanka Sanjeev XIII, XXI
- Shin, Jennifer Yunhee 80, XXII
- Shoemaker, Sam 138
- Simpson, Scott Austin 12, 102
- Song, Christine Yeasul 122
- Sorabjee, Maya 67, 116, 143
- Studebaker, Luke Claude 40
- Sutherland, Colin Hollingworth 145
- Taha, Dina XXI
- Tan, Si Hen Megan 23
- Tang, Sida 53
- Thibodeaux, Adam 25, 107, 138
- Thompson, Benjamin LaTour 56, 122
- Thompson, Brenna Leigh 66, 108
- Thompson, Seth Colburn 69, 121, XX, XXI
- Tritt, Christopher Dylan 41, 91, 133, XXII
- Tryon, Jerome John 25, 90, 103, 104, 116, 157, XXII
- Tsai, I-Ting 98, 103, 119, XXII
- Tsang, Hin Yeung Justin 94, 144, XXII
- Vathupola, Rukshan Eranga 66, 154
- Venditti, Lucia 44, 71, 110, XXII
- Wagstaffe, Matthew Leo 94, 119, XX, XXI, XXII
- Wang, Liwei XXI
- Wang, Minquan XXII
- Weigel, Melissa Kendall 52, 119, 150, XXII
- Weimer, Darryl Thomas 64, XX
- Weiss, Sarah Anna 15, 114, 139
- Wright, Shelby 59, 102
- Wu, Paul 124
- Wu, Ray 43
- Yi, Issy 39
- Yin, Xiaoyue Katrina 119, 134
- Yoshida, Millie 50, 76, XXII
- Yuen, Winston Gee Kong 98, XXI, XXII
- Zhang, Jingqiu XIV
- Zhang, Leyi 61, 112, 114, 123
- Zhang, Yuhan 122
- Zhao, Kaiwen Kevin 122
- Zisson, Ethan Norris 52, 105, XX, XXI
- Zwiebel, Sasha Fisher 101, 114, 131

Faculty

- Abruzzo, Emily 17, 30, 53, 69, 80, 120
- Acciavatti, Anthony 63, 70, 85
- Agran, Victor 104
- Alam, Maya 113
- Apicella, John 119, 127
- Bald, Sunil 157, 24, 54
- Barrett, Annie 17, 54
- Bellomio, Anibal 124
- Benner, Andrew 45, 85
- Bernstein, Phillip 119, 127
- Bloomer, Kent 108, XV
- Booth, Dorian 114
- Bouchard, Nikole 8
- Bradford, Kipp 118
- Bradley, Kyle 118
- Briggs, Laura 17
- Brooks, Miroslava 8, 38, 63, 100
- Brooks, Turner 6, 109
- Buck, Brennan 109
- Bulman, Luke 112
- Burnell, Nathan 104
- Caldeira, Marta 45, 139, 156
- Carnicero, Iñaqui 17,146

· Davies, Trattie 54, 62, 136
· de Bretteville, Peter 17, 54, 105
· Deamer, Peggy 49
· Dugdale, Kyle 26, 73, 100
· Dyson, Anna 24, 49, 89, 95, 118
· Easterling, Keller 144
· Eisenman, Peter 38, 101, 108
· Elliott, Alastair 124
· Etman, Mohamed Aly 118
· Finio, Martin 17,124
· Forster, Kurt 130
· Fuermann, Bryan 149, 150
· Gage, Mark Foster 110
· Gagliardi, Anthony 38, 101, 108
· Garvin, Alexander 148
· Gray, Kevin 149
· Harris, Steven 52
· Harwell, Andrei 30, 77, 153, 156
· Hatfield, Erleen 124
· Haughney, Robert 124
· Hawkins, Kristin 124
· Hayden, Dolores 52
· Hogben, Gavin 52
· Hopfner, Adam 121
· Hsiang, Joyce 26, 115
· Imperiale, Alicia 63, 70
· Iturbe, Elisa 63 , 38, 115
· Jacobson, John D. 124
· Jones, Larry 124
· Karimpour, Amir 103
· Kawai, Yoko 80, 134
· Keena, Naomi 95, 118
· Kim, Beom Jun 115
· Knight, George 89, 115
· Lan, Jennifer 124
· Lelyveld, Amy 54, 121,144
· McDermott, Nicholas 8
· Mendis, Bimal 63, 92, 100, 114
· Moon, Kyoung Sun 119
· Moore, Joeb 54, 121
· Narracci, Gina 124
· Newton, Timothy 104
· Nystrom, Kari 124
· Organschi, Alan 48
· Pelkonen, Eeva-Liisa 17, 30, 136
· Peterson, Miriam 54
· Pirie, Laura 124
· Plattus, Alan 63, 153, 156
· Ponce de Leon, Victoria 124
· Profeta, Daniele 113
· Purves, Alexander 49, 94
· Razza, Craig 124
· Reynoldson, Pierce 124
· Rotheroe, Kevin 106, 124
· Rubin, Elihu 63, 151
· Sanders, Joel 24, 26, 95, 137, 140
· Schlabs, Surry 25, 63, XXII
· Shahane, Aniket 63, 131
· Shieh, Rosalyne 34, 53, 63
· Shim, Brigitte 24
· Steiner, Philip 124
· Stern, Robert A.M. 89, 124, 132, 141
· Szivos, Michael 8, 54, 125
· Toche, Celia 124
· Trojanowski, Adam 124
· Tsien-Shiang, Lexi 26, 34
· Wiseman, Carter 140
· Wrzesniewski, Amy 140
· Zarin, Cynthia 135
· Zoric, Dragana 54, 63

Guest Critics
· Aeberhard, Beat 30
· Akhtar, Saima 92
· Albert, Ramona 54
· Aragüez, José 54
· Ayata, Kutan 8
· Bauman, Hansel 24
· Becker, Louis 17
· Bergdoll, Barry 34
· Berktold, Ruth 94
· Berman, Andrew 17
· Bernheimer, Andy 49
· Besler, Erin 8
· Betts, Stella 24
· Bevan, Jenny 88
· Bilbao, Tatiana 69
· Bingol, Ceren 77
· Bollack, Françoise 88
· Bonder, Julian 54
· Bucci, Angelo 69
· Buckley, Craig 69
· Bunge, Eric 63
· Busansky, Alex 17
· Butterfield, Brian 17
· Benjamin Cadena 8
· Canty, Sean 8
· Carpenter, James 74
· Carpenter, Tei 8
· Cobb, Henry 38
· Dallman, James 42
· Davidson, Cynthia 38
· Davidson, Stephanie 38, 63
· Day, Joe 63
· Decker, Tabitha 92
· DelVecchio, Melissa 88
· Fairbanks, Karen 54
· Frampton, Kenneth 69
· Galen, Timur 94
· Genevro, Rosalie 49
· George, Ashlee 17
· Gill, Leslie 54
· Goldstein, Elizabeth 63
· Goldstein, Jeff 24
· Gooden, Mario 34
· Gordon, Viviana 17
· Gray, Lisa 74, 81
· Harmon, Frank 74
· Hawkinson, Laurie 42
· He, Gary 69
· Heikkinen, Pekka 49
· Henry, Sia 17
· Hoerr, Theodore 63
· Holder, Andrew 8
· Hood, Walter 94
· Hoss, Gregory 88
· Huge, Elijah 17
· Hume, Abby Coover 8
· Ibañez, Mariana 8
· Jamaleddine, Ziad 17
· Jimenez, Carlos 26
· Ke, Zhang 42
· Khalili, Parsa 8
· Kolb, Jaffer 54
· Kuittinen, Matti 49
· La, Grace 42
· Lai, Jimenez 45
· Lamunière, Inès 69
· Lange, Alexandra 63
· Lehto, Antti 49
· Leven, David 54
· Lin, Stephanie 8
· Lori, Noora 92
· Lott, Jon 17
· Louie, Jonathan 8
· Luthi, Tanya 49
· Macapia, Peter 63
· Maleh, Nadine 17
· Mandrup, Dorte 8
· McVoy, Chris 34, 69
· Mergold, Aleksandr 8
· Middleton, William 34
· Mogilevich, Mariana 63
· Mori, Toshiko 81
· Newsom, Jennifer 17
· Oki, Toshihiro 54
· Ouroussoff, Nicolai 38
· O'Donnell, Caroline 38
· Panzano, Megan 54, 17
· Pinnell, Pat 88
· Price, Bill 30
· Prosky, Benjamin 17
· Puigjaner, Anna 30
· Raicovich, Laura 54
· Riano, Quilian 63
· Rice, Lyn 54
· Rich, Nathan 54
· Rickenbacker, Shawn 63
· Rieselbach, Anne 17
· Rocker, Ingeborg 38
· Rothko, Christopher 34
· Rothstein, Karla 54
· Sakamoto, Dean 69
· Schindler, Susanne 63
· Selldorf, Annabelle 81
· Serlin, David 24
· Sharples, Bill 94
· Shin, Jae 8
· Simon, Mark
· Simon, Sydney 34
· Smith, Timothy 88
· Starr, Ruth 24
· Sturges, Beka 74
· Tehrani, Nader 42
· Theodore, Georgeen 63
· Thompson, Joe 94
· Thompson, Maryann 26
· Tidwell, Philip 49
· Titus, Anthony 94
· Trone, Jennifer 17
· Tsao, Calvin 42
· Tsien, Billie 42, 69
· Tsurumaki, Marc 24, 54
· Vali, Murtaza 92
· Vobis, Yasmin 34
· Vrachliotis, Georg 30
· Vucic, Jelena 30
· Weisz, Claire 84
· Whiting, Sarah 38
· Williams, Tod 42
· Witt, Andrew 8
· Yao, Kim 49
· Young, Michael 8
· Zell, Mo 8
· Zuliani, Guido 38

....
Retrospecta 42

Editors
· Natalie Broton
· Ives Brown
· Colin Chudyk
· Sze Wai Justin Kong

Graphic Designers
· Maria Candanoza
· Nicholas Weltyk

Photography
· Sara Alajmi
· A.J. Artemel
· David Bruce
· Davis Butner
· Nicole Doan
· Kate Fisher
· Zelig Fok
· Norman Foster Foundation
· Michael Gasper
· Kerry Garikes
· Orli Hakanoglu
· Isabel Balda Moncayo
· Iven Peh
· Kassandra Leiva
· Jacob Schaffert
· Baolin Shen
· Christopher Tritt
· Kay Yang
· Issy Yi
· Winston Yuen
· Yale Manuscripts & Archives

Design Consultant
· Michael Bierut
· Pentagram, New York

Printer
· Rich Kaplan
· Allied Printing Services, Manchester, CT

Sincere Gratitude to
· AJ Artemel
· Deborah Berke
· Zelma Brunson
· Richard DeFlumeri
· Jessica Dooling
· Sheila Levrant de Bretteville
· Jessica Quagliaroli
· Nina Rappaport
· Rosemary Watts
· Donna Wetmore
· The faculty, staff, and students of YSoA

ISBN 978-1-948765-33-6

Distributed by Actar D
440 Park Avenue South
17th Floor
New York, NY 100016
www.actar.com

For more information and copies
of this book, please
write, call,
or visit us at:

Yale School of Architecture
Third Floor
180 York Street
New Haven, CT 06511
+1.203.432.2288
www.architecture.yale.edu

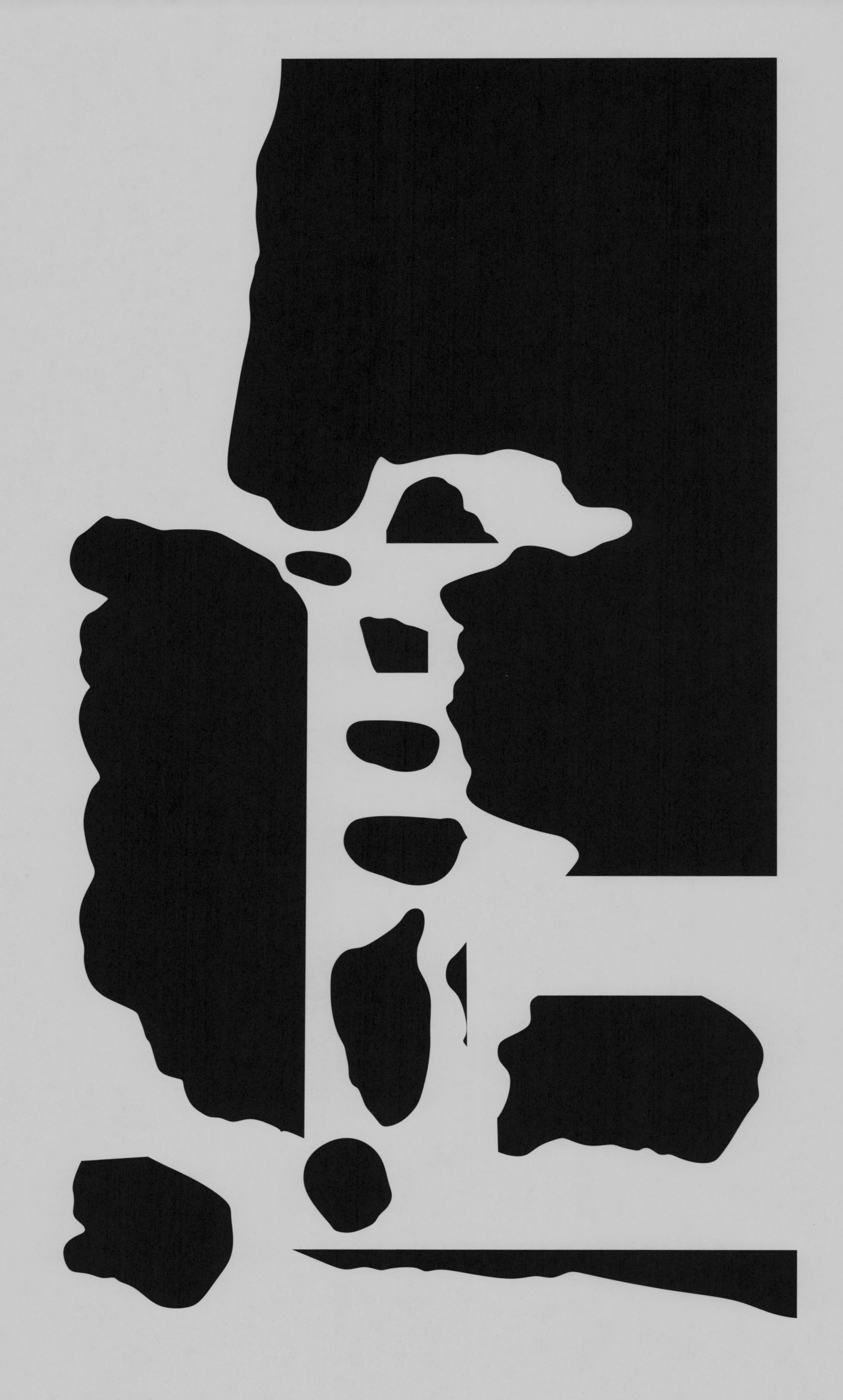

Studio
Spring 2019
1114b Advanced Design Studio
Yolande Daniels, Gary He

This studio studies "Thresholds" in Japanese architecture. The threshold is a potent architectural trope and physical demarcation of boundaries that reveals cultural approaches to space-making when examined across cultures. The studio focuses on a range of threshold conditions found in temple interiors and grounds, Zen gardens, and castles. Students studied the metaphorical and literal space of gates, the elongated pause of entry as shoe removal, material changes, and a step up demarcate the shift from exterior to interior spaces; and, the mechanics of sliding doors in temples, houses, and shops versus hinged doors in gates and military battlements.

Students researched in the form of hand drawings and photographs of architecture and details to represent the transitions inherent in crossing a variety of thresholds. The studio trip focused on examples found in both contemporary and traditional Japanese architecture and serve as a springboard for a semester long architectural exploration of thresholds for an assigned architectural project sited in Japan.

Participants
Kate Altmann, Lani Barry, Taiming Chen, Kate Fisher, Dimitris Hartonas, Jennifer Lai, Kassandra Leiva, Smit Patel, Abigail Smith, Vivian Tsai, Katrina Yin

Jury
Emily Abruzzo, Pier Vittorio Aureli, Joe Day, Lisa Gray, Walter Hood, Yoko Kawai, V. Mitch McEwen, Toshiko Mori, Annabelle Selldorf

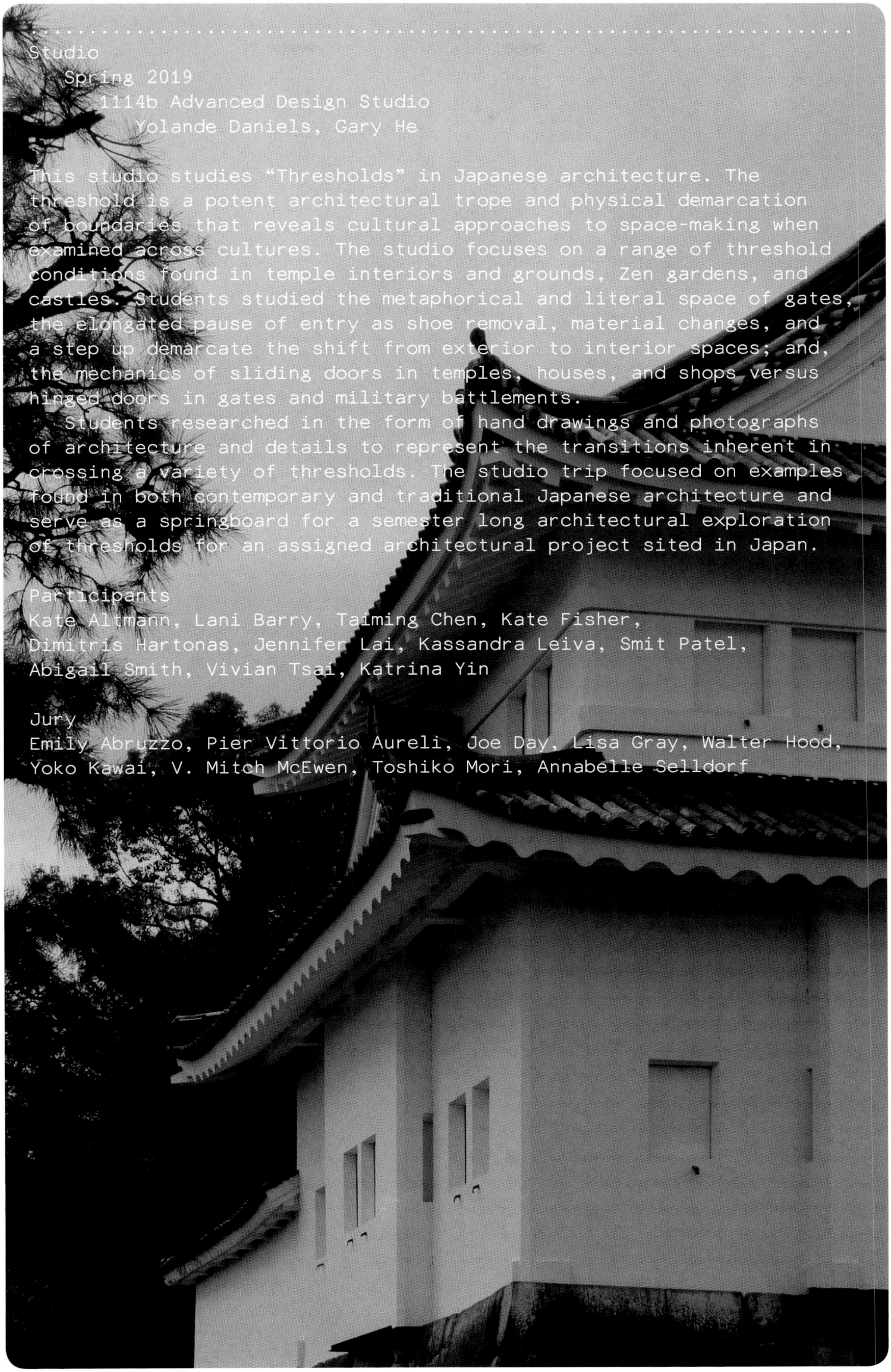

A series of simple small serial units

TM: Beyond the pragmatic, the site plan is a completely miniaturized version of Chiba; it's actually denser. It's more like minimal living, quite different from Chiba, of course, a very different lifestyle. It's like a cat house! *laughter*

EA: Well it's not a minimal dwelling, right? It's a dwelling that has a room to expand to other types of collective space, that are greater than the minimal dwelling.

PVA: I think the potential of the minimal dwelling idea, in Japan where domestic labor has been repressed, is to allow people to have their own private space, a respite from socialization. Many other functions that are not privatized within the home are opened up and shared among the inhabitants. I think your plan responds very well to that: they're gradients, gradients of privacy and gradients of sharing. If that is the principle, to me, there are too many kitchens.

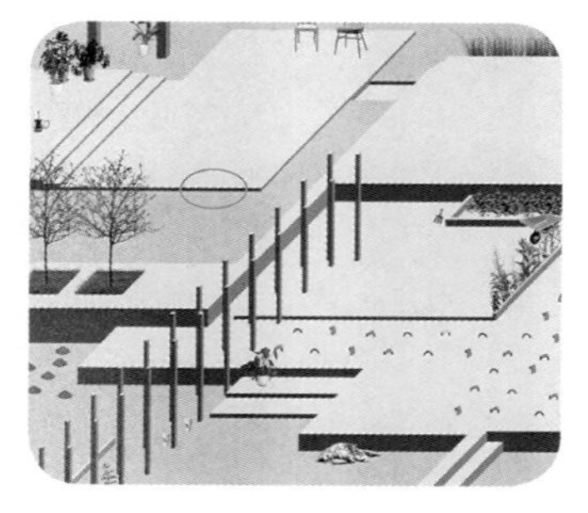

Fujimoto's project in Itabu aims to attract visitors to the quiet rural villages of Chiba, Japan. Beyond the unique and eccentric experience of the infamous and much photographed public toilet, the site of Itabu station offers a quiet and exquisite landscape. The relationship between the Shiriyama Shrine, just adjacent to the site, the existing train station, and Fujimoto's project are not considered as part of a coherent visitor experience. The project for the site formalizes the relationship between these elements, choreographing a path between them and highlighting particular views of the landscape. The path thus turns the current ten minute experience of Fujimoto's project into a much longer one, encouraging visitors to dwell for a greater period in the vicinity and venture into the amenities of Itabu proper. This project titled, "Thresholds: West | East", seeks to understand how a series of simple small serial units can be used as a system across the shifting topography of the site, in order to produce a distinct experience of the landscape.

A continuous, seamless series of threshold experiences

JD: Ten or twenty years ago there was the crisis of the library. Would books become obsolete and libraries become unnecessary? But since then, people have figured out that libraries are these incredible gathering spaces and social condensers for different generations, classes, public needs. I like your scheme a lot. In a way, I want to point to the reinvention of the library, acknowledge it, take on where you're taking that trajectory anew. But in this context, I have a feeling there may be more novelty to that move in Japan. Certainly, bringing older and younger residents together, given the demographic realities of Japan, is a huge issue you're taking on.

YD: You have such a sensitivity to the images you've studied to the relationship of the body through light and passage. It does seem like there could be a very specific initiation for the nature of transitioning from outside to inside. Right now, it seems that you want variety, but it's not clear that it's happening.

This project is based on the studies of threshold, which is defined as "LINKAGE/GREY SPACE", a space neither exterior nor interior. Located along the Biwa Canal in Kyoto and surrounded by the new Kyoto City University of Arts, the project is programmed as a library for the symbiosis of the community, which extends the university library and creates a threshold experience of life along the canal. The architectural design of the library itself is a grey space, which links different community programs for the young and old ages through a continuous, seamless series of threshold experiences. Guided by bookshelves embedded in walls, users perceive the grey space from subtle moments of moving from one space to another. The entire project has a constant interplay of solid and void, opaque and transparent to blur the boundaries between the inside and outside, as well as architecture and landscape along the canal.

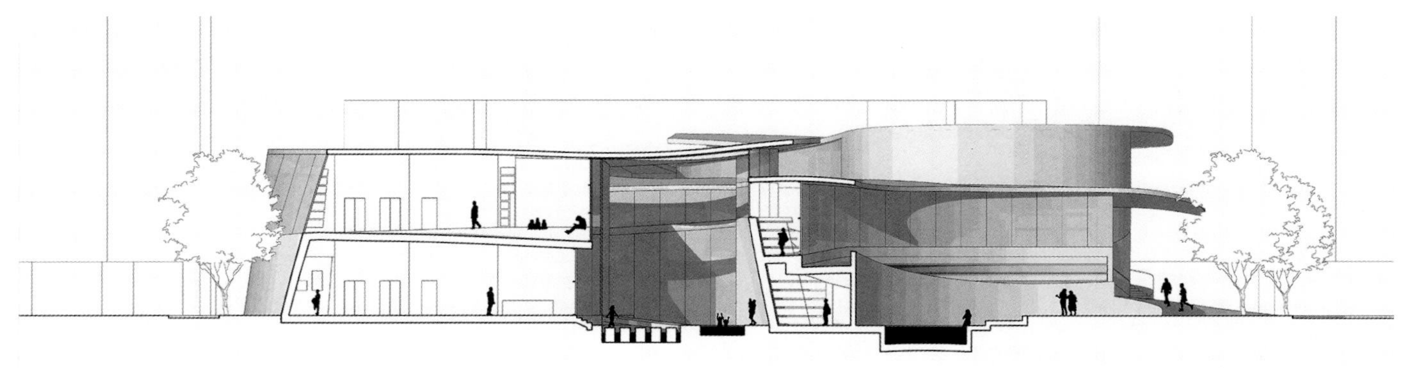

Speed as a phenomenon of thresholds

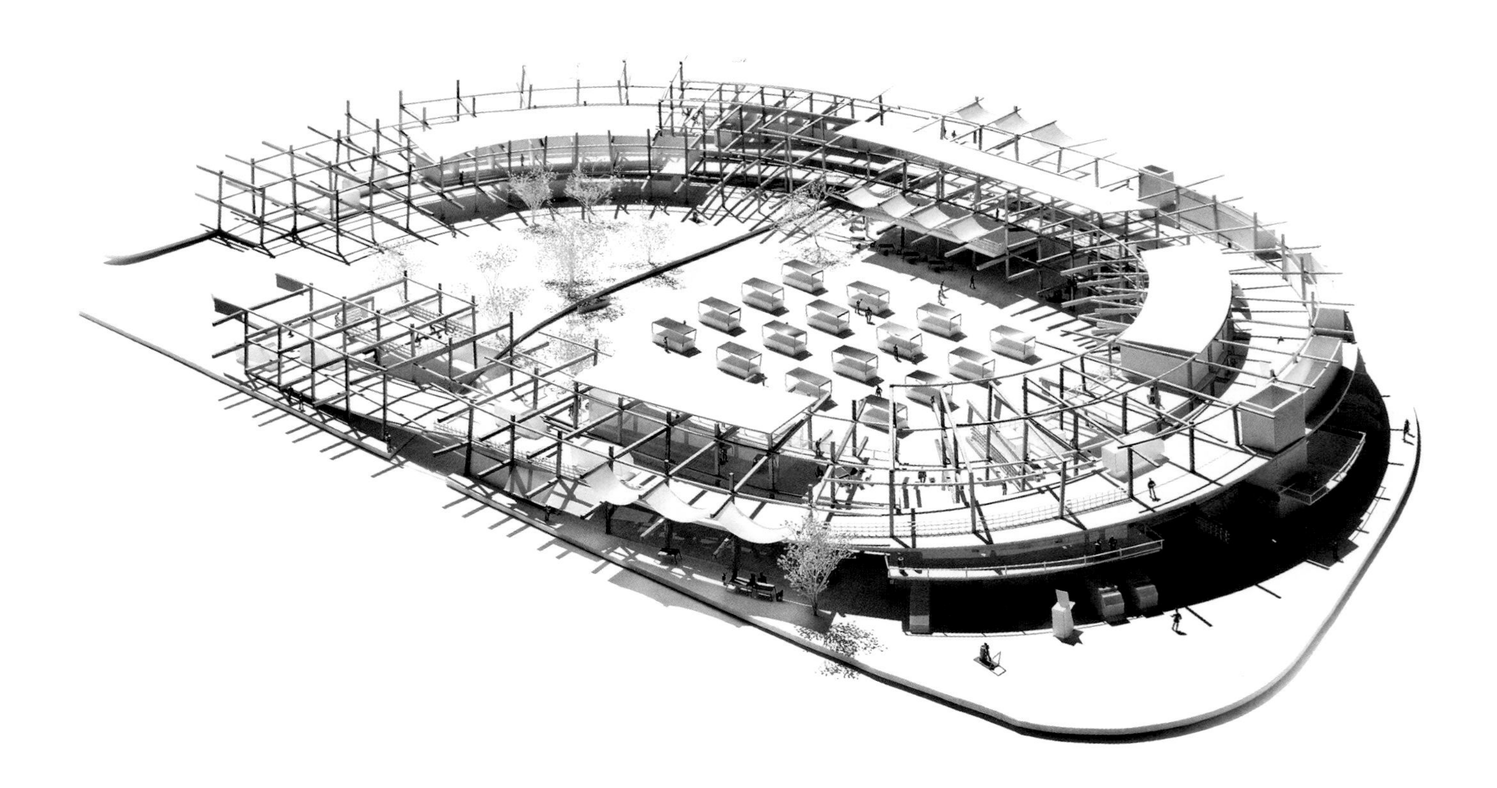

This project hosts different velocities of activities within an urban market as informed by an exploration of speed as a phenomenon of thresholds. It is an infrastructure that initiates interactions between locals, Burakumin, and newcomers (students and tourists) in Suujin, Kyoto. The project organizes people according to activities and requisite speed, replacing social categorization previously of this site.

The market is a place where all constituencies exchange goods, values, time, and experiences. The project encourages active participation through diminishing the distance between market front of house and back of house. Two vehicular ramps generate the armature of the project form. Burakumin and newcomers take on roles of market vendors, part timers, buyers, and auction participants. Different occupational speeds—sidewalk, stalls, cafeteria, offices—radiate offset from the two paths.

PVA: Actually, looking at your project, what's really interesting is the choice of the market. We know in many cultures, markets are places of loose relationships. In fact, many governments have always tried to formalize those markets because they knew that markets were always dangerous places: places of business, places of trade, of change, and often, of uprise. So with the market, it always has acted as a kind of hotbed where relationships between people are not controlled.

EA: I think her architecture points to that. Your building is a scaffold, correct? And I think that's super interesting for a variety of reasons. This is one question I have: could the temporary activities of the middle have a similar relationship to the scaffold as the more permanent programs of the edge? You could think of your scaffold as something that's not deterministic about the site, not deterministic about the ramp but rather, a way of analyzing neighborhoods. It is not just this site but other sites also. I'm thinking about this kind of market infrastructure that is maybe very light and not built up much at all.

Studio

Spring 2019

1115b Advanced Design Studio

Sandra Barclay, Jean Pierre Crousse, Andrew Benner

The Northern coast of Peru has been experiencing the effects of climate change for 5000 years. The El Niño-Southern Oscillation (ENSO) has created severe climatic and cultural disturbances in Peru and widely scattered areas all over the world. It has affected the civilizations that flourished there, causing both involuntary and organized migrations over centuries. Piura, a booming region in the North of Peru, has the potential to be a laboratory for responses to climate change. The resilience of its low-income rural population to recurrent ENSO phenomena can inform how traditional low-tech construction can be reinterpreted today to face global warming.

The studio analyzed how present inhabitants of Piura cope with extreme climate events in order to imagine a different approach to technology and the act of building. Students designed an Innovation Center for Resilient Building Knowledge in Narihualá (Piura), a village heavily affected by rain and flooding during the 2017 ENSO.

Participants

David Bruce, Gretchen Gao, Ryan Hughes, Minakshi Mohanta, Iven Peh, Anna Rothschild, Miguel Sanchez-Enkerlin, Priyanka Sheth, Luke Studebaker, Melissa Weigel, Ethan Zisson

Jury

Anthony Acciavatti, Marta Caldeira, Angelo Bucci, Thomas Phifer, Beka Sturges, Claire Weisz, Tod Williams

The architecture bobs on either side of the flood line

Once a decade, the El Niño phenomenon transforms the desert of Northern Peru into an inundated valley. In Narihaulá, one of the few spaces of communal refuge is the Huaca, an adobe pyramid—or artificial mountain—built by a pre-Incan Civilization called the Tallán. This project considers how reshaping the site's terrain can create multi-functional high-ground on the edge of the city. A cut-and-fill strategy establishes new ground above the flood line for community houses. Below, grade is closer to ground water for an agricultural research and natural-building material innovation center. The architecture bobs on either side of the flood line. Dry, technical research spaces are positioned above workshop spaces that can flood. During the Niño, void spaces of the artificial ridgeline are transformed into surface for refuge. After the Niño, the structure becomes a laboratory. Infill panels are rebuilt with material from agricultural spaces of the innovation center. This interplay requires a co-evolution; the building and its environment evolve and change on parallel courses. In this light, El Niño is not a catastrophic episode, but part of an ongoing and regenerative process of constructing and maintaining architecture. Inspired by Stan Allen's provocation in his introduction to Landform Building, "Architecture is situated between the biological and the geological—slower than living things but faster than the underlying geology", this project imagines that resilient architecture can emerge from a spectrum multitude of strategies: the geologic reshaping of ground and construction itself as a cyclical response to climate events.

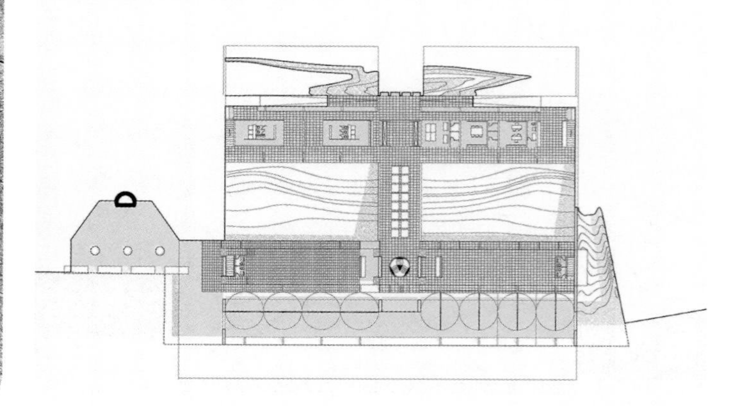

TW: It's wonderful.
I guess I'll come back to something I've said before: what would be the first unit you'd make and what would be the second?

DB: This might be a bad answer, but I've adapted the program to that existing frame of the housing. Tom had a comment during midterms, to be really aware of the east/west fabric. So each edge is rotated to speak to these natural channels. So I think there's an argument that this could be done incrementally and work in blocks, but then it loses effect if it's only one small piece.

BS: I'm intrigued by this discussion about how it is made. Because I do wonder about the idea that architecture could set up the front edge. How would you then backfill this new mesa? The way you would do it is not the way you'd do it here: just steal a bunch of dirt from somewhere else. Is there a way to think about the way they used to make this that may be a part of the industry that other places could use?

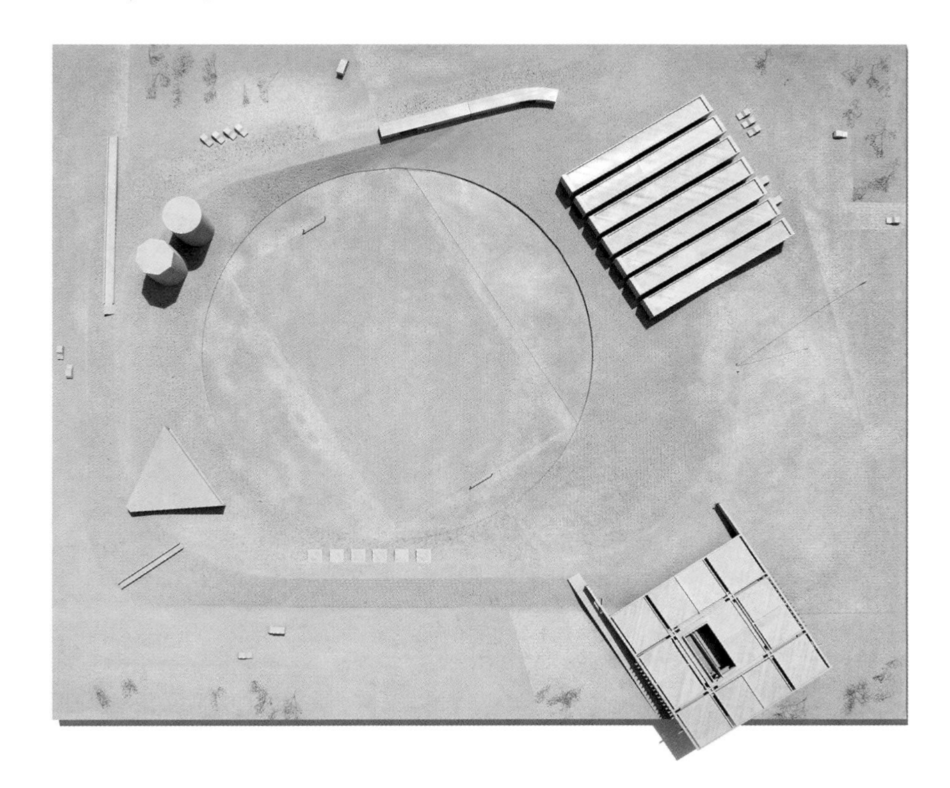

Bounded by its section, not its plan

Over the past three decades, climatic conditions associated with global warming have transformed the landscape in northern Peru. This is most clearly illustrated by an increased water supply from melting ice in the Andes which has accelerated the growth of new agricultural economies in the lower lying desert valley. These same conditions have also exacerbated the effects of El Niño related storm events, causing disastrous flooding in the region.

These key issues are illustrated clearly on our immediate site. Structured by an agricultural economy, the village of Narihuala is an informal settlement with very limited access to basic services. The majority of occupants in the village live without immediate access to clean drinking water or sanitation services. Furthermore, the entire village floods with upwards of three to four meters of water during the El Niño every ten to fifteen years causing most of the inhabitants to rebuild their homes from scratch.

The project is an earthen stadium, an inverted huaca, which protects a dry zone at its center. This place becomes a space for large community gatherings whether that is a football game or a farmers market. A series of community buildings sit on the rim of the mound. Characterized as utility buildings, material workshops, research labs, and a school, these buildings are elevated above the El Niño flood line. During storm events, these community buildings also provide space for an emergency command center, a health clinic, as well as water and food storage. Learning from past scenarios of sports stadiums as storm shelters, the project is characterized by an open perimeter which is bounded by its section, not its plan.

CW: I have a very emotional response to this project. In a lot of ways I'm just grateful for you putting it out there. It says, in a way, that we may have to build things that are very clear and important. They have all of the things that we need to have: a school, a market, a production of food, in places that honor the fact that we have to have dialogue about the things that we've done and forced poorer people to do that actually won't work and won't last. This is much more clear, but elegant, industrial—a substantial response. I guess I'm having a very positive but strong reaction. Just putting that out there—this level of environment in volume and investment in space.

TW: I agree. Super elegant presentation, elegant thinking. I love it. Now, you're planning to make more of these, but I can only afford half of this project. What are the first three to four things you would say are most solid in terms of things we must do? Does the whole composition have to occur, are all of the elements critical?

RH: I think it's shown clearly in the way I've designed this building, the shed. In that model it's shown as six modules. Here I simply added a seventh. But the idea was that the whole thing could start off with the mound and just one of these bars.

Digging down and piling up

Resiliency in architecture is not simply a question of buildings surviving severe rain, or dramatic flooding. Neither is it solely about the ability to host temporary housing for displaced human beings. Rather, it is about the permanence and enduring qualities that the form of architecture can offer, so that a building can have many lifetimes. This proposal is an undulating landscape upon which generic buildings are built. The landscape responds in section, taking precedent from the Waru Waru, digging down and piling up, to create fertile and safe ground intermittently. These site incisions set the stage for fertile agricultural areas and are the base for the five long bar buildings. All of them—the school, the community center, the workshops, and the labs—are rehearsals of the same type. A slab is elevated by a mound—the shaping of ground and differentiation of space. A ten meter grid of columns and walls, together with stair cores and service walls, supports the most potent element of the buildings: an overhanging roof whose hanging walls provide shading and calibrate views. Incisions into this roof ensure sufficient light and ventilation to all usable space. The top of this roof is readily accessible, inhabitable, and safely above the flood-line. Achieving a transcendent quality in the architecture is true resiliency. In its ability to adapt to a post-program period—be it an El Niño event, a dystopian future, or simply a future we cannot imagine—the building engages questions that we don't yet know how to ask.

CW: You keep talking about the paradigm, what architecture leaves... The cultural or deep questions are open-ended. The form itself leaves you with something, right? To me, that's a really interesting starting point. I love that model, maybe because I feel like it's about architecture questioning the shadow it makes. In this case, there's no question: the building depends on the landscape to be there. That's the statement. To me, the question is, what does that mean to you, actually?

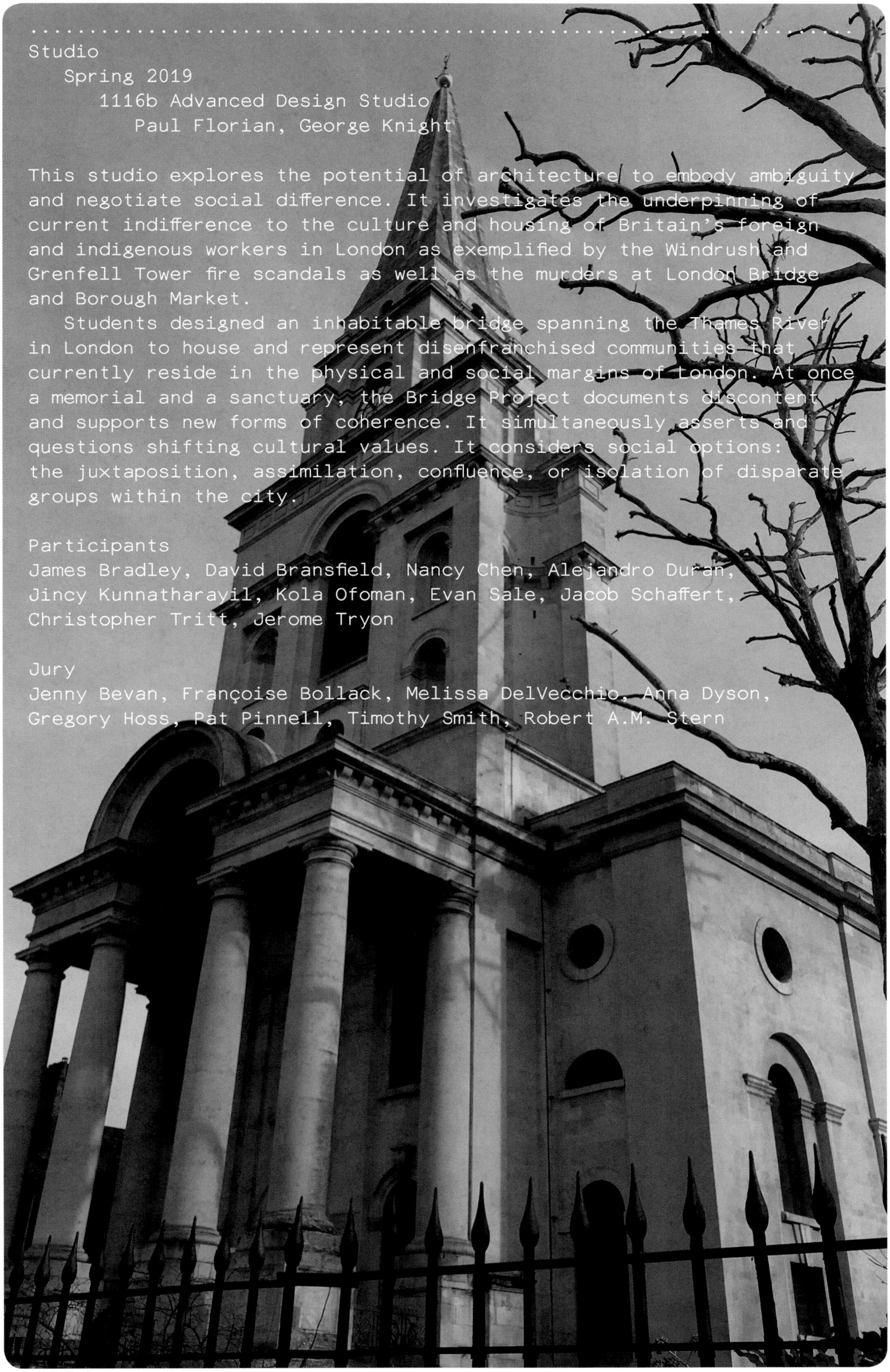

Studio
Spring 2019
1116b Advanced Design Studio
Paul Florian, George Knight

This studio explores the potential of architecture to embody ambiguity and negotiate social difference. It investigates the underpinning of current indifference to the culture and housing of Britain's foreign and indigenous workers in London as exemplified by the Windrush and Grenfell Tower fire scandals as well as the murders at London Bridge and Borough Market.

Students designed an inhabitable bridge spanning the Thames River in London to house and represent disenfranchised communities that currently reside in the physical and social margins of London. At once a memorial and a sanctuary, the Bridge Project documents discontent and supports new forms of coherence. It simultaneously asserts and questions shifting cultural values. It considers social options: the juxtaposition, assimilation, confluence, or isolation of disparate groups within the city.

Participants
James Bradley, David Bransfield, Nancy Chen, Alejandro Duran, Jincy Kunnatharayil, Kola Ofoman, Evan Sale, Jacob Schaffert, Christopher Tritt, Jerome Tryon

Jury
Jenny Bevan, Françoise Bollack, Melissa DelVecchio, Anna Dyson, Gregory Hoss, Pat Pinnell, Timothy Smith, Robert A.M. Stern

RS: I smell the coffee and I want another cup. *laughter* I think the drawings are amazing; they're beautiful. The scheme really answers many questions that were raised in the previous scheme. Your precedent study for the Acropolis really opened up a new direction, which was great. The multi-level concept–although I can't decide–will the bicycle level have natural light?

JK: There will be.

RS: Otherwise it would be ready for the Clockwork Orange movie–seems like a good idea. *laugher* But your scheme is a marriage of Schinkel and Behrens, which is great. The hous-ing seems, in an effort to make it more vernacular, to just fall flat. It's not architecturally up to the same level as the rest of it.

A potential theater of experiences

The bridge is a microcosm of the city itself. It is both a connector and a place. Multiple public spaces promote engagement to allow needed water access to London residents and new places to explore their own city. The bridge complements and respects city views, becomes an extended piece of the fabric of London, and provides a sense of belonging for its users. The bridge is a rich network of places that transforms space into a potential theater of experiences. Episodic moments on the bridge vary from fast to slow spaces and direct to indirect pathways. The simple action of walking across the bridge produces a multiplicity of experiences as the views compress and release. To cross the bridge is an ever-changing experience that remains unique with each encounter.

Medium: Pencil.

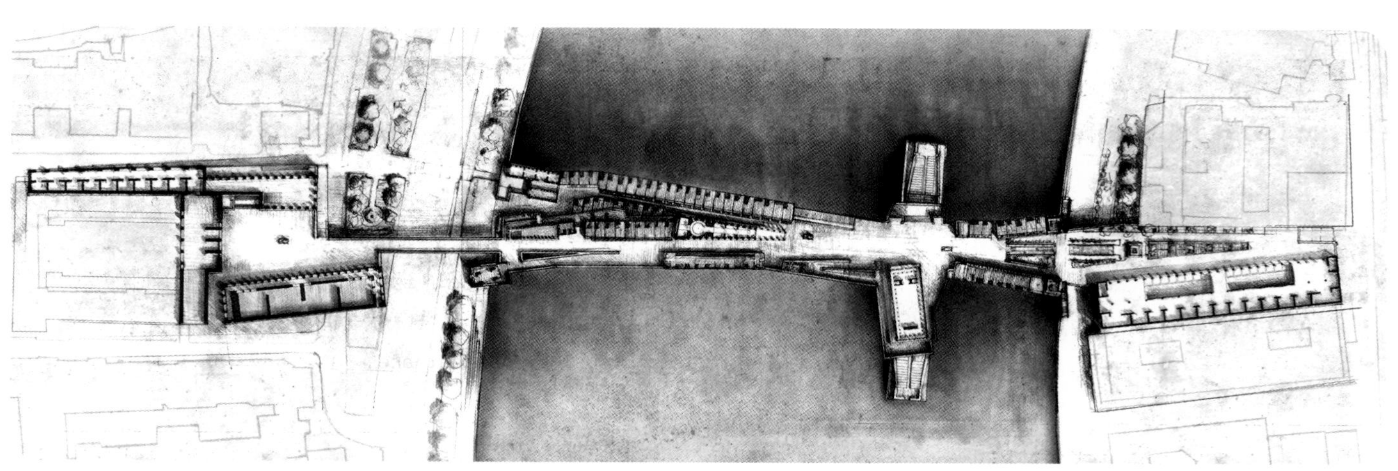

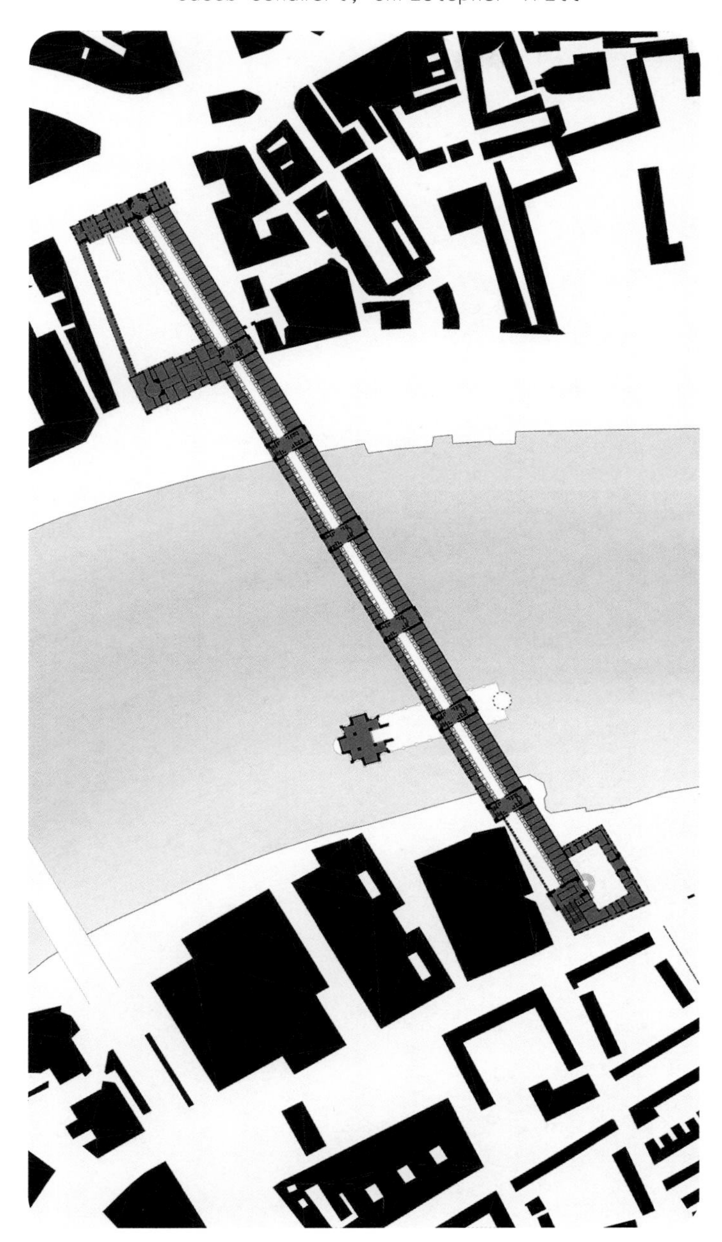

The bridge is a neighborhood

London is becoming a landscape of glassy skyscrapers, faceless giants, dipping their toes into the fabric of cities around the world. Our bridge is a counterpoint to these anonymous modern forms as a building that is embedded in the experience and place of the city of London. We utilize a classical architectural expression to emphasize our rejection of the glass skyscraper and reassert the prominence and importance of the residential block to the city center. The bridge is a neighborhood that spans the Thames, announcing itself to the Strand and integrating into the fabric of Southwark. Our proposal utilizes the latent forms of the urban fabric of the site. We looked to a lineage of English housing typologies, classical organization, and great works of British classical architecture to create moments of surprise and excitement along our modern interpretation of a London neighborhood.

RS: The hard thing to do is to interpret a language from any period in relationship to some of the annoying factors of 21st century life. One of which is the car. The other is need for recreational space. The third of which is the need for convenient shopping. You have this market that's there—but that seems—Saturday morning the farmers come in. It's not like you can't do it, but you haven't tried. That's the part that makes me a little unhappy.

JS: I think there are two attitudes to the city we've had. One, looking at the neighborhood and seeing what is necessary for the kind of local scale of the block. So we've included things like small businesses that are block-level urban infrastructure. And the market at either end is a larger version—a kind of bodega or corner store. As far as a much larger infrastructure, we've said that we see the rest of the city as part of it. We didn't want to make it completely self-contained so people still need to go into the city to go to other civic institutions or larger supermarkets.

Studio
Spring 2019
1117b Advanced Design Studio
Todd Reisz

This studio addresses the design of a new city that acknowledges the transient nature of city populations: configuring its rules of engagement, its economies, and, of course, its forms. This new city is based on the presumption that cities have been freed from their mythical sense of permanence. With that, they have been released from illusions of *belonging* and, in the end, might therefore be more humane and more welcoming for international migrants, refugees, and those crossing borders.

The studio's site is, in some ways, Dubai (United Arab Emirates). It was the semester's ongoing case study for investigating the temporary nature of urban living. A counter to Dubai will be Amman (Jordan), where the studio investigated an entirely different manifestation of the urban temporary. Dubai is not endowed with the myth of permanent cities. In fact, many critics have envisioned Dubai's collapse at cataclysmic scales, even its physical dismantling by the blowback from its own hubris. The studio inspected how the city has materialized over the last sixty years for and by a dynamic, global population, and how it can act as a precedent for a new city.

Participants
Sara Alajmi, Lara AlKhouli, Dana AlMathkoor, Isabel Balda Moncayo, Katherine Barymow, Brian Cash, Erin Kim, Melissa Russell, Mariana Sao Pedro Riobom Dos Santos, Justin Tsang, Matthew Wagstaffe

Jury
Saima Akhtar, Sultan Sooud Al Qassemi, Sandra Barclay, Tabitha Decker, Noora Lori, Bimal Mendis, Murtaza Vali

Beit means house

This project titled “Beit” is a transnational collective housing corporation that tackles the issues of housing and refuge on an international scale. The project is set in the future and is imagined to be founded in 2020 by a group of people in reaction to the struggles of economic migrants in Dubai, UAE. It was founded by using remittances from migrant workers and investing wealth in a shared property that transcended place, to make Beit users also shareholders. The purpose of the corporation is to expand the concept of ‘home’ across different properties and countries through a system that allows its users to move freely and live in different places. Thus, Beit owns and renovates affordable vacant buildings, whether abandoned or partially empty—even vanity height skyscrapers. The properties include Dubai Expo labor camp, which was empty after 2020 and thus renovated. Beit uses a platform with users profiles to facilitate their movement. Beit means house in Arabic.

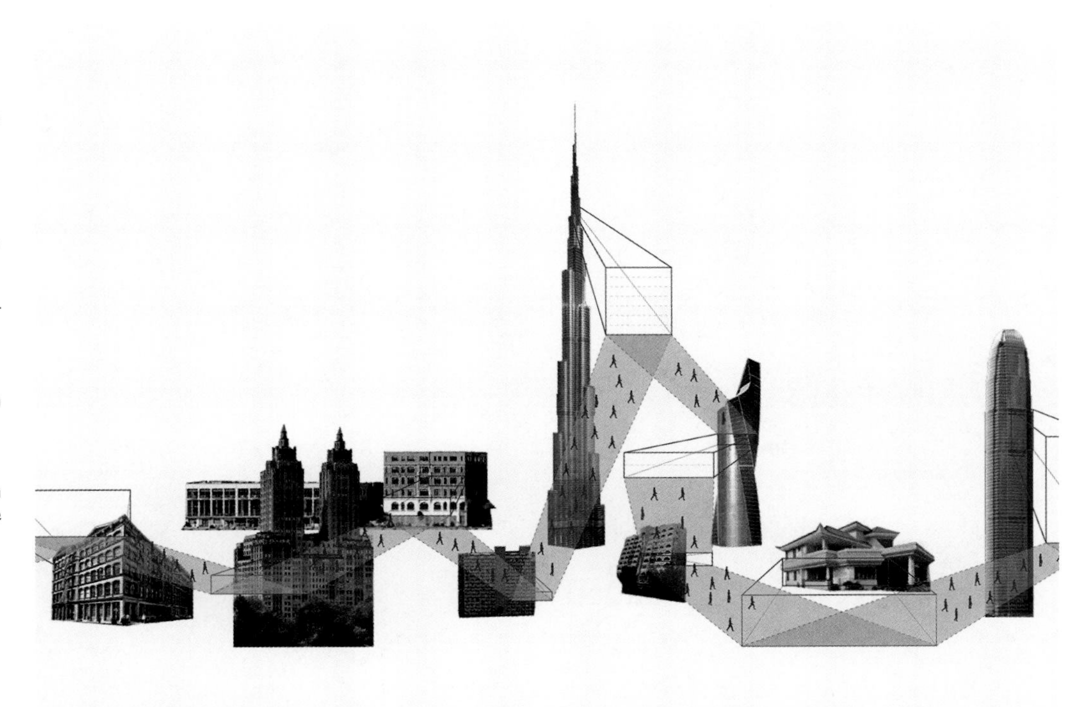

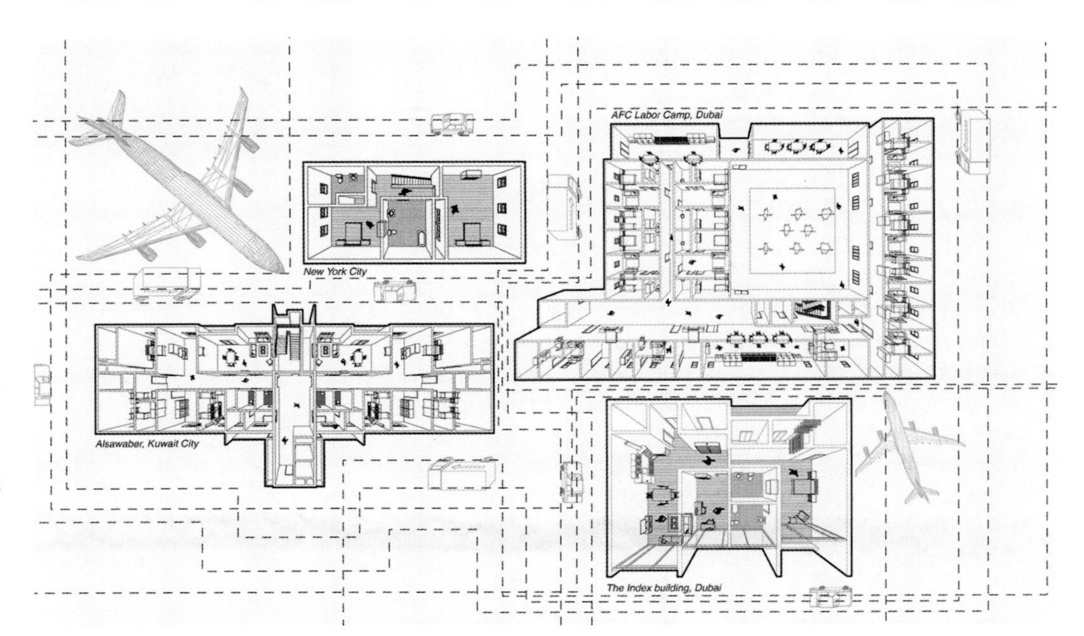

SAQ: I think this idea of reusing empty properties is something that can be a real way to recognize a citizen. Now the tendency is to work at home. I think it is important to integrate the unit, the place for work. When you are moving every two or three years, it opens the possibility to not only work in one office, but worldwide. Also, I think it is important—now that I am looking at how you organize the space in accordance to the idea. If this is a place to gather people, I think it’s important to think about how they live as a community. Also, little things, like common spaces must open to the outdoors. To connect them to the whole—this is very important.

NL: How do you propose to circumvent the segregation of communities? In the UAE, you have the Arabs who have segregated themselves. You have the South Asians, the Europeans, the Africans and now Latin Americans; and they all came to live in separate quarters. I think this is a missed opportunity for people to integrate and mix together. How do you propose, to number one, cater to the needs of different communities? I saw you used the Kuwait project in your presentation, which was heavily criticized for not taking into consideration the Kuwaiti needs. And now it’s being demolished.

SA: Some of the structures are adjusted to the sizes of the families. To the Kuwaiti project, the issue was—my first project in architecture school was a renovation of the project. What I did was I created an entire plot for a typical Kuwaiti family. But you can’t push the idea of creating communities because they’re going to happen no matter what. But if you give them a tool such as this, they might choose to live in a community.

Studio
Spring 2019
1117b Advanced Design Studio
Todd Reisz
Dana AlMathkoor, Brian Cash, Melissa Russell

Mass unexpected movement need not be unexpected

To the untrained eye, "The Passage" may appear to be nothing more than a train, a road, or a bridge. But to those who can lift the veil, The Passage is an unparalleled network of movement. Each day, millions of railcars, units of cargo, and people flow through the sovereign space of The Passage. It is in the spaces between major urban areas that the potential of The Passage is seen most clearly, where the profound impact on livelihoods of individuals is incontestable. The Passage allows cities and the spaces in-between to absorb the strengths and stressors that the region at-large has encountered in the past and will continue to encounter. Mass unexpected movement need not be unexpected. No longer is one city asked to solve all problems by itself; instead, a network of resources, revenues, and memories aid in that process continuing to develop before its eyes.

TB: Something that's very interesting to me in how you're framing this is that it could be shared among cities. Historically, this issue, especially in the 19th and 20th centuries, tended to develop as a national project. We haven't seen this take off in this region yet. What you're describing sounds more like a collaborative agreement and is now transcending that model. It is really interesting; it's still a little mysterious to me.

ML: First, I really like the focus on the city. Cities are the major host for migrant populations, and they often are even when national governments are not supportive. So you see that variation in the US context–you definitely see it in the Middle East. I think Istanbul is a really great example because Istanbul has a very large migrant population.The other thing I really like about this project is thinking about migrant populations and building something infrastructural as opposed to short-term gain that is meant to break down. So what you're providing is something that is actually an investment in these cities long-term for the host population. That is one of the strongest points.

Studio
Spring 2019
1117b Advanced Design Studio
Todd Reisz
Erin Kim, Mariana Riobom, Justin Tsang, Matthew Wagstaffe (Feldman Nominees)

We do not view our investments abstractly

Archinvest Global

We harness the power of novel financial instruments and high-level spatial analysis to fund and implement projects that expand the educational, financial, and social opportunities of populations in the developing world.

Unlike other financial portfolio managers, we do not view our investments abstractly. We believe that the financial success of a project is dependent on its spatial properties and urban location—that's why each project we invest in is co-led by a financial analyst and an architect/urban designer.

While our financial specialists undertake the quantitative analysis, ensuring that the numbers indicate a strong return on investment, our architects analyze the urban environment, confirming that the projects we invest in connect to the key transportation networks and social spaces that enable them to serve the populations for which they are intended. We connect high level investors in the social impact sector with crowdsourced donations from the excess remittance payments of migrant worker populations. Together this novel investor class is able to invest in social services.

NL: Congratulations on finding a way to harness capitalism for social good. *laughter* It's impressive. I'm wondering at what point of the massive amount of land you've acquired will raise concerns. What were some of the obstacles you must have faced to overcome that?

MW: We benefited from the expansion of the prequel zone areas. Dubai's ministry of architecture was not doing very well in 2019, so the rules for foreign ownership were becoming a little more porous. Once we acquired this land and our investment started to pay off and were ready to sell, there was an official in Dubai who explained that they couldn't really afford to kick us off [the land].

Studio
Spring 2019
1118b Advanced Design Studio
Anna Dyson, Chris Sharples, Naomi Keena

North Adams, a small city in Western Massachusetts, was at one time a booming manufacturing town. After a long decline in its economy, its vast industrial infrastructure was repurposed to form MASS MoCA. As we contemplate the future of North Adams, this studio investigates some fundamental questions about how we want to manufacture products and systems in the 21st century. We face a global challenge to shift manufacturing and building practices from the current toxic, energy intensive processes towards bio-compatible methods that promote healthy ecosystems and sustainable local communities.

Students designed an Innovation Hub for the center of North Adams that connects to and galvanizes the regional base for bio-based prefabricated and modular construction and manufactured products. This studio merged the existential question of what would constitute meaningful manufacturing in the 21st Century, and how North Adams could serve as a prototype for the galvanization of a new type of manufacturing base.

Participants
Olisa Agulue, Hamzah Ahmed, Gwyneth Bacon-Shone, Kunhee Chang, Miguel Darcy de Oliveira Miranda, Hojae Lee, Dhruvin Shah, I-Ting Tsai, Anna Yu, Winston Yuen

Jury
Ruth Berktold, Lise Anne Couture, Paul Florian, Timur Galen, Walter Hood, Alan Organschi, Alexander Purves, Joel Sanders, Bill Sharples, Joe Thompson, Anthony Titus

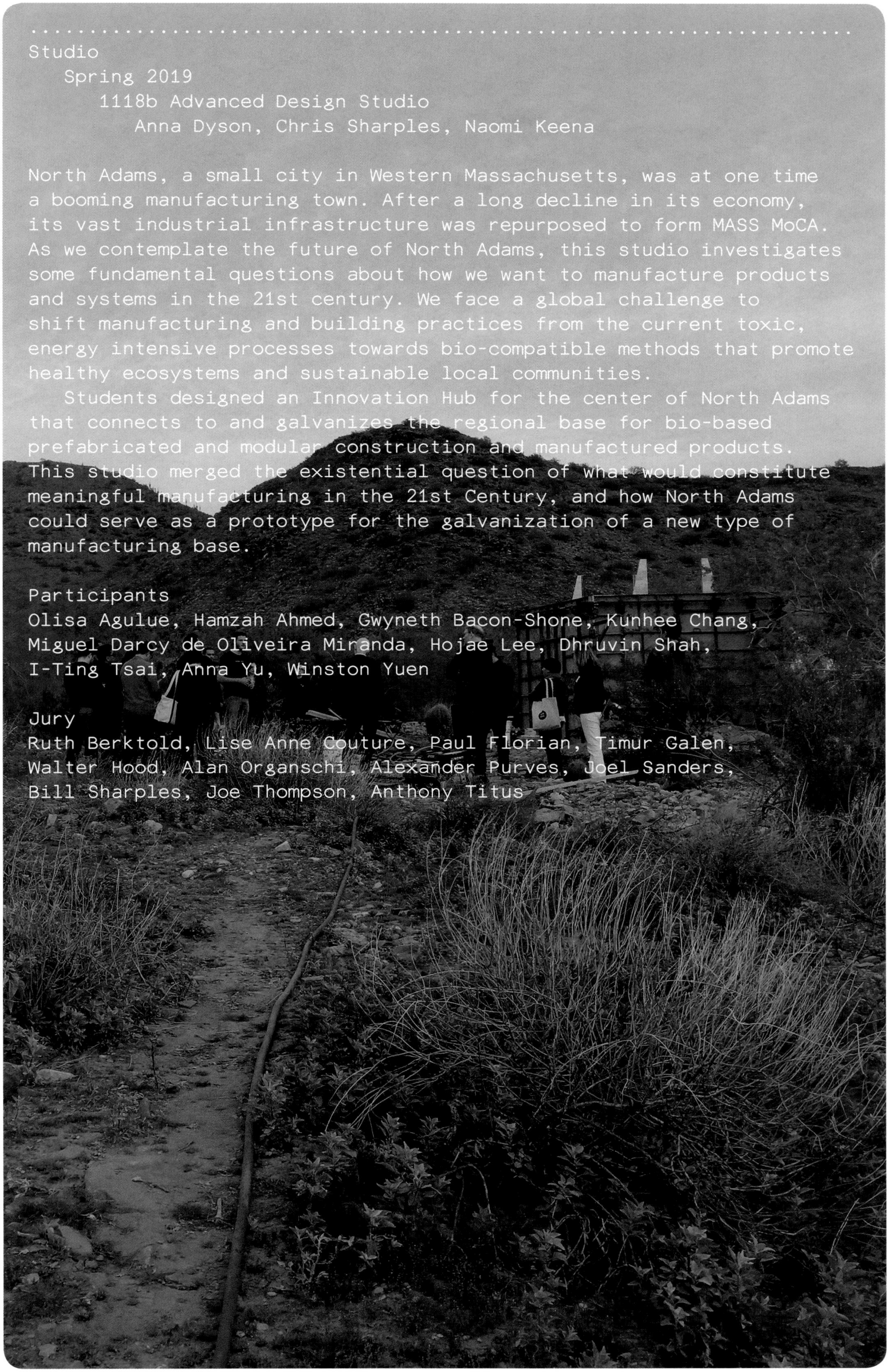

Parametric moulds of pins that shift and dance

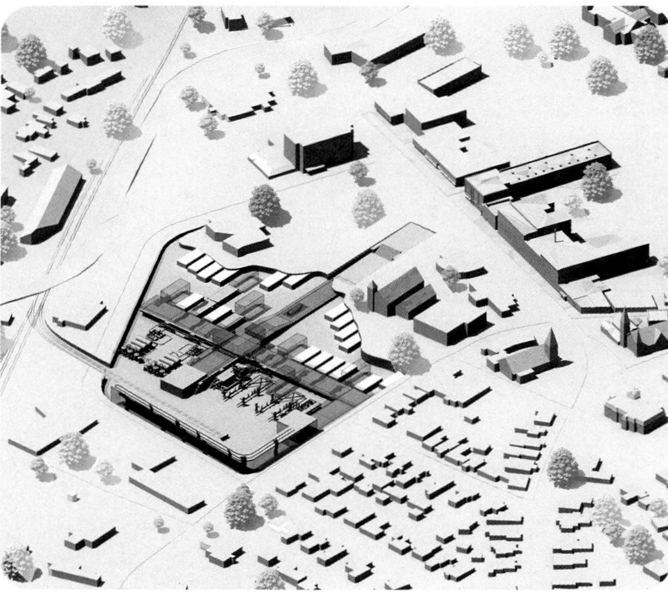

For too long, the approach towards industrial space has been to fetishise their aesthetic by either filling their historic shells with bars and art galleries or by displaying manufacturing as a sleek clean space by isolating it from its necessary "dirty" counterpart. This project instead creates a factory that embodies both its clean and dirty manufacturing in one location whilst also providing a spectacle.

On the site, the street gradually rises into an elevated public park. Below the park sits the production of a bio fibre plastic from agro waste. Above, like a forest of trees popping up throughout the park, large glass structures stand with parametric moulds of pins that shift and dance in order to press the material into any range of mass or bespoke products. The factory provides not only intrigue but also the economic and social benefits of a well designed space for the future of manufacturing.

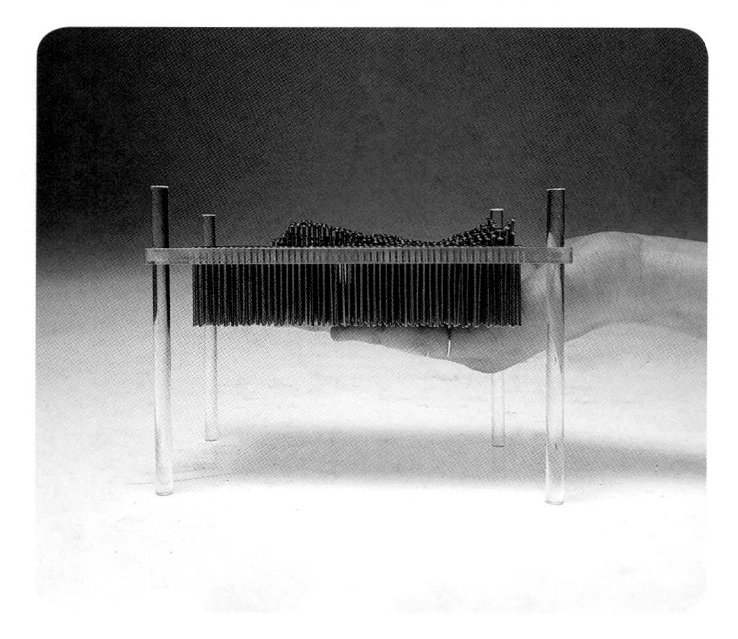

PF: I think there's a great elegance. The thing that could be added is to make this crystalline quality even better—and you'd never really be able to see into it. I was thinking if these cruciform forms actually penetrated into the landscape down into this single datum that connects all of them, this transit datum. You could use the landscape as a very generative layer to allow people to see things at different layers of construction. You could simply wander through. You could have it, very elegantly, pass through the landscape so the public can kind of see it at every stage. The site section is so intriguing in this project.

WH: It's essentially a tower in the park; a quintessential modernist tower in the park. That's it's strength. Also the strongest thing about it is the Achilles' heel to the extent that that gets challenged or infiltrated by conditions that are so multi-layered. How do you retain an idea? How do you allow an idea to have a certain amount of elasticity so that it can actually become more than the initial idea.

AO: It is interesting to me that you have, given my rough calculation, 15,000 square feet of area. Which is actually not that much for prototyping. It seems that there is this kind of hermeticism here through the closed ring. You could imagine that the architecture could allow for leakages of forms: expansions and contractions that try to program that kind of space to allow for flexibility and adjustment. So I'm wondering if that would be the next step in addressing these questions.

JT: There's not just an efficiency, but the momentum of connecting skills or accidental meetings that form directions of program. It just seems sort of like you've been very concerned with making visual connections with strangers who pass by, but less with the actual scaling of the things—the economic factor.

Prototyping campus

North Adam's close location to the Hoosic River and railroad enabled prosperity. Yet, due to the suburbanization of manufacturing facilities, North Adams has diminished into a small town with no industry. MASS MoCA is solely left in the center, occupying the remnants of industrialization. However, a museum is met with dubiety; locals claim a prison or a call center may bring more jobs. Is there a program attractive enough to revitalize the city center, as well as being reciprocal to the economy?

"NAIL—North Adams Innovation Lab" is a prototyping campus. Prototyping hubs are rapidly increasing within metropolises, and proving to be efficient business models. However, the scale is limited within typical building spaces forcing the experimental scale to be minute. Conversely, North Adams has the potential of providing generous spaces—unimaginable in city centers.

The design process involved researching machinery requirements, studying their interrelationships, and providing related public programs, all centrally towards an assembly campus that acts as a plaza, exhibition space, and cross-pollination space for innovation.

Studio
Spring 2019
1118b Advanced Design Studio
Anna Dyson, Chris Sharples, Naomi Keena
I-Ting Tsai, Winston Yuen (Feldman Nominees)

WH: So in your case, if you look at what distinguishes your scheme, you're essentially concentrating pretty much all of the interim programming under this snakeskin that covers it. In that snake you've absorbed existing programs and inserted others. So that's your idea: some existing, some new. This kind of rub between the two produces another condition which is about the future of this place. To me, that is what's interesting about the project. In regards to the site, you've said you've created a central park. What seems to me to be an interesting opportunity that I'm not yet seeing is that there is a very stark contrast between your park and your building.

A cultural corridor

Hardwood Cross-Laminated-Timber (CLT) has the potential to revitalize the manufacturing economy of the post-industrial North Adams and transform the asphalt and concrete identity of downtown with the warmth of wood. The folded timber roof, derived from origami, provides strength for the long-span roof vault that is manufacturable from flat-packable panels. The undulating form mirrors the rolling Adirondack mountains, recalling the large eaves of mountain cabins, and provides a seamless transition between disparate programs. By rethinking the factory typology into a compact and lean manufacturing model, the building is placed on an undesirable sliver of land next to the overpass. This creates a cultural corridor with MASS MoCA, Main Street, the new Train Museum, and allows for the development of a new central park in the heart of the city.

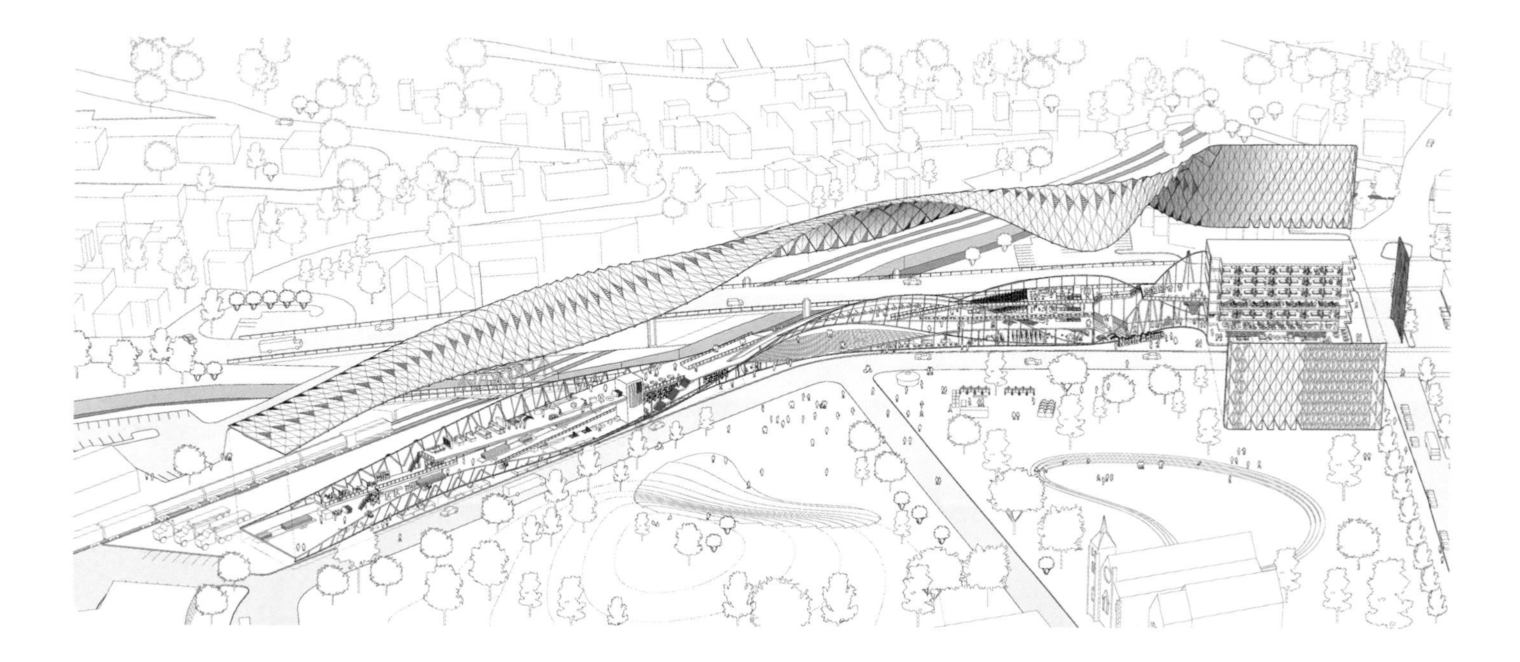

Design and Visualization

Design and Visualization Summer 2018

Design and Visualization
Summer 2018
1000c Architectural Foundations
Miroslava Brooks, Kyle Dugdale, Bimal Mendis

This summer course is an intensive, five-week immersion into the language of architectural representation and visualization, offering a basic framework upon which to build subsequent studies. Students are introduced to techniques and conventions for describing the space and substance of buildings and urban environments. In parallel to the visualization portion of this course, an introduction to architectural history and theory focuses on principal turning points of thought and practice through to the eighteenth century.

Design and Visualization
Summer 2018
1000c Architectural Foundations
Miroslava Brooks, Kyle Dugdale, Bimal Mendis
Malcolm Rondell Galang

Incomprehensible, but comprehensible

This viewing device heightens the uniquely human ability to perceive patterns of symmetry and asymmetry, and comprehend only what the human brain can make comprehensible. It brings specific parts of architecture into focus and recreates the sensation of an existing space or general environment on a smaller scale through the use of anamorphosis. By creating a distorted projection, the viewer, occupying a specific vantage point, can visually experience the intentions of the space at its original 1:1 scale. As the viewer observes one perspective, the rest of the physical model remains distorted and out of focus, helping the viewer to focus on one perspective at a time. This produces what may seem to be an incomprehensible, but comprehensible device.

Design and Visualization
Summer 2018
1000c Architectural Foundations
Miroslava Brooks, Kyle Dugdale, Bimal Mendis
Sasha Zwiebel

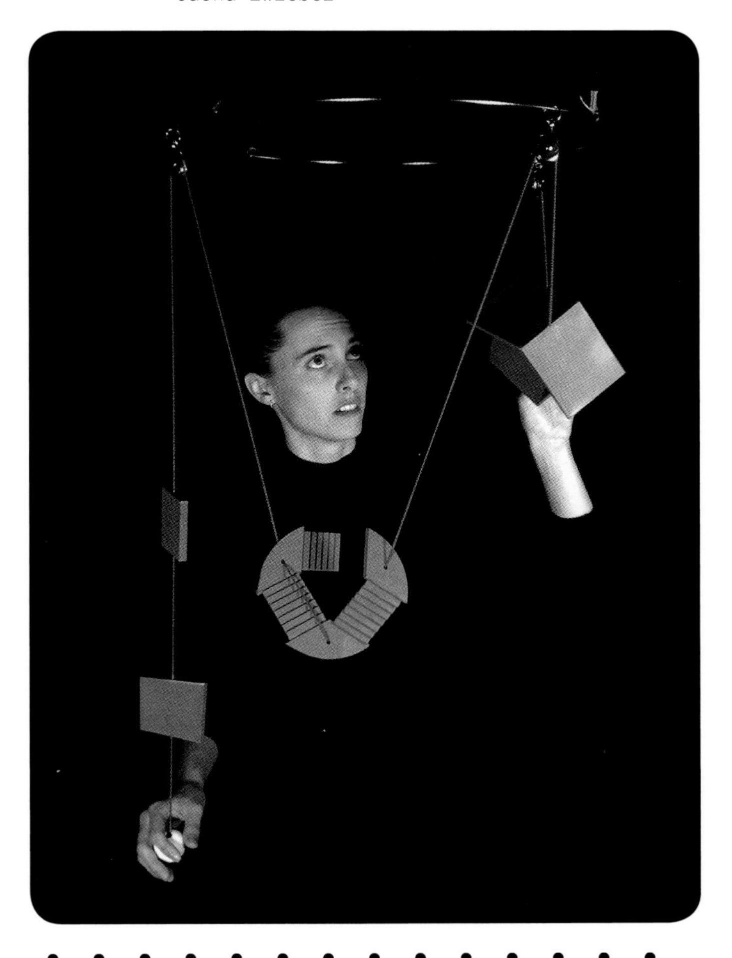

Two jewels tucked at the periphery

This project explores the relationship between the Tea Gate and the Serra sculpture garden via the Kahn staircase in the Yale University Art Gallery (YUAG). Both of these elements have a sense of discovery—they are two jewels tucked at the periphery of the museum's main circulation.

The model translates the linear circulation of the YUAG into three-dimensional space. The length of the string represents the to-scale distance between the sites. The model is ungrounded and malleable to explore the area between both objective and subjective space, and surveyed and remembered space.

Design and Visualization Fall 2018

Design and Visualization
Fall 2018
1018a Formal Analysis
Peter Eisenman, Anthony Gagliardi

This course studies the object of architecture–canonical buildings in the history of architecture–not through the lens of reaction and nostalgia but through a filter of contemporary thought. The emphasis is on learning how to see and to think architecture by a method that can be loosely called "formal analysis".

Design and Visualization
Fall 2018
1018a Formal Analysis
Peter Eisenman, Anthony Gagliardi
Ife Adepegba (A); Malcolm Rondell Galang, Niema Jafari (B); Ashton Harrell (C);
Tyler Krebs, Shelby Wright (D); Angela Lufkin (E); Rachel Mulder (F); Scott Simpson (G)

Canonical buildings through a filter of contemporary thought

Design and Visualization
Fall 2018
1062a Computational Analysis Fabrication
Amir Karimpour

This course investigates and applies emerging computational theories and technologies through the design and fabrication of full-scale building components and assemblies. Students investigate various modeling paradigms, computational-based structural and sustainability analysis, and digital fabrication technologies.

Design and Visualization
Fall 2018
1062a Computational Analysis Fabrication
Amir Karimpour
James Bradley, Taiming Chen

Two equivalent halves minutely excavated

The expression of the wall transforms as it is observed in motion. Passing by the wall reveals an innate quality of transparency and opacity. This expression is akin to the rising and setting sun or the myth of Sisyphus, the full expression is cyclical and rhythmic. The wall is built from a modular system, constructed from two equivalent halves minutely excavated for vertical and horizontal interlocking.

Design and Visualization
Fall 2018
1062a Computational Analysis Fabrication
Amir Karimpour
Jerome Tryon, I-Ting Tsai

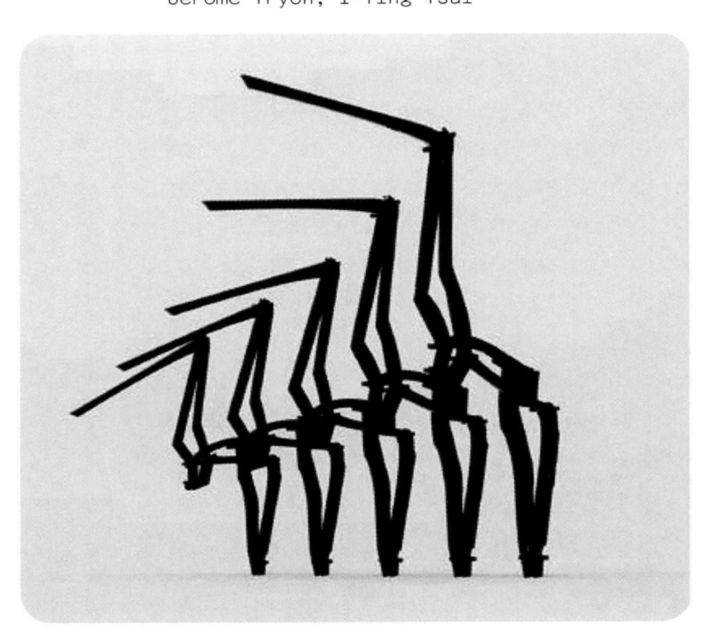

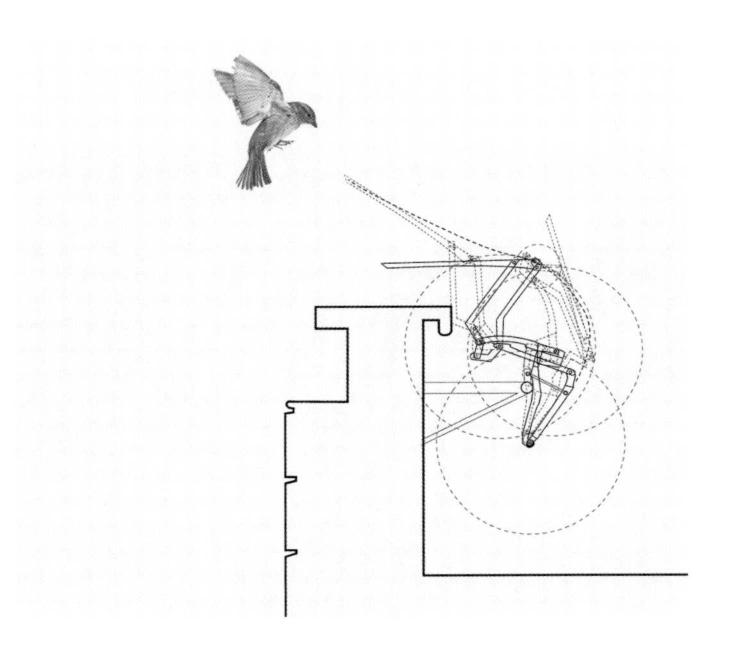

A dynamic element that elaborates upon natural movement

Taking inspiration from the fundamental and complex motions common in nature, we developed a dynamic element that elaborates upon natural movement. The Second Cornice can be mounted on a building parapet both to beautify the building and to protect its façade from unwanted aerial intrusions.

Design and Visualization
Fall 2018
1211a Drawing and Architectural Form
Victor Agran

The method of drawing for the means of generation, presentation, and interrogation of design ideas is currently ill-defined and under stress. This course examines the historical and theoretical development of descriptive geometry and perspective through the practice of rigorously constructed architectural drawings.

Design and Visualization
Fall 2018
1211a Drawing and Architectural Form
Victor Agran
Rosa Congdon

Hand drawing

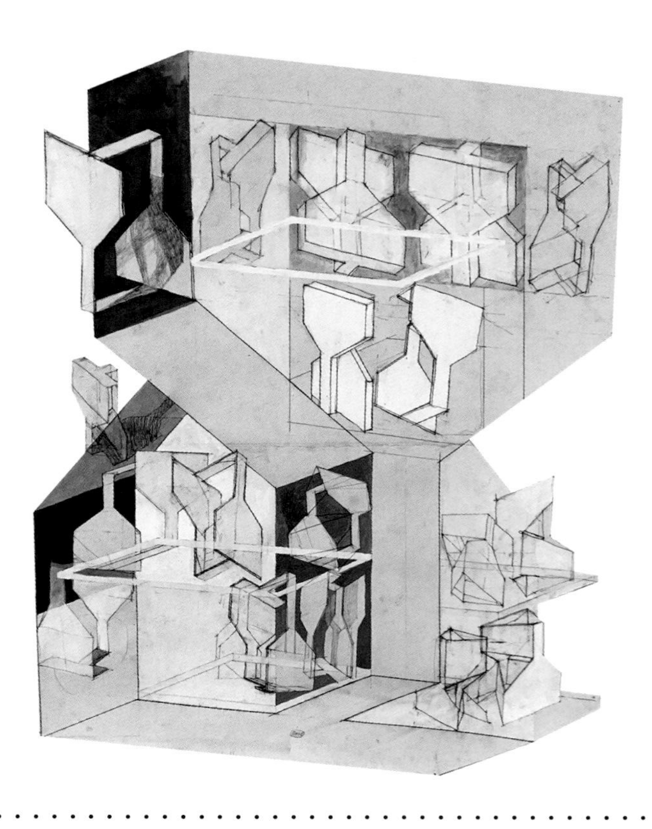

Design and Visualization
Fall 2018
1211a Drawing and Architectural Form
Victor Agran
Jerome Tryon

Ideas, perception, and memory

Design and Visualization
Fall 2018
1224a The Chair
Timothy Newton,
Nathan Burnell

The chair is both a model for understanding architecture and a laboratory for the concise expression of ideas, material, fabrication, and form. In this seminar, students develop their design and fabrication skills through exploration of issues involved in the design and construction of a full-scale prototype chair.

Design and Visualization
Fall 2018
1224a The Chair
Timothy Newton, Nathan Burnell
Jackson Lindsay

Hand-woven danish cord on a looping steel frame

Influenced by the furniture of Danish designer Hans Wegner, the Paperclip Chair is made of hand-woven danish cord on a looping steel frame.

Design and Visualization
Fall 2018
1224a The Chair
Timothy Newton, Nathan Burnell
Ethan Zisson

Breathable joinery

Made from locally sourced ash and cherry, this stacking chair is designed with sustainable principles in mind—no metal fasteners, an all natural Danish soap finish, and breathable joinery designed for a lifetime in seasonal climates.

Design and Visualization
Fall 2018
1233a Composition
Peter de Bretteville

In addressing architectural composition, this course leaves aside demands of program and site in order to concentrate on formal relationships and the impact of alternative strategies. Students develop techniques by which words, briefs, written descriptions, intentions, and requirements can be translated into three dimensions.

Design and Visualization
Fall 2018
1233a Composition
Peter de Bretteville
Sissi Guo

Possible Assemblies of Form

Design and Visualization
Fall 2018
1233a Composition
Peter de Bretteville
Javier Perez

Photoshoot

Design and Visualization
Fall 2018
1240a Custom Crafted Components
Kevin Rotheroe

This seminar encourages individual aesthetic expression through the craft of tangible, original, intimately scaled architectural elements. Students experiment with unusual combinations and sequences of analog and digital representation to produce objects, elements, or material explorations.

Design and Visualization
Fall 2018
1240a Custom Crafted Components
Kevin Rotheroe
Sharmin Bhagwagar

A fluid structured fabric
and a heavy concrete panel

Design and Visualization
Fall 2018
1240a Custom Crafted Components
Kevin Rotheroe
Hojae Lee

Inspired by the
crystallization of salt

Design and Visualization
Fall 2018
1241a Rendered: Art, Architecture, and Contemporary Image Culture
Brennan Buck

This course addresses the role of digital production and image making in art and architecture. Students speculate on the current and future role of the image as an architectural medium through research of the Internet's impact on contemporary art, and recent writing on aesthetic conceptions.

Design and Visualization
Fall 2018
1241a Rendered: Art, Architecture, and Contemporary Image Culture
Brennan Buck
Zelig Fok

Misuse the code

DeepFakes—a combination of "deep learning" and "fake", are images that use Artificial Intelligence based Human Image Synthesis, allowing for near seamless superimposition and mapping of images onto moving medium. Also known as FACS—Facial Action Coding System, these have been primarily used for facial manipulations in the movie industry. In this project, FACS was used to manipulate and misuse the code to read architectural façades and images, creating a new tool for form generation.

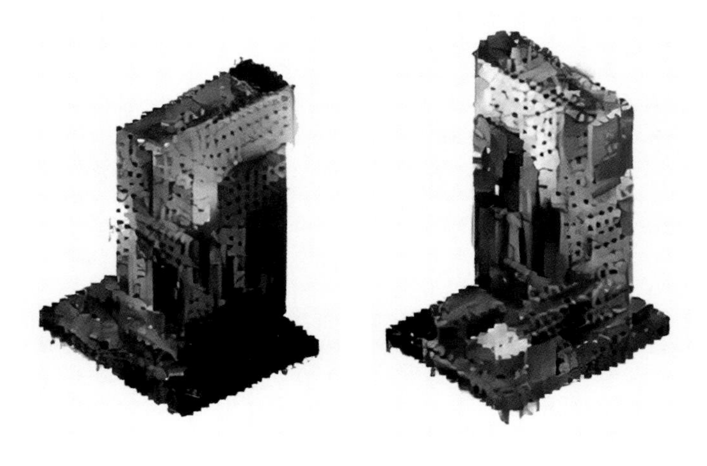

Design and Visualization
Fall 2018
1241a Rendered: Art, Architecture, and Contemporary Image Culture
Brennan Buck
Adam Thibodeaux

Pseudo-seamless false realities

The process of online product image mapping is juxtaposed by an intentionally manual process which re-inserts the cropped-out, or "forgotten" parts of the image back into the printing space. These reinserted fragments are manually manipulated to become pseudo-seamless false realities of new architecture, which are then mapped back onto the objects through the online service.

Design and Visualization Spring 2019

Design and Visualization
Spring 2019
1216b Ornament Theory and Design
Kent Bloomer

This seminar reviews the major writings and criticisms governing identities of and distinctions between ornament and decoration in architecture. After individual student analyses of Victorian, Art Nouveau, and Art Deco production, the course focuses on ornament in twenty-first-century design.

Design and Visualization
Spring 2019
1216b Ornament Theory and Design
Kent Bloomer
Varoon Kelekar

Ornament creates and lives in an "edge-world"

Design and Visualization
Spring 2019
1216b Ornament Theory and Design
Kent Bloomer
Brenna Thompson

Considering the body, in the round

Design and Visualization
Spring 2019
1222b Diagrammatic Analysis: Recon Modernism
Peter Eisenman, Anthony Gagliardi

Now that "the modern" is no longer the universalizing metric used to judge "the present", it can be treated as an historical phenomenon. This course rethinks what "the modern" was and what it is now through reading and drawing of modernism from 1914-1939 and postmodernism from 1968-1988.

Design and Visualization
Spring 2019
1222b Diagrammatic Analysis: Recon Modernism
Peter Eisenman, Anthony Gagliardi
Tayyaba Anwar

Trier Thermenmuseum, O.M. Ungers

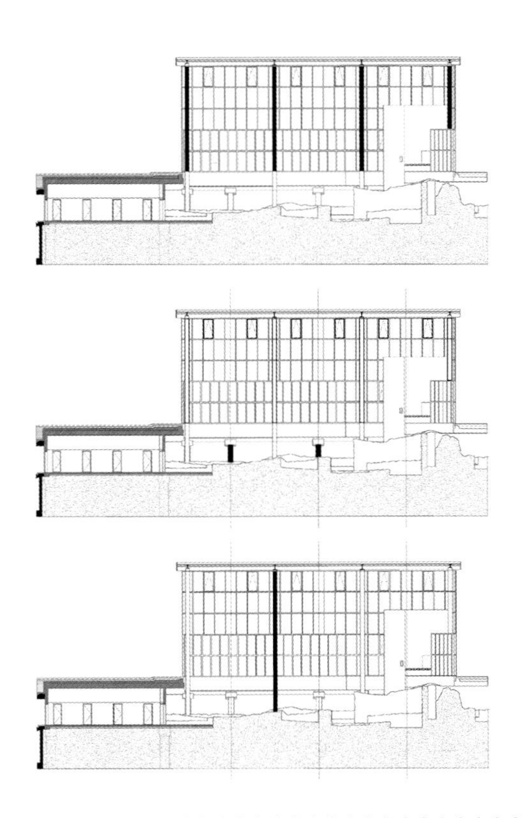

Design and Visualization
Spring 2019
1222b Diagrammatic Analysis: Recon Modernism
Peter Eisenman, Anthony Gagliardi
Zelig Fok

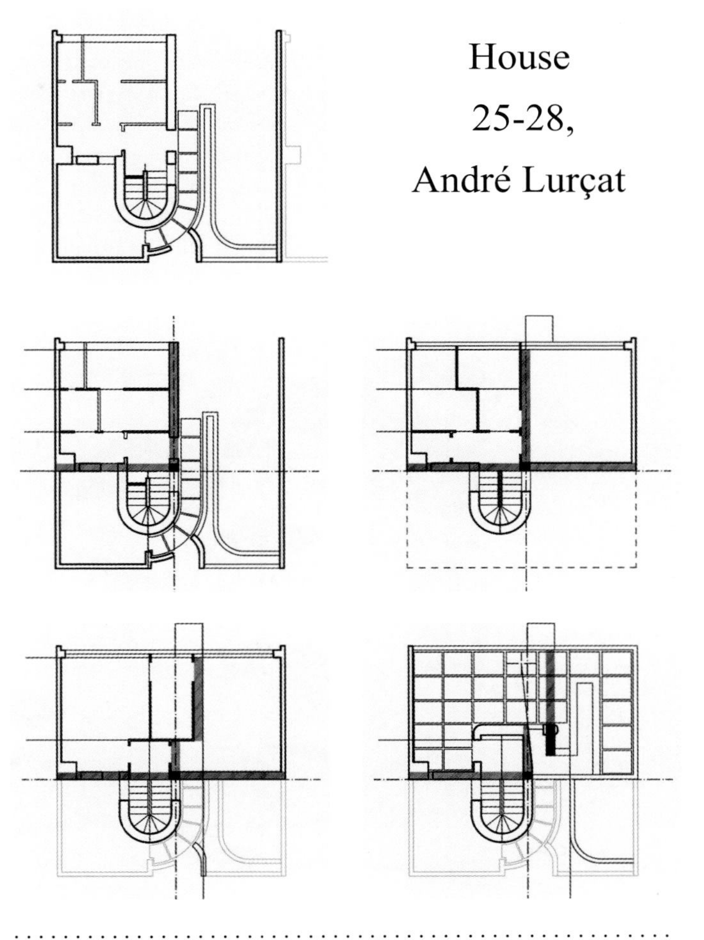

House 25-28, André Lurçat

Design and Visualization
Spring 2019
1227b Drawing Projects
Turner Brooks

Each student comes prepared with a particular subject that is investigated through the media of drawing for the entire term. There is a weekly evening pin-up with group discussion of the work in progress.

Design and Visualization
Spring 2019
1227b Drawing Projects
Turner Brooks
Nicole Doan

This seemingly unending world of color

This watercolor series stems from an initial study on the overlap of color and the potential to draw a seemingly infinite number of lines. White lines are drawn around distinct shapes and shades of colors, although this subjective act could produce a different result, based on how one interprets the placement and layering of paint on the paper. Individual splotches of color emerge from the bottom and reach out to the top edges of the frame, which implies a window into this seemingly unending world of color.

Design and Visualization
Spring 2019
1227b Drawing Projects
Turner Brooks
Iven Peh

Solidarity and flux, stillness and motion

Water always flows (horizontally) and falls (vertically). Often visualized as a graphic icon or still life landscape, the challenge is to depict water with an intuitive balance between illustrative and perspective modes. The uphill task to capture its dual characters (solidarity and flux, stillness and motion) in black and white sketches that tests one's imagination and reality. By observing constant rapid water flow to dissect the 'anatomy' of water within a split second, the result is a series of black ink blobs and streaks on grainy rice papers imbued with imagination and shapes.

Design and Visualization
Spring 2019
1227b Drawing Projects
Turner Brooks
Lucia Venditti

Ink and water

Design and Visualization
Spring 2019
1228b Disheveled Geometries: Ruins and Ruination
Mark Foster Gage

Architectural ruins index the failure of individual buildings, technologies, economies, or, at times, entire civilizations. The irony of late capitalism is that now these failures, through their ability to generate vast amounts of capital through tourism and regional identity, are more financially valuable than ever. This course researches ruination and architectural ruins on levels from the visual and formal to the philosophical and psychological.

Design and Visualization
Spring 2019
1228b Disheveled Geometries: Ruins and Ruination
Mark Foster Gage
Zelig Fok

Undermining the original monolithic form

In 1989, the New York Times ran the headline: "The Whitney Paradox: To Add Is To Subtract", an article expressing Paul Goldberger's distaste for Michael Graves' addition to Marcel Breuer building. "The Breuer building is resistant to all attempts to bring it into an urban dialogue along the street, but that alone should not be a reason not to build a work of architecture that attempts, gently and powerfully, to coax it into speaking."

The original Breuer building has been subject to several renovation proposals, from Michael Graves, OMA, Renzo Piano, and even a public sketch competition. This ruination examines an alternative to the current Whitney at the end of the High Line, in which Renzo Piano's proposal was approved with an additional alteration to the original Breuer building to establish a less internalized building, thus undermining the original monolithic form.

Design and Visualization
Spring 2019
1228b Disheveled Geometries: Ruins and Ruination
Mark Foster Gage
Sissi Guo

Michael Graves's Villa Savoye

Design and Visualization
Spring 2019
1242b Architecture and Illusion
Brennan Buck

This seminar examines the synthesis of architectural and representational space achieved during the Baroque period, specifically looking at trompe l'oeil, due to its renewed relevance. In this course, students develop a trompe l'oeil case study, speculating on the multiple implied volumes their precedent suggests and testing the threshold between representational and physical space.

Design and Visualization
Spring 2019
1242b Architecture and Illusion
Brennan Buck
Andrew Kim

An expansiveness of space and sight

The spatial illusions in the sixteenth century quadratura paintings of the Pitti Palace (Florence, Italy) suggest an expansiveness of space and sight. By multiplying both the spatial extent of the vaults and configuration of the painted illusions, the object explores the registration of infinite expanse on the modeled surfaces.

Design and Visualization
Spring 2019
1242b Architecture and Illusion
Brennan Buck
Leyi Zhang

The image that unifies drawn and built space

After developing a precise understanding of the physical and representational geometry of the Perspectives' Hall in Villa Farnesina, this project manipulates the geometry to produce alternative space rather than a single ideal. The final model is a projection of the image that unifies the drawn and built space, the virtual and the physical. It creates new special qualities that the original room never achieved.

Design and Visualization
Spring 2019
1243b Graphic Inquiry
Luke Bulman

This seminar explores how architects might use a wider array of communication processes to describe, develop, and release their ideas strategically. The inquiry includes, but goes beyond, graphic tools to explore alternate models of knowledge creation. Architecture in this sense is seen in the context of a wide variety of other subjects.

Design and Visualization
Spring 2019
1243b Graphic Inquiry
Luke Bulman
Emily Cass

Test flights of the NASA ultra-long duration balloon

This project is a collection of studies exploring how the surface of a balloon responds to being written on.

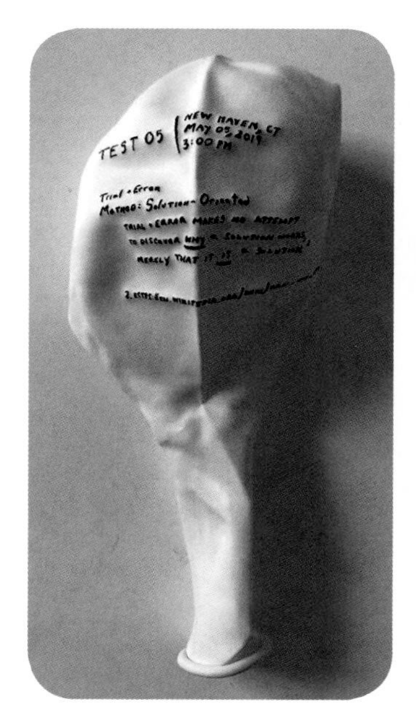

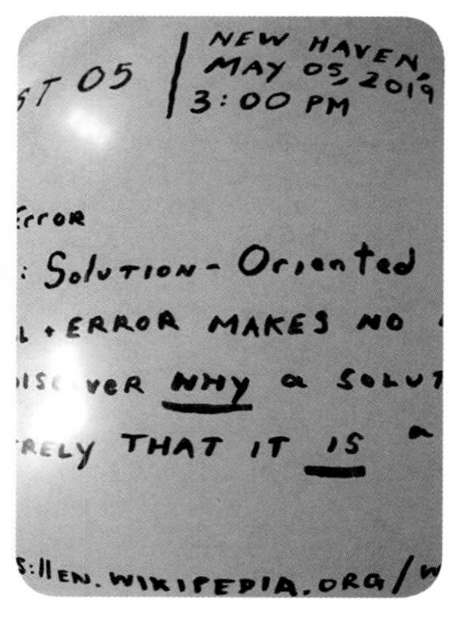

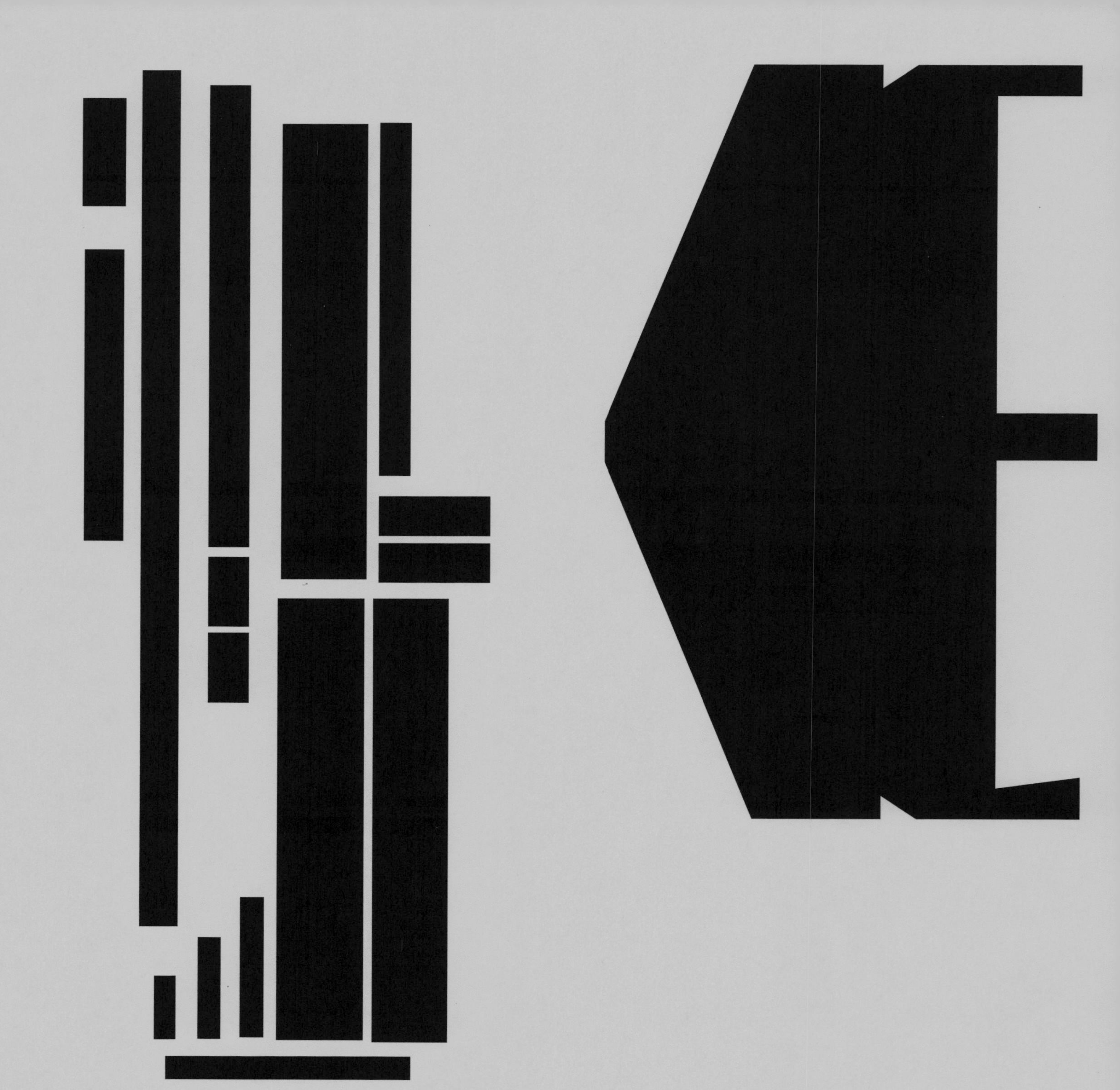

Design and Visualization
Spring 2019
1243b Graphic Inquiry
Luke Bulman
Michael Glassman, Christine Pan

x = sandwich

From the deli to the bodega, from tea sandwiches to the ploughman's lunch, from Dagwood to the Hamburglar, sandwiches nurture material culture at every level. The sandwich exists just on the border between abstract and concrete, image and sustenance. Stacking, layering, structure, portability—superimposition, orientation, adjacencies, permutations—bread, condiment, meat, cheese. We won't try to define a sandwich, but to borrow the words of Supreme Court Justice (and Yale alumnus) Potter Stewart, we know it when we see it.

Design and Visualization Summer 2019

Design and Visualization
Summer 2019
1019c Petite Planets: An Ecology of Digital Materiality
Maya Alam, Daniele Profeta

Since the late eighteenth century, from a newly acquired elevated point of view with mountaineering and air-balloon flights, panoramic views have shaped the way in which we engage with the world around us as well as produced experimental means of representing landscape. In this class we leverage immersive modes of representation, what we define as a series of 'Planetary Images', to reflect on our engagement with the built environment.

Design and Visualization
Summer 2019
1019c Petite Planets: An Ecology of Digital Materiality
Maya Alam, Daniele Profeta
Kate Fritz

The scoop of snow cone planet

Design and Visualization
Summer 2019
1019c Petite Planets: An Ecology of Digital Materiality
Maya Alam, Daniele Profeta
Malcolm Rondell Galang

Monoscopic

Design and Visualization
Summer 2019
1019c Scripting and Algorithmic Design: Grid Space
Dorian Booth

While recent trends in architecture have focused on constructions seemingly absent of or axmbiguously related to grids or regulating frameworks, these organizational strategies have significant historical importance and continue to play a central role in defining formal relationships. Beginning with the presumption that these formal or informal organizational systems may not be mutually exclusive, students study areas of overlap between them and how digital tools and computational techniques may facilitate their study.

Design and Visualization
Summer 2019
1019c Scripting and Algorithmic Design: Grid Space
Dorian Booth
Ives Brown, Leyi Zhang

Underlying matter

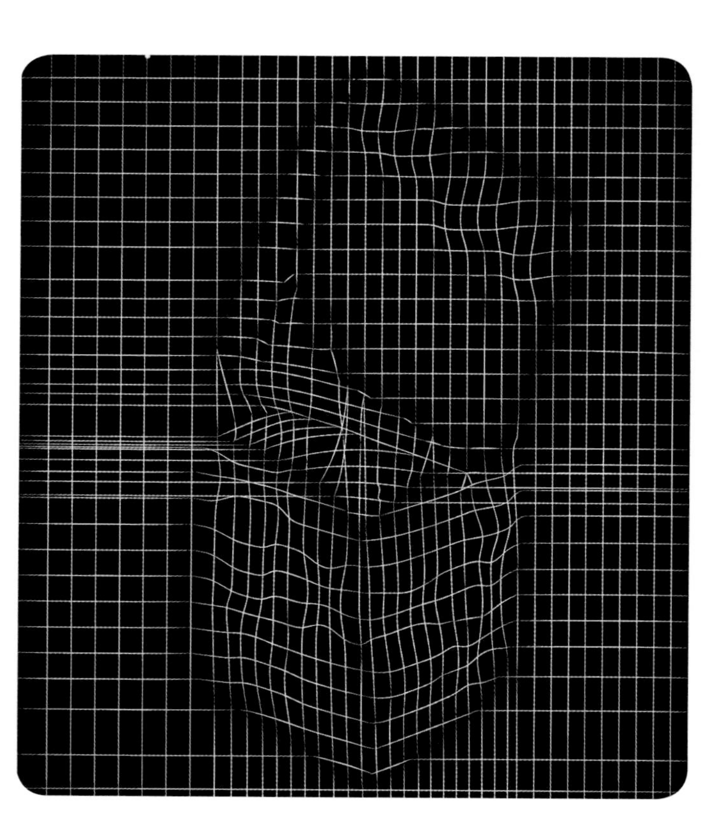

Design and Visualization
Summer 2019
1019c Scripting and Algorithmic Design: Grid Space
Dorian Booth
Sarah Weiss, Sasha Zwiebel

Algorithmic smocking, group v, no. 19

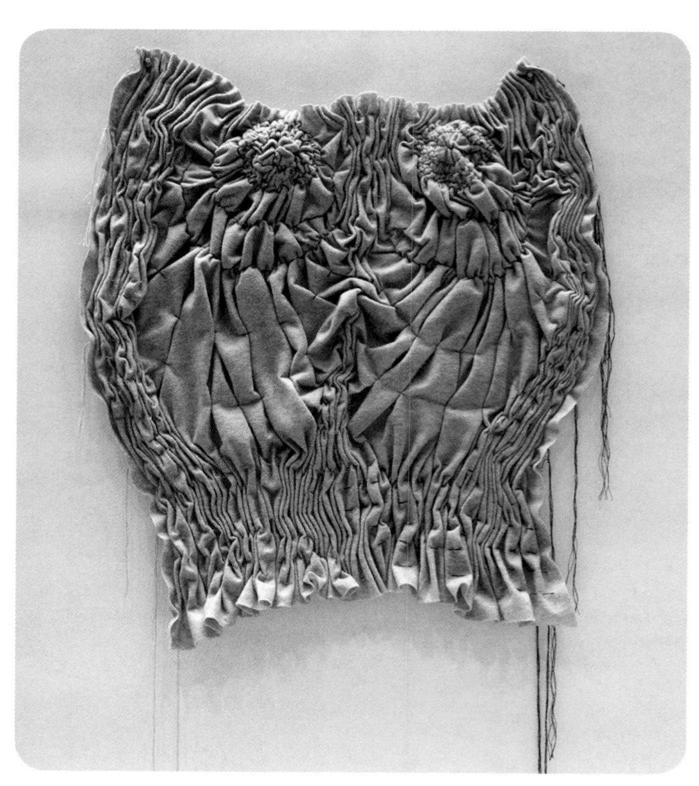

Design and Visualization
Summer 2019
1019c Virtual Reality: The Memory Palace
Beom Jun Kim

Parmenides gives us "the way of truth" (*aletheia*) that reveals the world as an unchanging unity or one, but he also presents us with "the way of seeming" (*doxa*) which describes how we receive phenomena that is subjective and thus represents an unreality. Students take on either "the way of truth" or "the way of seeming" in virtual reality, questioning notions of authenticity, subjectivity, perception, and ontology within a world of their creation.

Design and Visualization
Summer 2019
1019c Virtual Reality: The Memory Palace
Beom Jun Kim
Isabel Li

An inner space and an outer space

Design and Visualization
Summer 2019
1019c Virtual Reality: The Memory Palace
Beom Jun Kim
Naomi Ng

Spaces unbounded

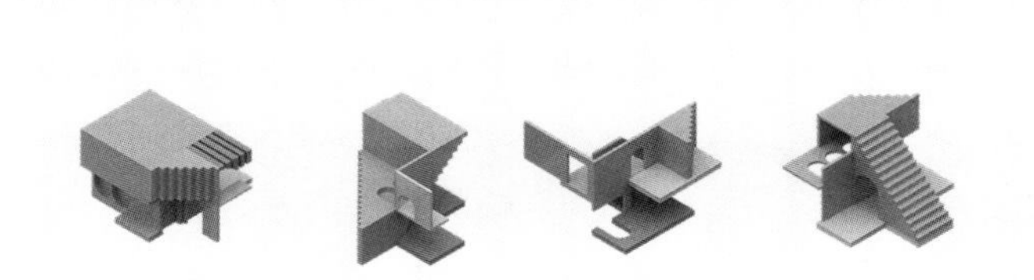

Design and Visualization
Summer 2019
1291c Rome: Continuity and Change
Bimal Mendis, Joyce Hsiang, Elisa Iturbe, George Knight

The seminar, taking place in Rome, examines historical continuity and change as well as the ways in which and the reasons why some elements and approaches were maintained over time and others abandoned. Examples from antiquity to the present day are studied as part of the context of an ever-changing city with its sequence of layered accretions. Hand drawing is used as a primary tool of discovery during explorations of buildings, landscapes, and gardens, both within and outside the city. Students devote the final week to an intensive independent analysis of a building or place.

1291c Rome: Continuity and Change

Bimal Mendis, Joyce Hsiang, Elisa Iturbe, George Knight

Phoebe Harris (A), Alix Pauchet (B), Rhea Schmid (C), Maya Sorabjee (D), Jerome Tryon (E)

An ever-changing city with its sequence of layered accretions

116

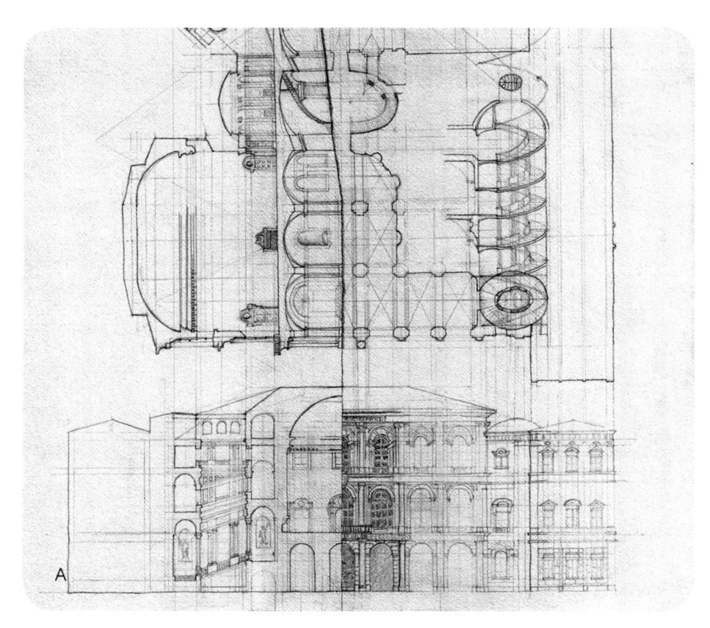

Technology and Practice

Technology and Practice Fall 2018

Technology and Practice
Fall 2018
2021a Environmental Design
Anna Dyson, Kipp Bradford, Mohamed Aly Etman, Naomi Keena

This course examines the fundamental scientific principles governing thermal, luminous, and acoustic environments of buildings. Students are introduced to the methods and technologies for creating and controlling the interior environment.

Technology and Practice
Fall 2018
2021a Environmental Design
Anna Dyson, Kipp Bradford, Mohamed Aly Etman, Naomi Keena
Kelley Johnson

An aesthetic of continuity

The main environmental design factor for this project is responding to the thermal needs of a building through a lattice and glass façade that is calibrated around solar angles. The louvers are at a series of rotations to maintain an aesthetic of continuity around the building, but still react to thermal comfort needs of the occupants.

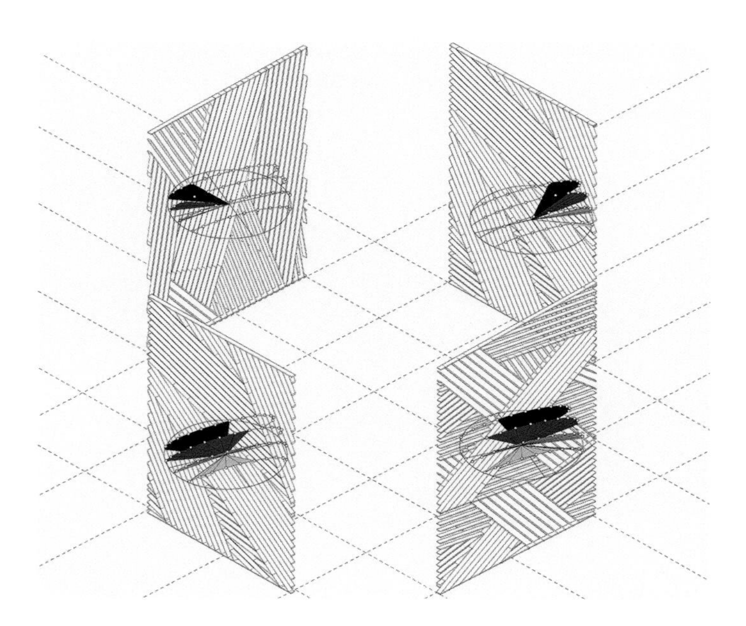

Technology and Practice
Fall 2018
2021a Environmental Design
Anna Dyson, Kipp Bradford, Mohamed Aly Etman, Naomi Keena
Rachel Lefevre

Particular rooms at particular times of day

This design project consists of a community justice center without any walls and is comprised only of doors which are all operable. By combining wind, thermal heat gain, and seasonal climate data to create a set of guidelines for opening and closing doors, the project could achieve thermal comfort within particular rooms at particular times of day with particular occupancies.

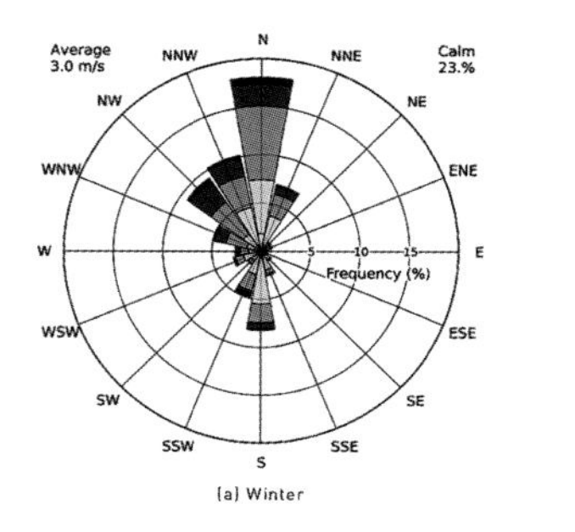

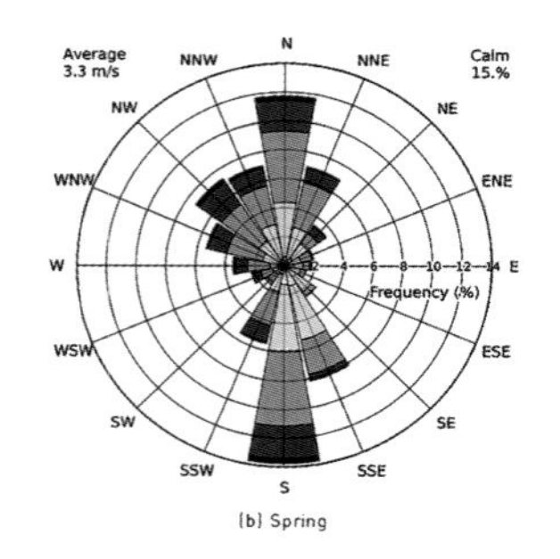

Technology and Practice
Fall 2018
2031a Architecture Practice and Management
Phillip Bernstein, John Apicella

The process by which an architectural design becomes a building requires the architect to control many variables beyond pure aesthetics. This course provides an understanding of structure, organization, management, and execution related to the profession and its resulting built projects.

Technology and Practice
Fall 2018
2031a Architectural Practice and Management
Phillip Bernstein, John Apicella
Sunny Cui, Jincy Kunnatharayil, Larkin McCann, Miguel Sanchez-Enkerlin, Jacob Schaffert, Melissa Weigel

The totality of the building process

The practice of architecture, being the totality of the building process from conception to completion, requires more than design intent. The role and responsibilities of architects in the twenty-first century are rapidly evolving under the influence of broad building industry changes in sustainability, digital technology, globalization and integrated project delivery. Understanding architectural practice as the mechanism that realizes design, and subsequently project management as means of executing design intent, is as critical as form and character to the success of the building. Effective architects master both aesthetic and managerial issues to guide their projects through the currents of professional practice, the vagaries construction, and political forces of planning and approval. The creation of a business and project delivery method is as much of an exercise in design as the architectural work these constructs service.

Technology and Practice
Fall 2018
2031a Architectural Practice and Management
Phillip Bernstein, John Apicella
Ryan Hughes, Hsin-Ju Lai, Martin Man, I-Ting Tsai, Matthew Wagstaffe, Katrina Yin

Construction alone will require 13 months

The School of Global Affairs is set to be fully operational for the 2021/2022 academic year. We understand this to be a non-negotiable deadline due to the university-wide operational consequences of a late opening. At the time of this report, the maximum length provided for all design, construction, and occupancy phases is 2 years and 8 months. We estimate that construction alone will require 13 months. Given the complexity of program and square footage, this creates significant stress on our project schedule for the degree of coordination we hope to achieve. The accelerated pace of work will result in less contingency in the schedule for any unforeseen interruptions, higher procurement costs due to shortened lead times, and less time to create working rapport between parties working together for the first time.

Technology and Practice
Fall 2018
2211a Technology and Design of Tall Buildings
Kyoung Sun Moon

This seminar investigates the dynamic interrelationship between technology and architecture in tall buildings. Students research structural and facade systems, the separation of which led to modern architecture and allowed the emergence of tall buildings.

Technology and Practice
Fall 2018
2211a Technology and Design of Tall Buildings
Kyoung Sun Moon
Dana AlMathkoor, Smit Patel

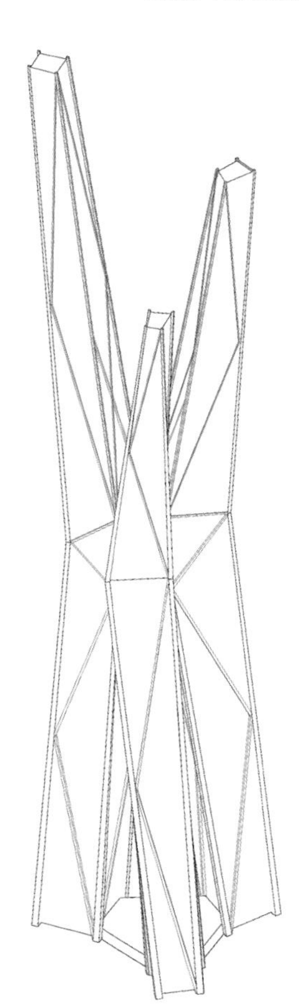

Joined at the hip

The Trio Tower represents a fundamentally new way of looking at the integration of public space into complex super-tall building structures. The inherent structural efficiency of the tripod results in three unique towers: residential (700 meters), hotel (850 meters) and office/mixed-use (1000 meters). Joined at the hip, these towers use the Cultural Band at 500 meters to embrace diversity by juxtaposing hyper-public space, semi-public and private space. The Trio Tower conceals parts of itself depending on the elevation, allowing for it to have a dynamic presence in Chicago's historic skyline, acting almost as a compass because of the city's cardinal street grid.

Technology and Practice
Fall 2018
2211a Technology and Design of Tall Buildings
Kyoung Sun Moon
Taiming Chen

Subtleties of interior spatial adventures

The project "M.O.M.A +" is a mixed-use tower including residential apartments, offices, and gallery extensions to the current MoMA museum in New York City. As part of the museum block, the tower is designed as a sculptural object constructed by steel tubes and braces, which harmoniously connects to the adjacent buildings. Each corner of the mass is cut away, where pockets of public spaces are inserted to extend the MoMA experience throughout the building. The public spaces are continuous atriums, where MoMA visitors, office workers, and residents can all congregate in a shared experience. The entire building is wrapped by gradient screen facade to not only provide shading and privacy, but also reveal the subtleties of interior spatial adventures.

Technology and Practice
Fall 2018
2234a Material Case Studies
Emily Abruzzo

This seminar focuses on the intuition for material use in both the execution and generation of design. In this course students investigate the relationship between a material's substance and its performance qualities, and propose a site specific design-build project.

Technology and Practice
Fall 2018
2234a Material Case Studies
Emily Abruzzo
Thomas Mahon, Max Ouellette-Howitz, Seth Thompson

51 pieces of wood leaning against the side of Rudolph Hall

This installation features a linear array of 51 pieces of wood leaning against the side of Rudolph Hall, interwoven at various angles. Each 8' length of red oak is capped with an 8" piece of square-cut steel. This wood-metal joint produces a natural blue stain when exposed to water. Outside the building, the wood pieces are darkened from the staining and the steel is rusted. Inside the building, the wood-metal dowels are pristine. Through the window, one can contemplate the junction between Rudolph Hall and the Loria Center, the effect of time and weathering on standard building materials, and the memory of Rudolph's bush-hammered concrete construction.

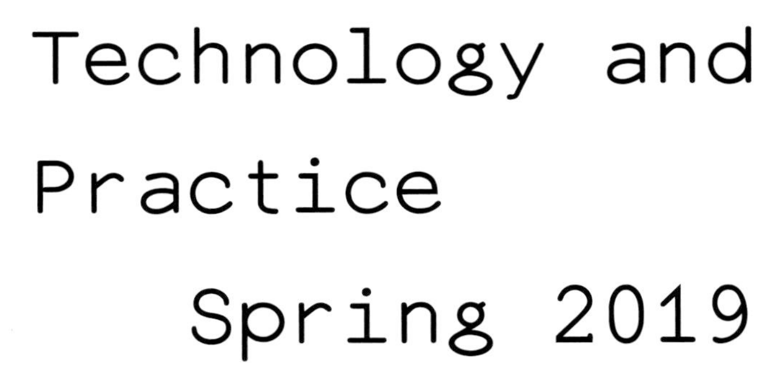

Technology and Practice
Spring 2019
2016b Building Project I:
Research, Analysis, Design
Alan Organschi,
Kyle Bradley, Adam Hopfner,
Amy Lelyveld, Joeb Moore

This course explores the conception and construction of dwelling space in the city. Student teams examine the specific relationship of the human body to its environment, the elemental concerns of inhabitation, and the formation of building. This year the final project is a three unit home in New Haven. Students and professors worked with Columbus House—a New Haven-based shelter and permanent supportive housing provider for the homeless—to select one scheme to house three men who have experienced homelessness.

Alan Organschi, Kyle Bradley, Adam Hopfner, Amy Lelyveld, Joeb Moore
Ife Adepegba, Martin Carrillo Bueno, Jiachen Deng, Hyun Jae Jung, Dreama Lin, Naomi Ng

A fluid connectivity

The rituals of sanitation, rest and nourishment are essential in order to dwell. This design starts with the analysis of critical surfaces in which these daily rituals transpire.

Spaces are configured through a process favoring functionality, spatial economy, and connectivity between the aforementioned rituals. Negotiation occurs as one surface experiences a push from within, and the adjacent surface experiences a subtractive pull. Whether it be the transition from interior space to exterior enclosure, or transitioning between interior spaces, a certain memory, or porosity of the adjoining element becomes evident within the scheme.

A fluid connectivity is produced through the insertion of bedroom volumes into the living space, both completing the dwelling and connecting the dwelling to the next as a collective aggregation.

Alan Organschi, Kyle Bradley, Adam Hopfner, Amy Lelyveld, Joeb Moore
Jiaming Gu, Liang Hu, Christine Song, Ben Thompson, Yuhan Zhang, Kaiwen Zhao

A gentle elevational transition

Our homes sit humbly among the neighborhood fabric on Plymouth Street. As one travels down the street, they are greeted by the low roof line of our dwelling which bows down at a sympathetic angle to the viewer. Our one story units are bridged to the neighboring two story homes by a row of trees just larger than our roof line and lower than our neighbor's eave, orchestrating a gentle elevational transition for the eye. Our interior offers opportunities to imbue identity within the space; a series of pull-out shelves reside in a cavity below the bed. From the bed above, one may survey the extent of their home before slipping into rest for the night, knowing fully the protection of its enclosure and also what may wait beyond.

Alan Organschi, Kyle Bradley, Adam Hopfner, Amy Lelyveld, Joeb Moore
Malcolm Rondell Galang, Louis Koushouris, April Liu, Louisa Nolte, Leyi Zhang
(Selected for Construction)

The first principle is a power cell

The first principle is a power cell, a mechanical core that holds the bathing and cooking configuration, which is an efficient means of organizing interiors between public and private. The second principle is the delamination of the building envelope. A typical floor plan is stacked and rotated. Stairs are added which allow a potential for borrowed space below. The addition of these two principles yields a third condition: the garden. Akin to the New Haven triple-decker vernacular, the garden is instrumental in connecting residents with the neighborhood.

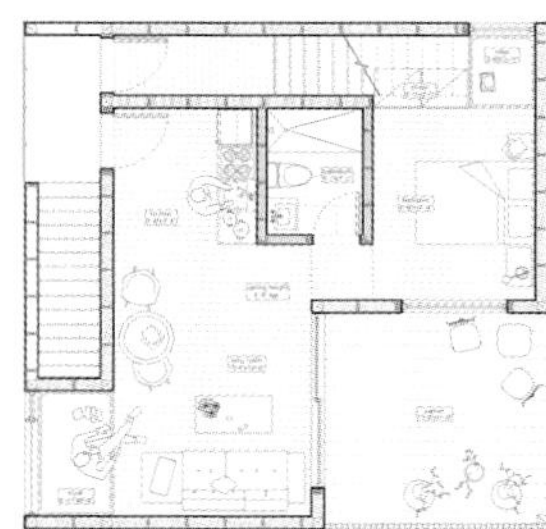

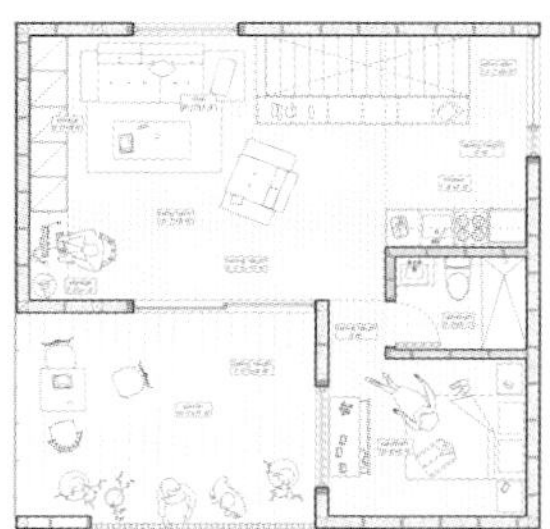

Technology and Practice
Spring 2019
2022b Systems Integration and Development in Design
Martin Finio, Victoria Arbitrio, Anibal Bellomio, Alastair Elliott, Erleen Hatfield, Robert Haughney, Kristin Hawkins, John D. Jacobson, Larry Jones, Jennifer Lan, Gina Narracci, Kari Nystrom, Laura Pirie, Victoria Ponce de Leon, Craig Razza, Pierce Reynoldson, Edward Stanley, Philip Steiner, Celia Toche, Adam Trojanowski

The careful advancement of structural form and detail, environmental systems, egress, accessibility, and envelope design are all approached systematically as elements of design to achieve technical and performance goals and reinforce the conceptual origins of student designs.

Technology and Practice
Spring 2019
2022b Systems Integration and Development in Design
Martin Finio, et al.
Alex Pineda Jongeward, Matthew Liu, Paul Wu

Structurally articulating the seemingly complex

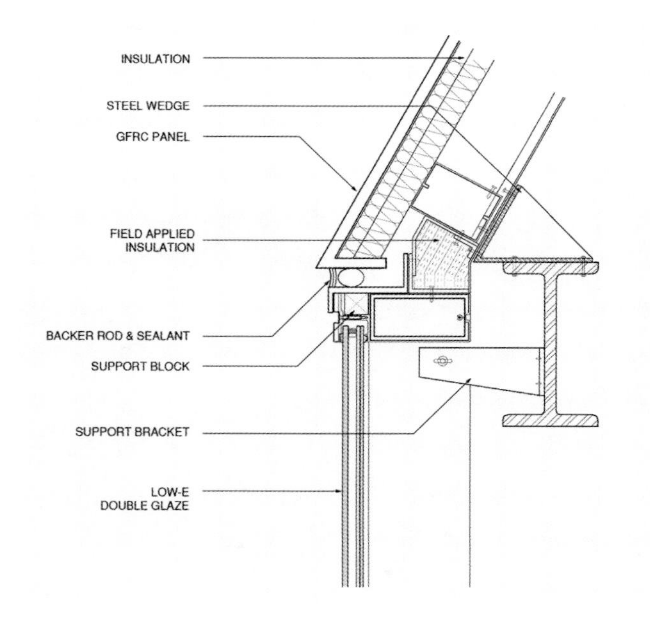

Technology and Practice
Spring 2019
2022b Systems Integration and Development in Design
Martin Finio, et al.
Page Comeaux, Alix Pauchet, Deirdre Plaus

Carving away of a solid to bring light from above

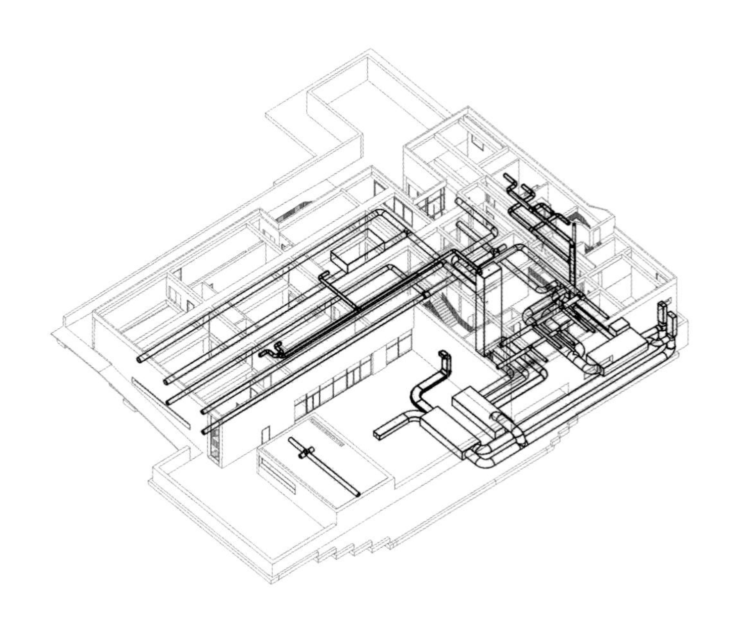

Technology and Practice
Spring 2019
2219b Craft, Materials, and Digital Artistry
Kevin Rotheroe

This course reviews materials and manufacturing processes especially suited for digitally crafting unique architectural components and surfaces. Cross-fertilization of digital and conventional modes of representation and making is emphasized, as this approach often enables economically viable, highly original artistic creative expression.

Technology and Practice
Spring 2019
2219b Craft, Materials, and Digital Artistry
Kevin Rotheroe
Natalie Broton

Laminated maple and pistachios

Technology and Practice
Spring 2019
2219b Craft, Materials, and Digital Artistry
Kevin Rotheroe
Tayyaba Anwar

The natural processes of corrosion

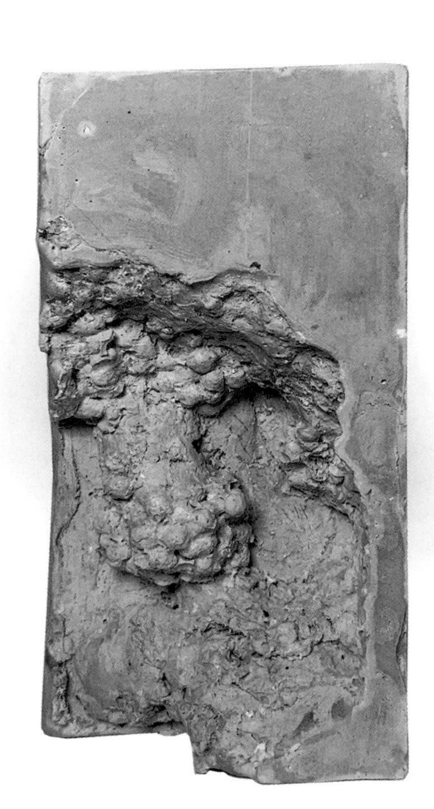

Technology and Practice
Spring 2019
2226b Design Computation
Michael Szivos

The capabilities and limitations of architects' tools directly influence the spaces they design. This seminar introduces design computation as a means to enable architects to operate exempt from limitations of generalized commercial software; to devise problem-specific tools, techniques, and workflows; to control the growing complexities of contemporary architectural design; and to explore forms generated only by computation itself.

Technology and Practice
Spring 2019
2226b Design Computation
Michael Szivos
James Bradley

The algorithm saw 507,747 pixels, and painted 17,603 strokes

"AlphaP" is an algorithmic painting developed to closely mimic the style and application of oil paint to canvas. Within the algorithm are meticulously crafted routines that give the script an authorship and agency that expresses itself in the final painted work. Each stroke is drawn out through a vectorized noise field, jittering the brush and mixing paint on the digital canvas. While the algorithm can technically see the full array of pixel input, the image that it sees versus the image it paints are miles apart. In essence, the painter only knows the image by what it samples. Of the 2,304,000 pixels in the lake scene that were painted, the algorithm saw 507,747 pixels, and painted 17,603 strokes.

Technology and Practice
Spring 2019
2226b Design Computation
Michael Szivos
Eunice Lee, Jewel Pei

Animated raindrops falling down each string

This project explores the relationship between digital projection, a three-dimensional display surface, and human interaction. A dense volume of 150 strings were installed in the staircase as a display surface. With processing, we developed a tool that controls the offset and spacing of each column of light that would be mapped onto each string. This tool allows us to map the projection accurately onto a manually fabricated object, which is difficult to measure digitally. For the simplicity of testing, we animated raindrops falling down each string. A Kinect detects users in the space, and sends the spatial data to Processing. Processing then translates the proximity of users to the speed and density of raindrops.This tool can be further developed for future projects that explore three-dimensional projection and communicate different sets of data or images.

Technology and Practice
Spring 2019
2230b Exploring New Value in Design Practice
Phillip Bernstein, John Apicella

How do we make design a more profitable practice? This seminar redesigns the value proposition of architecture practice, explores strategies used by better-compensated adjacent professions and markets, and investigates methods by which architects can deliver—and be paid for—the value they bring to the building industry.

Technology and Practice
Spring 2019
2230b Exploring New Value in Design Practice
Phillip Bernstein, John Apicella
Kate Altmann, Alejandro Duran, Javier Perez

Common sense

At Common Sense, our goal is to take advantage of existing, undervalued real estate to produce new, affordable, and flexible housing opportunities.

By entering in an equity partnership with a developer partner, our practice can increase the value captured from real estate development for both the designer and the investor.

127

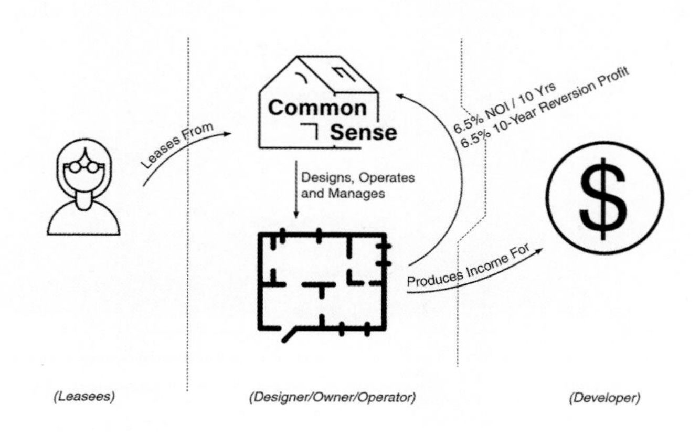

Technology and Practice

Summer 2019

Technology and Practice
Summer 2019
2017c Building Project II: Construction
Adam Hopfner, Kyle Bradley

This course examines the materialization of a building, whereby students are required to physically participate in the construction of a structure that they have designed. The course demonstrates the multiplicity of forces that come to influence the execution of an architectural intention, all the while fostering an architecture of social responsibility, providing structures for an underserved and marginalized segment of the community. This project is realized through the participation of students, the contributions of Columbus House, the donations from many sponsors, the hard work of student interns, and the support of the Plymouth Street community.

Plymouth Street

History and Theory

History and Theory

Fall 2018

History and Theory
Fall 2018
3011a Modern Architecture and Society
Kurt Forster, Gary He

As architecture gained importance in advancing social and industrial agendas, it also built a basis for theoretical reflection and visionary aesthetics. This course embraces the last century and a half of architecture, when traditional fables began to yield to more scientifically conceived ideas of architecture's role in the creation of civilizations.

History and Theory
Fall 2018
3011a Modern Architecture and Society
Kurt Forster, Gary He
Kevin Gao

The Individuality, Acceptance, and Ignorance of the New "City"

A formal analysis of a building, regarding, whether depending on its formation, geological location, material, or particular interests in architectural history, a conceptual, religious, and cultural background about the architects with the relationship to the architecture must be carefully studied. In this case, the discussion would be based on the specific issues presented by the architect Ma Yansong using his iconic "language" inserted in the heart of Beijing, our target architecture piece—the Chaoyang Park Plaza.

The development of modern and contemporary architectures in China, specifically in the city of Beijing was tightly related to the changes of political attention, lifestyle, and the dramatically vanishing natural environments in terms of both natural and cultural (man-made). Since the 1980s, Beijing was targeted as the center of development in China, which expansion, renovation, and gentrifications were introduced. It was far from being an abstract issue for one who has experienced the entire process. Born and raised in Beijing, I am driven to explore the transformation of the city through its architecture after witnessing this shift taking place since I was a kid. The 20 million settlers create an endless construction and development movement. Rapid changes take on a faster pace when stepping into the 21st century: my childhood playground was turned into the "Bird's Nest"; my grandparents' bungalow was demolished for a subway station; historic façades were torn down for emerging café shops and bars. This undesirable urbanization converted the city into a net of chaotic compounds, which fundamentally destroyed the identity of the architecture. It could only be described as being traded in an entangled market that some people were fulfilling their wishes to see far in a high rise while others died to protect their foot on the ground. The "solatium" from the government was significant which our acceptance was majorly forced to gather the belongings accumulated by generations within that 60 square meter bungalow. There is not much to bring anyways. If anything, really sincerely precious, it would be that old plum tree in the shared courtyard with three other families who are placed to outside the city after the movement; the smell of the lamb shashlik next door in the summer night; the "one yuan store" (equal to 0.15 USD, the entire store sells items that cost one yuan) across the street with trite ice-cream; and of course, the taste [...]

History and Theory
Fall 2018
3011a Modern Architecture and Society
Kurt Forster, Gary He
Sasha Zwiebel

Acceptance Letters: The Dialogue Between Louise Bethune and the WAA and AIA in the Late 19th Century

Daniel Burnham, Louis Sullivan, W. L. Plack, Sidney Smith, and S. A. Treat as the board of directors of the Western Architects Association at their second annual convention in St. Louis on November 18, 1885, all agreed and "were very much in favor" of admitting women to their organization. After taking a poll of the current members, the president, C. E. Illsley, declared, "The motion is made and seconded that this lady applicant be admitted to membership [...] Mrs. Louise Bethune is the applicant. [...] She has done work by herself, and been very successful. She is unanimously elected a member", (fig. 1). [1]

In the late 19th century, Louise Bethune was one of few female architects in the United States and the only woman with a full-time, profitable practice. [...]

1. "The Convention: Official Report of the Second Annual Convention of Western Association of Architects, held at St. Louis, November 18, 19 and 20, 1885". The Inland Architect And Builder 6 5 (1885): 66–67.

FIRST DAY—AFTERNOON SESSION.

The president called the meeting to order and said: There is a bit of unfinished business before we can proceed. All the members recommended by the directors for admission were voted in except one, and nothing was done on that subject.

Mr. Burnham: That was with reference to a lady.

The President: Now, I will ask if the committee are prepared to recommend that party in all respects except the fact that she is a lady?

Mr. Sullivan: Yes, sir.

The President: What shall be done with this question?

Mr. Burnham, of the Board of Directors: May I say that what the board desires is to be instructed upon the principle of admitting women as members of this association. That is the thing. If this decision is given us to admit women, we will make the recommendation. We would like the decision, now, of the convention, as to whether it desires to admit women as members of the association. We want the By-Laws interpreted.

A member: I would like to know what the opinion of the Board of Directors is.

Mr. Burnham: We are all agreed; we are very much in favor of it.

Mr. Cochrane: Then I would recommend that the secretary cast the ballot for the lady.

A member: Is the lady practicing?

The President: Yes, sir.

Mr. Cochrane: Let the secretary cast the ballot as he did for the others.

The motion was seconded.

Mr. Sullivan: What we desired was a vote of instructions as to the admission of women as a general thing.

A member: It seems to me that if you carry the motion as made by Mr. Cochrane, that it will suggest a precedent for future consideration. If the lady is practicing architecture, and is in good standing, there is no reason why she should not be one of us.

The President: The motion is made and seconded that this lady applicant be admitted to membership. All in favor of this will say aye.

Motion was adopted.

The President: Mrs. Louisa Bethune is the applicant. Her husband was an applicant, but withdrew. She has done work by herself, and been very successful. She is unanimously elected a member.

131

History and Theory
Fall 2018
3071a Issues in Architecture and Urbanism: Practice
Aniket Shahane

By investigating a broad range of projects and practitioners that have impacted the discipline of architecture, this course fosters a discourse among post-professional students on the notion of practice.

History and Theory
Fall 2018
3071a Issues in Architecture and Urbanism: Practice
Aniket Shahane
Kate Altmann

A Reimagining of the Sanctuary of the Home

The asylum occupies a unique position within culture. The term originates from the Greek word *ásȳlon* meaning sanctuary. Today, the word is fraught with an array of confused and sometimes misunderstood connotations which speak of "Otherness". This project, "Architecture as Asylum", revisits notions of asylum through a study of both the hospital and the home. The investigation posits that the home might be seen as the setting from which to redress perceptions of mental health. In a reimagining of the sanctuary of the home, we might see a housing model which goes some way to address concerns of loneliness, social isolation and economic barriers to housing associated with mental illness.

History and Theory
Fall 2018
3071a Issues in Architecture and Urbanism: Practice
Aniket Shahane
Sharmin Bhagwagar

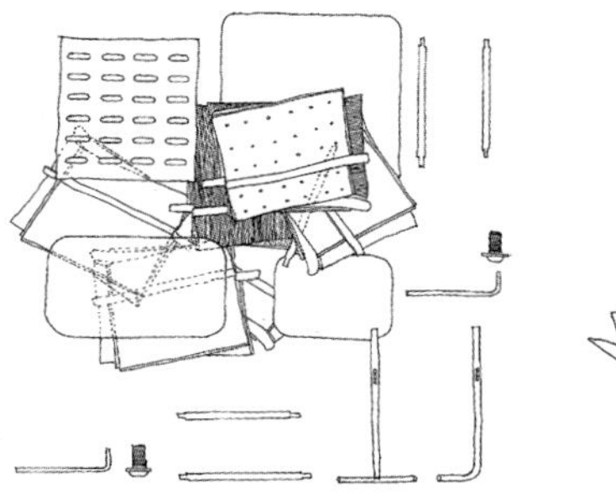

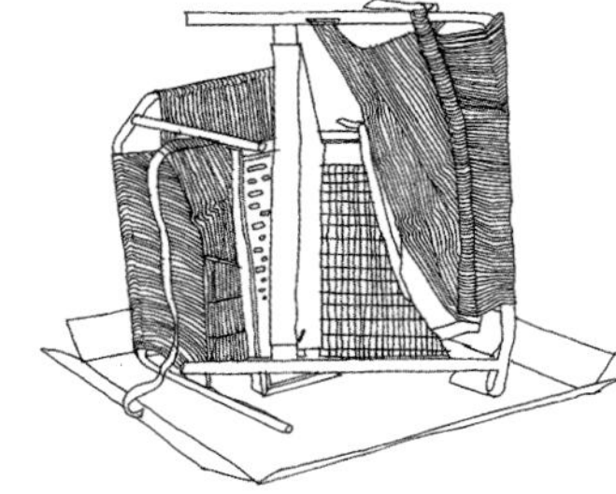

How to

This how-to manual presents itself as a rigid, overbearing, and a rather comical instruction document. Often associated with assembling furniture, setting up devices and building homes, the manual occasionally presents itself as a disciplining tool for human behavior. Building a manual is the single most important step in production and reproduction within society and is the entity through which we allow consumers to create and creators to consume. Each manual comes with a set of standardized components to ensure efficient communication.

History and Theory
Fall 2018
3223a Parallel Moderns: Crosscurrents in European and American Architecture, 1880-1940
Robert A.M. Stern

This seminar examines the argument that the exclusive discourses of tradition and innovation in the modern architecture—respectively identified as the *New Tradition* and the *New Pioneers* by Henry-Russell Hitchcock—share common genealogy and are integral to an understanding of modern architecture as a whole.

History and Theory
Fall 2018
3223a Parallel Moderns: Crosscurrents in European and American Architecture, 1880-1940
Robert A.M. Stern
Deo Deiparine

Strong geometrical voids punched through the pyramidal figure

For his façade in the Strada Vecchia, Plečnik would allude to the historical program of the Arsenale's rope-factory by using braided columns, supported below by a monumentalized Tuscan order. The ground level portal of this facade echoes the strong geometrical voids punched through the pyramidal figure, 'dressed,' following Semperian principles with an expressive masonry finish.

History and Theory
Fall 2018
3223a Parallel Moderns: Crosscurrents in European and American Architecture, 1880-1940
Robert A.M. Stern
Christopher Tritt

The balance of abstraction, technology, and tradition

Auguste Perret pioneered a synthesis of the technology of reinforced concrete with the French Classical tradition. This studied façade follows after Perret, playing back and forth between the three elements of the frame, the panel, and the vertical opening. The façade is a triumphal arch motif centered on a blank square. The composition draws on Perret's works such as the 1928 Salle Cartot and the 1931 Musée Bourdelle to celebrate the balance of abstraction, technology, and tradition so particular to his modernism.

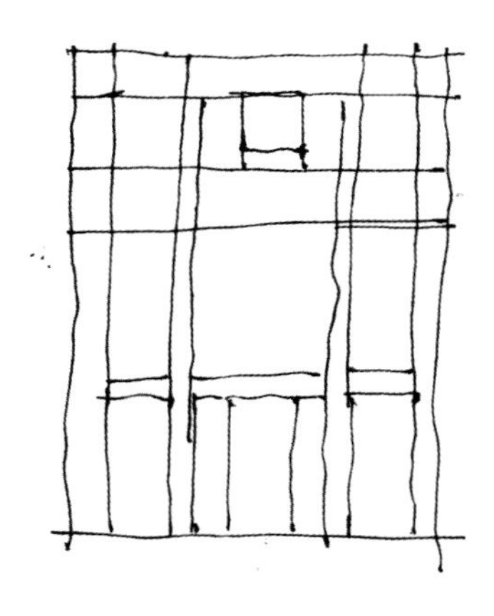

History and Theory
Fall 2018
3228a The Autobiographical House
Kurt Forster

Architects and artists have long built dwellings for themselves as showcases of their art, as sites of collecting and teaching, and as retreats from professional life. From Thomas Jefferson to Philip Johnson, from John Soane to Eileen Gray and Frank Gehry, this seminar examines key examples of architects and buildings as well as wide-ranging readings in autobiography.

History and Theory
Fall 2018
3228a The Autobiographical House
Kurt Forster
Kelley Johnson

Aino Marsio Aalto

Alvar and Aino Aalto designed their house and office near Helsinki, Finland in 1936. The house is a good example of the main ideals that the Aalto's architecture represented. The building is mostly made of natural materials with consideration of how they would age over time. The larger massing of the office is integrated into the more domestically scaled residence. Most importantly, it is integrated into the backyard gardens, with cascading green spaces to make a more fluid connection between indoor and outdoor. The house was designed not by Alvar Aalto alone, but, like most projects in their firm, it was a collaboration between Alvar and his wife, Aino Marsio-Aalto, and it is a representation of both their work. Aino is often described as stern and quiet, but she was also creative and focused on design that was affordable and humanist. Much of Aino Aalto's individual work is well known and correctly credited to her as her own work. However, she was a partner to Alvar in his work, and her influence on their work is a large part of why it was a more humanist modernism. Aino was a creative and experimental designer in her own right, and her influence on architecture in collaboration with Alvar is overshadowed by Alvar Aalto himself, just as her [...]

History and Theory
Fall 2018
3228a The Autobiographical House
Kurt Forster
Evan Sale

Moore Houses

To Charles Moore, the late Modern city's failure to provide distinct places disrupted the formation of the self and manifested a cultural crisis. His 1967 essay "Plug it in, Rameses" implicated architects:

> "[T]heir proper concern must be, as it has always been, the creation of *place*, the ordered extension of man's idea about himself in specific locations on the face of the Earth to make what Susanne Langer has called "ethnic domain". This, supposedly, will be useful to help people know where they are which will aid, by extension, in helping people know who they are." [1]

For the importance he gave the rooting of identity in place, in his own life he seemed dogged by a contradictory urge to pull up stakes, to shed the constraints of whatever he had most recently built. He traveled constantly, founding several architectural practices and designing eight houses for himself over a period of 30 years. The cycle of relocation suggests that he believed a changing self demanded a changing environment, or that new environments were necessary to professional [...]

1. Charles Moore. "Plug It in, Rameses, and See if It Lights Up, Because We Aren't Going to Keep It Unless It Works", in *Perspecta 11*. (MIT Press, 1967). 34.

History and Theory
Fall 2018
3265a Architecture and Urbanism of Modern Japan: Destruction, Continuation, and Creation
Yoko Kawai

This course examines how design philosophies and methodologies were developed in Japanese architecture during the 130-year period from the Meiji Restoration until the postmodern era.

History and Theory
Fall 2018
3265a Architecture and Urbanism of Modern Japan: Destruction, Continuation, and Creation
Yoko Kawai
Serena Ching

Spiritual Confrontation in Tadao Ando's Churches

Tadao Ando implements his own understanding of spirituality in the design of Western churches, namely Rokko Chapel and the Churches of Light and Water. The church as a typology has long existed in the Western world, from the early basilicas to gothic cathedrals and modern mega-churches. The church type had been introduced into Japan through early Portuguese missionaries, as early as the 16th century. Rather than an 'importation' of the Western church type into Japan, Ando intertwines his spiritual disposition and study of Western precedents to create his own internalized interpretation of the Christian church that is widely accepted as a 'sacred' or 'sublime' space by the Japanese and foreign, Christians and non-Christians alike.

Japanese Spiritual-Religious Philosophy

To begin, it is important to state the distinction between Western and Eastern philosophies of spirituality and religion. The Western Judeo-Christian belief had so often emphasized the dualism and opposition of mind and body. St. Augustine so clearly illustrates the torment between what he believes is righteous in spirit [...]

History and Theory
Fall 2018
3265a Architecture and Urbanism of Modern Japan: Destruction, Continuation, and Creation
Yoko Kawai
Katrina Yin

Railways and Retail: the Depāto as an Enduring Urban Chronicle

"Our city is never fixed; it is always in a state of transition. City is process—no concept is more certain than that" [1]

Few would disagree with the above observation of the Japanese city by Arata Isozaki. The quintessential Japanese city's voracious appetite for the new is balanced with reverence for the old. Of the many spatial endeavors that have formerly or currently contribute to the Japanese city in process, the Japanese department store is an exceptional model that embodies both stability and transition. There is little else of in modern history that can compete with the endurance, inventiveness, and proliferation of the Japanese *depāto*.

The *depāto*, or department store, is a cornerstone of Japanese urbanity—a typology that withstands wars and disasters through the sheer force of will of their truly resilient parent corporations. Each time resurrecting established infrastructure to house new, contemporaneous needs. The *depāto*'s close integration into public transit, social hierarchy, urban fabric, and communal needs have—until now—cemented its place as a precondition to urban life.

"The final section of 'Process Planning' sets forth the way in which architecture that has grown in reverse from the terminal minute is frozen in an instant. In other words, the building ceases to progress towards growth and instead begins moving in the direction of ruin. For this reason, my doctrine...is closer to the Buddhist doctrine of the impermanence of all things" [2]

The department store as we know it has fully undergone the first sections of what Isozaki characterizes in his Theory of Process Planning—of genesis and development. It is through chronicling the past and present of this singular infrastructural phenomenon that insight can be gained about the factors metabolized into its inception and growth. We will also consider an instance of the typology removed from its native context, briefly surfacing in America, as a foil for determining the efficacy of the model detached from said factors.

Finally, some thought must be given to the future outcomes of physical and architectural space left [...]

1. Isozaki, Arata in "Japanese Urban Space"; excerpted from Kira, Moriko, and Mariko Terada's *Japan Towards Totalscape: Contemporary Japanese Architecture, Urban Planning and Landscape*: NAI Publishers, 2000.
2. 25, Isozaki, Arata. *The Island Nation Aesthetic*. Academy Editions, 1996.

History and Theory
Fall 2018
3284a Architectural Writing
Cynthia Zarin

This course introduces students to how writers have addressed and described places and their relationships to such spaces to help students learn to write clearly about place themselves. The seminar treats the page itself as a place in which ideas about place, including current projects and proposals, can be articulated and made legible to readers both inside and outside the architectural community.

History and Theory
Fall 2018
3284a Architectural Writing
Cynthia Zarin
Michael Glassman

Yale Bowl

In 1914, at the advice of Yale graduate and architect Charles A. Ferry, the University dug a giant hole in the ground a mile west of campus. In the hole they would play a game they called football. As they dug they piled the earth around them in an oval, creating a berm forty feet tall in all directions. They cut thirty tunnels through the berm, linking the field at the center of the hole to the grounds outside, and built enough stands on the interior slope of the berm to hold over 60,000 people. The stadium resembled a giant basin. They called it the Yale Bowl. It was the largest stadium in the world and a testament to Yale's status as the greatest football team anywhere to be found.

Yale's climb to the top of the football world began before the game properly existed. They say that it was Princeton and Rutgers who played the first football game, but like most details of early histories, this point is debatable. The game that Princeton and Rutgers played in 1869 much more closely resembled rugby than football. Players were prohibited from touching the ball with their hands and play was continuous, with possession decided by a scrum. It would not be until 1882 that Walter Camp, former Yale player and then Yale coach, [...]

135

History and Theory
Fall 2018
3284a Architectural Writing
Cynthia Zarin
David Schaengold

A Ghost Story

I was assigned the Beam Room the Summer I moved into the house. The room was small, but its ceiling sloped down to the dormer window in a way that reminded me of Balzac. It was the room, I thought, of someone who would later be the subject of a monograph. This poetic aspect was compromised by the six-inch-wide steel beam that bisected the room. The beam entered at the upper molding on the north side and plunged into the floor about a foot away from the baseboard on the south side. I never managed to fit any more furniture into the room than a bed, a desk with a chair, and an electronic keyboard.

The friend who had found me the room lived off the same landing, in the Ghost Room. His room had two windows, an air conditioner, and a couch. I always accepted his invitations to walk across the landing for a nightcap, but the couch annoyed me, and my envy of it almost spoiled our friendship.

I never discovered who owned the house legally, but the priest who lived on the second floor seemed free to do as he pleased with it. Since it was vastly too large for his own needs, he rented out rooms to any unmarried young man who could get a current resident to vouch for him. While I was living in the house the tenants included two of my friends, a few other recent college grads [...]

History and Theory
Fall 2018
3286a Architecture after the Rain: Theory and Design in the Post-Atomic Age
Anthony Vidler

This seminar examines architectural, literary, and critical responses to war, threat, anxiety, and dystopia between 1945 and the present. The theories and practices of surrealism and counter-surrealism provide a foundation in the critical and psychoanalytical construction of and influence on post-atomic architectural practices from World War II to the present.

History and Theory
Fall 2018
3286a Architecture after the Rain: Theory and Design in the Post-Atomic Age
Anthony Vidler
Sheau Yun Lim

Printing, Painting, Architecture: Constant's New Babylon

What is it to study the prints of Constant's New Babylon?

In an essay on the 2000 Drawing Center exhibition of Constant's New Babylon in New York, Mark Wigley posed a parallel question on the role of drawings in his oeuvre, drawing defined as "a unique work on paper". [1] Much critical attention has been paid to the models and, to a lesser extent, drawings of New Babylon. For the specific purposes of this paper, I thus pose the question, what is it to isolate the prints of New Babylon, a single medium, in a project that is "polemically multimedia for a multimedia life"?

While the tradition of drawing has long been held sacrosanct in the making of architecture, the printed form of architecture—as it relates to a modern movement—has largely been confined to studies of the architectural book or studies of mass media. The focus is thus placed on the effect of the object's ability to travel, rather than the considerations of the making of the printed object. This is not to overlook the printed form's distinctive feature [...]

1. Mark Wigley, "Paper, Scissors, Blur", *The Activist Drawing*, (Cambridge, MA: MIT Press), 27.

History and Theory
Fall 2018
3286a Architecture after the Rain: Theory and Design in the Post-Atomic Age
Anthony Vidler
David Schaengold

The Liturgical Ruin: Rudolf Schwarz's Annakirche

As an architectural figure, the ruin is ambiguous; it has both a historical and a trans-historical mode. The trans-historical mode is well represented by the European 18th century's enthusiasm for visiting and making pictures of ruins. Piranesi's Roman vedute do not arise from nor do they provoke interest in the specific cataclysms that turned building into ruin, even in the cases when the buildings depicted were destroyed in historically identifiable ways; History itself is the cataclysm. His Campo Marzio map is neither historical reconstruction nor proposal, but an atmospheric generator, and the atmosphere it generates is essentially non-specific; it belongs to no particular time but rather to the passage of time as such.

The non-specificity of ruin as an architectural figure has sometimes produced something more than the delectation Piranesi offered to the buyers of his books; in the 20th century it became useful for political purposes, as WG Sebald writes in his *Natural History of Destruction*, describing the reaction of the German people to the Allied bombing campaigns of World War II. If the [...]

History and Theory
Fall 2018
3289a Bauhaus @ 100
Eeva-Liisa Pelkonen, Trattie Davies

In celebration of the centennial of the 1919 founding of Bauhaus in Weimar, students conducted a series of material and formal experiments expanding the physical explorations of form, color, texture, and space conducted in the legendary Vorkurs program, taught by Josef Albers from 1923 to 1933. Students examine the writings of Anni Albers and Herbert Bayer, addressing textiles, installations, and graphic experiments and their role in architecture.

History and Theory
Fall 2018
3289a Bauhaus @ 100
Eeva-Liisa Pelkonen, Trattie Davies
Emily Cass

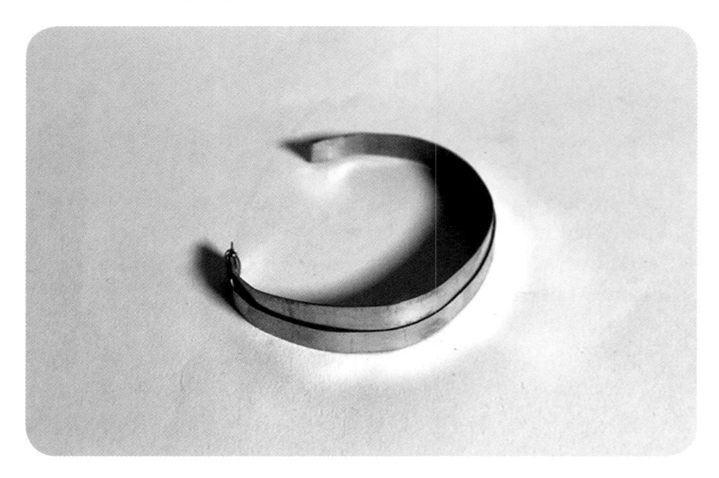

Wearable quote

This wearable quote was inspired by the Bauhaus' commitment to the economy of means and their dedication to the inherent properties of materials. These bracelets were conceived by exploring the memory of a material (metal) and how it responds over time. I first created the simple brass band, which then served as a mold for the following bracelet. After wrapping wire around the brass band, I removed the newly formed coil from the mold. Its ultimate expression was the memory of having once been coiled.

History and Theory
Fall 2018
3289a Bauhaus @ 100
Eeva-Liisa Pelkonen, Trattie Davies
Orli Hakanoglu, Rachel Mulder

Pliable Surface: Anni Albers and the Bauhaus Weaving Workshop

[Excerpt, edited, from Orli's essay Pliable Surface: Anni Albers and the Bauhaus Weaving Workshop]

The Josef and Anni Albers Foundation in Bethany, Connecticut is dedicated to the life and work of husband and wife Josef and Anni Albers, pioneers of modernism and key figures at the Bauhaus school of art and design in Germany. Anni Albers and other members of the workshop helped re-position the medium as a part of the school's avant-garde design ethos by considering its performative, functional, and structural dimensions. In this sense, textiles were seen as not only an integral component of a complete building conceived as a total-work-of-art, but also the very foundation of its material and spatial logic.

Students in the Bauhaus at 100 seminar traveled to the Foundation on October 24 where they studied original textile samples by Anni Albers and were introduced to manual textile experimentation of their own. Working in pairs, students constructed backstrap looms (a tradition Anni took back with her from Central America where she learned from artisans' weaving methods), and were encouraged to explore a variety of interlocking patterns of the warp (vertical) and weft (horizontal) threads while experimenting with the interaction of different yarn colors, thicknesses, and compositions. In many ways the exercise from start to finish was true to how Anni thought one should learn weaving: "Unburdened by any practical considerations, this play with materials produced amazing results, textiles striking in their novelty, their fullness of color and texture, and possessing often a quite barbaric beauty. This freedom of approach seems worth retaining for every novice." [1] Having struggled with relatively simple weave patterns to work on their own backstrap looms, students returned to school with 'barbarically beautiful' textiles and a deepened appreciation for the technical mastery and creative extents of Anni Albers' work.

1. Anni Albers, "The Weaving Workshop", in *On Weaving* (Middletown, CT: Wesleyan University Press, 1965), 141.

History and Theory
Fall 2018
3289a Bauhaus @ 100
Eeva-Liisa Pelkonen, Trattie Davies
Louis Koushouris

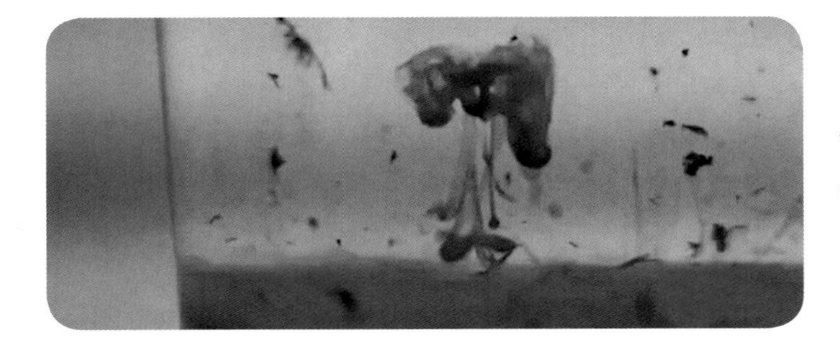

Liquid color

Experimentation is a means of understanding the illusory effects of color, due to its instability and relativity. It is perceived by contrast of adjacent colors. By changing the measure of a single color in a composition, the entire perception changes as well. The effect comes from complementary comparison, by the relationships between colors. Liquid color is an experiment imbuing water with pigment to study movement, magnification, and the relationships of color.

History and Theory
Fall 2018
3290a Body Politics: Designing Equitable Public Space
Joel Sanders

This seminar explores the design challenges triggered by an urgent social justice issue: the imperative to create safe accessible public spaces for people of different races, genders, and disabilities. Students proposed alternative design strategies that allow a spectrum of different embodied people to productively mix in public space.

History and Theory
Fall 2018
3290a Body Politics: Designing Equitable Public Space
Joel Sanders
Robert Coombs, Hojae Lee, Lissette Valenzuela

More inclusive toward different bodies

Two group members, one being a user of a wheelchair and another being an able bodied person, visited the Yale University Art Gallery with gopro cameras attached to their head to record and compare their experience. The raw footage was juxtaposed and played simultaneously to show the dramatic differences between the two users. Each experience was traced upon an identical axonometric drawing of the museum to show the building design limiting one's experience. Based on these two drawing methods, three areas were selected, proposed with a separate intervention that could be more inclusive toward different bodies visiting the gallery.

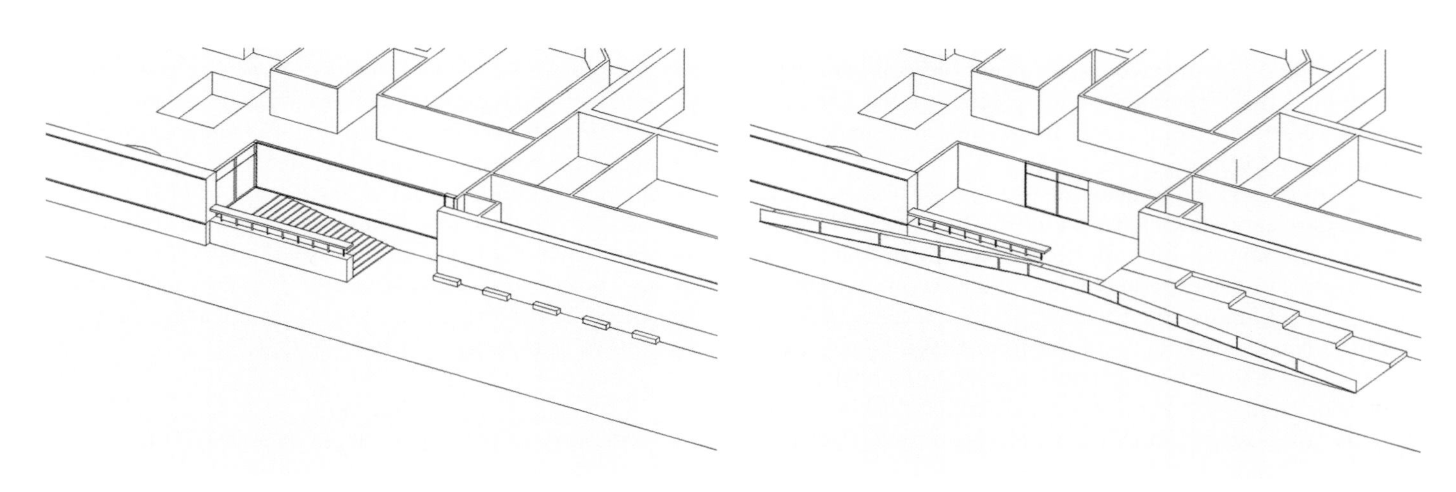

History and Theory
Fall 2018
3290a Body Politics: Designing Equitable Public Space
Joel Sanders
Amanda Hu, Jenny Katz, Sam Shoemaker, Adam Thibodeaux

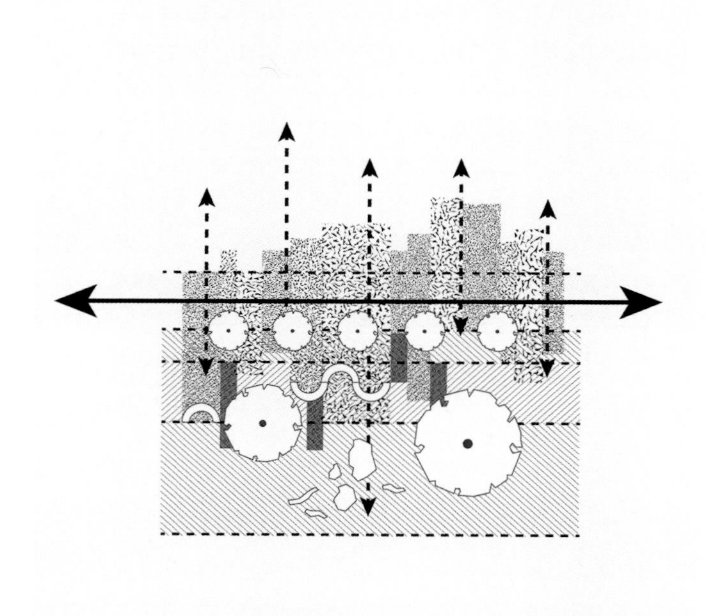

Reimagining the path as a porous assembly of uses

The proposal uses the New Haven Green as a case-study for the urban park, acknowledging the path as a link between directional movement and the intersection of divergent bodies. The proposal starts by maintaining the existing width of the pathways to allow directional flow through the site, and then identifies additional programmatic zones that run parallel to it. By reimagining the path as a porous assembly of uses, the proposal provides a stimulating and multi-generational vision for the New Haven Green, as well as a prototypical case study for a re-imagined public pathway.

History and Theory

Spring 2019

History and Theory
Spring 2019
3012b Architectural Theory
Marta Caldeira

This course explores the history of Western architectural theory, from 1750 to the present. Topics include theories of origin, type and character, the picturesque, questions of style and ornament, standardization and functionalism, critiques of modernism, as well as more contemporary debates on historicism, technology, and environmentalism.

History and Theory
Spring 2019
3012b Architectural Theory
Marta Caldeira
Christine Pan

Chinoiserie in the Garden: Power and the Picturesque

The prominent incorporation of "Chinese" elements in British landscape gardens of the late 18th to 19th century corresponds to a contemporaneous interpretation of the picturesque that mediates between nature and man, a view that reflected cultural power dynamics and allowed the expression of political ideas through landscape.

The Anglo-Chinese Garden

The first recorded European writing on the architecture of the Chinese empire can be traced to Marco Polo's accounts, circa 1300, of the imperial palace of Kanbaluc (Beijing). [1] A few centuries later, the *Historia del Gran Reyno de la China*—published in Rome in 1585 by Spanish Augustinian Juan Gonzalez de Mendoza—also contains a brief mention of Chinese building as follows: "In this kingdom in all places there be men excellent in architecture" who built "mightie buildings and verie curious." [2] Almost an entire century following that [...]

1. Lothar Ledderose, *Chinese Influence on European Art, Sixteenth to Eighteenth Centuries.*
2. Ibid.

History and Theory
Spring 2019
3012b Architectural Theory
Marta Caldeira
Sarah Weiss

Marcus Garvey Park Village: Fragments of a Radiant City

Architecture has a limited capacity to address the quality of life of its inhabitants. It is not that practitioners of architecture are at a loss for observations on how people use and respond to architectural space—in fact the opposite is true. Rather, it is difficult to traverse the disconnect that exists between these observations and the output of design. Architects are painfully aware of what they would like to improve, in how buildings fail to contribute to their inhabitants' quality of life, but such efforts are often thwarted by the difficulty inherent in translating between sociological concerns and formal ones. The chasm that exists between these two modes of architectural thought requires a bridging mechanism that mediates between what motivates progress towards better architecture and how the shape of it is operated upon.

The Marcus Garvey Park Village apartments confront this insurmountable void between theory and praxis that inhibits architecture's ability to effectively ameliorate the lives of its inhabitants. Though bloated with theoretical underpinnings that address quality of [...]

History and Theory
Spring 2019
3216a Case Studies in Architectural Criticism
Carter Wiseman

This seminar concentrates on issues that influence the way modern buildings and their architects are perceived by critics, scholars, and the public. The careers of such architects as Frank Lloyd Wright, Eero Saarinen, Louis Kahn, Philip Johnson, Robert Venturi, and Frank Gehry provide a framework for the examination of how patronage, fashion, social change, theory, finance, and politics affect the place of prominent designers and their work in the historical record.

History and Theory
Spring 2019
3216a Case Studies in Architectural Criticism
Carter Wiseman
Dimitris Hartonas

What Makes a Good Building?

Slowness. Slowness makes a good building; but let me explain.

During the eight years I have been actively dealing with architecture, I have studied and become fascinated by more than a wide range of architectural styles. Although I would not identify them as such at the time, as I believed their claims of being architecture instead of a specific style, it became evident that good and bad buildings were to be found across the spectrum. Whether I tried to put the different approaches into practice myself, or delved into understanding their inner workings from a historical or theoretical perspective, I was always able to reach a conclusion regarding an individual building's success. My main criterion for making such judgements, apart from my instinct that I still trust, was the degree to which a building was adhering to the principles of the architectural style, language, current or theoretical framework it was associated with. During my time at Yale, I came to realize that the more one knows about the specificities of a style or current, the easier it becomes to argue both sides; in favor and against a building. My own tool was coming back to haunt me and render me unable to reach a conclusion. [...]

History and Theory
Spring 2019
3216a Case Studies in Architectural Criticism
Carter Wiseman
Zack Lenza

A Building I Dislike: Luis Barragán's Casa Gilardi

Near the end of a tree-lined avenue in Mexico City sits Luis Barragán's Casa Gilardi. Like many other houses on the block, it presents a fortress-like façade, exchanging gated doors and grilled windows for solid doors and black stone. On top rests a hot pink rectilinear volume, attempting to make up for its lower counterpart's muteness by screaming its personality. A single square window with opaque yellow glass asserts itself into the streetscape but affords no views in or out.

Throughout the house, color is treated as the primary element. Windows such as the one described above bring in obnoxiously large swaths of colored light; walls are painted hot pink, red, blue. The whole house appears like a three-dimensional painting; a building that wishes it did not have to be a building. This can be seen in the dining room, which features a pool roughly the size of the walkable floor adjacent to it. The room is completely white, save for a red, free-standing wall in the pool whose sole function appears to be to contrast with the blue-painted sections on the walls behind it. This is the location of a slice of light from a thin window above. All the visual interest in the room comes from the paint on the walls. Putting a pool in a dining room is [...]

History and Theory
Spring 2019
3272b Exhibitionism: Politics of Display
Joel Sanders

This seminar uses the resources of Yale's art collection to map the intertwined histories of art and gallery architecture from the 16th century to today. The past will allow us to imagine alternative futures for making museums interactive environments that promote multi-sensory experience among people of different races, genders and abilities.

History and Theory
Spring 2019
3272b Exhibitionism: Politics of Display
Joel Sanders
Allison Minto, Deirdre Plaus, Rhea Schmid

Systems of Power at (dis)Play

How to Unpack White Supremacy
in the 21st Century Museum through an Analysis
of Human and Non-Human Hierarchies

Museums are portrayed as beacons of culture and knowledge; however, closer examination reveals motivations that are less agreeable. Museums are and continue to be deeply rooted in a history of othering, supremacy, and control. These complex power dynamics, especially as they relate to the effect of white supremacy, are at play from the scale of a painting to how a museum sits within a city. By focusing on one of the BAC's galleries on 18th century art, our project addresses the following questions: How do we begin to interrogate the predominant lens through which we have been conditioned to view works of art? How do we make sense of the national museum as an institution, rooted in racism? By bringing the discussion around race and animals, we look to unpack the power dynamics at (dis)play, where matters of race cannot be ignored, while challenging our anthropocentric assumptions. Finally, our design proposal addresses the physical space in which these pieces are displayed more critically through specifically designed 'filters'. [...]

History and Theory
Spring 2019
3283b After the Modern Movement
Robert A.M. Stern

Postmodernism should not be seen as a style, but rather as a condition that arose out of the ahistorical, acontextual, self-referential, materialistic modernism that prevailed in the post-WWII era. This seminar is motivated by conditions in contemporary practice, including the renewed interest in postmodernism and the return of precedent to the design process. Students explore a number of architects who have been overlooked and deserve renewed consideration.

History and Theory
Spring 2019
3283b After the Modern Movement
Robert A.M. Stern
Alejandro Duran

A heretic among heretics

I found myself wondering what Eric Moss would have submitted to the Strada Novissima at the 1980 Venice Biennale when I realized, "that's just the problem; to think, to prefigure, to operate in a categorized world of discreetly circumscribed Platonic ideas, that is exactly what Moss would never do."

This hypothetical façade for the 1980 Biennale draws upon the formal language of some of Moss' projects from around that time. Around the time of the Biennale, Moss's was a young and fledgling practice, but he nonetheless was exploring instincts and intellectual methods that have persisted throughout his career. A destabilizing figure even in the context of the "L.A. Ten", Moss's work shows a propensity toward what Vidler cites as "Giedion's progressive hope and Benjamin's melancholic pathology". Truly, Moss remains a heretic among heretics.

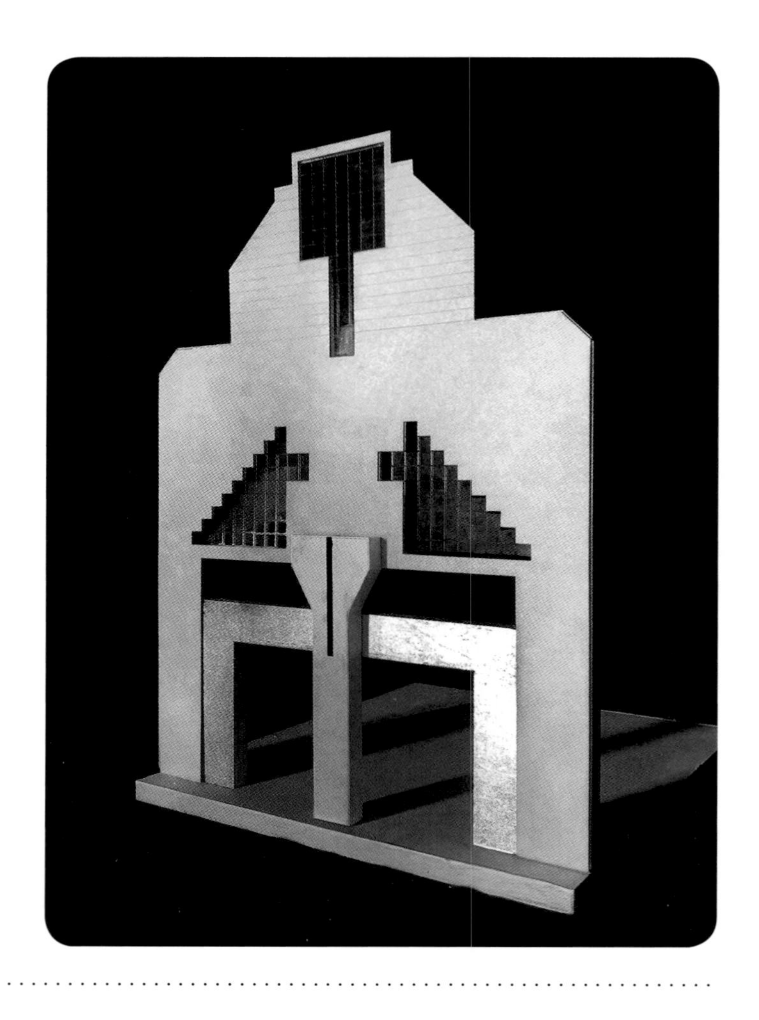

History and Theory
Spring 2019
3283b After the Modern Movement
Robert A.M. Stern
Evan Sale

A fusion of Miesian steel construction and Schinkelesque neoclassicism

The façade emulates Thomas Beeby's language of around 1980, a hybrid of Neoclassicism and Miesian Modernism. The nearest precedent is the Conrad Sulzer Library in Chicago, which inverts the Miesian play of solid core and thin envelope. A solid ground floor has both Miesian reveals and arched openings that resemble those of H.H. Richardson's Marshal Fields Warehouse. The upper story is a fusion of Miesian steel construction and Schinkelesque neoclassicism. Literal references are sparing: windows with acroteria, a wide-flange beam sitting in for an entablature. In the design for the *Strada*, a massive arcade supports an attenuated *piano nobile*. Reentrant corners acknowledge Mies, and at the top an entablature and pediment are rendered in steel. The façade pursues what Beeby called "the hidden part of Mies, the suppressed romanticism that lies within neoclassicism."

History and Theory
Spring 2019
3287b Havana's Architecture: Recent Past and Possible Future
Esther da Costa Meyer

This seminar covers architecture and urbanism in Havana: the old colonial city, Art Deco, the International Style, the footprint of the American presence (from the mob to nearby sugar mills), and buildings from the Cuban Revolution and the Soviet period. At the heart of the course are the main challenges facing the city's extraordinary architectural heritage.

History and Theory
Spring 2019
3287b Havana's Architecture: Recent Past and Possible Future
Esther da Costa Meyer
Manasi Punde

Being Connected

Wifi & Public Space in Havana

Like many cities around the world, the history of urban planning in Havana has been greatly guided by its ambitions to address increasing population density. Most of Havana's significant urban moves have been an attempt to solve this problem. As the city got denser, and solutions to housing were arrived upon, the role of public space grew significantly. Like in most dense cities, these spaces provide the city dwellers with a space for respite and social and cultural exchange.

In Havana, however, they also play a very different and specific key role. The urban spaces of Havana are not just the key to social engagement for its people, but they are also its physical portals to the world of digital information and exchange; the primary connecting place to the world wide web. This is where people are increasingly coming together, physically, to wonder at a digital world, individually. Making public spaces synonymous with the internet has affected the use of urban space dramatically. This paper seeks to understand the different changing relationships between public space, people, and the internet. [...]

History and Theory
Spring 2019
3287b Havana's Architecture: Recent Past and Possible Future
Esther da Costa Meyer
Maya Sorabjee

The Social Practice of Housing in Old Havana

Never Finished, a short story by Cuban writer Nancy Alonso, tells the tale of a couple living in a dilapidated yet beloved house in Havana. Carmen and Manolo face a leaking roof above their kitchen and have decided to swap their home in order to escape the daily struggles of seeking waterproofing, filling roof cracks with asphalt, and fearing falling chunks of ceiling. At the end of the story, however, they decide not to *permutar*; instead, they don hard hats and sit together in their leaking kitchen. Carmen's own invented adage hovers above their heads: "In a house, you never finish, and if you don't take care, it'll finish you."[1]

Many residents of Old Havana face similar daily predicaments as the built fabric of the historic centre has worsened in physical condition due to increasing densification in the years since the Revolution and a destabilizing global climate. But despite the extreme decay of the housing stock, or perhaps because of it, the social bonds that stitch together Old Havana are as strong as ever. Informal systems of mutual aid exist in [...]

1. Nancy Alonso, "Never Finished". *Closed for Repairs*, translated by Anne Fountain, (Curbstone Press, 2007), 53.

History and Theory
Spring 2019
3288b MANY
Keller Easterling

This University-wide interdisciplinary seminar is designed to bring together graduate, professional, and undergraduate students to research and develop MANY—an online platform to facilitate migration through an exchange of needs. MANY rethinks cosmopolitan mobility for all those who might say, “We don’t want your citizenship or your victimhood or your segregation or your bad jobs. We don’t want to stay.”

History and Theory
Spring 2019
3288b MANY
Keller Easterling
Sara Alajmi, Michelle Badr, Holly Bushman, Phoebe Harris, Limy Rocha

MANY + Construction Labor

The US is currently facing a labor shortage in construction due to an aging population and societal shifts away from vocational training. Today, 42% of the workforce is comprised of migrant workers. Due to the current political climate, we believe this group is at risk and aim to develop a model that brings both value and legal status to skilled construction laborers. Our scenario calls for an exchange between individuals who hold valuable environmental or technical construction knowledge and people living in at-risk areas. The skills learned through these technical collaborations can elevate the value of construction laborers and lead to enhanced building practices across climates.

144

History and Theory
Spring 2019
3288b MANY
Keller Easterling
Robert Jett, Minakshi Mohanta, Claudia Mezey, Justin Tsang

MANY_mirri

MANY is a platform designed to enable skills exchange; *mirri* proposes a new layer on MANY that enhances MANY’s function in facilitating connections. It’s grassroots, agnostic to types of exchange or learning and thus a testing ground to observe the potential of new contexts for learning. With *mirri*, we add a layer of credentialing to the MANY platform, allowing for the visualization of users’ credentials and recognition of skills transferred through MANY exchanges.

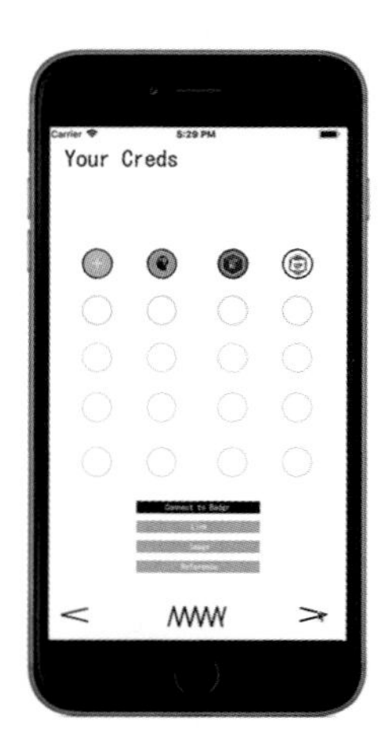

History and Theory
Spring 2019
3291b GREATS: China’s Big Projects 1949–1980
Amy Lelyveld

This seminar focuses on the large-scale experiments in new Chinese building during the tenure of Mao Zedong. Over this time span, many fundamental notions of daily life—language, expression, family, education, countryside, and city—were redefined and radically tested. These new representations of culture included a paradox for architecture: how to both reflect progress while remaining place-specific.

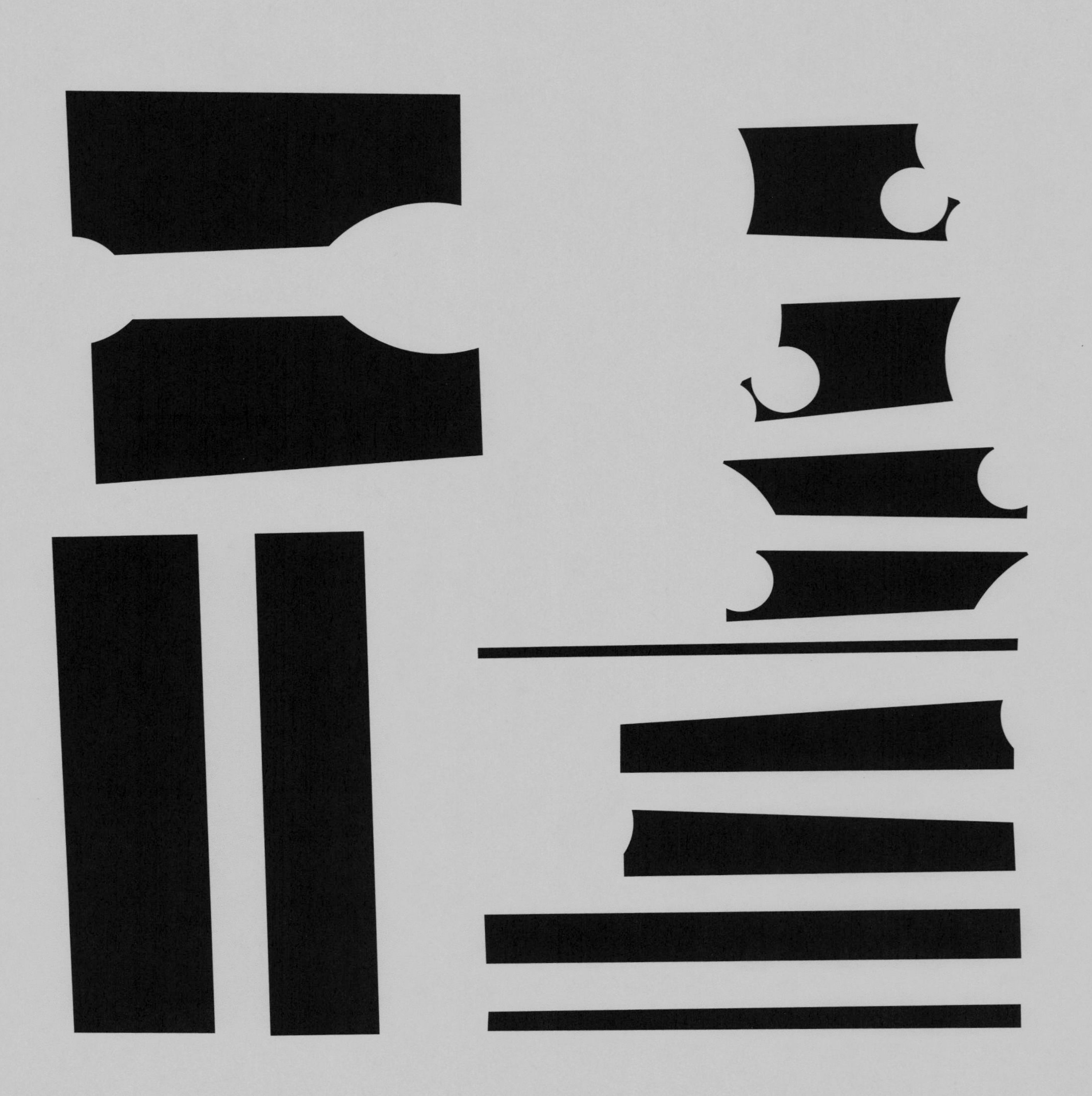

History and Theory
Spring 2019
3291b GREATS: China's Big Projects 1949-1980
Amy Lelyveld
Rachel Lefevre

Daqing: A Failed Model (Organism)

In the winter of 1913, M.L. Fuller and F.G. Clapp, petroleum geologists for Standard Oil, arrived in China to begin their oil finding expedition in the Northern provinces. [1] They set out across the plains and the mountains of China on horseback, in wheelbarrows, and Peking cart. Travelling along ancient roads dug out of loess and thick sandstone, they stayed in local villages, visited temples and encountered Mongolian bandits. [2] Along the way, they noted geologic formations, researched soil composition and eventually began drilling experimental oil wells, calculating their output. [3] In the three years prior, Standard Oil had begun the process of establishing a private partnership between itself and the Chinese Nationalist Government in an effort to re-assert itself into the Asiatic oil markets. [4] In the end, Standard Oil was granted exclusive prospecting and discovery rights to Oil found in the North-eastern Provinces in exchange for $15,000,000 in investment in China [...]

1 Fuller, M. L. "Explorations in China".
2 Ibid.
3 Ibid.
4 Pugach, Noel H. "Standard Oil and Petroleum Development in Early Republican China". 454.

History and Theory
Spring 2019
3291b GREATS: China's Big Projects 1949-1980
Amy Lelyveld
Colin Sutherland

Radio in China: Power and its Discontents

The emergence of radio communication in the twentieth century opened up new opportunities in the transmission of information and power. News no longer travelled at the speed of the fastest messenger, but rather could cross an entire country instantaneously. The potential for radio broadcasting as a political tool was quickly recognized by both Republican China and the Communist Party of China. Following the victory of the Communists and the establishment of the People's Republic of China in 1949, the Chinese government focused on building a national broadcasting system to help consolidate its authority and legitimacy. With the onset of the Cultural Revolution in 1966, systems of authority were upturned, and the political role of radio and broadcasting fell into flux, between leftist, rightist, and ultraleftist uses. The distancing between speaker and listener reinforced the "imperial" aura of the speaker, and privileged a speaker as the deliverer of the truth, making it a valuable asset for the many factions that emerged during the Cultural Revolution. Between functioning as a regulator of daily life, as a tool for the raising of class consciousness, and as a means of inciting the masses into popularv revolt, radio as a medium easily transitioned across the contradictions [...]

History and Theory
Spring 2019
3291b GREATS: China's Big Projects 1949-1980
Amy Lelyveld
Jingqiu Zhang

Reconsidering the "Informal" and its History from the 1950s–1980s in Beijing's Hutongs

From the 1950s to the beginning of 1980s, most of the urban fabric in Beijing's inner city have been altered through a series of transformations. The extreme housing shortage and overpopulation in the inner-city area have exerted a great pressure on the traditional courtyard houses and alleyways, which lead to series of "informal" constructions. This research attempts to trace the concept of "informality" in China using inner City of Beijing as context. It intends to understand the political-social-economic mechanism behind the "informal" constructions around the hutong districts. The research will examine the functional, social and economic roles that those informal constructions play in the ecology of urban environment based on specific historical background. It intends to fully understand the negotiation between individual and state power, private and public, and their implications for the future improvement of the district. The research will be divided into three parts chronologically: before Culture Revolution, during the [...]

History and Theory

Summer 2019

History and Theory
Summer 2019
3000c Madrid Summer Program: Deploying the Archive
Iñaqui Carnicero

This summer program focuses on the potential of the Archive to stimulate new strategies for design. Our base camp is located in the heart of the city of Madrid at the Norman Foster Foundation, a new cutting-edge institution that promotes interdisciplinary thinking and research. Each student explores, re-appropriates, and re-arranges the available documentation to discover new narratives to inform their architectural thinking.

History and Theory
Summer 2019
3000c Madrid Summer Program: Deploying the Archive
Iñaqui Carnicero
Page Comeaux

Previously unseen commonalities

Inspired by the *Twelve Around One* exhibition of Buckminster Fuller's work in 1981, this exhibition proposal delaminates patent drawings from photographs in order to retain the autonomy of each, but allows the user of the exhibition to manipulate their arrangement in order to create a new narrative for each of the projects. By suspending panels from tracks on the ceiling of the exhibition space, new configurations of photographs and drawings are possible, generating previously unseen commonalities between projects by Fuller and Foster. Using patent drawings of architectural work, *On Precedent* shifts attention away from the heroic image of an architect as the inventor of a building or design, to the sources from which they draw inspiration as a more honest depiction of the architectural design process.

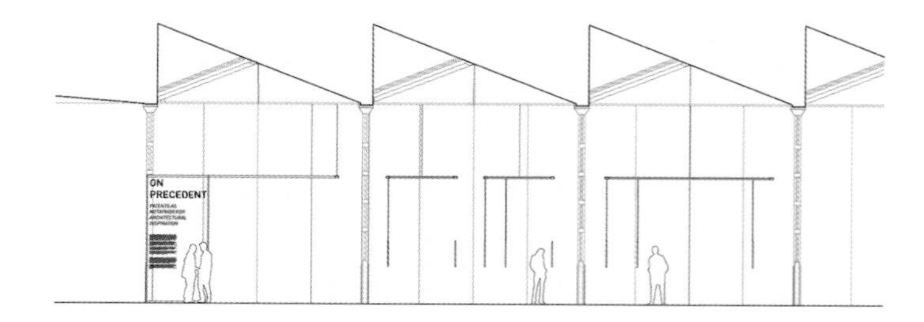

History and Theory
Summer 2019
3000c Madrid Summer Program: Deploying the Archive
Iñaqui Carnicero
Rachel Lefevre

Subverting notions of the hi-tech

In March of 2018, The Sainsbury Centre hosted an exhibition entitled *Superstructures: The New Architecture 1960–1990*, an homage to the "hi-tech". The focal point of the exhibition, rather than being an object held within, was to be the Sainsbury Centre itself, which celebrated its 40th Year in March of 2018. The Sainsbury Centre, like much of Foster's work, is celebrated as the pinnacle of the hi-tech in architectural criticism and practice alike. Yet, this hi-tech narrative is a myopic one, backed by easily made observations of discrete pieces rather than holistic thinking. "[Tech]stile" re-examines the archive in relation to representations of 1900s British textile manufacturing practices in order to re-consider Foster's connection to the hi-tech. The pairing of Foster's drawings with illustrations from well-known textile and basket making manuals writes a new narrative, one which subverts notions of the hi-tech through understandings of the low-tech and provides a new lens through which to view the work of Norman Foster.

Urbanism and Landscape

Urbanism and Landscape

Fall 2018

Urbanism and Landscape
Fall 2018
4021a Introduction to Planning and Development
Alexander Garvin

This course demonstrates the ways in which financial and political feasibility determine the design of buildings and the character of the built environment. Students propose projects and then adjust them to the conflicting interests of financial institutions, real estate developers, civic organizations, community groups, public officials, and the widest variety of participants in the planning process.

Urbanism and Landscape
Fall 2018
4021a Introduction to Planning and Development
Alexander Garvin
Michael Glassman, Christine Pan, Rhea Schmid

183 State Street

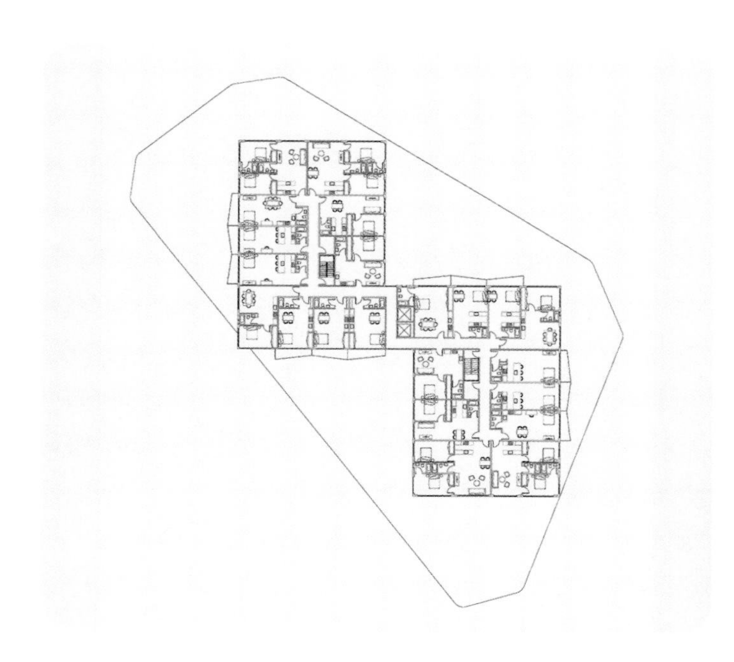

Urbanism and Landscape
Fall 2018
4021a Introduction to Planning and Development
Alexander Garvin
Michael Glassmann, Jewel Pei

Mixed-use development focused on technological innovation

The Partnership for New York City has designated the area surrounding Court Square—44th Drive, 45th Avenue and 45th Road—as an appropriate area for mixed-use development focused on technological innovation. With the creation of the Long Island City Innovation Corridor along 44th Drive, LIC will become the center of New York's Innovation Economy.

Urbanism and Landscape
Fall 2018
4221b Introduction to Commercial Real Estate
Kevin Gray

This course examines five basic types of commercial real estate–office, industrial, retail, multifamily, and hotel–from the standpoint of the developer, lender, and investor.

Urbanism and Landscape
Fall 2018
4221b Introduction to Commercial Real Estate
Kevin Gray
Misha Semenov

Prepared by Semenov Advisors for Spinnaker

This report, prepared by Semenov Advisors for Spinnaker, analyzes the potential returns from acquisition of parcels on the Broadway retail strip. One portfolio includes the 14 properties owned by Yale, totalling 234,200 SF, while the second is comprised of the 8 properties owned by other entities, totalling 55,500 SF. Within each of these portfolios, the parcels are subdivided into square footages of five categories: Class A and B retail; second-floor office spaces; multifamily residential; and parking garage. Each of these five components is treated as its own investment, with appropriate cap rates, income, and expenses factored in. Each portfolio is then combined into a blended total and assigned an overall mortgage. The initial run of these numbers suggests that buying the non-Yale portfolio may yield a slightly higher IRR, but other factors, such as higher risk and lower building quality, need to be factored in.

Urbanism and Landscape
Fall 2018
4222a History of Landscape Architecture: Antiquity to 1700 in Western Europe
Bryan Fuermann

This course presents an introductory survey of the history of gardens and the interrelationship of architecture and landscape architecture in Western Europe from antiquity to 1700. Students examine the evolution of several key elements in landscape design including architectural and garden typologies; the boundaries between inside and outside; issues of topography and geography; etc.

Urbanism and Landscape
Fall 2018
4222a History of Landscape Architecture: Antiquity to 1700 in Western Europe
Bryan Fuermann
Shiyan Chen

Flowing from one built structure to another

Water, marked in black, takes various forms of underground canals, contained streams, pools, and fountains throughout Hadrian's Villa. Flowing from one built structure to another and following the topography of the site, water is employed as an artistic device connecting independent parts of the villa and activating its whole.

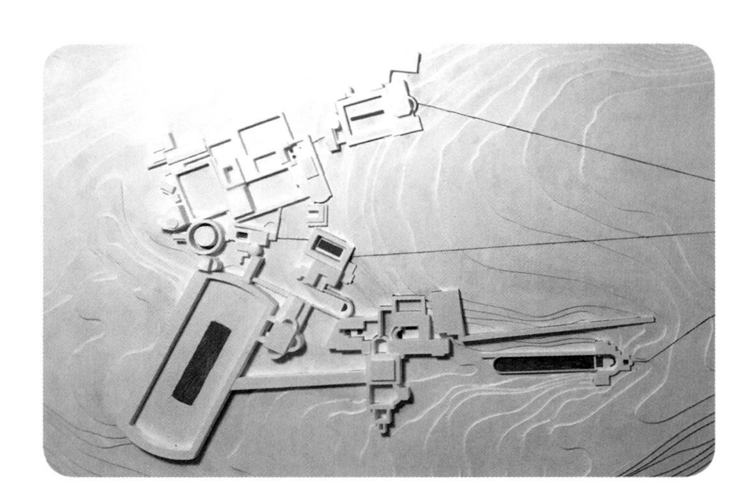

Urbanism and Landscape
Fall 2018
4222a History of Landscape Architecture: Antiquity to 1700 in Western Europe
Bryan Fuermann
Nicholas Miller

"Casinum" tea set

A tea set, in the tradition of Swid Powell, based on a reading of Marcus Terentius Varro's "De Re Rustica" and elements of the ancient Roman garden.

From Left to Right: Tholos (Hot Water), Skyphos (Tea Cup), Herma (Cream), Avis Caveam (Tea Bags), Labrum (Sugar Bowl).

Urbanism and Landscape Spring 2019

Urbanism and Landscape
Spring 2019
4223b History of British Landscape Architecture: 1600 to 1900
Bryan Fuermann

This seminar examines chronologically the history of landscape architecture and country-house architecture in Britain from 1500 to 1900. The collection of the Yale Center for British Art is used for primary visual material, and a trip to England over spring break, allows students to visit firsthand the landscape parks studied in this seminar.

Urbanism and Landscape
Spring 2019
4223b History of British Landscape Architecture: 1600 to 1900
Bryan Fuermann
Melissa Weigel

Bridge at Blenheim Palace

This is a model of the Bridge at Blenheim Palace, designed by John Vanbrugh. The flooding was done at a later stage by Capability Brown.

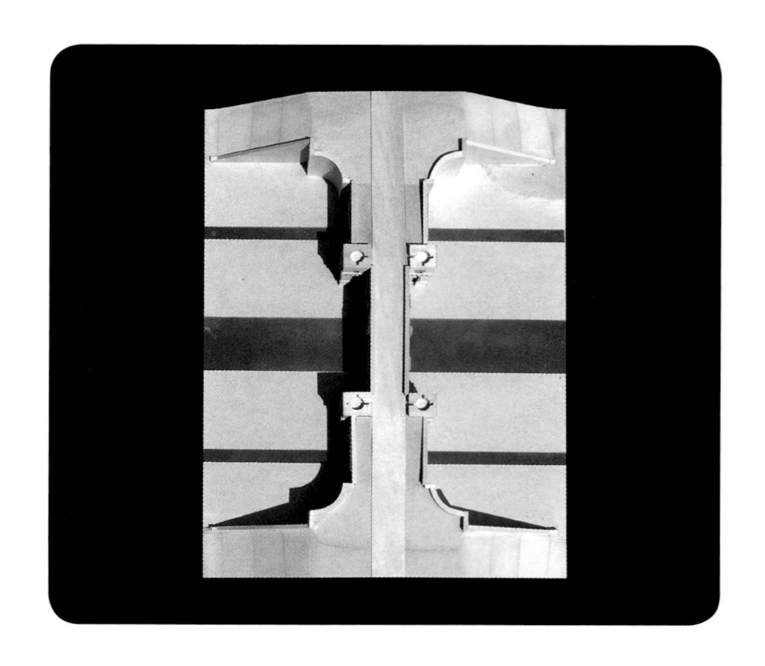

Urbanism and Landscape
Spring 2019
4223b History of British Landscape Architecture: 1600 to 1900
Bryan Fuermann
Kola Ofoman

Mausoleum at Castle Howard

The model depicts the Mausoleum at Castle Howard, designed by Nicholas Hawksmoor. It is based on a drawing by Hawksmoor showing a comparison between the colonnaded scheme (which was eventually built in 1736) and an earlier arcaded scheme.

History and Theory
Spring 2019
4233b Ghost Towns
Elihu Rubin

Looking at a broad spectrum of failed or almost-failed cities in the United States and across the globe, this seminar uses the "ghost town" and its rhythms of development and disinvestment to establish a conceptual framework for contemporary urban patterns and processes.

Urbanism and Landscape
Spring 2019
4233b Ghost Towns
Elihu Rubin
Rachel Lefevre

Astounding architectural bones

In the 1930s, New Haven had a new beacon added to its skyline. The towers of the Yale campus and the taller office buildings rising downtown were joined by the smoke stacks of English Station. At night, English Station lit up with the United Illuminating logo for all to see, from harbor to downtown, where United Illuminating projected a different but equally important image through its classical revival buildings.

In 1992, English Station was decommissioned and today it sits empty atop a toxic brownfield site. With its remediation underway, it is the perfect time to reconsider English Station's status as a beacon and what it would mean to re-invigorate its past image with a projection of the future. This project is a proposal for literally projecting English Station's future onto its astounding architectural bones, in the process restoring its status as a beacon, and building a constituency for its preservation by visually re-connecting it to the surrounding community.

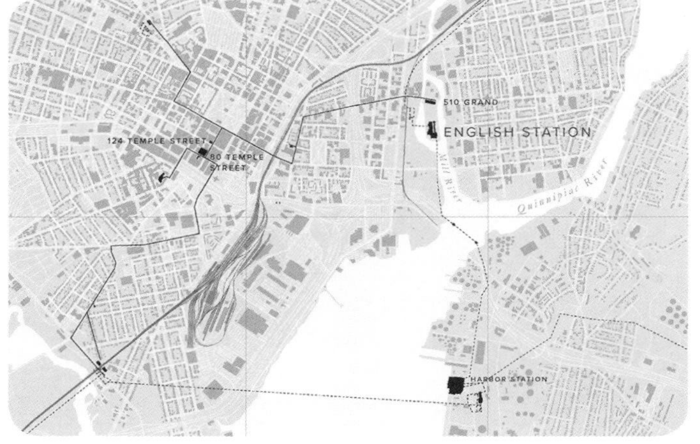

Urbanism and Landscape
Spring 2019
4233b Ghost Towns
Elihu Rubin
Davis Butner

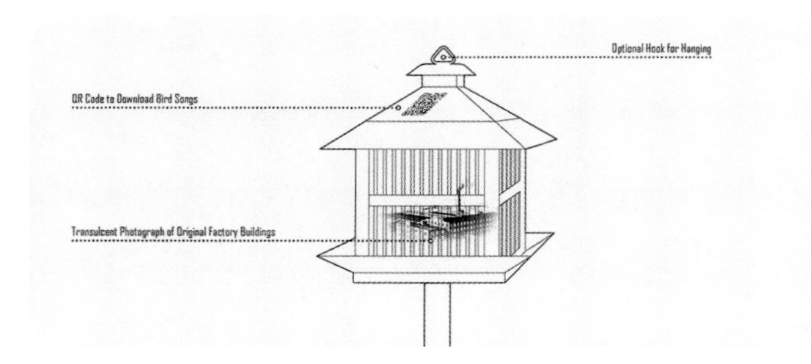

Sonic sanctuary

While often overlooked, sonic pollution at the turn of the 20th century represented a major concern for urban planners across the US, spawning a flurry of inventive solutions to combat this growing modern nuisance.

The Hendryx Company cleverly positioned themselves as a genuine solution to the growing urban noise crisis afflicting residences across growing American industrial cities such as New Haven. Through catalogs and posters, the company boldly proclaimed its solution through birdsong, bringing sounds of nature into the home through the use of their ornately designed birdcages.

This project proposes a sonic sanctuary along New Haven's Audubon St. Park, reflective of the industrial presence and rich social history of the Hendryx Birdcage Company which used to exist on the site.

History and Theory
Spring 2019
4240b Landscape of Fulfillment: Architecture and Urbanism of Contemporary Logistics
Jesse LeCavalier

Once the domain of the industrial engineer or the quartermaster, logistics now affect increasingly large areas of everyday life, including significant aspects of architecture and urbanism. This seminar examines the historical and theoretical sources of logistics before looking more closely at a series of corporate actors that define themselves through logistics in significant ways, including Walmart, Amazon, IKEA, and Tesla.

Urbanism and Landscape
Spring 2019
4240b Landscapes of Fulfillment: Architecture and Urbanism of Contemprary Logistics
Jesse LeCavalier
Thomas Mahon, Nicholas Miller

Somewhere in the mournful depths of the Athabasca tar sands

"Suncor Firebag" is a video game that begins at the 2016 North American Supply Chain Management Expo (NASCME) and ends somewhere in the mournful depths of the Athabasca tar sands. You are a third-party logistics consultant. You have come to NASCME at The Westin Peachtree Plaza in Atlanta for the fantastic networking opportunities. You meet professionals and build strategic relationships. You attend presentations and round-tables. You learn about various products and services. You collect business cards. Perhaps you meet Christian B. and Peter. They are interested in your products and services. You give them your business card. Christian B. emails you at a later date. You can accept his offer or ask for more information. You fly from Norfolk to Edmonton with a layover in Toronto. You travel by bus from Edmonton to Suncor Firebag. You arrive in your new office. You turn on the computer. You open documents that were created by the person who last held your position. The documents provide ominous and disquieting suggestions.

Urbanism and Landscape
Spring 2019
4240b Landscapes of Fulfillment: Architecture and Urbanism of Contemprary Logistics
Jesse LeCavalier
Rachel Mulder

Handscapes of Fulfillment

"The hand is the tool of tools."
– Aristotle

What is the role of the hand in the landscape of fulfillment? Following an interest in how humans fit into vast and illusive logistical systems, this project offers an investigation of the hand and the fulfillment center through representation. The hand is complicated figure. As a symbol of the worker, it represents a problematic relationship both in terms of a public image (Amazon workers have made strenuous working conditions public knowledge) [1] and how the worker is incorporated into the fulfillment system.Amazon's global workforce employs over 613,000 workers and roughly 100,000 temporary workers. On average, US employees are paid $15/hr and during peak season will work up to 60 hrs per week. [2] The worker in monitored and production is quantified. Workers are expected to "pick" 120 [3] to 400 items per hour, seven seconds per item. [4] At peak season, workers can be expected to pick 4000 items [...]

1. Press, "Whats It Like to Work at Amazon?"
2. Sainato, "We Are Not Robots"
3. "IamA I Pack Your Things at an Amazon Fulfillment Center AMA!"
4. Sainato, "We Are Not Robots"

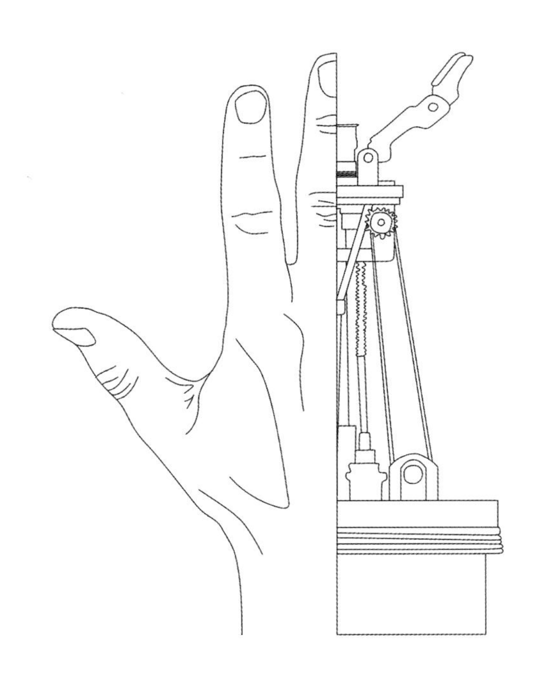

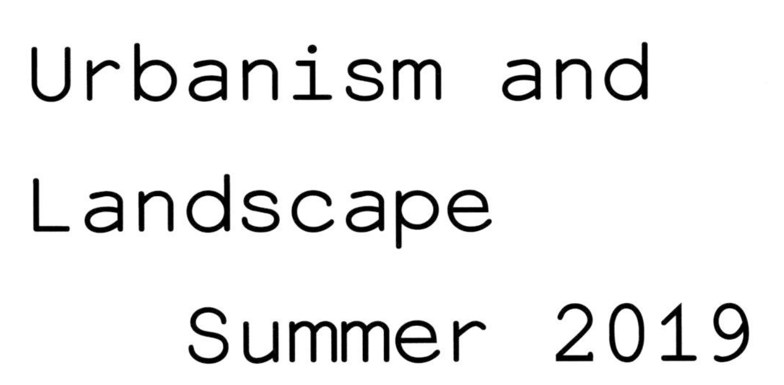

History and Theory
Summer 2019
4291c Gothenburg Summer Program: The Urban Atlas
Alan Plattus,
Andrei Harwell

This program is based on the collaboration between YSoA and the Architecture Department at Chalmers University of Technology in Gothenburg, Sweden. The program involves a month-long residency in Gothenburg, with frequent field trips to other Swedish, as well as neighboring North Sea and Baltic cities. Students research the representation, analysis, and design of urban form and space in the context of historic and contemporary architecture and urbanism in the northern Europe. The program is an ongoing project of Yale and Chalmers, contributing to the building of a new Urban Atlas of North American and Northern European Cities.

4291c Gothenburg Summer Program: The Urban Atlas
Alan Plattus, Andrei Harwell
Hamzah Ahmed, Will James, Baolin Shen, Rukshan Vathupola (A); Michelle Badr, Serena Ching, Alex Pineda Jongeward, Eunice Lee (B); Gioia Connell, Kelley Johnson, Jackson Lindsay (C); Deo Deiparine, Miriam Dreiblatt, Thomas Mahon, Manasi Punde (D)

Morphology, typology, and thick space

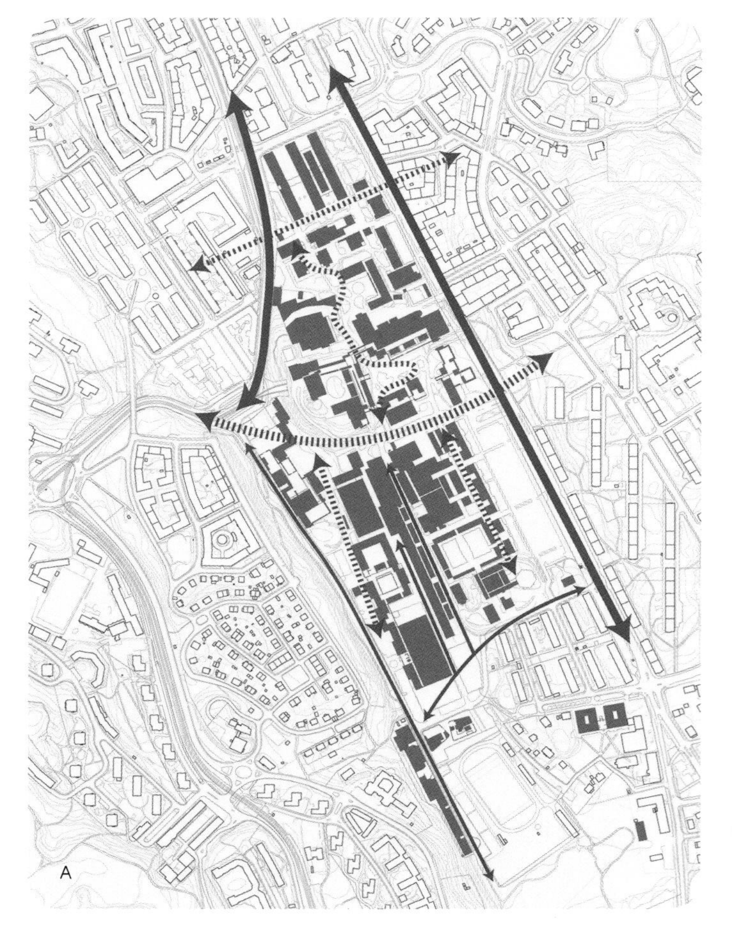
A

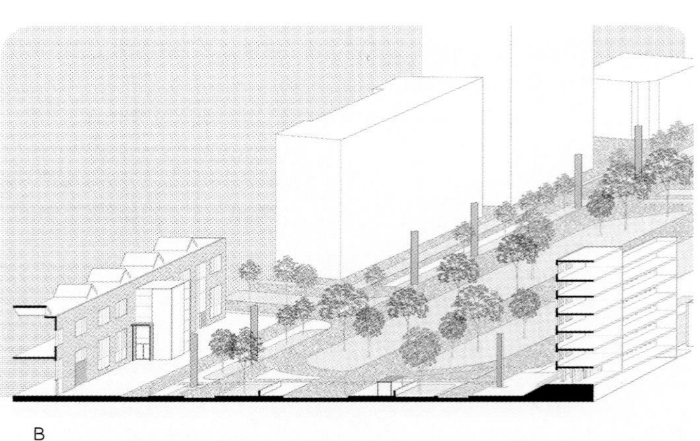
B

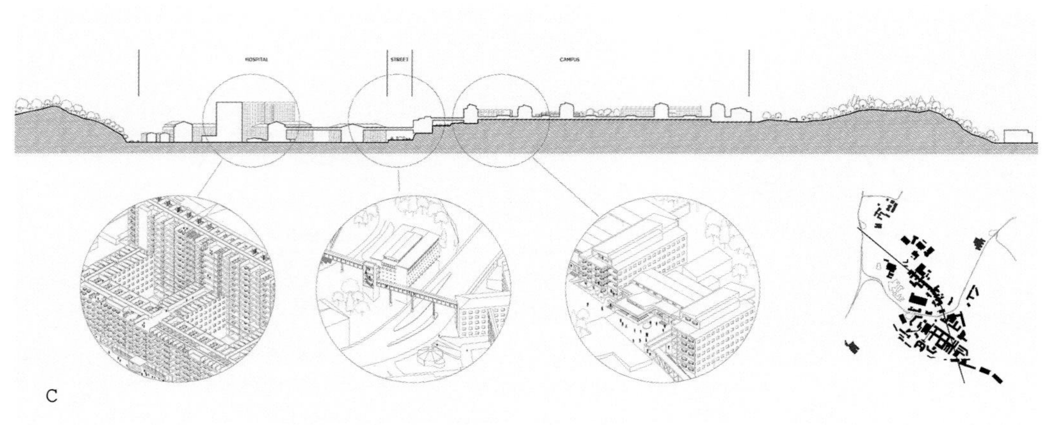

C

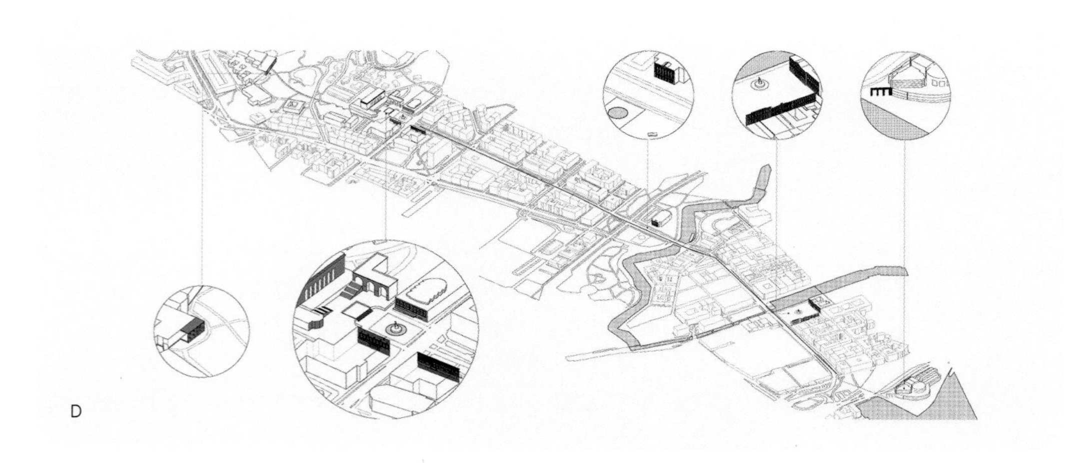
D

Other Academics

Other Academics
Yale Urban Design Workshop

The Yale Urban Design Workshop (YUDW) is a community design center based at the School of Architecture. Since its founding, the YUDW has worked with communities across the state of Connecticut and around the world, providing planning and design assistance on projects ranging from comprehensive plans, economic development strategies, and community visions to the design of public spaces, streetscapes, and individual community facilities. Much of the work and research of the YUDW has focused on strategies for regeneration in Connecticut's small post industrial towns and cities in promoting the intersection between preservation, cultural heritage, redevelopment, tourism, and identity.

Founding Director
Alan Plattus

Director of Design
Andrei Harwell

Director of Research
Marta Caldeira

Postgraduate Associate
Jared Abraham

Student Fellows
Gioia Connell, Jincy Kunnatharayil

Other Academics
Independent Study

Independent study allows students whose interests go beyond the available course options to pursue and develop deeper architectural interests with the guidance and criticism of a faculty member.

Other Academics
Independent Study
Brad Gentry, Alan Organschi, Andy Ruff
David Bruce

Processes specific to New England's forest stocks

"Building Biogenic" mapped the Northern Forest's species composition and diagrammed processes specific to New England's forest stocks, manufacturing capacities, and urban building demands. This project is a guide to alternative processes, products, and assemblies specifically suited to the Northeast's unique forest stocks.

Other Academics
Independent Study
Sunil Bald
Jerome Tryon

Deconstructing fabricated memories

This series of drawings is a graphic exploration of the composition of memories. Through drawing, I deconstructed and codified the different elements of memory, including natural memory and reconstructed or fabricated memories. I used an object buried deep in my childhood memories as a catalyst for exploration.

157

Other Academics
M.E.D. Program

The Master of Environmental Design program is a two-year research-based program culminating in a Masters thesis. Today that scope informs many crucial contemporary issues from climate change and global inequality to digital ubiquity and the influence of large socio-technical organizations. MED students generate a rich interdisciplinary discussion of social, political, economic, technical, and aesthetic material. Below are the authors and titles of theses completed this year.

Other Academics
M.E.D. Program

Holly Bushman
"Aesthetics of Control: Architecture, Surveillance, and Migration in a Socialist Model City"

Jack Hanly
"Managing the Well/ Managing the Town: Petro-capital, Late Modernism, and the Environmental Professional"

Jonathan Hopkins
"Democratizing Development: Addressing Wealth Inequality and Exclusionary Urbanism in the American city Through Popular Sector Participation in Real Estate"

Maia Simon
"Reconstructing the Nation: Large-Scale Architectural Projects in Astana 1998-2018"

Dina Taha
"What is the Time in Mecca? Clock Towers and the Transformation of the Temporal Culture in Mecca, Saudi Arabia"

Jia Weng
"Waste in the Water Machine"

Jingqiu Zhang
"Representing the City: Visual Media and Interdisciplinary Inquiry in Urban Research and Experiments 1954-2019"

Other Academics
Ph.D. Program

The doctoral program prepares candidates for careers in university teaching, cultural advocacy and administration, museum curatorship, and publishing. It educates teachers capable of effectively instructing future architects in the history of their own field. The program forges a unique combination of professional knowledge with a historical and analytical grasp of key phases in the history of architecture. Below are the current candidates and their research topics.

Christina Ciardullo

Christina has held research positions at Columbia University's Graduate School of Architecture's Space Architecture Lab and the Habitability Design Center at the NASA Johnson Space Center. In addition to terrestrial practice, including a resilient waterfront development and the Shanghai Planetarium with Ennead Architects, she has consulted in the lunar and martian endeavors of Foster+Partners and is founding member of SEArch, a consortium of architects designing for habitats for life in other atmospheres.

Gary Huafan

Gary is currently investigating theories of ornament in the context of the proliferation and development of several concurrently emerging disciplines since the late 18th-century, moving through the rise of modern architecture and culminating in an examination of 20th-century theories of society.

Theodossis Issaias

Theodossis is interested in the history of modern architecture and planning and their intersection with humanitarian interventions. By focusing on the resettlement commissions of refugees in interwar Europe, his dissertation explores architecture in relation to international law and the politics of nation-states.

Iris Giannakopoulou Karamouzi

Iris is investigating the unique cultural, technological, and ideological formations that came to prominence during the beginning of the twentieth century with special attention paid to the experimental compositional, inscriptive, and interpretative processes employed by the literary and artistic avant-gardes of that period.

Ishraq Khan

Ishraq is studying the role of literature, culture, and gender politics in shaping architectural histories in South Asia. Her research projects have included the institutionalization of architectural education in the region, the work of the architect Muzharul Islam, and recording oral histories of Modern architecture in Bangladesh.

Phoebe Mankiewic

Phoebe illustrates and develops the connections and disparities between "wild" and "human" ecologies. With a background in Biology spanning Neurobiology and Invasive Ecology, and a masters in Architectural Science out of RPI, her thesis work in Yale's CEA focuses on ecologically-influenced strategies for indoor ecologies, and solutions to urban ecological problems.

Zachariah Michielli

Zachariah's research focuses on questions surrounding Benjamin's notion of the Loss of Aura and Marx's theory of Alienation of Labor. Zach brings elements of Behavioral Economics, Logic, Philosophy, and Cognitive Psychology to bear on the relationship between architects and their work, and is developing an understanding of boredom and its implications within the field of architecture.

Nicholas Pacula

Nicholas studies the sociotechnical apparatuses directing the production, dissemination and interpretation of architectural imagery. His scholarship deals with the space in-between images and buildings, ranging from the history of drawing and the unbuilt to popular culture and digital media.

Mandi Pretorius

Mandi focuses her research on how the building envelope makes provision for the multiple roles of water (in vapor and liquid phases) as a thermodynamic and photoelectric medium, a human need and equitable scarcity, and as a biophilic affordance in the built environment.

Gabrielle Printz

Gabrielle explores landscapes of detention and the spatial and performative networks which connect border and prison in her research. This exploration manifested most recently in the web-based project C-A-R-TRIP.US, an award-winning thesis for the Critical, Curatorial and Conceptual Practices in Architecture Program (MS.CCCP) at Columbia University GSAPP.

Summer Sutton

Summer's research agenda includes: Surveys of Mosque Development in Sub-Saharan Africa; Contemporary University Campus Design in Iran; as well as Urban Development in Iran during the Safavid Dynasty and its implications on modern urban development in present day Iran.

Aaron Tobey

Aaron is currently conducting research on how the relationship between digital tools, forms of representation, and political agency in architecture informs collective social imaginations of space and processes of subjectivization. A major focus of this work is a combined historical and contemporary analysis of the social, political, and economic dimensions of software development and operation.

David Turturo's

David's dissertation, Caryatid: A Genealogy of the Architectural Subject, identifies and critiques the power structures that shape dominant histories. The subject is architectural in both a disciplinary and corporeal sense. Simultaneously, David is developing a critical monograph on the work of the American architect and educator John Hejduk.

Jane Jia Weng

Jane's research focuses on how the environment and its subject reciprocally molds each other through architecture. By tracing historical developments of weather control technologies, such as refrigeration, air-conditioning, and weather modification, her current work explores the role of modern architecture in the endeavor of reinventing weather.

9 781948 765336